M000087776

NEW DIRECTIONS IN ANTHROPOLOGICAL KINSHIP

Linda Stone, Editor

ROWMAN & LITTLEFIELD PUBLISHERS, INC.
Lanham • Boulder • New York • Oxford

ROWMAN & LITTLEFIELD PUBLISHERS, INC.

Published in the United States of America
by Rowman & Littlefield Publishers, Inc.
4720 Boston Way, Lanham, Maryland 20706
www.rowmanlittlefield.com

12 Hid's Copse Road
Cumnor Hill, Oxford OX2 9JJ, England

British Library Cataloguing in Publication Information Available

Library of Congress Cataloging-in-Publication Data

Stone, Linda, 1947–
  New directions in anthropological kinship / Linda Stone.
    p. cm.
  Includes bibliographical references and index.
  ISBN 0-7425-0107-8 (alk. paper) — ISBN 0-7425-0108-6 (pbk. : alk. paper)
    1. Kinship.   I. Title.

GN480 .S83 2000
306.83—dc21   00-040303

Printed in the United States of America

♾™ The paper used in this publication meets the minimum requirements of American
National Standard for Information Sciences—Permanence of Paper for Printed Library
Materials, ANSI/NISO Z39.48–1992.

NEW DIRECTIONS IN ANTHROPOLOGICAL KINSHIP

Contents

Preface

This book attests to a revival of kinship in anthropology. Even Schneider, whose own work contributed to the demise of kinship in the 1970s and 1980s, remarked in the 1990s that kinship had "risen from its ashes" (1995: 193). There are different reasons for this revival, some explored in this volume. In addition to those, it may well be, as Holy (1996: 165) suggested, that "too much theoretical effort has been invested" in kinship for its abandonment to be realistic, or as Parkin noted, "to neglect kinship is to disregard a good deal of what any society explicitly recognizes" (1997: ix). In any case, kinship in anthropology has changed significantly since mid-century and it is headed in interesting new directions.

This book grew out of a conference panel, "New Directions in Kinship Studies," at the 1997 meeting of the American Anthropological Association in Washington, D.C. Though the conference papers were all by cultural anthropologists, as are most of the chapters in this book, kinship has been also receiving attention from anthropologists in other subdisciplines. I then decided to broaden the book to include contributions from archaeology, primatology, evolutionary anthropology, and sociolinguistics, aiming to approximate an anthropological "four field" approach to contemporary kinship. Sociolinguistics is the only subfield from which, unfortunately, I did not find contributors.

The collected papers present new research, analytical reviews of new directions in kinship studies, or theoretical contributions to the field. Theoretically, the contributions represent diverse perspectives. However, a major preoccupation with several "new directions" in kinship have to do with debates over the relationship between biology and culture in kinship studies. This topic is discussed at length in the introduction.

This kinship collection has been compiled for professional anthropologists. It also will be useful as a supplementary text in graduate courses in anthropology or advanced undergraduate classes that cover kinship or combine it with social organization, gender, or anthropological theory. Contributions deal with the history of kinship, the influence of feminism in leading kinship into "new directions," an overview of primate kinship, neoevolutionary approaches, kinship and gender, new family forms, and kinship and state politics. Students will find here both in-depth treatments of the history of kinship in anthropology and examples of contemporary research in this field.

I am grateful to Nancy E. Levine for suggesting and co-organizing the "New Directions" kinship panel that laid the basis for the book. I would like also to thank Dean Birkenkamp, executive editor for Rowman & Littlefield Publishers, not only for his considerable help in producing the book, but for inspiring its creation.

References

Holy, Ladislav. 1996. *Anthropological Perspectives on Kinship*. London: Pluto.
Parkin, Robert. 1997. *Kinship: An Introduction to Basic Concepts*. Malden, Mass.: Blackwell.
Schneider, David M. 1995. *Schneider on Schneider: The Conversion of the Jews and Other Stories*, edited and transcribed by Richard Handler. Durham, N.C.: Duke University Press.

Chapter One

Introduction: Theoretical Implications of New Directions in Anthropological Kinship

Linda Stone

In the latter half of the twentieth century, kinship fell from a position of theoretical centrality to one of marginality in the discipline of anthropology. Amid the attacks on the viability of "kinship" as an analytical category were two interrelated themes. The first was that kinship studies had been based on an unwarranted assumption that people everywhere devise kinship systems on the basis of the "natural facts" of procreation. Although variations in kinship terminology, systems of descent, and marriage were abundantly noted in the ethnographic literature, all were presumed to be derived from universal human concerns with relationships founded upon biological reproduction. Led primarily by Schneider and his students, the past several decades have seen growth of the idea that this view of kinship as a system of relations reflecting actual (or assumed) biological connections is peculiar to Western and especially American culture. These scholars argued that from this fundamental flaw, the basis for compounding misconceptions about "kinship" and its meaning in non-Western societies was laid.

A second, related theme in the demise of kinship was the growing concern that anthropological analyses of kinship had fed into the demarcation between "advanced" Euro-American societies and the exotic primitive "Other." In Euro-American ideology those societies with "more kinship" (complicated clan structures, extended families, deep lineages, or even the large families of immigrant groups to the United States) were contrasted with "modern" industrialized societies with trim nuclear families, societies in which social institutions have taken over the functions that more primitive kin units and networks provide elsewhere. Thus, anthropological kinship became tainted by the analytical and judgmental Eurocentrism that the field of anthropology has been seeking for decades to transcend (Peletz 1995).

An additional problem with kinship was the feeling in the anthropological community that its models were too rigid and formalistic, the analyses too grounded in legalistic rules and pedantic jargon, all of which led kinship to be seen as tedious and boring, especially by students.

For all this, kinship did not die out in anthropology. On the contrary, it now appears to be undergoing a revival. After a period spanning more than twenty years during which not a single textbook on kinship was published, Holy's *Anthropological Perspectives on Kinship* appeared in 1996, as did the reader *Gender, Kinship, Power: A Comparative and Interdisciplinary History* by Maynes et al. The next year saw the publication of three new texts: Parkin's *Kinship: An Introduction to Basic Concepts*; Pasternak, Ember, and Ember's book *Sex, Gender and Kinship*; and my book *Kinship and Gender: An Introduction*.

In revived forms, kinship studies have moved away from formalism and have become more sensitive to the problems of Eurocentric impositions. With this, kinship is now taking new directions that overall parallel other changes that we see in the discipline as a whole (see Brettell, chapter 3 in this book). These include greater attention to (1) historical context, (2) inequalities of power and strategies of resistance to dominant cultural ideologies, (3) multiple ethnographic "voices," (4) human agency, (5) the influence of state policies and transnational forces on cultural constructions, (6) intersections of ethnicity, gender, and class, (7) the incorporation of feminist perspectives, and (8) new perspectives on the relationship between biological and cultural approaches to human behavior. Far from dying out, kinship has remained what it was all along: a special mirror in which both the failings and the promise of anthropology are reflected.

This book captures some major new topical directions in anthropological kinship. Although most authors are cultural anthropologists, the collection includes a primatologist, an archaeologist, and an evolutionary anthropologist. Following a section on kinship in the history of anthropology, the collected articles cover primate kinship, neoevolutionary approaches to human kinship, new reproductive technologies, kinship and gender, new family forms, and relations between kinship and the state. Theoretically speaking, the focus of the book is intentionally wide. One trend from the past that I, for one, seek to avoid is polemical debates where the topic of kinship is concerned. With the book, I rather seek to give voice to different approaches within anthropology that are using and reformulating kinship, and to foster communication between them. For professional anthropologists and graduate students, the book provides a wide spectrum of the new directions that kinship is now taking. Some theoretical positions may be currently more prominent than others, but, as before, kinship continues to be an arena in which many different theoretical perspectives are represented.

At the core of both previous and current theoretical differences and controversies is the relationship between kinship and biology. Other kinship debates (for example, that between alliance and descent theory) have come and gone, but this one remains and is taking new forms. In many respects the history of these debates underlies most of the contributions to this volume and so merits some review. While all authors would agree that debates about biology and culture are at the heart of kinship theory, not all authors would agree with the interpretation of the history I outline. I did not ask the contributors to this book either to adopt or to critique this perspective.

In the nineteenth century, Morgan (1877), a founder of kinship studies, set forth that systems of kinship terminology reflected people's understandings of their biological relationships as based on their marriage practices. Morgan imagined that classificatory terminological systems (where lineal and collateral relatives are merged) reflected an earlier state of "primitive promiscuity" and brother–sister marriage. People did not know who their fathers were and thus devised no special terms to distinguish real fathers from a larger class of potential fathers. Since all women of one's mother's generation were equally wives of these men, they too were lumped together with a single term. A later stage of monogamy brought about descriptive terminological systems that distinguished fathers and mothers from other collateral relatives. Aside from denouncing this kind of evolutionary speculation, later anthropologists came to see kinship not as human recognition of actual biological bonds but as social interpretation of assumed biological bonds (Holy 1996; Schneider 1984).

From the beginning, anthropologists had of course noted some slippage between real or presumed biological relationships and "kinlike" relationships that did not correspond to biological ones. Adoptions, descent groups formed through common residence, and the assigning of children to deceased persons, as in the levirate, were common examples. But how this "slippage" (or what some came to call a difference between social and biological kinship) was to be understood was another matter. An early debate was that between Needham (1960) and Gellner (1960). Needham had argued that "Biology is one matter and descent is quite another, of a different order" (1960: 97). Gellner, by contrast, argued that kinship, as most anthropologists implicitly define and analyze it, lies in the connection between kinship systems and the actual facts of human biological reproduction. In this sense, so-called social kinship may be seen to select from and even distort the realm of human biological reproduction, but anthropologists always specify social kinship with reference to physical kinship. For example, in the case of the levirate, Gellner said,

> The anthropologist's kinship term "leviratic" is only applicable when certain real kinship relations obtain. The relationship, and its offspring, can only be identified by the anthropologist *as* "leviratic" because the anthropologist knows that the fiction by which the offspring are raised "in the dead man's name" is indeed a fiction. (1960: 188)

On another level, Gellner asserted that it would be impossible for anthropologists to refer to kinship in any other than biological terms. He wrote:

> Suppose an anthropologist observes, in a society he is investigating, a certain kind of recurring relationship between pairs of individuals or of groups. (It may

be a relationship of authority, or a symmetrical one of, say, mutual aid, or of avoidance, or whatnot.) Suppose the autochthonous term for the relationship is *blip*. The crucial question now is: Under what conditions will the anthropologist's treatment of the *blip*-relationship fall under the rubric of kinship structure? It will be so subsumed if the anthropologist believes that the *blip*-relationship overlaps, in a predominant number of cases, with *some* physical kinship relationship. Otherwise, naturally, the *blip*-relationship will be subsumed under some other rubric, such as "authority" or "economy." What, other than at least partial overlap with physical kinship, *could* conceivably lead a relationship to be classified as a part of "kinship structure"? (1960: 187)

In Gellner's view, kinship is an anthropologist's category and what matters is whether the anthropologist believes a relationship to involve what he or she sees as physical kinship. He does not consider biology or reproduction in relation to people's own (emic) views or consider what difference it would make if these were taken into account. Scheffler (1973), by contrast, based his definition of kinship directly on native perceptions, and in doing so, took a position somewhat between that of Gellner and Needham. In Scheffler's formulation, a *blip*-relationship in a particular culture would be classifiable as "kinship" if the people themselves understand it as a "genealogical connection," that is, a connection based on the people's own folk-culture theory of human reproduction. Scheffler distinguished genealogical connections from genetic ones as understood in scientific biology.

[T]he "kinship relations" of interest to the social or cultural anthropologist are those "genealogical" connections whose existence is presumed by or "known" to any people, not those posited by or known to any scientific discipline. Thus the foundation of any kinship system consists in a folk-cultural theory designed to account for the fact that women give birth to children, i.e., a theory of human reproduction. (1973: 749)

Scheffler noted the considerable variation in folk-cultural theories of reproduction but he held that a mother–child genealogical connection was a human universal and a father–child connection very likely so as well. These primary links then form the basis of other genealogical connections, which may be drawn in various ways by different groups. Thus for Scheffler, in contrast to Gellner, actual physical kinship was not the issue; what was important is how people draw connections among themselves based on local ideas about reproduction. In contrast to Needham, kinship is not entirely detached from "biology" in the sense that an emic view of biological reproduction is a foundation for genealogical connections.

Scheffler's position was probably all along closer to the way in which most anthropologists were implicitly viewing kinship than to Gellner's formulation. But his explicit attention to emic views contributed to new debates over what kinship is. It was Schneider, who by delving further into the emics of kinship, escalated the debates, and in the process, nearly swept kinship off the anthropological horizon. His ideas were formulated by the early 1970s and culminated in his later book, *A Critique of the Study of Kinship* (1984).

Schneider (1984) saw Scheffler's view of kinship as essentially a return to Morgan—kinship reflects people's understanding (or, for Morgan, misunderstanding) of their own reproduction. He claimed that most anthropologists had in one way or another persistently defined kinship in relation to human biological reproduction. They did so because of an implicit and erroneous assumption, namely, that their own Western cultural notion that "Blood Is Thicker Than Water" is a human universal. They assumed that human reproduction everywhere establishes links between people that are imbued with special qualities and importance as distinct from other social relationships formed in some other way. Anthropological kinship was defined and founded on this specific cultural notion: "[T]he study of kinship derives directly and practically unaltered from the ethnoepistemology of European culture" (1984: 175). Thus, with their studies of kinship anthropologists were merely imposing their own cultural notions on the lives of other peoples; as a result, kinship theory produced an ethnocentric distortion of other people's cultural realities.

From these unexamined assumptions came the equally unwarranted idea of the Genealogical Unity of Mankind, that relationships based upon human reproduction can be organized into categories (such as "mother" and "father") that are comparable cross-culturally. Schneider himself claimed to seriously doubt the universality of these assumptions of anthropological kinship. He concluded that kinship cannot cross-culturally be considered a distinct domain, and indeed, for anthropological purposes, "there is no such thing as kinship" (1984: vii). Deprived of a basis in universally acknowledged "facts of life," the whole edifice of anthropological kinship concepts—descent groups, patrilineality, matrilineality, marriage, genealogy, and so on—comes tumbling down. Using his own material on the Yap, Schneider attempted to show, for example, that "motherhood" and "fatherhood" cannot be posited for the Yap in any way comparable to anthropological (Western, biologically rooted) categories. He claimed the Yap (at the time of his fieldwork) did not believe that men in any way contribute to the conception of a child, that although the Yap acknowledge that women give birth, the child in her womb is given life by ghosts, and that in any case, production of human beings is not highly valued among the Yap (1984: 201).[1] He also described that what he himself had noted earlier as a patrilineal descent group for the Yap was in fact a unit based on land use and ownership.[2]

With all this, Schneider turned "kinship" upside down in at least one sense. While formerly, anthropologists had emphasized kinship as fundamental and pervasive in tribal and peasant societies and relatively insignificant in Western industrial ones, Schneider suggested that, on the contrary, kinship might *only* exist in Euro-American society. Properly investigated, kinship might turn out to be "a special custom distinctive of European culture, an interesting oddity at worst, like the Toda bow ceremony" (1984: 201).

Schneider left little room for the possibility of recovery or reform in anthropological kinship. Thus, even in cases where cultures recognize relationships based on biological reproduction, we cannot assume that reproduction ("engendering another human being" [1984: 198]) is always highly valued. He claimed that such an assumption could be tested, "But it cannot be done on the literature that is generally available to us today, for almost all of that literature assumes that these are the facts instead of asking if they are not" (1984: 198). In a similar vein, he wrote that it would make little difference if the notion that Blood Is Thicker Than Water turned out to be universally true: "[C]ulture, even were it to do no more than recognize biological facts, still adds something to those facts," the value and meaning of which is still problematic.

What got everyone's attention was, of course, the charge of ethnocentrism. Kuper (1999: 149) noted that "It took some gall to accuse all his colleagues of ethnocentrism (the most serious sin of all in anthropology)," although, as Kuper noted, Schneider included his own previous work in this accusation. In addition, Schneider was not only undoing anthropological kinship, but by implication, anthropology itself. "Not only the science of kinship but all of anthropology, sociology and biology were revealed to be not false science but ethnosciences" (Kuper 1999: 145–46). His work, then, was in line with broader currents of postmodern self-criticism and internal charges of ethnocentricism that were being felt throughout the discipline of anthropology.

Anthropologists had before Schneider documented cases of "kinship" constructed along lines other than the "biological reproduction" in either Western scientific or locally emic terms. In countless ways, human groups structure units and define "kinship" relations on bases other than biological connections, such as residence, ritual, adoptions, or even certain patterns of food sharing or other material transactions. The Nuer plotted "fatherhood" along lines of cattle paid as bride wealth for the mother. In some New Guinea groups, people became members of descent groups through common residence, reinforced by food sharing (Strathern 1973). Indeed, all along there had been ideas of kinship as "shared substance" (not only "blood" and semen, but also food), a concept much broader than kinship as shared biogenetic substance (to use Schneider's [1980] phrase in his cultural account of American kinship) or kinship as stemming from procreation, however culturally conceptualized.

Could shared substance and/or other kinds of transfers be used to construct a cross-culturally valid analytic category of kinship? Cucciari (1981) said yes, but then his own model brings us right back to biology and to a view of kinship similar to that of Scheffler. Cucciari held that "What distinguishes kinship, as a social system, from other systems is its underlying notion of shared substance: 'consubstantiation' " (1981: 35). There are two kinds of consubstantiation: procreative and nurturing. All kinship systems will make use of both procreative and nurturing notions of sharing (e.g., blood, semen in the former; food, breast milk, in the latter), though some may be "procreative dominant" while others are "nurturing dominant." Either way, however, notions of shared substance through nurturing rely on a procreative model.

Despite the fact that kinship systems can and do stress either a nurturing or pro-creative notion of consubstantiation, everywhere, kinship categories have procre-ative referents: Indeed, kinship systems seem universally able of being expressed in terms of some *cultural* model of procreation rather than nurturing. That is, even where parents are defined more as the people who protect, feed, and raise the child, the relationship is still expressed in a genealogical idiom. (1981: 35)

Cucciari notes as an example the idea of motherhood among the Navajo. For them, a mother can be a woman who bore the child or a woman who raised it; but either way, only a *woman* (a person capable of bearing a child) can be a mother. If the cultural model of "motherhood" were completely based on nur-turing, it could include men. This ultimate reliance of all kinship on a model of procreation was seen as needed "in order to map the total kinship system" (1981: 36). Otherwise kinship boundaries would be blurred and kinship cate-gories could not be reproduced from generation to generation. Thus,

If the defining characteristic of the category "parent" is the one who feeds and cares for the child, even the generational distinction would be weakened as par-ent and grandparent cooperated in child rearing. Indeed, all categories . . . would tend to be semantic domains with variable boundaries and include no fixed cat-alogue of relationship. (1981: 37)

Thus, even the idea of kinship as nonbiological shared substance entails a bi-ological referent and so is vulnerable to a Schneiderian attack.

More recently, a few others have attempted to reformulate kinship in a way that would avoid (Western) notions of biology and so might constitute a cross-culturally valid category. Carsten (1995) has tried to "rescue" kinship by redefining it as "relatedness," but as Holy (1996: 168) points out, broadening the definition of kinship in this way fails to specify how "kinship" is then to be distinguished from any other type of social relationship. For a new attempt to reformulate kinship, see Galvin, chapter 6 in this book.

This brings us back to the heart of the issue raised by Schneider: "kinship" can be a distinct domain only in relation to biological reproduction. Other-wise, if we open the definition to include relationships established on some other bases, what distinguishes kinship from other types of relationships—neighbors, friends, or coworkers? Schneider made it quite clear that "Robbed of its grounding in biology, kinship is nothing" (1984: 112). He further wrote that "[I]t is simply not possible to conceive of genealogy without the model of the pedigree" (1984: 55). He would have agreed, then, with Gellner's point that a *blip*-relationship can only be subsumed under "kinship" when it is under-stood to overlap with physical kinship. To put Schneider's view another way, one cannot take "genealogy" out of kinship, and one cannot take biological re-production out of genealogy, without of course destroying the category of kinship itself. Schneider did not encourage a redefinition of kinship to fit bet-ter the ethnographic observations we might make in less culturally biased in-vestigations. Any broadening of the concept destroys it as a distinct domain.

Schneider advised those who wished to continue to study "kinship" (a group in which he did not include himself [1984: 199–200]) to take the propositions such as Blood Is Thicker Than Water and the Genealogical Unity of Mankind as hypotheses to test rather than as givens (1984: 200). In a similar vein, he advocated that we first study each culture emically on its own terms as a prerequisite to any cross-cultural comparison (1984: 184).

Schneider's ideas were influential in that, in the wake of his critique, nearly a whole generation of anthropologists largely forgot about kinship as a distinct domain. A telling development was that undergraduate courses on kinship were often deleted from the curriculum in departments of anthropology.

The demise of kinship and yet, in another way, also its revival, was fostered by the work of some feminist anthropologists who joined the ranks of what Scheffler (1991: 361) called the "antikinship school." Specifically, Collier and Yanagisako (1987) tried to do for the categories of "gender" and "sex" what Schneider had done for "kinship." They argued against an earlier view (articulated by Oakley [1972], Shapiro [1981], and others) that "sex" refers to the universal biological differences between women and men, whereas "gender" refers to the relative and variable ways in which different cultural groups interpret and evaluate those differences. Collier and Yanagisako's position was that the categories "male" and "female," and any presumed biological differences between them, are themselves culturally constructed. Thus, not only gender but also sexual difference needs to be understood within each specific cultural context. As Schneider had exposed Western cultural bias in the concept of "kinship," so Collier and Yanagisako exposed Western cultural bias in the concept of "gender," which earlier had implied a base of universal biological sexual difference, specifically a male/female difference in reproduction.[3] Sexual difference could not be taken for granted; rather each culture's notion of sexual difference needed to be explored. Collier and Yanagisako also argued that kinship and gender are "mutually constituted."[4]

> We argue that gender and kinship have been defined as fields of study by our folk conception of the same thing, namely, the biological facts of sexual reproduction. Consequently, what have been conceptualized as two discrete fields of study constitute a single field that has not succeeded in freeing itself from notions about natural differences between people. (1987: 15)

The Collier and Yanagisako position has been criticized by Scheffler (1991) who, among other issues, pointed out that studying each culture on its own terms is "an impossible project" since "ethnographic inquiry begins and ends as a theory-laden act of comparison" (1991: 37). I also did not adopt the position of Collier and Yanagisako in *Kinship and Gender* (Stone 1997). Following more closely Scheffler's (1973) views, I held that women universally do bear children, that men and women universally do play different roles in reproduction, and that upon this "fact of life," cross-cultural comparisons of kinship and gender can be made.

Regardless of one's position on this issue, there is no question that the revival of kinship is in large part due to feminist anthropology (see Lamphere, chapter 2 in this book). Equally important is that Collier and Yanagisako's call to consider each culture "on its own terms" following upon Schneider's critique of kinship has inspired richer ethnography of both kinship and cultural notions of sexual difference. The meaning and universality of basic concepts in kinship studies is no longer taken for granted and this by itself has reinvigorated the field.

Even before Schneider's critique, another view of kinship, one that linked it more directly with scientific biology than most cultural anthropologists ever had, was in the making. This view was set within the framework of neo-Darwinian evolutionary biology. An early approach, represented and led by Fox (1980, 1989a, 1989b; and Tiger and Fox 1971), studied kinship from the perspective of human ethology. Here, kinship systems are varied answers to humans' (and other primates') problems of survival and reproduction. To Fox, kinship systems have very much to do with the "facts of life" ("[g]estation, impregnation, domination and the avoidance of incest" [1989a: 31]) but ultimately are based in the evolved human capacity to conceptualize and classify. This capacity was for humans as important to survival as "the claws of the tiger or the neck of the giraffe" (1989a: 31) were for those species. Fox sees human kinship as a species-specific form of assortative mating and the most basic kinship categories as pertaining to marriageable or nonmarriageable divisions. Human kinship derives from a primate baseline, but in the course of our evolutionary history, it shifted to a categorizing, rule-bound way of mate allocation that entailed new and distinctively human links between affines or in-laws. Another important development in evolutionary theory was Hamilton's (1964) hypotheses regarding kin selection, or the idea that an individual can promote his or her own reproductive success through altruistic acts that favor the survival and reproduction of close kin who share at least some of his or her own genes (see Silk, chapter 4 in this book).

Schneider himself mentioned this more explicitly biological view of kinship (he uses the earlier term, "sociobiology"), but with little comment. He noted that "the most recent, explicit, detailed, and developed commitment to the premise that Blood Is Thicker Than Water is made by the sociobiologists" (1984: 173). This may be true with respect to the concept of kin selection, but not necessarily true with respect to how evolutionists understand the construction of human kinship systems. Most contemporary theorists emphasize the importance of context or environmental conditions to explain mothers', sisters', or others' reproductive decisions (Hrdy 1999).

These ethological and evolutionary approaches do not imply that kinship systems are necessarily founded on a calculation of actual biological or genetic relationships (Fox 1989b: 174). In other words these approaches see *humans* (not their kinship systems) as biologically rooted and therefore subject to natural selection, a fact which in their view will affect human kinship systems (see

Hewlett, chapter 5 in this book). The kinship systems humans create can be based on anything; neoevolutionary theory only posits that the constructions and uses of kinship will reflect individual striving for fitness maximization. Neoevolutionists are, however, necessarily concerned with the biological outcomes of human behavior; in this sense, their position is perhaps most comparable to that of Gellner in that they are interested in the overlap between "social kinship" and (etically) presumed biological relationships.

In the main, most cultural anthropologists have either ignored or criticized (e.g., Sahlins 1976) sociobiological or evolutionary approaches to kinship. In this they have been aided by a now voluminous feminist criticism of evolutionary approaches to gender (see Gotway 1997 for a review of the issues). An important concern underlying these criticisms is that linking what feminists see as pervasive (if not universal) gender inequality in the world with biological forces is seen as a thinly veiled attempt to "naturalize" and so perpetuate that inequality (Bernstein 1997). On the other hand, a few anthropologists have argued against the growing split between biological and cultural (or "constructivist") approaches. Thus, Peletz wrote in a review of kinship studies in the late twentieth century: "Most (cultural) anthropologists . . . have turned their backs on sociobiologists rather than involve them in serious discussion. This seems a strategic mistake" (1995: 366). And from Scheffler (1991: 367): "As feminists we should seek to transform the study of human biology, not to turn our backs on it."

Thus, the relation between biology and kinship is by no means settled in anthropology, as seen in the various perspectives of authors in this volume. The debates, however, have shifted ground. And while Schneiderian efforts to dismantle kinship have not succeeded, in one sense, Schneider has won: kinship is no longer a "distinct domain" in terms of how and for what purpose it is studied. Regardless of our varied theoretical persuasions, kinship is today studied in relation to other aspects of social, cultural, and biological life, addresses contemporary social issues, and reflects anthropology's current concerns with process, variation, and history, as seen in the contributions to this book.

Kinship in the History of Anthropology

Part 1 opens with two chapters that cover the history of kinship in anthropology from the middle of the twentieth century to the present. In chapter 2, Louise Lamphere traces the transformation of kinship through her own work with the Navajo, working-class families, and immigrants in the United States. She argues that kinship never really disappeared in anthropology; it was rather gradually transformed by the approaches of feminism and political economy. It was the feminism of the 1970s, in which Lamphere's own work was a leading force, that kept kinship "alive and well" and in which the transformation of kinship began. With feminism, the interest in kinship shifted from that of rights and duties embedded in kinship structures to questions of women's subordination and women's strategies for power and autonomy. Attention to history and political economy later provided the larger framework that many feminist anthropologists needed to understand the dynamics of power that had become the focus of their work. Lamphere's chapter then moves to an analysis of the personal narratives of three Navajo women whose lives span three generations in one family. With these narratives, she criticizes earlier static and abstract approaches in kinship studies to the understanding of domestic group cycles, arranged marriages, and the meaning of matrilineality among the Navajo. The use of these narratives exemplifies the new trends that Lamphere sees in kinship studies, such as the close attention to history, colonialism, and the placing of the anthropologist in the narrative-based text.

The third chapter by Caroline Brettell also covers the history of kinship studies, but from the angle of pedagogical issues in graduate student training in anthropology. Brettell suggests that a graduate course on kinship is one way to provide students with a sense of continuity, breadth, and depth in anthropology in face of the current trend toward increased specialization in our field. She describes the aims and coverage of her own graduate course on kinship and social organization, showing how it is able to cover the history of anthropological theory and its central controversies, provide students with a range and depth of ethnographic knowledge, and show how kinship and social organization have been reformulated in terms of current theoretical paradigms. The chapter develops a theme of "old wine in new bottles" with respect to the history, demise, and revival of kinship studies. Around this theme, Brettell's course traces topics such as segmentation, kinship terminology, and incest, illustrating how concepts once central to kinship studies of the past are being reformulated around new questions and issues. Through kinship, the course reveals a major shift in anthropological theory from static models to historical and processual approaches. This chapter is not only an instructive guide to the teaching of kinship and social organization at the graduate level, but is itself a cogent review of the centrality of kinship in the history of theory in anthropology.

Biology and Culture in the Study of Kinship

Part 2 concerns relationships between biology and culture in the study of kinship. Chapters 4 and 5 present some new directions that kinship studies are taking in primatology and within neoevolutionary perspectives in cultural anthropology. Joan Silk's chapter 4 opens this part with a review of kinship in primate societies. Silk discusses the concept of kin selection in evolutionary theory and how it is held to shape the evolution of behavior. Focusing on a set of Old World primate species (macaques, baboons, and vervets), she discusses the parameters of primate knowledge of kinship and how kinship shapes social organization in these primate groups. Particularly interesting are the ways in which primates apparently recognize not only their own kin but each

other's kin as well. Also intriguing is Silk's discussion of matrilineal dominance hierarchies and how power differences among matrilines may be perpetuated through the reproductive advantages they confer. This chapter
demonstrates the roots of kinship in the primate order, but as Silk cautions,
there are "no simple analogies" to be drawn with human behavior, which is
complicated by the capacity for culture. The challenge that lies ahead is to explain how and why humans have maintained certain features of kinship that
they share with other primates and how in our species other kinship behaviors have been transformed.

In chapter 5, Barry Hewlett shows how evolutionary theory is being applied
to studies of human kinship. For Hewlett, "neo" evolutionary theories are
those that use recent contributions to Darwinian evolution, specifically kin selection, parental investment, sex ratio theory, reciprocal altruism, and life history theory, all of which are clearly outlined in this article. He further shows
the diversity of approaches to kinship even within neoevolutionary thought,
covering the somewhat different perspectives of evolutionary psychology, behavioral ecology, and dual transmission theory. This chapter concludes with
some results concerning kinship patterns of Hewlett's ongoing research with
other colleagues on cultural transmission and diversity in Africa. As Hewlett
notes, neoevolutionary approaches to kinship are "relatively new and controversial"; they take the position that while kinship is "cultural" in many respects, it is not purely so. But as his chapter makes clear, culture is neither
downplayed nor ignored in neoevolutionary thought. Indeed, he demonstrates that neoevolutionary approaches are consistent with other theoretical
developments in kinship studies, such as the interconnection of gender with
kinship relations; neoevolutionary approaches also emphasize how individuals manipulate their cultural environments, which is consistent with current
"practice theory."

The final chapter in part 2, by Kathey-Lee Galvin, returns us to the concept,
and the problem, of "biology" in Schneider's critique of kinship. Analyzing others' recent work on kinship in Ecuador, Malaysia, and Nepal, Galvin suggests that
"kinship" can be reformulated for cross-cultural comparison. Her article develops a new model of kinship that revises and expands Schneider's (1980) "Order
of Nature" and "Order of Law" in his cultural account of American kinship.

Kinship and New Reproductive Technologies

Relationships between biology and culture take on a new twist in kinship studies when the recent assisted reproductive technologies are considered (see
Lamphere and Brettell, chapters 2 and 3 in this book). Work in this area covers
the confrontation of Euro-American kinship with new "biological facts" and
the ways that individuals construct kinship in relation to new technologies of
reproduction (Strathern 1992; Ragoné 1994; Franklin and Ragoné 1998; Ed-

wards et al. 1999). In part 3, two chapters address kinship and new reproductive technologies. Lynn Åkesson's chapter 7 focuses on genetic counseling sessions as sites for the constructions of kinship in Sweden. She then moves to a discussion of how genetic investigations of kinship are complicated by the new reproductive technologies. Placing this case of European kinship in historical context, she discusses how the themes of individuality, individual variation, and "blood" as a basis for kinship have changed and are changing through modern technical interventions.

Susanne Lundin's chapter 8 covers patients' experiences at an infertility treatment center, also in Sweden. Similar to Åkesson's analysis of genetic counseling sessions, Lundin sees the clinic as a site not only of medical procedure but also for the cultural construction of sexuality, the body, parenthood, and gender identity. Using the case of one infertile couple, supplemented by interviews with others, she focuses on men's reactions to discoveries of and treatments for their own infertility. Through their experiences at the clinic, these men come to understand their masculinity as bound to biology, even though this perception may be at variance with changing gender norms in the broader society.

Kinship and Gender

Nearly all chapters in this book show connections between kinship and gender, but those in part 4 explicitly focus on these interlinkages. Karen Sinclair's chapter 9 draws out the relations between gender and cognatic descent among the precolonial Maori of New Zealand. Her analysis is based on parallels in the marginal and threatening positions of women and younger brothers in a Maori social structure that valued descent through males and primogeniture. This parallel is reflected in Maori mythology and in rituals for firstborn males. Sinclair analyzes the social and mythological positions of women and younger brothers in terms of the cognatic descent group's lack of control over the "creativity" of younger brothers and women. In the case of women, this concerns the descent groups' uncertain control over female fertility in relation to descent group continuity.

Whereas women and younger brothers were categorical problems for Maori descent, it is the mother-in-law who is the "problem" in American society, as seen in chapter 10 by Allen Ehrlich. By combining scholarly findings from research on in-law relations with materials from popular culture such as newspaper advice columns, Ehrlich shows how the "mother-in-law problem" usually refers not to the relation between a man and his wife's mother, but primarily concerns a triangle of relations between a woman, her husband, and her husband's mother. Based on interviews and questionnaires from middle-class respondents, Ehrlich links the mother-in-law problem to gender role socialization and to ways that husbands negotiate a position of noninvolvement in the tensions of this kinship triangle.

Lisa Anderson-Levy's chapter 11 focuses on the intersection of race, class, and gender in Jamaican family systems. Raised in Jamaica, Anderson-Levy refers to her own family and experiences in Jamaica to show how the categories of race, class, and gender are productive of one another. She then shows how these often colluding and colliding axes of identity intersect with kinship in lower-class and middle-class families. In her analysis, we see how colonialism in Jamaica entailed a racial, class, and gender hierarchy that continues to shape Jamaican kinship systems.

The final chapter in this section is a contribution from archaeology that shows the influence of recent kinship theory from cultural anthropology. Here, Cynthia Robin uses a "discourse analysis" to examine the narrative texts of ancient Maya kings and from this draws connections between kinship and gender in ancient Maya society. This work shows the application in archaeological investigations of the new approach to kinship that emphasizes kinship as a social and historical process rather than as an abstract system. Thus, rather than using archaeological data to reconstruct genealogies and kinship models, Robin shows how the social reality of kin and gender relations was created by the ancient Maya through their publicly circulating discourse.

New Family Forms and New Formulations of "Family"

The chapters in part 5 concern new forms and formulations of kinship and family within the United States. The first three chapters deal with changes that are profoundly affecting household formation and kin relationships throughout the country and are the focus of much recent research in anthropology and other disciplines (see especially Stacey 1990; Weston 1991; and Modell 1998). Chapter 13, by David Jacobson, Joan Liem, and Robert Weiss, discusses problems of parenting from separate households. More and more children in the United States grow up in separate households, not only because of the high rate of divorce, but also because divorced or separated parental couples are increasingly sharing parental responsibilities. The study by Jacobson, Liem, and Weiss is based on interviews with two-household parental couples in twelve middle-class, mostly white families in the greater Boston area, along with interviews and projective tests administered to children of these parents. The authors concentrate on the problems of co-parenting experienced by fathers, mothers, and children, covering issues such as the logistics of moving children between households, the emotional problems of regular absences of children from a household, and the advent of a new partner in one or both households. This chapter analyzes these problems in terms of the challenges that two separate households pose to mainstream cultural constructions, which concern household boundaries, familial roles, and distribution of parental resources. The variation the study found in the reported difficulty of parenting from separate households is discussed in terms of parents' abilities to tolerate or negotiate more permeable household boundaries and more flexible parental roles.

As separate parental households threaten the physical boundaries of the traditional family in mainstream America, so "open adoption" weakens the boundaries of the family as defined by kinship. Judith Modell covers open adoption in chapter 14, based on her research with an adoption agency and its clients in the United States. Open adoption covers a range of situations, from a one-time exchange of nonidentifying information between adoptive and biological parents, to a face-to-face meeting, or to ongoing contact. But all varieties are a challenge to the "consanguineal core of kinship" that a policy of closed adoption previously defended and replicated in the United States. At the same time, although open adoptions are often presented positively as an extension of kinship, Modell found that, in fact, open adoptions are about gaining control over information, enhancing individual choice, and constructing "a permanency missing in a post-modern society." Discussing the importance and value of information and individual choice in U.S. society, Modell shows how adoption can no longer automatically replicate and support customary ideas of consanguineal kinship.

The United States has increasingly grown more tolerant of alternative families and marriage forms, as seen in William Jankowiak's chapter 15 on fundamentalist Mormon polygynous families. Based on his fieldwork in a fundamentalist community in the West, Jankowiak pinpoints a phenomenon of "father glorification" as a core feature of Mormon fundamentalist theology and constructions of kinship and family. He explores the theological roots and cultural expressions of father glorification in this community. Cultural expressions cover public testimonials glorifying fathers, forms of status competition through references to fathers, positive (and sometimes negative) childhood memories of fathers, and household dynamics. Of particular interest is his analysis of how father glorification arises in part from a polygynous family system that centralizes the father/husband; in addition, the competition of co-wives further promotes adoration of the father as co-wives draw their children into their strategies to secure their husband's attention.

Chapter 16 approaches a formulation of "kinship" in the United States from a new angle. Here, Richard Maddy takes a category from conventional kinship studies—fictive kinship—and applies it to his study of professional relationships within American biomedicine. The result is a new understanding of how American biomedicine actually operates as cultural system. His analysis shows how "fictive kinship" ties in biomedicine link participants in social networks that confer benefits, entail moral obligations, and provide access to social and economic power, much as fictive kinship relationships do in many other societies. Based on interviews and participant observation with biomedical practitioners, Maddy identifies several "fictive kinship clusters" whose internal relationships typify a kinlike organization. He presents three cases of these clusters, each revealing different aspects of fictive kinship in biomedicine. With these cases, Maddy discusses how such clusters form, the rituals and rites of passage they entail, and the ideological bases for their cohesion.

Kinship and the Politics of Nations

Intersections between kinship and the state, including not only kinship in relation to social structure but also kinship in relation to personhood, national identity, and political struggles are the focus of current research (Goody 1990; Ginsburg and Rapp 1995). In part 6, the book's final chapters touch upon this topic from two different angles. The first one by Ilana Gershon deals with Samoan migrant families in New Zealand, showing the conflicts between how the New Zealand government bureaucracy imagines "families" and their roles in the production of "good citizens" and the realities of Samoan migrant family life. Around this conflict she raises an important general question: Can liberal democratic governments genuinely support multicultural diversity while at the same time pursue their goal of helping families raise productive citizens? Focusing on the New Zealand government's intervention in bureaucratically defined cases of child abuse and juvenile delinquency, Gershon shows how this bureaucracy sees Samoan extended families through a European nuclear family lens, assuming them to be egalitarian systems for the circulation of knowledge and resources, a vision that masks the intricacies and realities of Samoan kinship.

Chapter 18 by Rosa De Jorio focuses on the role of kinship as metaphor in struggles for political power. Based on her research on women's associations in postcolonial Mali, De Jorio shows how both Malian women and state officials are employing kinship ideology (in particular, ideas of motherhood) to reformulate women's relationship to the state. Government officials employ a kinship idiom that enforces gender and status difference, while women use ideas of both kinship and gender to effectively "politicize the domestic sphere" and open new political avenues for themselves. On this basis, De Jorio proceeds to a discussion of the role of women elites and patron–client relations among women in Malian national development. Once again her discussion highlights the centrality of kinship in structuring power relations among group members within women's associations.

Conclusion

Together, these chapters reflect some distinctive new themes and approaches in kinship studies, with the history of the emergence of these new directions provided in the chapters by Brettell and Lamphere and in this introduction. Perhaps most prominent is that in current research, kinship is no longer a separate topic unto itself. It is focused outward on a diversity of other issues, with relationships of gender and power leading the list.

A second theme is the situating of kinship in historical context. No longer do we hear about "Navajo kinship," for example, in terms of a timeless structure of matrilineal clans and matrilocal residence, but instead, through Lamphere's chapter, we are acutely aware of process and change in Navajo meanings of matrilineal descent. In many of the chapters, and especially those by Lamphere, Sinclair, Anderson-Levy, Gershon, and De Jorio, colonialism and its aftermath are a crucial dimension of the broader historical framework within which kinship is approached.

A third theme is an emphasis on kinship with respect to the sociopolitical position of diverse actors. Within any culture, anthropologists no longer see one kinship "system" into which human actors fit and play out their allotted roles, but rather different kinship vantage points that depend on actors' particular positions. Thus, De Jorio shows how different segments of Malian society articulate "motherhood" to their own political ends. Jankowiak contrasts the different views of the Mormon polygnous family held by fathers, children, and co-wives, whose separate strategies support a cultural emphasis on "father adoration." Ehrlich's chapter shows the various vantage points and strategies of husbands and wives in the tangled "mother-in-law problem" of American middle-class couples. The chapter by Jacobson, Liem, and Weiss shows the different viewpoints of mothers, fathers, and children in American post-divorce parenting from separate households.

A fourth theme evident in these chapters, reflecting the legacy of Schneider and others, is that kinship studies are now more culturally contextualized; the focus is clearly on how local persons construct kinship and the meaning they attribute to these constructions. No one any longer takes for granted that kinship is constructed on the basis of biological procreation, and several of the chapters draw attention to culturally specific kinship constructions on other bases. A review of recent research along these lines is provided in Galvin's chapter and a discussion of the issue in relation to archaeological data on ancient Maya is provided by Robin.

The chapters by Lundin and Åkesson discuss "biologized" perceptions of kinship as specific to Western society and the ways that this perception in fact deviates from a Euro-American past. Equally important, as seen in both of these chapters, is that Western biologized kinship is itself now changing under the impact of new reproductive technologies. And from another angle, we see in Modell's chapter how "open" adoption in the United States fosters new constructions of parent–child ties. Indeed, process, change, and diversity in Euro-American kinship itself constitutes a separate theme in new kinship research as seen here in the chapters by Åkesson, Lundin, Ehrlich, Jacobson et al., Maddy, Jankowiak, and Modell.

One issue that was a fundamental part of past kinship debates and continues into the present is the relation between biology and culture in the study of kinship. As already discussed here, past arguments over so-called "social" and "biological" kinship focused on whether or not human kinship constructions grew out of "real" biological ties, or over what we should mean by "kinship" if they did not do so. These debates continue. Research in primate studies and neoevolutionary approaches to human kinship, as seen in the chapters by Silk and Hewlett, are shifting the debate, however. Today there is a much larger question being raised in the whole of anthropology: To what extent do biological and evolutionary forces guide human behavior? And to the extent that they are considered to do so, what are the implications for our understanding of human culture? If evolutionary forces shape human mating preferences, marriage strategies, and reproductive behavior, what are the implications for our understanding of human kinship? These questions are significant quite apart from local, culturally specific, emic bases of "kinship" construction, the focus of earlier debates. A kinship theory that integrates evolutionary approaches with other cultural ones is a challenge for the future.

There are other challenges ahead. Anthropologists still have not answered (or at least not answered with any unanimity) Gellner's question: On what basis should we consider a *blip*-relationship to be one of kinship? Meanwhile, and perhaps paralleling the anthropologists' concept of "culture," research and writing on "kinship" continues in spite of lack of agreement on what "kinship" really is.

With all of the chapters in this volume, we see not only the new arenas into which kinship is spreading and new approaches to the study of kinship, but also what in kinship studies has been retained from the past. While kinship study has been reformulated and historicized, and is less ethnocentric and better grounded in cultural context, we still see the use of some basic concepts of descent, marriage, reproduction, parenthood, adoption, polygyny, polyandry, fictive kinship, and families. We still see an interest in figuring out what "kinship" is to others and to ourselves as anthropologists. To this, we owe a continuing debt to all of our anthropological ancestors from Morgan through Schneider in the study of kinship.

Notes

1. For a critique of Schneider's use of Yap data and his earlier use of data for his 1968 study of American kinship, see Kuper 1999.

2. Leach (1961: 305) had expressed a similar concern much earlier when he noted of kinship in Pul Eliya, Sri Lanka, that "kinship systems have no 'reality' except in relation to land and property."

3. Collier and Yanagisako followed Schneider's ideas closely, but they did not take "gender" along quite the same path that Schneider took "kinship," which was to a statement of its nonexistence. They did not argue that, robbed of biology, gender is nothing. This leaves the problem of specifying what, then, gender is.

4. It appears, then, that kinship and gender are a single field because they are both based on the same error. Collier and Yanagisako also note that "Although the two [kinship and gender] are mutually constituted as topics of study in *our* society, this does not mean that they are linked in the same way in all societies" (1987: 34). It is not clear to me what, according to the authors, the basis for linking gender and kinship should be once the error is corrected.

References

Bernstein, Irwin S. 1997. Females and Feminists, Science and Politics, Evolution and Change: An Essay. In *Feminism and Evolutionary Biology: Boundaries, Intersections, and Frontiers,* ed. Patricia Adair Gotway. New York: International Thomson Publishing.

Carsten, Janet. 1995. The Substance of Kinship and the Heat of the Hearth: Feeding, Personhood, and Relatedness among Malays in Pulau Langkawi. *American Ethnologist* 22:223–41.

Collier, Jane Fishburne, and Sylvia Junko Yanagisako. 1987. *Gender and Kinship: Essays Toward a Unified Analysis.* Stanford: Stanford University Press.

Cucciari, Salvatore. 1981. The Gender Revolution and the Transition from Bisexual Horde to Patrilocal Band: The Origins of Gender Hierarchy. In *Sexual Meanings: The Cultural Construction of Gender and Sexuality,* ed. Sherry B. Ortner and Harriet Whitehead. Cambridge, U.K.: Cambridge University Press.

Edwards, Jeanette, Sarah Franklin, Eric Hirsch, Frances Price, and Marilyn Strathern. 1999. *Technologies of Procreation: Kinship in an Age of Assisted Conception.* 2d ed. London: Routledge.

Fox, Robin. 1980. *The Red Lamp of Incest.* New York: Dutton.

———. 1989a. *Kinship and Marriage: An Anthropological Perspective.* New York: Penguin, 1967. Reprint, Cambridge, U.K.: Cambridge University Press.

———. 1989b. *The Search for Society: Quest for a Biosocial Science and Morality.* New Brunswick, N.J.: Rutgers University Press.

Franklin, Sarah, and Heléna Ragoné. 1998. *Reproducing Reproduction: Kinship, Power and Technological Innovation.* Philadelphia: University of Pennsylvania Press.

Gellner, Ernest. 1960. The Concept of Kinship. *Philosophy of Science* 27:187–204.

Ginsburg, Faye D., and Rayna Rapp, eds. 1995. *Conceiving the New World Order: The Global Politics of Reproduction.* Berkeley: University of California Press.

Goody, Jack. 1990. *The Oriental, the Ancient, and the Primitive: Systems of Marriage and the Family in the Pre-Industrial Societies of Eurasia.* New York: Cambridge University Press.

Gotway, Patricia Adair, ed. 1997. *Feminism and Evolutionary Biology: Boundaries, Intersections, and Frontiers.* New York: International Thomson Publishing.

Hamilton, William D. 1964. The Genetical Evolution of Social Behavior. *Journal of Theoretical Biology* 7:1–52.

Holy, Ladislav. 1996. *Anthropological Perspectives on Kinship.* London: Pluto Press.

Hrdy, Sarah Blaffer. 1999. *Mother Nature.* New York: Pantheon.

Kuper, Adam. 1999. *Culture: The Anthropologists' Account.* Cambridge, Mass.: Harvard University Press.

Leach, Edmund R. 1961. *Pul Eliya, A Village in Ceylon: A Study of Land Tenure and Kinship.* Cambridge, U.K.: Cambridge University Press.

Maynes, Mary Jo, Ann Waltner, Birgitte Soland, and Ulrite Strasser, eds. 1996. *Gender, Kinship, Power: A Comparative and Interdisciplinary History.* Routledge: New York.

Modell, Judith S. 1998. *A Sealed and Secret Kinship: Politics and Practices in American Adoption.* Providence, R.I.: Berghahn Books.

Morgan, Lewis Henry. 1877. *Ancient Society.* New York: Holt.

Needham, Rodney. 1960. Descent Systems and Ideal Language. *Philosophy of Science* 27:96–101.

Oakley, Ann. 1972. *Sex, Gender, and Society.* New York: Harper and Row.

Parkin, Robert. 1997. *Kinship: An Introduction to Basic Concepts.* Oxford, U.K.: Basil Blackwell.

Pasternak, Burton, Carol R. Ember, and Melvin Ember. 1997. *Sex, Gender and Kinship: A Cross-Cultural Perspective.* Upper Saddle River, N.J.: Prentice Hall.

Peletz, Michael G. 1995. Kinship Studies in Late Twentieth-Century Anthropology. *Annual Review of Anthropology* 24:343–72.

Ragoné, Heléna. 1994. *Surrogate Motherhood: Conception in the Heart.* Boulder, Colo.: Westview.

Sahlins, Marshall. 1976. *The Use and Abuse of Biology: An Anthropological Critique of Sociobiology.* Ann Arbor: University of Michigan Press.

20

Chapter 1: Stone

20   *Chapter 1: Stone*

Shapiro, Judith. 1981. Anthropology and the Study of Gender. *Soundings: An Interdisciplinary Journal* 64, no. 4:446–65.

Scheffler, Harold W. 1973. Kinship, Descent, and Alliance. In *Handbook of Social and Cultural Anthropology*, ed. John J. Honnigman. Chicago: Rand McNally.

———. 1991. Sexism and Naturalism in the Study of Kinship. In *Gender at the Crossroads of Knowledge: Feminist Anthropology in the Postmodern Era*, ed. Micaela di Leonardo. Berkeley: University of California Press.

Schneider, David M. 1980. Reprint. *American Kinship: A Cultural Account.* 2d ed. Chicago: University of Chicago Press. Original edition, Englewood Cliffs, N.J.: Prentice-Hall, 1968.

———. 1984. *A Critique of the Study of Kinship.* Ann Arbor: University of Michigan Press.

Stacey, Judith. 1990. *Brave New Families: Stories of Upheaval in Late Twentieth Century America.* New York: Basic.

Stone, Linda. 1997. *Kinship and Gender: An Introduction.* Boulder, Colo.: Westview.

Strathern, Andrew. 1973. Kinship, Descent and Locality: Some New Guinea Examples. In *The Character of Kinship*, ed. Jack R. Goody. Cambridge, U.K.: Cambridge University Press.

Strathern, Marilyn. 1992. *Reproducing the Future: Essays on Anthropology, Kinship, and the New Reproductive Technologies.* New York: Routledge.

Tiger, Lionel, and Robin Fox. 1971. *The Imperial Animal.* New York: Holt, Rinehart and Winston.

Weston, Kath. 1991. *Families We Choose: Lesbians, Gays, Kinship.* New York: Columbia University Press.

Chapter Two

Whatever Happened to Kinship Studies?
Reflections of a Feminist Anthropologist

Louise Lamphere

In one of the last chapters of the book *Schneider on Schneider*, Richard Handler asked Schneider, "Whatever happened to kinship?" In typical Schneider style—a style of argument that comes through clearly and evocatively in this rich set of interviews, Schneider set off on a long conversational discussion. "First," he answered, "until recently, kinship had ceased being a major popular subject in anthropology. Papers on kinship clearly fell off. They became fairly rare. Now, of course, phoenix-like, it's risen from its ashes. This is due to people like Marilyn Strathern . . . and the new work in gay and lesbian studies, like that of Kath Weston and Ellen Lewin, and to feminist work, from people like Sylvia Yanagisako." Then in the next paragraph, Schneider fastened on a second factor, "Another answer is that it isn't just kinship. It's the whole idea of discrete, functionally specific institutions—that is, the whole idea that institutions are the major things of which society is made up, and the cultural categories of institutions are really what it's about. That, I think, was abandoned" (Schneider 1995: 193).

In this chapter, I want to amend and expand on Schneider's ideas. I will argue that kinship did not rise "phoenix-like" from its own ashes. Rather, as anthropologists shifted to new ways of looking at societies, our study of kinship transformed. In other words, there was more continuity than disjuncture.[1] If we mean by "kinship studies" the old dichotomy between alliance and descent theory, or how residence rules or domestic group cycles operate, then kinship did die out. But if we are looking for the ways in which people utilize kin ties, conceive of family and sexuality, and shape marriage arrangements, then the study of "kinship" did not disappear so much as move to new arenas of study and new conceptualizations driven by the work of a new set of theorists. Feminism and political economy were the twin approaches that had the most impact on altering kinship studies. I can best discuss these transformations through the history of my own research on the Navajo, U.S. working-class families, and new immigrants, although I will mention other research throughout the course of this chapter. Most recently, using the insights from feminist ethnography, the narratives of three Navajo women in one family allow me to rethink older topics within the study of kinship and provide a different angle of vision on residence patterns, marriage, and matrilineality.

Critiques from Inside Kinship Theory

Even from within kinship studies by the mid-1960s, there was a sense that something was wrong. Schneider's essay "Some Muddles in the Models" (1965) charged that Needham's analysis of matrilateral cross-cousin marriage was too rigid and inflexible (a "total system model"), while Needham was moving toward a position that kinship was not a unique phenomenon and therefore did not exist, at least as a distinct type of theory (Needham 1971). Schneider's analysis in *American Kinship* (1968) led him to argue that our own Euro-American models of kinship were based on ideas about biological reproduction (and the assumption that "blood is thicker than water") and thus led anthropologists to misconstrue the ways other cultures conceptualized the social relations we define as "kinship." In other words, all our models of kinship were hopelessly biased by our own system.[2]

I had my own sense during the mid-1960s that carefully crafted models did not work, though I could not have mounted the attack that Schneider did in emphasizing the Western bias of the genealogical method. Trained by two anthropologists who had been schooled in British social structure (David Maybury-Lewis and Tom Beidelman), I went to the Navajo Reservation in New Mexico after two summers of preliminary fieldwork in order to study Navajo residence patterns. Since Navajo social organization was notoriously "flexible" (to use Aberle's term), I wanted to know under what conditions Navajo families might choose to live matrilocally (meaning that daughters when married remain with their mothers) and when they might choose a virilocal (where sons when married remain with their natal group) situation. I was already well armed with concepts like Jack Goody's "developmental cycle of domestic groups" to study the kind of flexibility one finds in residence patterns (Goody 1958). However, my carefully constructed "problem," extracted from the literature on domestic groups and residence rules, was still much too abstract and removed from everyday Navajo life. Informants were particularly vague on why they had moved from one residence group to another and I soon reached a dead end. Instead, my strategy of living with different families and driving them from residence group to residence group or into Gallup for groceries or to pick up schoolchildren was much more conducive to the study of everyday cooperative patterns—the subject I finally took up for my dissertation.

During my first four years as an assistant professor at Rochester and at Brown (where I taught kinship to both Linda Stone, the editor of this volume, and Karen Sinclair, a contributor), I rewrote my dissertation as a book (Lamphere 1977). I took my analysis even further away from British structuralism, borrowing the notion of social network from British anthropologists working in urban Zambia where rigid models of lineage systems or domestic groups also did not work. The flexibility of Navajo social organization and the continuous change brought about by Anglo-American institutions pushed me beyond rigid models as I joined the critique coming from inside kinship studies itself. Yet my dissertation and book were still founded on the assumption that "the Navajo" were a discrete, bounded "society," one where the kinship system still dominated and anthropological characterizations of the Navajo as matrilineal and matrilocal still seemed appropriate.

The Feminist Transformation of Kinship

Beginning in the early 1970s, much more radical approaches to kinship theory began to come from those at the margins of the discipline. And here, I place myself among a group of younger women anthropologists who were heavily influenced by second-wave feminism. The feminist critique, at first embodied in *Towards an Anthropology of Women* (Reiter 1975) and *Woman, Culture, and Society* (Rosaldo and Lamphere 1974), was a response to our desire to bring feminism's newfound analysis about women and power into anthropology. The first issue, of course, was "Where were women in our ethnographic accounts?" For many of us, it was a shock to realize that we had spent most of our time in the field with women, but had not analyzed women's activities, much less contrasted them with men's. We needed to make women more visible and to theorize about them. This brought us to an analysis of power and autonomy, sexual asymmetry, and subordination. Kinship and lineage relations thus became construed not in terms of rights and duties but in terms of power and strategies to gain power. Here, Collier's (1974) work on patrilineal systems was particularly important. She emphasized women as strategists and argued that "wives are the worms within the apple of a patrilocal domestic group," advancing their own interests as they worked through their sons and husbands to break up domestic groups. Collier's point of view and that of Wolf (1974) as outlined in her article "Chinese Women: Old Skills in a New Context" had a big impact on my own article "Strategies, Cooperation, and Conflict among Women in Domestic Groups" (Lamphere 1974).

In my article, I broadened the analysis of women's strategies beyond patrilineal, patriarchal systems to include an analysis of women in foraging and horticultural/pastoral cultures, many of which had bilateral or matrilineal kinship systems. In contrast to peasant women (such as those in Taiwan in the 1950s and Chiapas in the 1970s), Navajo women live in a social world where

domestic and political spheres are relatively undifferentiated and, until recently, most crucial decisions were taken within the domestic group rather
than in a wider political arena. Authority within domestic groups (often a
cluster of households around a mother and her married daughters and sometimes married sons) is egalitarian. These "matrilocal grand families" are structured around female bonds, matrilocal residence, a system of matrilineal clanship, and a positive cultural valuation of the role of the mother. Under these
conditions, Navajo women have a great deal of control over their lives. Unlike
the women Collier and Wolf described who lived in patrilineal, patrilocal families, Navajo women do not need to wrest power from others who hold positions of authority or attempt to influence decisions that are not theirs to
make. At no time do a Navajo woman's interests conflict with those of her
close female kin. Women rarely "work through" men, but are themselves
mediators between men as, for instance, between a young husband and his
father-in-law.

Many of the contributions to *Woman, Culture, and Society* thus put gender
at the center of analysis and emphasized the variety of women's strategies
within kinship systems, viewing kinship in terms of the dynamics of power relations and negotiation rather than as more abstract systems of descent and
alliance. The thrust of our analyses was to view women as actors rather than
as bodies over whom men had rights and whose major function was to knit
together kin groups. While some may have perceived a declining interest in
kinship in the early 1970s, these articles indicate that kinship analysis was
"alive and well" within feminist anthropology.

Adding History and Political Economy

Still missing from many of the articles in *Woman, Culture, and Society* was a
historical perspective, one that could be wedded to an economic analysis that
would situate strategies in a larger context. We needed a better framework
than the one provided by British structural functionalism or American cultural anthropology.

For me, dependency theory first provided that framework. I initially used
this particular brand of political/economic analysis to rethink Navajo society
and history in my article "The Internal Colonization of the Navajo People"
(Lamphere 1976). I was, of course, cognizant of the impact of white society on
the Navajo Reservation in the mid-1960s. In the preface to my book *To Run
After Them: Cultural and Social Bases of Cooperation in a Navajo Community*,
I noted that "Anglo institutions—schools, hospitals, churches, government
agencies, and certainly Anglo business interests—dominate the reservation
and continue to shape the lives of the Navajo" (Lamphere 1977: xi). In fact,
one chapter of my book examined the impact of the pickup on Navajo cooperation: how those without cars or trucks got rides from those who owned ve-

hicles. What I did not have was a way of framing this impact, but the notion of an "internal colony" helped me to historicize and analyze some of the changes evident in Navajo society as a whole.

Drawing on Frank's (1967) model of underdevelopment in Latin America, on Jorgensen's (1971) analysis of the dependency fostered on American Indian reservations, and on Aberle's (1966) research on Navajo economic history, I reviewed the creation of the Navajo Reservation as an internal colony. This process entailed military defeat, the establishment of a reservation under Bureau of Indian Affairs (BIA) control (a relatively inexpensive method of administration), the integration of the Navajo economy into the rural satellite economy of the Southwest (through the establishment of the railroads and a network of trading posts), and the creation of a Tribal Council during the 1920s in order to grant oil leases to U.S. companies. This last set of events established a precedent of allowing non-Navajos to exploit natural resources on Navajo land. The trend continued into the 1960s and 1970s when leases for coal reserves on the Navajo Reservation became an important issue. On the one hand, the construction of power plants and strip mining at the Black Mesa, Pittsburgh-Midway, and Utah International mines provided needed resources for economic development and jobs. On the other hand, the mines removed families from homesteads and grazing lands and created environmental damage.[3] This historical analysis clarified for me the impact of larger economic and political forces in shaping the Navajo economy and in creating growing class differences on the reservation (between Tribal Council members and employees in the larger tribal, BIA, and Indian Health Service bureaucracies and local Navajo communities whose members depended on some traditional sources of income along with low-wage jobs). However, the analysis did not connect with the lives of Navajo families and how the changing political economy affected kin ties and the position of women.

Kinship, Urban Research, and Political Economy

It was not until I began to conduct urban research that I was able to link a political economy analysis with kinship. But here, my work on domestic group cycles and social networks stood me in good stead. I also turned from dependency theory to a straightforward analysis of the history of capitalism and the development of class relationships in my study of a New England working-class community, Central Falls, Rhode Island. In my book *From Working Daughters to Working Mothers* (Lamphere 1987), I was able to analyze census data on French Canadian, Irish/English, and Polish immigrant households in 1915 and 1935 using the construct of a domestic group cycle. But I argued that the cycle was in turn shaped by the expanding and then declining textile mill economy of Rhode Island. For example, as the cycle operated in 1915, at a first stage, young families were dependent on only the wages of working husbands.

Young wives either took in boarders or simply stretched their husband's wages. Middle-aged families, in a second stage, were able to send their teenage children into the mills, increasing household income, as the family came to depend on multiple wages. Yet, this strategy failed during the Depression as indicated in the 1935 census when fathers, teenage sons, and teenage daughters suffered unemployment as mills laid off workers or shut down.

Through long interviews with contemporary immigrants it was possible to understand the role of support networks for working families, a topic that could not be broached with historical census data. But even these networks had a kind of "developmental cycle," depending on a group's potential kin networks on entering the United States and the wage opportunities of the local political economy. Portuguese families came to the United States through kin who had migrated earlier, while Colombians had no such ties. By 1975, the dense networks of Portuguese kin were dispersing as layoffs and new job possibilities spread a sibling group throughout the region. In contrast, the Colombians, by bringing over parents and siblings, were creating denser kin networks in the same period. It was among these recent immigrants that the impact of wives' participation in the labor force had altered the domestic division of labor, with immigrant men taking a greater role in child care and some household tasks.

The micropolitics of domestic units and the importance of kin networks also continued to be of crucial importance in our Albuquerque study of women employed in the new Sunbelt industries (Lamphere, Zavella, Gonzales, and Evans 1992). Here we interviewed Anglo and Hispano couples where both the husband and the wife worked in blue-collar jobs in newly constructed apparel and electronics plants. Kin networks were supplemented with important friendship ties for Albuquerque working mothers. In all three of these studies (my dissertation book, the Rhode Island monograph, and the Albuquerque study), my interests have continued to be in household or domestic group organization and the use of kin networks for social and economic support. But the way I treated these organizing concepts changed as I paid more attention to gender differences and to the way in which the local political economy shaped support networks. For my research, kinship did not disappear as an interest but was reformulated through the impact of feminism and Marxist theory.

New Trends in Feminist Kinship Studies

During the late 1990s, feminist approaches to kinship gained wider recognition within mainstream anthropology as the work of Martin (1987, 1997) and Strathern (1992) began to have an impact and several important collections were published (Yanagisako and Delaney 1995; Franklin and Ragoné 1998; Edwards et al. 1999). A Wenner-Gren Conference on "New Directions in Kinship Study" took place in 1998, and at the American Anthropological Association meetings, two sessions were devoted to kinship theory, and other sessions on reproduction, gender, and family touched on issues of kinship. What seems at first glance to be the "reemergence of kinship" is a result, primarily, of the broader legitimacy (through graduate seminars, publication of university press books, and attendance at meeting sessions) that feminist research has acquired.

There has been an outpouring of research on the new reproductive technologies that has provided a new space for thinking about American and British kinship as women themselves (along with medical personnel, textbook writers, and family members) have confronted situations where the "biological facts" no longer have the appearance of being "natural." Anthropologists have studied amniocentesis (Rapp 1999), maternal serum alpha-fetoprotein screening (Press et al. 1998), ultrasound (Taylor 1998), infertility and assisted conception (Cussins 1998; Franklin 1997, 1999), and surrogate motherhood (Ragoné 1994). In some cases, as Martin's work shows, American metaphors of industrial capitalism or gender relations shape the way the medical establishment presents biological processes to women patients (Martin 1987, 1997). In others, women bring their own, often ethnically based, notions about biology and kinship to the medical encounter that surrounds a new technology such as amniocentesis (Rapp 1997). And in a third group of situations, cultural meanings concerning kinship (e.g., who is a mother?) are reshaped to meet new circumstances. Thus, in Ragoné's study *Surrogate Motherhood: Conception in the Heart* (1994), surrogates and adoptive mothers distinguish between the biological mother (the surrogate) and the social mother. Surrogates override their genetic contribution and view the adoptive mother as someone who has conceived the child "in her heart," not through her body (Ragoné 1994: 126). Both women adopt a set of practices (sharing shopping trips, baby showers, and birthing classes) that cement their relationship and help them redefine motherhood as based on nurturance rather than a biological tie.

Euro-American ideology tends, on the one hand, to naturalize both kinship and power and, on the other, to utilize the dichotomy between nature and culture. The tendency is to assimilate kinship to biology and to see it as "natural." Even anthropologists took the view that kinship was "based" on the natural facts, at least until Schneider and his students persisted in showing us that even these ideas are part of a cultural model. What Yanagisako and Delaney bring to the table is the important point that power is embedded in kinship as well as in other domains such as politics, religion, ethnicity, and nation (Yanagisako and Delaney 1995: 1–21).

Historical analyses of kinship theory and research into the Human Genome Project, cloning (Edwards 1999), and computer-generated models of artificial life (Helmreich 1998) examine notions of "substance" that lie behind conceptions of kinship in Euro-American culture. Feeley-Harnik (1999) shows that in the nineteenth century, Morgan's notion of "channels of blood" actually linked land, animals, water, roads, and indigenous peoples. In the twentieth century, rather than "blood relations," we have come to talk about kinship in terms of genes and, more recently, as "information" and "code." All of these ways of thinking of kinship as substance entail the dichotomy between nature and culture, whether "nature" is seen as the bedrock on which kinship is "added on" or culturally constructed (Yanagisako and Delaney 1995), whether nature is the ground or context for culturally constructed notions (such as that of the person or individual) (Strathern 1992), or whether culture and nature are mutually constituted (Edwards 1999). Recent approaches all generated by research on new reproductive technologies have given kinship theory a much more subtle and nuanced set of theoretical constructs, ones that seek to interrogate and make visible Euro-American assumptions and interventions as well as those of other cultures.

Another site for analysis of kinship has been the family, particularly new forms of partnership and domestic life in the United States. Stacey's *Brave New Families* (1990) probes the impact of the electronics industry in Silicon Valley on the upward mobility of two white families in the early days of economic boom. Then she follows their stories and those of their children as they experience divorce, death, religious conversion, feminism, drugs, and unemployment. Her study explores the changing nuclear family as it evolves into different household and kin forms. Weston's *Families We Choose* (1991) and Lewin's *Lesbian Mothers* (1993) examine gay and lesbian family, household, and relationship forms. These studies show how gays and lesbians (often rejected by their own nuclear families) borrow from American notions of kinship and reshape them, creating new definitions of kin relations. For example, Lewin's chapter on single lesbian mothers and their children emphasizes the phrase "that permanent roommate," citing the ways in which mothers develop "companionate," almost friend-like relations with their dependent children (Lewin 1993). Sherman's book *Lesbian and Gay Marriage: Private Commitments, Public Ceremonies* (1992) takes up this same theme in a different way, examining the myriad ways in which gays and lesbians create families through commitment ceremonies. Adoption is another area where Americans construct kin ties through both exclusion and inclusion, but here, adoptive parents create "as-if-begotten" kinship (Modell 1998) and thus suppress biological relations. In transnational adoptions, there are also negotiations around issues of class and race. Upper middle-class white Euro-Americans both erase and exclude the birth parents from what counts as family and yet retain the right to return a child who is in some way "defective" (Gailey 1998).

Finally, feminist anthropologists have examined kinship and family in connection with colonialism. Stoler's work emphasizes the changing colonial role in shaping sexual relations and family formation between Europeans and natives. At first, regimes encouraged concubinage and then later, with the immigration of European women to the colonies, created segregated European settlements where white women upheld sexual standards (Stoler 1997). Gailey takes a seemingly traditional analysis of the Tongan kinship system (of conical clans or pyramidal ramages) and uses it to explore both gender relations and the transformation of the kin system under missionary activity and colonial dependence (Gailey 1987). These analyses place kinship at the heart of analyses of power, a very different approach from early anthropological work that separated kinship from the domain of politics and ignored the importance of gender ideologies.

All of these studies have been powerfully informed by feminist anthropology, placing gender at the center of analysis, yet paying attention to race, class, and power. Most interrogate Euro-American conceptions of kinship and in the process lay bare the cultural logics involved in both utilizing these notions and/or restructuring them. Most studies also elucidate the daily practices Americans construct as they confront new situations (brought about through the new reproductive technologies, the increasing instability in wage, jobs, or marriages, and the increased acceptance of gay/lesbian relationships).

Navajo Kinship and Personal Narratives

In my present work *Weaving Together Women's Lives: Three Generations in a Navajo Family,* a biography of three women in a Navajo family, I am using personal narratives (gathered in long, life-history style interviews) to forge a story informed by both feminism and political economy (Lamphere n.d.). My approach owes a great deal to feminist ethnography where anthropologists have interrogated their own positionality vis-à-vis their subjects. A number of essays have examined the ways in which race, class, and colonialism shape the fieldwork situation, which nevertheless usually remains one in which the anthropologist has more access to power than do her subjects (Zavella 1993; Limón 1989; Wolf 1996; Narayan 1993). Several recent monographs focus on women's lives using dialogical forms that place the anthropologist and her subjects in the text as interlocutors (Behar 1993; Abu-Lughod 1993; Briggs 1998). What these narrative-based texts lack is specific attention to the historical context and political economy in which women's lives are carried out, something I attempt to remedy in my book, which spans the period from 1930 to the present.

I see my own life, as someone who grew up in Colorado, as part of the same political economy that has shaped the lives of Eva Price, her daughter Carole Cadman, and granddaughter Valerie Johnson. I first met Eva when I was conducting research for my dissertation in 1965 on the Eastern Navajo Reservation. I lived several months with Eva, her husband (who was often away working for the railroad), and four young boys. Her daughter Carole, who was much closer to my age, was attending a boarding school near Gallup, New Mexico. Over the past thirty-five years, I have kept in close touch with Eva and

Carole. During these decades, the children have grown and married, and Carole has had her own children, including Valerie, her oldest daughter, who attends the University of New Mexico where I teach.

One of the foci of the biography has become tracing the mutual and contrasting themes that separate our lives by class and race, as well as generation. There are aspects of my own family history that intersect with Navajo history, including my grandfather's role in the discovery of oil on the Navajo Reservation and our Presbyterian church's support of a mission in Tuba City. Eva's family experienced the impact of both oil development and missionization, in the former case through the family's interaction with a couple that ran an oil pumping station near their homestead in the 1930s, and in the latter case through Eva's conversion and active participation in the Church of Jesus Christ of Latter-day Saints (the Mormon religion). Both Carole and I vividly remember reading "Dick and Jane" as young grade-school students, but the gap between these texts and our everyday lives was quite different. I may have felt alienated from the silliness of the text and "blondness" of baby Sally, but those children looked much more like me than like Carole, who started school knowing only Navajo and who spent summers herding sheep with her grandmother. Our cultural and class backgrounds even more fundamentally shaped the way divorce and drinking have impacted our respective families. Finally, as I have watched Carole's experiences in the labor force and on welfare, and Valerie's passage through the reservation public school system into the state university and into a series of part-time jobs, our differing class position and life trajectories within the same state economy have become more marked, even as we have continued to interact across economic and racial divides.

In addition to the analysis of class, culture, and race, Eva's narratives have allowed me to rethink several aspects of Navajo kinship and reassess the value of kinship models that were prominent in the 1960s and 1970s within anthropology. I have approached kinship from a much more internal, narrative standpoint than I did thirty years ago, much like Abu-Lughod did in her book *Writing Women's Worlds* (1993). In what follows, I will use three examples from topics that have traditionally been at the heart of anthropological analysis of kinship. The first topic—domestic group developmental cycles—illustrates the way a more narrative, life-history approach uncovers the cultural and personal logics for postmarital residential moves. This exposes the weakness of abstract models of postmarital residence and the developmental cycle of domestic groups, prevalent in my own dissertation research and anthropological studies of the 1960s that relied heavily on one-time census analyses (Fortes 1949; Goody 1958; Richards 1950). The second topic—that of arranged marriage—can be used to critique not just the literature on kinship, but the models of assimilation and acculturation so common in the research on Native Americans. Finally, Eva's narratives, along with Schwarz's (1997a) recent writing on Navajo personhood, lead to a reconsideration of matrilineality, place, and the substance of kinship. The Navajo construction of kinship, which I argue does not utilize the dichotomy of nature and culture, contrasts with Euro-American forms of relationship. Rather than kinship as something constructed on top of or out of the "natural facts," (e.g., the processes of conceptions and birth, genetic relationship between parents and children, and so on), among the Navajo so-called "natural" forms, sacred beings, and humans all partake in the same structure, including those relationships that are included under the English term "kinship" and the Navajo term *k'é*, a term that means compassion, cooperation, friendliness, peacefulness, and unselfishness. Relationships of *k'é*, birth, and place are all intertwined so that aspects Euro-Americans would see as distinct (e.g., the creation of links between humans and the connections between humans and a particular landscape), are conceptually connected and inseparable.

Rethinking the Developmental Cycle of Domestic Groups

My earlier analysis of the developmental cycle of domestic groups looks much different when viewed from a narrative approach where the dynamics of family interaction and powerful cultural beliefs about death and illness play into decisions to move. More recently, economic forces, largely emanating from the U.S. political economy and the incorporation of Navajos into it, have pushed Navajos to move more frequently and to move to a variety of new contexts (suburban housing tracts near stores, schools, or chapter houses on the reservation, or to urban apartments or trailer courts). The search for wage jobs as well as new forms of housing and urban or border-town migration now enter into the mix of factors important in shaping residence and family developmental cycles.

In the past, anthropologists have conceptualized Navajo residence patterns in terms of matrilocality or, more technically, uxorilocality (a young couple resides with the wife's relatives). However, most non-Navajo observers wrote that there was considerable "flexibility" in these rules so that married sons often remain with their mothers and bring their wife to live with them (Aberle 1961, 1963). Witherspoon has summarized what his Navajo consultants told him in the following way, "A Navajo may live wherever his or her mother has the right to live. A mother has the right to live wherever her mother lived. In addition, a Navajo may live wherever his or her spouse has the right to live. Residence rules are therefore based on the mother-child and husband-wife relationships and residence rights are acquired from one's mother and one's spouse" (Witherspoon 1975: 74). However, these rules do not consider how new residence groups are formed (e.g., couples hive off from a mother or parental homestead), or how residence groups of middle-aged siblings or individual couples are moved.[4]

Through Eva's narratives of her childhood and young adulthood, it is possible to see how the dynamics of what we used to think of as domestic group

formation, development, and fission are played out in relation to Navajo beliefs surrounding illness and death, rather than through the application of abstract residence rules. For example, Eva's parents moved from their homestead
at Black Rock Standing in the early 1930s, after their eldest son was burned in
a fire that erupted when a kerosene lantern was overturned. They established
a new residence at Yellow Hills, where Eva still lives today.

As she explained, "And then my late older brother [Frank Sandman] . . . was
building a fire with the coals still in there. He poured white gas on it. It made
a 'ts'ibag' sound, and he caught on fire. . . . He became crippled, and his liga-
ments burned on one side. . . . Most of his hand was burned, and that is the
reason why his hand was like that. He was in critical condition when they
transported him to the hospital in Shiprock. He was on the edge of death.
That is what they were saying. Somehow he came back to life. That is how I
remember it.

"As for me, someone threw me out of the hoghan and I was standing outside. . . . At that time they didn't have cars, but the only person that had a car
was Hastiin Bitsii Be'estł'nii [Mr. Tied Hair]; he had a Model T. That's how
they took him to the hospital."

The fire that burned Frank Sandman provided a narrow escape for Eva, who
was pulled from the burning hoghan. Eleanor, Eva's sister who was eight years
older, remembered that Hastiin Tł'aai performed a Blessing Way for Eva, who
was only about four years old at the time. "He did an all night ceremony for this
one, at Black Rock Standing. . . . When my older brother burned up, my father
had [had] a bad dream then . . . [5] about two days later, my older brother
burned. So it was then that her grandfather [Tł'aal] performed the ceremony
for her. This is what I remember. . . . And then he also performed the Chiri-
cahua Windway for her too." The fire prompted the family to move from Black
Rock Standing to the base of a low hill near a larger yellow bluff, an area called
Yellow Hills, about three miles across the plains to the southwest. Clearly, the
bad dream and the subsequent fire meant that Black Rock Standing had become dangerous (*báhádzid*), and not where the family should rebuild and stay.
A new place would be *hózh*, not filled with *hoch* (evil, difficult, unpleasant conditions), but blessed, harmonious, balanced, and beautiful.[6]

Later, in the 1950s, this same older brother was involved in another fire, one
that took his life. Carole, Eva's daughter, was in Utah at the time, living with a
Mormon family (on the Mormon Placement Program). She recalled what
family members told her about the fire, after she returned to Yellow Hills that
next spring. "But I understand, they were saying that he was drinking, and
some of them, like Leonard Sandman [Frank's stepson] was drinkin' also at
the time. . . . He [Frank] tipped over the kerosene lamp. . . . And the only person that was in there with him was his daughter [Elizabeth] . . . and of course,
Elizabeth was young at the time . . . four or five. . . . And I guess the only thing
he said to her was, 'Run out. Get out,' while he was tryin' to find his way out
through the door. I don't know, but I think he was pretty drunk at the time.

He didn't make it out. That's what they were telling me when I came back [from Utah]. And when I came back, you know, people didn't live over here [at Yellow Hills]. See, I left when people were over here, against this hill. Real nice—a horse corral and houses and everything. . . . So, when I came back from Utah, you know, things were a little bit different than they used to be. People used to tell 'em, you know, 'You can't live over there' . . . everybody else just . . . moved across [the road]. And then over here, I guess Joe didn't wanna move this house; he just wanted to stay here . . . So that's how we stayed. We were a little distance from where those . . . people were, see?. . . [7] They used to say, 'It [will] affect you guys or something later in the future' . . . but it hasn't affected anybody yet."

In this narrative, Carole reiterated the Navajos' aversion to living near a place where someone has died, since the ghost may trouble those who remain and bring bad dreams or illness. Frank's widow Anita, her grown son Leonard, his wife, and their children moved across the road to a new residence site.

Later, Eva moved for a while across the road and had a hoghan built there (near her sister's house), because she had become very ill. The first phase of her illness led to a conversion to the Native American Church (also known as the Peyote Religion) and to the discovery that Joe, her husband, was performing witchcraft on her and was thus the source of her illness. As Carole told the rest of the story, "After she [had] gotten better, you know, maybe like a year or something like that, she started feeling very funny . . . like . . . something was burning on her body. . . . She felt absolutely funny to where she couldn't stand going into this old house over here. And they had to build her a new hoghan across the road. And she used to feel better when we stayed over there. For every time she entered this house . . . something would start bothering her. And she said that up in the mountain when she was young she used to live with my uncle Frank Sandman and Frank Sandman told her to go up to the cornfield; she said that somebody's eating corn and . . . she had a .22 gun, and she found out that it was a porcupine. So . . . when the porcupine was sitting on top of a tree, she aimed at it and she killed him . . . she got him in the heart and maybe, you know, that started affecting her because that's got something to do with the . . . Mountain Top Way Chant [*dziłk'ijí*] . . . and she burned the poor porcupine also. And that was what was starting to bother her. . . . They did all kinds of medicine men singing on her." Only after she was well again, and after she had separated from her husband, did she return to her mother's area and her former house.

In the next two generations, Eva's children and grandchildren have often moved because of wage jobs or new housing opportunities that have become available in federally funded neighborhoods where two-, three-, and four-bedroom, all-electric homes have been built. Timothy, the oldest, has adhered to the more traditional pattern. He moved to the residence group of his wife's mother, building a hoghan there, and remaining in that site for more than twenty years, although both he and his wife have commuted to wage jobs in

Shiprock and Farmington. Another son, Rudolph, also has lived with his wife's family, but primarily at their summer residences in the Chuska Mountains. As his children became of school age, he and his wife would spend the school year at Eva's home. For a number of years, they lived in the ceremonial hoghan built for Valerie's *Kinaaldá* (girl's puberty ceremony),[8] and then later they built a large hoghan just north of Eva's house. Then, in the early 1990s, they moved to a newly constructed home in a tribal housing area near Newcomb, fifteen miles away from Eva's. In 1998, they divorced and Rudolph moved back to the hoghan next door to his mother. Randy, the youngest son, often lived with his mother after his marriage to Barbara. The housing program sponsored by the tribe built a one-bedroom home for Eva and for Randy's family, next door to the remodeled log cabin that Carole and her children occupied in the late 1980s. A few years later, Randy and Barbara moved to Salt Lake City where Randy works in a warehouse. He and his family (often including one of Barbara's aunts) have lived in a series of apartments and a rented home. Erica, Carole's middle child, immigrated to Salt Lake City after high school and lived with Randy and his family before sharing several apartments with co-workers and then living on her own. Valerie and her younger brother J. R., as of 1999, were living in Albuquerque where Valerie lived in a rental apartment and J. R. stayed in the dormitory at Southwestern Polytechnic Institute where he attends classes.

While a narrative approach reveals the importance of Navajo notions of illness and death in residential decisions in the period 1930–70, recent changes in the Navajo economy and the prevalence of wage work away from the reservation have propelled Navajo people away from traditional residential groups. These decisions are not just about "neolocality" but are negotiated through kin ties, which are often crucial in allowing a family member to immigrate to an urban area or to return home to his or her mother's residence site if a job is lost or a relationship breaks up. Narratives unveil the cultural logic behind such residential choices, even as fluctuations in the availability of jobs or schooling mean that Navajo individuals are moving as often as families following their herds moved in the late nineteenth century.

Marriages and "Models of Acculturation"

Anthropological analysis of marriage in the 1950s and 1960s was rooted in a model emphasizing marriage as the glue between two kin groups. The transfer of rights over women's reproductive capacity and labor was the main vehicle for forging such affinal relations (Fortes 1949; Radcliffe-Brown and Forde 1950; Radcliffe-Brown 1952; Lévi-Strauss 1969). Such a view seemed compatible with the study of small-scale populations in the colonial contexts often studied by anthropologists. But with the increasing impact of Western notions of romantic love, egalitarian gender relations, and "individual choice," so-called "traditional" views of marriage are changing. It is all too easy to view these changes within the context of an assimilationist model, one that is particularly prevalent in the literature on Native Americans. In this view, Native Americans or Navajos progress along a continuum from "traditional" to "assimilated." They lose their culture and language and become more and more "white" or "American," not only in terms of material culture (housing, dress, food) but also in terms of cultural knowledge and identity. Individual Native Americans and Navajos can thus be classed as either "traditional," "semi-traditional," or "assimilated" or "acculturated" (i.e., "modern"). A variant of this model posits that Navajos or other Native Americans are "between two worlds" or have one foot in the nineteenth century and the other in the twenty-first (see Benedek 1995: 7–12). Such a model assumes an incompatibility between "tradition" and "modernity." It emphasizes the impossibility of new patterns of integration and it leaves the impression that Navajos are "torn" between two opposites, or "stuck" in a "no-win" situation. An analysis of narratives within one family allows me to use a much more dynamic and less teleological approach to the intersection of Navajo culture with the larger American political economy and culture. By examining the way marriage was experienced by Eva, Carole, and Valerie, we can see that there is no simple unidirectional change from arranged marriage to relationships of "choice" as an acculturation model would suggest. Rather, there are both radical transformations and fascinating continuities over a seventy-year period, as each woman forged relationships within the possibilities presented to her and forms a narrative analysis of her own relations and that of her other kin.

Eva's mother Mary Sandman and Eva both had arranged marriages, as did Eva's sister Eleanor. Each was arranged when the girl was thirteen or fourteen, just after her *Kinaaldá*, to a man several years older. Eva recalled how her mother described her relationship with her father. "This is what my mother used to say, when I was small, when I was about twelve years old. 'He had already become a man. I was given to him.' This is what she used tell us. 'And so I was afraid of him, and I didn't want him.' [S]o she was left by herself with him, and he would tie her up next to a pole and wrap the rope around her. So that she wouldn't run away from him. 'He did that to me,' my mother used to tell me. That's how it was. And somehow she got used to it."

Very often these early relationships broke up, even in Mary Sandman's generation. This was also the case for both Eva and her sister Eleanor. Like their mother, their narratives indicate they attempted to avoid these marriages, or once married, resisted their husband's advances. Eva explained that "I was scared of him, for four years . . . I was still little and he was a man. . . . It was my mother who actually did it, not my father. Well, he [Aaron] was with another woman—Betty's mother. Betty's mother passed away. . . . You'll be given to him, they told me.

"Yes, I was afraid of him, and they were saying that I should marry him, and they cooked and prepared food and I was told to take out some cornmeal

mush in the four directions, and so I ate some. Then people spoke to me." [9]
After the marriage ceremony, the couple lived in the hoghan with Eva's parents. "I used to run away from him [to stay with a clan sister]. Her name was Elsie. She was Shoemaker's wife's daughter, the youngest one. We would go around together. In the summers, I would herd sheep with her. 'Why did they do that to you?' she asked. So I would run away from him. Sometimes I would even spend the night over there."

Eva reiterated, "I was scared. He told my mom. He told my mom and his mother, Cross Hills Lady, that he was not wanted by me. That's the reason for it . . . I was not used to him . . . He was a man. I was just a child. [10] At that time, my older brother Grant was in the army, World War II, 1940, '41 and '42. That is how I remember, when he came back, he really got mad at my mother. 'Why did you give her away to a man? Are you crazy?' he scolded her. 'You should have let her go to school.'" [11]

Eleanor, Eva's older sister, had an arranged marriage as well. When she heard about the pending ceremony, she also ran off to a clan sister who was herding sheep, but this woman counseled her to go through with the marriage even though she was "scared." In both cases, the marriages broke up. Later, Eva and Eleanor formed other relationships that were consensual and not marked by a ceremony where the couple eats cornmeal mush from a traditional Navajo wedding basket.

In contrast to her mother and aunt, Carole had two significant relationships (one with Valerie's father) before her mother arranged a marriage for her in the mid-1970s. Carole herself was very ambivalent about the marriage and tried to avoid it. "It was a forced marriage," she said. Carole ran away to a girl-friend in Shiprock where she stayed all night, but then she returned. "Well, she forced me . . . my mom forced me." Her mother and a man named Elton who was trying to arrange the marriage made a lot of promises. "He'll take care of you. I'll be wealthy after . . . he starts helping me. . . . But I found out that . . . it was a totally different story after [about] three months later. . . . He was an alcoholic." The marriage lasted several years before Carole left. Clearly, female resistance to arranged marriage, in this family at least, was not simply a response to acculturation or the impact of Western notions of "individual choice." Resistance and acquiescence had a great deal to do with the kinds of economic resources and social support each woman could marshall in a particular context.

The meanings of marriage are often negotiated between generations that have very different understandings, as clearly was the case for Eva as she resisted her mother's arrangements, and for Carole when she resisted those of her own mother. Both "gave in" in the short run, but through different paths, they eventually extricated themselves from these marriages. Valerie, a full-time student living 200 miles from home with scholarships and, later, a steady part-time job, has been more successful in defining her own path. During her college years, Valerie had a long-term relationship with Duane whom she met in high school, but she was not married. The divergence between her views and the experiences of her mother and grandmother was not apparent to her until the day she lay on the bed listening to my interview with Carole and Eva concerning the role that arranged marriages played in her own family. Her surprise and disagreement with these marriages emerged on that Sunday morning in January 1996. This four-way conversation illustrated the ways that a more narrative approach to kinship and marriage uncovers the interpretive meanings of differing conceptions of marriage and illustrates the ways women negotiate across generational differences, often incorporating another's point of view into their own thinking.

Eva explained the old system as one based on respect. "That's what it was for; that was how it was done. Now it seems like we don't have any worth. Like when they just get together these days. Later on, they split. Anyway, inside a church is also a marriage that has worth [meaning]. . . . That is how it was." Valerie objected, saying, "I'm going to marry who I want to marry. Not what nobody, what everybody else wants . . . for me . . . I mean, once you think about it, if somebody were to pick a husband for you, it's like disrespectful to you. . . . It's like you're saying, 'You're not . . . old enough or you're not mature enough to find your own husband,' so somebody else has to do it for you. You know what I mean?"

My own role in this conversation was to explain, as an anthropologist, that lots of other cultures had arranged marriages. But I also suggested to Valerie that we (meaning the larger American society) agreed with her. "That's the way we think about it, but I think other systems think . . . what marriage is really about is ties between two families. And what they're trying to do is make an arrangement between two families who will . . . provide kids for both families." Eva returned to the issue of worth and respect. "And probably after you are bought like that, and paid for, then you also become of worth to the relatives as you go among them. That was the reason for that price, so that you earn the right to go among the male's and the female's family, out of respect for them and respect for one another."

In a later interview in 1997, Valerie commented on her views of arranged marriage that seemed to incorporate her new understandings of her own family history, even as she used the language of individual choice. An acculturation model that views assimilation as taking on the dominant culture's values seems too simplistic to register the nuanced way in which Valerie thinks about her own situation, yet validates her grandmother's, mother's, and uncle's experiences. "I never understood the concept behind those arranged marriages. Maybe they just thought that person was good for you and they were wealthy, they owned cows, or horses, or whatever. Maybe that could have been a factor. Maybe their family was well-off, and you wanted your daughter to go and be part of that wealthy family. But my views are definitely different over arranged marriages. I, myself, maybe if I lived back in the 1960s . . . wouldn't have minded so much, but now I'm my own individual, and I'm free to make my own choices. I don't think I would agree to it if my grandma or my mom would ever suggest it to me. I don't think I would want to. I would never impose that on my children. I think it just has a lot to do with the changing times. That's how they did it back then and today it's like, these kids these days are growing up and they choose for themselves. They have choices. Back then, you didn't have a choice only because you couldn't get off the Reservation. There was no way you could get off the Reservation. You had to stay . . . and learn to weave . . . either you were weaving, or you bore children, or you kept up with your farm. That was your life, that was the way of living back then. But now there's this difference. There's more opportunities for people these days. My Uncle Bean's marriage was arranged, and his arranged marriage seems to be working. . . . I don't really know. There's just a lot of factors that played a large part on why they did it back then as opposed to today."

Matrilineal Clanship, Place, and the Substance of Kinship

Finally, these narratives shed light on the nature of matrilineal clanship and the importance of place in relation to the conceptions of kinship. The outlines of Navajo kinship have been best worked out by Aberle (1966) and Witherspoon (1975), the former drawing more heavily on a social structural approach, and the latter on a more cultural, interpretive one. Witherspoon writes that Navajos think of kinship in terms of k'é. Following the terminology of his mentor Schneider, Witherspoon called this "intense, diffuse, and enduring solidarity" (Witherspoon 1975: 37). "My relatives," or shik'éí, are the particular ones with whom one shares such intense enduring relationships. They are relatives through what anthropologists call clans (open-ended collections of kin descended from a common ancestor where the actual genealogical links are not traced). K'é is anchored in birth, since it is through birth that a baby becomes affiliated with relatives on both the mother's and father's side. First, every Navajo is born of a woman (coming up and out of her womb). Birth affiliates a child with her or his mother and the mother's relatives or clan. These would include the mother's mother, the mother's sisters, and women of the same clan as well as one's own siblings (those who came up and out of the same womb) and children of any women in the same clan. Other important relatives would be males of the same clan, including mother's brothers, sister's sons, and mother's mother's brothers. It is birth from women linked directly to the births of other women that is central to identifying one's clan.

Second, each Navajo is "born for" his or her father. This notion of being "born for" affiliates each child, male and female, with the father's matrilineal clan. Third, each individual is further related to those their father was "born for," that is, the father's father's clan (called da shináli). Finally, the individual is also affiliated with the relatives his or her mother was "born for," that is, the mother's father's father's clan (called da shichei). Some clans are "related to each other" and, hence, members of these clans address each other by kin terms and assume relationships based on *k'é*.

Birth and, hence, clanship is located in space. Clan names derived most likely from places, for example, *Tódích'íí'nii* or Bitter Water describes a place where the water perhaps had a distinctive taste. Others are *Kii'yaa' áanii* or House in the Rocks, *Tábaa'há* or Water's Edge, *Haltsooí* or Meadows, and *Tó baazhní'ázhi* or Two-Came-To-Water. Even clan names like *'Áshiihí* (Salt People) or *Haashtl'ishnii* (Mud People) could refer to places where there was a salt deposit or a particularly muddy area. Eva's clan *Dziłtł'ahnii* is often translated as "Mountain Corner," but another possible translation is "Mountain Recess." The name indicates a corner in a rocky landscape, a place where two ridges come together at an angle, creating a recessed area in the shadow of uplifting rocks. Although clans do not hold territory or property in common, clan members often visit, extend hospitality, or go out of their way to help clan relatives. *K'é* and clan relationships are the primary way in which the Navajo people locate themselves in the social universe. There are connections to the physical universe as well. Even though generations of movement and post-marital residence patterns have separated sisters and their descendants and even though links to the original places have been severed, clanship ultimately leads back to the land. Birth, motherhood, *k'é*, and landscape are intimately connected.

Place, Clanship, and the Metaphor of Corn in Eva's Narratives

These connections can be seen first in Eva's stories of her own clan history, and second, in her narratives about her birthplace and her own identity. Eva is a matrilineal relative of *Hastiin Tł'aaí*, a well-known medicine man whose relationship with the local trader's wife, Franc Newcomb, led to a published biography, and whose connections with Mary Wheelwright resulted in the founding of the former Museum of Navajo Ceremonial Art in Santa Fe. In tracing Eva's relationship to *Hastiin Tł'aaí*, the importance of clan relations (in this case, the *Dziłtł'ahnii* or Mountain Recess Clan) has emerged much more clearly than in my dissertation. Furthermore, these narratives locate the various groups of *Dziłtł'ahnii* in space. This amounts to a placing of people who are *k'é* or *shik'éí* (my relatives) in the landscape. Such "emplacement" is also interwoven with the colonization of the Navajo. For example, one of the most important "placing" narratives is that of *Hastiin Tł'aaí*'s mother's escape from Fort Sumner (where the Navajo were held between 1864 and 1868), and her long walk back to the Chuska Mountains to her homestead on "Fuzzy Mountain." Eva tells the end of the story in the following way:

"It took her seven days to return home. She went up the Chuska Mountains, and as she was coming back, she noticed someone behind her [a black spot in the distance]. So then she thought that this would be the end of her life, because she thought that it was one of the Mexicans.[12] But as he came closer, she could see that it was a Navajo. It was her uncle. Her feet were puffy and swollen, she could barely walk, but she did. So then he threw her on top of the horse. Then he took her back to where they lived somewhere on top of that mountain range. And so this is where our grandmother came from and so did we. Just like corn, we have spread out and we are of the many that have sprouted."

Elsewhere she said, "Based on that, I believe we are from the *Dziłtł'ahnii* clan. His late mother had been taken captive at Fort Sumner. After she escaped and returned home *Tł'aaí* came into existence [was conceived, came into being] and from that birth, we came into existence, and to this day we of the *Dziłtł'ahnii* clan have grown [like plants]. This did not take place somewhere else. It took place here on this mountain ridge, on 'Chuska Mountain,' [said in English] on this land we call 'Washington Pass' [also in English]. This is how it is, and from this mountain ridge, our ancestors have traveled back. And also, we who are of the *Dziłtł'hnii* clan have grown [come to maturity as a corn plant comes to maturity]."

Eva mingles her memories of *Tł'aaí*"s mother with her strong sense of how her clan is rooted in the Chuska Mountains, placed there in a landscape that has defined them and also allowed them to expand and grow. She uses the word *diniit'* which is associated with plant life, especially corn, growing to maturity. The metaphor of the cornstalk is just below the surface of this description, but it is also a metaphor of growth that is "emplaced," put down in a certain locale associated with members of a matrilineal clan, kinsmen, or relatives. There is an unbroken link (subsumed in the metaphor of the growing cornstalk) between *Tł'aaí*'s mother, *Hastiin Tł'aaí*, Eva's mother, Eva and her children.

When we first began working on these narratives, Eva took me to her birthplace, *Dzil 'Zéé'aasgai* (White Neck Mountain). There, we found the ruins of her parents' hoghan. Then we walked to a grove of oak trees just down a slight hill near an old cornfield. There, Eva told me she was born under a ramada or shade (*cha'a'oh*) that had been built for outdoor living during the summer months. She bent over and took some of the earth and blessed herself with it.

Afterwards, Eva recorded her thoughts about being back at her birthplace. "This mother earth, you put it on like this; [then] you will live a good life. And when it rains, you put that on your body or you bless yourself with the rainbow. And early in the morning you have to bless yourself [with corn pollen]. These are holy places. I am very glad I have returned to my birthplace. I am very grateful. There is where I was raised, the place I was born. If you just forget and go any old way, I don't think you will last long that way. You won't live very long. You must return to your birthplace and say prayers for yourself and state how you will be and how you will live. These days, babies are born in hospitals. What did they do with that thing that comes out with the baby [the placenta]? What do they do with that now? They probably burn it and then trash it. Not me. They say you should roll around on the dirt on the place where your placenta is buried. They would say 'Go back over there and roll around the area where you are born.'"

Burying the placenta is done so it can "become one with Mother Earth again" (Knoki-Wilson as quoted by Schwarz 1997a: 138). The baby's umbilical cord is even more important. The parents or grandparents often bury the cord in a location considered to be beneficial to the child's future. A boy's cord was usually buried in a sheep, cattle, or horse corral, or in the family fields when it was desired that he be concerned with livestock or with farming. Likewise, a girl's cord might be buried in a sheep corral to ensure that her thoughts were with the livestock or inside the hoghan so that she would become a good homemaker. Also, a girl's cord might be buried where the loom is erected in the hoghan if the family wished her to become an expert weaver (Schwarz 1997a: 138).

As Schwarz explained, "Burial of the cord in the earth anchors the child to the 'belly button' of Mother Earth and establishes a lifelong connection between a person and a place, just as the cord anchors a child to its mother while in the womb and establishes a lifelong connection between mother and child. The presence of this anchoring cord is evidenced by spirals on the human body that represent an anchoring force that forms a continuous connection from Mother Earth to the person" (Schwarz 1997b: 48).

This connection between a person and place was clearly explicated by Eva. "I was not raised anywhere else but around the Washington Pass area. On that mountain was where I was born. And to this day, I am a woman from this place, the one called Sheep Springs. From a certain point, the white people and the Navajo have been aware of me, and that is how I walk around. And for that reason, my thinking has been laid down. That's how I think about it, to this day and from this time on."

Euro-American kinship, as I have already pointed out, always implies a distinction between nature and culture, although there have been several ways of characterizing the relationship between the two. In contrast, among the Navajo, there is no definitive split between nature and humans. In Navajo thinking, moisture, air, substance, and heat are the four elements needed for life to exist. A fifth element—vibration—which is often talked about as sound, is also necessary.[13] These elements often manifest themselves in a range of phenomena from rain (a form of moisture), to soil (a form of substance), to zigzag lightning (heat), and wind (air). Baskets, hoghans, cradles, and looms are composed of these elements just as persons are. Thus, in the Navajo formulation there is no distinction between the human, the supernatural, and the natural. All are constructed of the same elements and all are equally rooted in space.

It is not surprising, therefore, that Eva's narratives make these connections between the growing corn, birth, and place. Matrilineality is not, as most conventional anthropological models would suggest, an issue of building on the biological facts and tracing kin through females (using a particular cultural construction of kinship). Such an analysis misses the importance of place in the constitution of the person and those who are *k'é*. Birth and growth are the twin processes that apply to the making of kinship, but these processes are also located on the land. The emergence of the ancestors of the Navajo through several layered worlds on to the earth surface (the earth referred to as "our mother") parallels the emergence of siblings up and out of a mother's womb (and the emergence of clan relatives through the wombs of related mothers) at a particular place. Just as the Earth as Mother sustains the corn plants so they can grow, Navajo mothers give sustenance to their children (see Wither-spoon 1975: 20–21). And again, these processes of growth occur in individual cornfields and at particular places of residence.

The substance of kinship is at once about the natural and the cultural.[14] The particularity of place, where one was born, where one's placenta and cord are buried, and the land where one grew up, or where one's clan relatives have lived are intimately connected to the creation of the person and to the consti-tution of a whole social universe.[15] Personal narratives are a particularly good source for bringing out these mutually constituted connections. They not only give a sense of kinship in relation to historical meaning, personhood, and the substance of kinship, they outline the ways Navajos put the cultural meanings of kinship to work in their own lives.

Conclusion

Whether we think of kinship as having disappeared and then, more recently, "risen from the ashes" or whether, as I have argued, it has "been there all along," the kinship that anthropologists study in the 1990s is a transformed subject. Its center is perhaps in the Euro-American system and the contact of that system with others. Research on kinship has shifted over to the exploration of repro-duction and sexuality, the analysis of new forms of family, and the impact of colonialism and transnational forces on populations across the globe. We are studying kinship through examining ideologies, using narratives, and placing the anthropologist among his or her subjects (rather than as an aloof analyst). Feminism and political economy have been the twin orientations that have fu-eled these changes. As we look toward the study of kinship in the twenty-first century, we should expect that the frameworks we use will continue to change, but that anthropological interest in those intimate family and social relation-ships that are the "stuff" of everyday lives will continue to thrive.

Notes

1. This same theme has been developed in the Wenner-Gren international symposium, "New Directions in Kinship Study: A Core Concept Revisited," which took place March 27 to April 4, 1998, organized by Sarah Franklin and Susan McKinnon. The organizers argue that kinship

studies have "neither declined nor been displaced from the center of anthropological inquiry. Rather kinship studies continue to be crucial to the discipline—but this is, in part, precisely because they no longer look quite the same as they once did" (Franklin and McKinnon 2000).

2. Schneider's impact on feminist analysis of kinship is seen in Yanagisako's and Delaney's collection *Naturalizing Power: Essays in Feminist Cultural Analysis* (1995). A recent reconsideration of Schneider's impact on kinship studies is being edited by Richard Feinberg. Several papers from this volume were presented at the 1998 American Anthropological Association Meetings in a session titled "The Cultural Analysis of Kinship: The Legacy of David Schneider and Its Implications for Anthropological Relativism," organized by Martin S. Ottenheimer and Richard Feinberg.

3. Although the tribal government has always favored leasing coal reserves to outside interests, the Navajo Tribe has attempted at several times in the past to renegotiate the terms of leases from Peabody Coal. On June 16, 1999, the Navajo Tribe sued Peabody for $600 million for monies owed because royalty rates were not promptly raised in the late 1970s and because Peabody pressured BIA officials to keep rates as low as possible (*Navajo Times*, June 24, 1999, pp.1, 2, 6).

4. Witherspoon *does* discuss the possibility that a divorced or widowed woman who is part of a couple that had already established a residence group may remain as head of that family (in the use area of the husband's kin) rather than move back to her relatives. He gave an example of one divorced woman and said the following about the impact of death: "If the husband dies, the wife is expected either to remarry into the unit or to return with her children to her mother's unit. She can also remarry elsewhere and take her children with her. In the leadership generation, the wife will remain without remarrying into the unit, because she will likely be the head of the unit" (Witherspoon 1975: 76).

5. A dream is often an indication that something dangerous, or *bahadzid*, is going to happen.

6. The terms *hózh* and *hoch* are perhaps the two most important concepts in Navajo thought and worldview. *Hózh* has been translated as beauty, harmony, blessing, balance, and pleasant conditions. It describes a state of all that is positive—the way things should be. Its opposite is *hoch*, a state that has been described in English as one of disharmony, disorder, evil, or unpleasant conditions.

7. Eva's house is about 150 yards from the site of the hoghan that burned.

8. The *Kinaaldá* is performed when a young girl reaches menarche. It is a four-day ceremony during which the girl runs towards the East three times each day (to ensure a strong body later in life). A large corn cake is baked overnight in the ground on the last night of the ceremony, and songs from the Blessing Way are sung. What the girl does during these four days has an impact on her later personality, health, and well-being. The ceremony celebrates Navajo values of womanhood and ensures that a girl will live a long life (see Frisbie 1967; Schwarz 1997).

9. The core of the Navajo wedding ceremony consists of having the couple eat cornmeal mush served in a Navajo wedding basket before an assemblage of the groom's and bride's relatives. Afterwards, speeches are given urging the couple to take good care of each other.

10. Carole thought that her father had stayed until shortly after her birth in 1948, probably six years after Eva was married. "My grandmother used to tell me that he stayed around until I was one or two months old because he made that cradle board for me."

11. Carole added, "In those days, you know, they used to say, 'Oh, that man,' you know, 'will help you within your future life . . . and buy you things, and, you know, keep you well off.' Those are the things that I used to hear a lot. From my *grandmother*, you know. And I don't . . . know if that's right, but . . . they would just give you anybody else that they think, you know, is capable of . . . marrying you."

12. At the beginning of this narrative, Eva said that '*Asdz Hashké* (Angry Woman), *Hastiin Tl'aaí's* mother, had been kidnapped by Mexicans and enslaved. One of them made her his wife. There were two Mexicans watching her when she escaped. A very large dog that was tied up outside escaped with her and led her safely back towards Navajo territory. When she reached the Rio Grande, she evoked the names "Collected Waters" and "Water's Child," which caused the waters to recede so that she could cross. These waters, like all parts of the plant, animal, and

worldly environment, have the same homologous properties as humans. They are animated, move, and in this case, provided assistance and help. This is significantly different from the story recorded in Newcomb's book *Hosteen Klah* (1964). According to Newcomb *Hastiin Tł'aaí*'s mother was called '*Asdz Tsósí* (Thin Woman) and later '*Asdz Tso* (Tall Woman). At Fort Sumner, she worked for the wife of an army lieutenant, but left this employment in the summer of 1865 to marry Hoskie Nolyai. She was pregnant when she traveled with her uncle *Dził tł'ahnii Yázhí* and his wife, her aunt, and this woman's Apache husband to Fort Wingate. They were allowed to leave Fort Sumner and were accompanied by American soldiers as far as Wingate, where they camped in the piñon trees. *Hastiin Tł'aaí*, according to this account, was born near Wingate in December 1867.

13. "The fundamental living elements take a variety of forms when they are formulated and reformulated depending on the particular entity under construction. This variety includes, but is not limited to, the following manifestations: Moisture can take the form of water, rain, mist, snow, blood, or saliva. Air can appear as wind, breath, or voice. Substance can take the form of soil, pollen, skin, cornmeal, *ntł'iz* [hard goods], wood, or stone. Heat can appear as sunlight, zigzag lightning, sunrays, or fire. Vibration can take the form of song, prayer, speech, or melody. Individual persons such as baskets, hoghan, cradles, looms, songs, and masks are formed from a variety of manifestations of these basic elements. Regardless of the particular forms these elements take, one thing remains constant: some type of moisture, air, substance, heat, and vibration must be included in the formulation for life to exist" (Schwarz 1997a: 37–38).

14. Schwarz used the term "homology" to describe how parts of the whole are constructed on the same building blocks or processes (Schwarz 1997a: 4).

15. Basso has recently explored the importance of place among the Apache. His book has a great deal of relevance to the Navajo case, although he does not make the connection between kinship and place that I am making here (Basso 1998).

References

Aberle, David. 1961. The Navaho. In *Matrilineal Kinship*, ed. David Schneider and Kathleen Gough. Berkeley: University of California Press.

———. 1963. Some Sources of Flexibility in Navaho Social Organization. *Southwestern Journal of Anthropology* 19:1-8.

———. 1966. *The Peyote Religion Among the Navajo*. Chicago: Aldine.

Abu-Lughod, Lila. 1993. *Writing Women's Worlds: Bedouin Stories*. Berkeley: University of California Press.

Basso, Keith. 1998. *Wisdom Sits in Place*. Albuquerque: University of New Mexico Press.

Behar, Ruth. 1993. *Translated Woman: Crossing the Border with Esperanza's Story*. Boston: Beacon.

Benedek, Emily B. 1995. *Beyond the Four Corners of the World: A Navajo Woman's Journey*. New York: Knopf.

Briggs, Jean. 1998. *Inuit Morality Play*. New Haven, Conn.: Yale University Press.

Collier, Jane Fishburne. 1974. Women in Politics. In *Women, Culture, and Society*, ed. Michelle Zimbalist Rosaldo and Louise Lamphere. Stanford, Calif.: Stanford University Press.

Cussins, Charis. 1998. Producing Reproduction: Techniques of Normalization and Naturalizatioin in Infertility Clinics. In *Reproducing Reproduction*, ed. Sarah Franklin and Heléna Ragoné. Philadelphia: University of Pennsylvania Press.

Edwards, Jeanette. 1999. "Making Nature Explicit: English Kinship in the Light of New Reproductive Technologies." Paper presented at the 1999 American Ethnological Society Meeting in March 1999, Portland Ore.

Edwards, Jeanette, Sarah Franklin, Eric Hirsch, Frances Price, and Marilyn Strathern. 1999. *Technologies of Procreation: Kinship in the Age of Assisted Conception*. 2d ed. New York: Routledge.

Feeley-Harnik, Gillian. 1999. "Communities of Blood": The Natural History of Kinship in Nineteenth Century America. *Comparative Studies in Society and History* 41, no. 2:215–62.

Fortes, Meyer. 1949. Time and Social Structure: An Ashanti Case Study. In *Social Structure: Essays Presented to A. R. Radcliffe-Brown*, ed. Meyer Fortes. Oxford, U.K.: Clarendon Press.

Frank, Andre Gundar. 1967. *Capitalism and Underdevelopment in Latin America.* New York: Monthly Review Press.

Franklin, Sarah. 1997. Making Sense of Missed Conceptions. In *Situated Lives: Gender and Culture in Everyday Life*, ed. Louise Lamphere, Heléna Ragoné, and Patricia Zavella. New York: Routledge.

———. 1999. *Embodied Progress: A Cultural Account of Assisted Conception.* New York: Routledge.

Franklin, Sarah, and Susan McKinnon. 2000. New Directions in Kinship Study: A Core Concept Revisited. *Current Anthropology* 41, no. 2:275–79.

Franklin, Sarah, and Heléna Ragoné. 1998. *Reproducing Reproduction.* Philadelphia: University of Pennsylvania Press.

Frisbie, Charlotte. 1967. *Kinaaldá: A Study of the Navaho Girl's Puberty Ceremony.* Middletown, Conn.: Wesleyan University Press.

Gailey, Christine. 1987. *Kinship to Kinship: Gender Hierarchy and State Formation in the Tongan Islands.* Austin: University of Texas Press.

———. 1998. "New Directions in Kinship Study." Paper presented at Wenner-Gren Conference, March 27 to April 4, 1998, Palma de Mallorca, Spain.

Goody, Jack, ed. 1958. *The Developmental Cycle in Domestic Groups.* Cambridge Papers in Social Anthropology 1. Cambridge, U.K.: Cambridge University Press.

Helmreich, Stefan. 1998. Replicating Reproduction in Artifical Life: Or, the Essence of Life in the Age of Virtual Electronic Reproduction. In *Reproducing Reproduction*, ed. Sarah Franklin and Heléna Ragoné. Philadelphia: University of Pennsylvania Press.

Jorgensen, Joseph G. 1971. *Indians and the Metropolis.* In *The American Indian in Urban Society*, ed. Jack O. Waddell and O. Michael Watson. Boston: Little, Brown.

Lamphere, Louise. 1974. Strategies, Cooperation, and Conflict among Women in Domestic Groups. In *Woman, Culture, and Society*, ed. Michelle Zimbalist Rosaldo and Louise Lamphere. Stanford: Stanford University Press.

———. 1976. The Internal Colonization of the Navajo People. *Southwest Economy and Society* 1, no. 1:6-13.

———. 1977. *To Run After Them: Cultural and Social Bases of Cooperation in a Navajo Community.* Tucson: University of Arizona Press.

———. 1987. *From Working Daughters to Working Mothers: Immigrant Women in a New England Industrial Community.* Ithaca, N.Y.: Cornell University Press.

———. n.d. *Weaving Together Women's Lives: Three Generations in a Navajo Family.* Manuscript, forthcoming.

Lamphere, Louise, Patricia Zavella, and Felipe Gonzales with Peter Evans. 1992. *Sunbelt Working Mothers: Reconciling Factory and Family.* Ithaca, N.Y.: Cornell University Press.

Lamphere, Louise, Heléna Ragoné, and Patricia Zavella, eds. 1997. *Situated Lives: Gender and Culture in Everyday Life.* New York: Routledge.

Lévi-Strauss, Claude. 1969. *The Elementary Structures of Kinship.* London: Eyre and Spottiswoode.

Lewin, Ellen. 1993. *Lesbian Mothers.* Ithaca, N.Y.: Cornell University Press.

Limón, José. 1989. Carne, Carnales, and the Carnivalesque: Bakhtinian Batos, Disorder, and Narrative Discourses. *American Ethnologist* 16, no. 3 (August): 49–73.

Martin, Emily. 1987. *The Woman in the Body: A Cultural Analysis of Reproduction.* Boston: Beacon.

———. 1997. The Egg and the Sperm. *Signs* 16, no. 3 (1991): 485–501. Reprinted in *Situated Lives*, ed. Louise Lamphere, Heléna Ragoné, and Patricia Zavella. New York: Routledge.

Modell, Judith. 1998. *A Sealed and Secret Kinship: Policies and Practices in American Adoption.* Providence, R.I.: Berghahn Press.

Narayan, Kirin. 1993. How Native is a "Native" Anthropologist? *American Anthropologist* 95, no. 3 (September): 671–86.

Needham, Rodney. 1971. Introduction to *Rethinking Kinship and Marriage*, ed. Rodney Needham. Association of Social Anthropologists (ASA) Monograph no. 11. London: Tavistock.

Newcomb, Franc. 1964. *Hosteen Klah: Navaho Medicine Man and Sand Painter*. Norman: University of Oklahoma Press.

Press, Nancy, Carole H. Browner, Diem Tran, Christine Morton, and Barbara Le Master. 1998. Provisional Normalcy and "Perfect Babies": Pregnant Women's Attitudes toward Disability in the Context of Prenatal Testing. In *Reproducing Reproduction*, ed. Sarah Franklin and Heléna Ragoné. Philadelphia: University of Pennsylvania Press.

Radcliffe-Brown, A. R. 1952. *Structure and Function in Primitive Society*. London: Cohen and West.

Radcliffe-Brown, A. R., and Daryll Forde, eds. 1950. *African Systems of Kinship and Marriage*. New York: Oxford University Press.

Ragoné, Heléna. 1994. *Surrogate Motherhood: Conception in the Heart*. Boulder, Colo.: Westview.

Rapp, Rayna. 1997. Constructing Amniocentesis. In *Situated Lives: Gender and Culture in Everyday Life*, ed. Louise Lamphere, Heléna Ragoné, and Patricia Zavella. New York: Routledge.

———. 1999. *Testing Women, Testing the Fetus: The Social Impact of Amniocentesis in America*. New York: Routledge.

Reiter, Rayna. 1975. *Towards an Anthropology of Women*. New York: Monthly Review Press.

Richards, Audrey. 1950. Some Types of Family Structure Amongst the Central Bantu. In *African Systems of Kinship and Marriage*, ed. A. R. Radcliffe-Brown and Daryll Forde. New York: Oxford University Press.

Rosaldo, Michelle Zimbalist, and Louise Lamphere, eds. 1974. *Woman, Culture, and Society*. Stanford: Stanford University Press.

Schneider, David. 1965. Some Muddles in the Models: Or, How the System Really Works. In *The Relevance of Models for Social Anthropology*, ed. Max Gluckman and Fred Eggan. London: Tavistock.

———. 1968. *American Kinship: A Cultural Account*. Englewood Cliffs, N.J.: Prentice-Hall.

———. 1984. *A Critique of the Study of Kinship*. Ann Arbor: University of Michigan Press.

———. 1995. *Schneider on Schneider*. Durham, N.C.: Duke University Press.

Schwarz, Maureen Trudelle. 1997a. *Molded in the Image of Changing Woman: Navajo Views on the Human Body and Personhood*. Tucson: University of Arizona Press.

———. 1997b. Unraveling the Anchoring Cord: Navajo Relocation, 1974–96. *American Anthropologist* 99, no. 1:43–55.

Sherman, Suzanne, ed. 1992. *Lesbian and Gay Marriage: Private Commitments, Public Ceremonies*. Philadelpia: Temple University Press.

Stacey, Judith. 1990. *Brave New Families: Stories of Domestic Upheaval in Late Twentieth-Century America*. New York: Basic.

Stoler, Ann. 1997. Making Empire Respectable: The Politics of Race and Sexual Morality in Twentieth-Century Colonial Cultures. *American Ethnologist* 16 (November 1989): 4. Reprinted in *Situated Lives: Gender and Culture in Everyday Life*, ed. Louise Lamphere, Heléna Ragoné, and Patricia Zavella. New York: Routledge.

Strathern, Marilyn. 1992. *After Nature: English Kinship in the Late Twentieth Century*. Cambridge, U.K.: Cambridge University Press.

Taylor, Janelle S. 1998. Image of Contradiction: Obstetrical Ultrasound in American Culture. In *Reproducing Reproduction*, ed. Sarah Franklin and Heléna Ragoné. Philadelphia: University of Pennsylvania Press.

Weston, Kath. 1991. *Families We Choose: Lesbians, Gays, Kinship*. New York: Columbia University Press.

Witherspoon, Gary. 1975. *Navajo Kinship and Marriage*. Chicago: Chicago University Press.

Wolf, Diane. 1996. *Feminist Dilemmas in Fieldwork*. Boulder, Colo.: Westview.

Wolf, Margery. 1974. Chinese Women: Old Skills in a New Context. In *Women, Culture, and Society,* ed. Michelle Zimbalist Rosaldo and Louise Lamphere. Stanford: Stanford University Press.

Yanagisako, Sylvia, and Carol Delaney, eds. 1995. *Naturalizing Power: Essays in Feminist Cultural Analysis.* New York: Routledge.

Zavella, Patricia. 1993. Feminist Insider Dilemmas: Constructing Ethnic Identity with "Chicana" Informants. *Frontiers: A Journal of Women Studies* 13, no. 3:53–76.

Chapter Three

Not That Lineage Stuff: Teaching Kinship into the Twenty-First Century

Caroline B. Brettell

Thirty years ago, in his little Bible on kinship, Fox claimed that "kinship is to anthropology what logic is to philosophy or [the] nude is to art" (Fox 1967: 10). This statement encapsulated the fact that during the first half of the twentieth century, almost every anthropologist worked on the topic of kinship and made some contribution to theoretical developments in the area. But as Holy (1996) rightly observed in his book *Anthropological Perspectives on Kinship*, this is no longer the case. "Recent reviews of anthropological theory and the current state of anthropology (Ortner, Clifford and Marcus, Marcus and Fischer, and Borofsky) hardly make references to the theoretical problems in the study of kinship which exercised the imagination of our predecessors" (Holy 1996:172).[1] The demise of kinship studies is certainly understandable given the rigorous and incisive critique contained in Schneider's reevaluation of his own analysis of kinship on Yap in the Caroline Islands (Schneider 1984). In this book, Schneider questioned the assumptions and presuppositions that undergird "classic" kinship theory.

Despite the supposed "cooling of anthropology's love affair with kinship" (to borrow a phrase from Peletz [1995: 345], a required course on kinship and social organization is still part of many programs of graduate training in anthropology in the United States. At the university where I hold an appointment, the responsibility of teaching this course, at least every other year, lands in my lap. When I teach it, I am often confronted with skeptical young scholars who see little relevance of descent and alliance theories, the incest taboo, the matrilineal puzzle, the segmentary lineage, or parallel cross-cousin marriage to the anthropology of the twenty-first century in general and to their own research interests in particular. Many of them view the course as a painful rite of passage, similar to prelims or qualifying exams, that must be endured if one is to become a professional anthropologist.

This chapter is therefore about pedagogical method.[2] It is about some of the strategies I have developed to convince the unconvinced, and perhaps even myself, that the material on kinship and descent continues to be worthy of serious exploration and consideration in graduate education in anthropology. I focus in particular on the relationship between the study of social organization and the history of anthropological theory, the development of a breadth of ethnographic knowledge, the innovative application of central concepts, and the recasting of kinship and social organization in relation to current theoretical paradigms in our field. This discussion of how I teach this one course provides an opportunity to explore new directions in the study of kinship that are, in my view, reinvigorating not only our understanding of social organization, but the ethnological enterprise more generally. At the outset, I want to emphasize that the way I teach this course, and hence what I include in this chapter, reflect to a great extent my own interests and biases.

Depth and Breadth: Kinship Studies and the History of Anthropological Thought

It is undoubtedly a cliché to observe that the twentieth century has been an age of information explosion. The discipline of anthropology has itself grown exponentially, and increasing specialization has been the direct result. The debate over the continued compatibility of the four subfields is perhaps one outcome of the unmanageable expansion of knowledge. How, under these conditions, do we continue to offer depth and breadth to the students we train? The systematic study of kinship and social organization is one vehicle, not only because it offers a historical perspective, but also because it exposes students to a range of ethnographic contexts.

Most graduate programs still require a course in the history of anthropology, and many students consider one course sufficient. My position is different because I think that the critical evaluation skills that we hope our students acquire necessitate a sound footing in history. Hence, I have no qualms about teaching students more history (to give them more depth) in the course on kinship and social organization. Although they may hear about or read Morgan or Radcliffe-Brown twice, there is often little overlap with the contributions of many other anthropologists because they are either ignored, or only briefly treated in "History of Anthropology," or because their work in the area of kinship and social organization is not the primary focus in the history course. For example, in "History of Anthropology," French structuralism may be introduced through Lévi-Strauss's work on myth, and not through *The Elementary Structures of Kinship*.

In my course titled "Social Organization" I carry the historical approach throughout the semester, although not necessarily in a chronological sequence. As we move from one topic to the next, I assign the "classic" statements. Thus, students read Fortes, Evans-Pritchard, and Richards when we are dealing with lineages and descent theory; the early work of Smith (1973) and Gonzalez (1965, 1970) on the matrifocal family; John Campbell's (1963) thorough ethnographic description of the kindred in a Greek mountain village as we begin consideration of bilateral kinship; and Marshall Sahlins's classic 1963 article "Poor Man, Rich Man, Big Man, Chief" when we discuss social ranking and sociopolitical organization.

When appropriate, I generally assign a few critical pieces to begin to expose students to specific theoretical controversies. We deal, for example, with the debate surrounding African and New Guinea models (J. A. Barnes 1962; La-Fontaine 1973; Andrew Strathern 1973; Karp 1978; J. F. Weiner 1982; Feil 1984; Keesing 1987). J. A. Barnes (1962) first raised the disadvantages of an African orientation emphasizing descent for understanding highland New Guinea and pointed to a range of additional criteria for group membership that are important in this cultural context—residence, utilization of garden land, participation in exchange, feasting, or house building. In many New Guinea societies, Barnes argued, descent groups are hard to find and the proliferation of ties of the individual are more important. LaFontaine (1973), on the other hand, by emphasizing that kinship is a system of symbols rather than a set of rules, has argued that African models are relevant for the New Guinea Highlands. J. F. Strathern (1973: 29) positioned himself somewhere in the middle by suggesting that kinship in the Highlands "is a combination of filiative rules and ideas based on upbringing, nurturance, and consumption of food." Keesing (1987) carried on this debate between individual-centered and corporate lineage-centered approaches, while Karp (1978) has pursued a more theoretical argument, distinguishing between explanatory and analytical models. Finally, Rivière (1993), in an extremely interesting analysis of the "Amerindianization" of descent and affinity, moved the discussion to a different continent. Like Barnes, he noted many additional criteria beyond shared substance that influence group membership. "The widest social world of the Amerindian is not predicated on the narrow-range exchanges of spouses and things, but on symbolic exchanges which even incorporate unknown people" (Rivière 1993: 513). Clearly, a thorough consideration of this particular debate generates discussion of the definition of kinship, of units of analysis in anthropology, and of the diverse bases for group formation and, hence, social organization in a cross-cultural context.

A second major debate emerges from Evans-Pritchard's work on the Nuer. After addressing the ethnography itself, we explore some of the critiques, beginning with Gough (1971), and continuing with Verdon (1982, 1983), Karp and Maynard (1983), Kelly (1985), Hutchinson (1985), and Evens (1989). Although Gough dealt with a number of issues, one of her main concerns was the supposed supremacy of the agnatic principle. She conceded that this may be important for aristocrats but not for the society as a whole. "Agnation affiliates [a Nuer] to a minimal lineage usually only three generations deep or less, whose members may be scattered through one or more tribes, and who are therefore of little use to him in disputes, when he must rely for assistance on local matrilateral, conjugal, or natural ties. Agnation gives him little prestige, which he derives rather from cognatic attachment to aristocrats of his locality" (Gough 1971: 113–14).

Verdon (1982) rejected outright the idea of descent groups among the Nuer, arguing instead that group aggregation is based on economic survival and the need to preserve cattle trading. Verdon also focused on the multiple meanings of "native" terms and ultimately raises very current questions about partial truths and bounded cultures. Kelly (1985), like Gough (1971) and Marshall Sahlins (1961) before him, insists on careful attention to historical context.[3] Critics of Evans-Pritchard have argued that to suit the static functionalist models that were in vogue at the time, he paid little attention to the fact that shortly before he arrived, the Nuer had been involved not only in internal warfare but also in the conquest and displacement of the closely related and neighboring Dinka. This critique, in particular, permits initial consideration of how historical and political-economic frameworks that characterize much of contemporary anthropology can improve our understanding of ethnographic data.

Both Hutchinson (1985) and Evens (1989) took on the issue of incest among the Nuer, thus allowing me to at least raise that subject as a focus of intense anthropological attention. Hutchinson adopted a historical perspective, tracing the redefinition of various categories of incest by the Nuer over the past half century as well as crucial differences between Eastern Nuer and those west of the Bahr al-Jabal (White Nile). Evens offered a critique of the universal application of Western modes of thought by showing "how the Nuer might find kinship where we find none" (1989: 324). He offered a model of "alter-logical" reckoning. "[The Nuer] do not hold that incestuous congress between persons is incestuous because these persons stand to each other in particular social relationships. Instead, they say that 'marriage to persons standing in certain relationships, is forbidden because it would be . . . incestuous'" (Evens 1989: 329, and Evans-Pritchard [1951] quoted in Evens 1989: 329). Finally, Karp and Maynard (1983) offered a postmodern reading of interpretations of *The Nuer*. They argued that the diverse constructions of this text "are the result of a tendency to privilege one factor or another of what is in reality a multicausal explanation" (Karp and Maynard 1983: 481) and that discrepancies in interpretations can be resolved by returning to the text itself. Their analysis raises a host of provocative questions about interpretation.

Ultimately, of course, discussion of African models in New Guinea and the ethnography of the Nuer leads to the broader critique of lineage theory (Kuper 1982) and launches careful thinking about the formulation of analytical models, their continued application to the ethnic groups from which they were initially developed, their cross-cultural validity and, ultimately, the goals and possibility of a comparative anthropological science. Another result is an illuminating illustration of what Appadurai (1986) means when he points to "gatekeeping" concepts in the discipline of anthropology; that is, the privileged objects of anthropological attention in certain regions—lineages in Africa, hierarchy in India, exchange in Melanesia, honor and shame in the circum-Mediterranean.[4]

I balance this more critical approach by including, wherever possible, reasonably current scholarship on a particular issue in order to illustrate to students that a piece of work written thirty years ago can still generate serious ethnographic research and/or theory building. This is best exemplified by the topic of segmentary lineages, for which there is a rather extensive literature of reformulation and refinement (Combs-Schilling 1985; Dresch 1986, 1988; J. W. Fox 1989; Munson 1989, 1993; Sandstrom 1996); by research that continues to be informed by concepts of exchange, alliance, dualism, and dual organization (e.g., Borneman 1992; Bowden 1988; Cooper 1993; Fricke, Axinn and Thornton 1993; Gottlieb 1986; Hoskins 1990); by studies that describe and analyze cognatic kin groups in the ancestral houses of Bali (Boon 1990), among middle-class American Protestants who participate in family reunions (Neville 1987), or among upper-class families in contemporary Lima (Gilbert 1981) and Mexico City (Lomnitz and Pérez-Lizaur 1984); and by explorations of "new men," "big men," and "big women" in Melanesia (Brown 1987; Chowning 1987; Counts 1992; Harrison 1993); or among the dynastic rich in North America (Marcus and Hall 1992).

In the case of the segmentary lineage, discussion moves invariably from the description and analysis of a particular sociopolitical system based on descent that may or may not be characteristic of specific ethnic groups or geographic regions to a broader consideration of the structural principles of segmentation and complementary opposition and their relevance to studies of the construction of situational social identity and a sense of belonging. Students read, for example, Maynard's (1988) intriguing analysis of the organization of Protestant churches in Ecuador, Cohen's (1982) discussion of the layered nature of social association in the Shetland Islands community of Whalsay, and Herzfeld's insightful work on segmentation in modern nation-states (Herzfeld 1987, 1992).[5] I also introduce some of the literature on ethnicity among immigrant populations in Europe and America, as well as Bringa's (1995) study of *Being Muslim the Bosnian Way.* "The expression of identity," Bringa argued, "varies according to whether relations are enacted in the household, neighborhood, village, or outside the village, and . . . Bosnian Muslim identity both includes and excludes communality with non-Muslim Bosnians" (Bringa 1995: 83). Theoretically, this discussion also allows us to address issues of structure and agency, drawing on the work of Bourdieu (1977) and Giddens (1984). Clearly, this approach helps students to become more conversant with critical issues, concepts, and terminology in anthropology in general and kinship studies specifically, but also provides a breadth of ethnographic knowledge.

Old Wine in New Bottles

The diverse applications of the principle of segmentation offer a good example of putting old wine in new bottles. Indeed, there are numerous ways to illustrate how subjects that were of interest in the heyday of kinship studies have been reconceptualized in order to encompass topics of current ethnographic interest, including those in our own backyard. Needless to say, the archetypal example is kinship terminology. Although I introduce students to the work of Morgan and Kroeber—and the social and psychological frameworks of analysis that underlie their respective approaches to kinship terminology— I spend no time reviewing the various terminological systems. Rather, what I attempt to do here is deal with the issue at another level, focusing on the general topic of the language of kinship and, more specifically, on idioms of reference and address. I do this in a number of ways. First, beginning with Schneider's (1969) observation that the categories of kinship, religion, and nationality are conceptually similar, we explore the use and meaning of kinship terminology in these domains. We read, for example, Delaney's (1995) analysis of how Turkish national identity is conveyed through the images of Father State and Motherland. "Father State epitomized Ottoman rule. The state was both patriarchal and paternalistic, and the people, organized into *millet* ('nations'), were dependent on its benevolence and its protection. . . . Motherland was a generalized medium of nurture, under the control of the state but without specific boundaries of identity" (Delaney 1995: 179). Similarly, Williams (1995) examines kinship and nationalist ideologies in the United States, focusing in particular on the processes whereby nature is socialized and power is naturalized.

Second, students read literature on the inheritance of given names and nicknaming that is well developed in the ethnography of Europe (Brandes 1975; Breen 1982; Herzfeld 1982; Pina-Cabral 1984, 1994). Here I suggest not only that systems of classification have broader applications, but also that place may be just as important as substance in situating people in relation to one another. Third, I present and analyze ethnographic data from my own fieldwork. For example, I pose the question of what it means when a Portuguese wife uses the word *filho* (son) as a term of endearment when addressing her husband. I pose the question of what it means when a Portuguese employer says to her former maid, who has made some money as an emigrant in France, "but you will always be Maria to me." And I pose the question of what it means when the term of address *tia* (aunt) is replaced by the term *madrinha* (godmother) when a biological aunt becomes a godparent. This latter example segues nicely into a discussion of fictive kinship, beginning with Mintz and Wolf's classic statement on *compadrazgo* (1950), and moving to other discussions of godparenthood (Du Boulay 1984; Gudeman 1975; Nutini and Bell 1980; Shapiro 1988) or "cousinship" (Baumann 1995). As Holy (1996: 167) has suggested, the study of fictive kinship not only brings into consideration

a range of societies where performance and code of conduct rather than genealogical links determine who is or is not related, but also because in the
form of ritual kinship, it raises issues about the relationship between religion
and the forging of social relationships.

There are other good examples in kinship research of putting old wine in
new bottles. One is LaFontaine's (1988, 1990) attempt to shift anthropological discussion from the incest taboo to incest and thereby bring theory and
practice together. LaFontaine (1988: 15) viewed incest not merely as "a symbolic violation of kinship but [also as] the sexual abuse of children. It is behavior which must be considered in a total social context." McKinnon (1995),
in a powerful article that begins with a critique of Schneider's (1980) separation of the core symbol of sexual intercourse from cultural understandings of
gender and sexuality, showed how hierarchy and power are manifested in the
"ungrammatical" form of sexual intercourse—incest—and can explain the
prevalence of one form (father–daughter) over another (mother–son).
"Where sexual intercourse is thought to involve the 'naturally' assertive, even
aggressive, agency of men and the equally 'naturally' passive acquiescence and
'mandatory tenderness' of women, it follows that paternal incest would be
viewed in terms that stress its relative 'normalcy' at the same time that maternal incest would be viewed in pathological terms" (McKinnon 1995: 42).

Yet another example is provided by Simpson's (1994) work on what he calls
unclear families. Unclear (as opposed to nuclear) families have emerged as a
result of high rates of divorce and remarriage in late twentieth-century Western society and are characterized by linkages between households created
through the movement of children and/or property, as well as through the
renegotiation of economic and emotional relationships between former
spouses, their families, and children.[6] Simpson's analysis of these families
could not proceed without the conceptual tools formulated many years ago to
help us make sense of phenomena like "female–husbands," or "ghost marriage." I refer specifically to the distinctions between a genitor, a biological father, a fostering father, and a pater.

Similarly, it seems that the more fluid notions of motherhood and marriage
that cross-cultural study has forced us to consider may be illuminating to
analysis of the impact of reproductive technology on the family or of the new
kinds of families forming in the gay and lesbian community (Franklin and
Ragoné 1998; Hayden 1995; Ragoné 1994, 1996; M. Strathern 1992a, 1992b,
1993; Weston 1992, 1995). At the roots of much of this work is one of the
questions of broadest concern in anthropology—the relationship between biology and culture. Ragoné's (1994) work on surrogate motherhood is quite
provocative in this regard. It addresses the biogenetic basis for parent–child
relationships and the role of reproduction in marriage. The tension between
biology and culture is most apparent in the discomfort expressed by one male
informant, who is both genitor and pater, about the fact that the woman carrying his child is not his wife. Similarly, one adoptive mother interviewed by

Ragoné states quite forthrightly that the child was conceived in her heart before it was conceived in the surrogate's body.

Equally as powerful as Ragoné's work in demonstrating how the biology of kinship is culturally constructed is Hayden's analysis of Zook and Hallenback's (1987: 90) description of at-home donor insemination. "The jar [of semen] was handed over, hugs exchanged, and he was on his way. With Nancy's hips on pillows at a forty-five degree-angle, Rachel, taking a quick breath, inserted the semen into Nancy's vagina with a sterile syringe. . . . Rachel's participation in conception was crucial to us, as this was to be her child as well." "The act of begetting," comments Hayden (1995: 52), "is separated from authorship; shared parenthood can be demonstrated through active participation in the process, without necessarily laying claim to a genetic relationship as well."

Weston has also worked extensively on gay kinship ideologies. Weston first challenged the supposed enduring and involuntary nature of kinship through her descriptions of the severing of ties when relatives learn that a member of their family is gay. "Coming-out stories consistently focused on the prospect of 'losing' kin and highlighted the devastating emotional impact when rejection ensued. . . . Perhaps more important than the incidence of rejection was the generalized *fear* of being 'cut off' that pervaded these narratives" (Weston 1995: 96). Weston then turns to the forging of ties based on friendship and argues that such ties are much more than fictive kinship. "To categorize some forms of friendship as fictive kinship—or even 'alternative' families—is to presume that 'blood' relations, organized through procreative heterosexuality, not only constitute 'true' kinship but also provide a model for all possible derivative forms of family. When viewed through the lens of an ideology that refuses to recognize biology and marriage as the foundation for all conceivable types of kinship, however, gay families no longer appear as 'alternative', 'fictive', or 'substitute' formations" (Weston 1995: 99).

All of this work is intriguing not only because it challenges us to think in very complex ways about a model of kinship that is grounded in genealogical relationships and the natural fact of procreation (Holy 1996),[7] but also because it revives friendship as a legitimate area of research within anthropology. Wolf (1966) and Paine (1969) drew our attention to this topic more than thirty years ago, but it is largely in the ethnographic work of Europeanists (Gilmore 1975; Kennedy 1986; Uhl 1991) that it has sustained attention. Publication of a new book edited by Bell and Coleman (forthcoming) is certain to generate further work on the topic of friendship. Another "revival" that I see emerging from the pathbreaking research on the impact of new technologies on family and kinship is in the area of fosterage and adoption, well documented in the ethnography of Oceania (Brady 1976; Carroll 1970) and West Africa (Bledsoe 1993; Bledsoe and Isiugo-Albanihe 1989; Etienne 1979; E. N. Goody 1982; Schildkrout 1973), but in need of much more rigorous analysis by anthropologists interested in applying insights developed in a cross-cultural context to the study of our own society. Indeed, some time ago, Marshall (1977) discussed both adoption and friendship as forms of created kinship, arguing that the essence of kinship as a general cross-cultural construct is sharing. Students can test this idea through exposure to a number of excellent studies of adoption and fosterage in a variety of ethnographic contexts. I refer in particular to Weismantel's (1995) work in Ecuador, Altorki's (1980) study of milk-kinship in Arab society, Carsten's research in Malaysia (1991), Modell's (1994) work on the United States, and Waltner's (1996) more historical analysis of adopted sons in imperial China. The latter, in particular, raises the issue of legal fictions that were, of course, part of original descent theory.

One additional topic of interest here is the renewed focus on social networks (Brudner and White 1997; Scott 1991; Schweizer and White 1998). Although there were early formulations based on research in Europe (J. A. Barnes 1954; Bott 1957), the anthropological study of networks emerged most rigorously in connection with the development of urban anthropology, particularly in the African context where ethnographers trained in the structural-functional tradition and heavily influenced by descent theory found themselves bereft of concepts to describe adequately the social organization of "tribesmen" in towns (J. A. Barnes 1972; Boissevain 1979; Boissevain and Mitchell 1973; Gulliver 1971; Mitchell 1971, 1974; Sanjek 1978). After students are introduced to some of these classic examples, including Boissevain's (1968) more theoretical piece on "non-groups," we explore some of the more contemporary applications (Johnson 1985), including the rich literature on immigrant networks (Garrison and Weiss 1979; Ho 1993; Massey et al., 1987; O'Connor 1990; Zavella 1985; Zimmer and Aldrich 1987) and Hannerz's (1992) attempt to integrate networks with the ideas of global and unbounded cultures. "The network remains useful as a root metaphor when we try to think in a reasonably orderly way . . . about some of the heterogeneous sets of often long-distance relationships which organize culture in the world now. . . . One may indeed think of the global ecumene as a single large network, and perhaps the chain of even rather personal existing links that it would take to connect any two randomly chosen individuals within it may turn out to be surprisingly short" (Hannerz 1992: 51). This discussion of networks leads easily to an exploration of other forms of social organization that are characteristic of both rural and urban populations—voluntary associations, committees, cliques, and factions (Bestor 1985; Okamura 1983; Weinberg 1976).

Models, Rules, and Typologies: The Emergence of Historical and Processual Anthropology

Ortner (1984) has argued that after 1960, anthropological theory shifted from a static to a more processual approach. This is reflected, as Holy (1996:172) has recently observed, in contemporary studies that "tend to be historically grounded, emphasizing how local experiences of kinship have been affected by state politics, trade, colonialism or nationalist discourse." I teach students about the importance of dynamic models and historically grounded research in my course on kinship, beginning the discussion with yet another classic example—the debate between Goodenough (1956) and Fisher (1957) over residence patterns on the island of Truk. Goodenough and Fisher carried out similar censuses within three years of one another and came up with distinctly different incidences of residence forms. Concluding that he and Fisher interpreted the data differently, Goodenough (1956) moved to a more general discussion of the use of typologies in anthropological theorizing and to a preliminary consideration of the relationship between description and comparison that he went on to develop in his 1970 book *Description and Comparison in Cultural Anthropology.* "If I wish to apply the label 'patrilocal' to one of the real choices within a culture, I must recognize that it means something different from patrilocal residence in the context of ethnological comparison" (Goodenough 1956: 29). It is out of this debate that early thinking about emic categories emerged.

In my course on social organization, I move from residence rules to the concepts of household and family. Students begin by reading Berkner's (1972) analysis of the stem family in eighteenth-century Austria. Like Goodenough, Berkner focused on the interpretation of statistical frequencies. However, he also raised intriguing questions about time in anthropological and historical research. Continuing in a historical vein, I also introduce students to the typology developed by Hammel and Laslett (1974) to describe household composition in past societies. I talk a good deal here about my own research, particularly that focused on family history in Portugal (Brettell 1986, 1991a, 1999). This gives me the opportunity to expose students to the rich archival material that can be mined by anthropologists to study kinship through time.[8] It allows me to explore the varied meanings of family, household, and house as units of analysis (Kertzer 1991; Rubinstein 1983; Yanagisako 1979; Carsten and Hugh-Jones 1995) and the processual dimensions of coresidence (Verdon 1980). It also opens discussion of the life course (Elder 1975, 1977, 1987) as an alternative approach to the domestic or family cycle, which, although it shifted the focus of analysis from structure to process when it was first introduced (J. Goody 1958), cannot deal adequately with variation. As Kertzer (1984:194) stated, "a life course perspective involves simultaneous study of processes of individual aging and study of how historical forces affect the individual aging experience. The norms themselves (whether statistical or ideological) for what is appropriate behavior and what are the appropriate roles for an individual of a given age change over time. These changes are closely associated with changes in the structure of the economy, but also reflect . . . political facts." I can also introduce the interesting and varied literature that addresses the relationship between kinship and property in the form of marriage prestations (dowry and bride wealth) or in the form of inheritance (whether premortem or postmortem) (Brettell 1991b; Goody, Thirsk and Thompson 1976; Goody and Tambiah 1973; Hann 1998; Harrell and Dickey 1985; Hirschon 1984). Here, too, thinking has evolved from the typological to the processual. Finally, because we are dealing with issues of locality, we can return to some of the critiques of descent theory, which, it has been suggested, did not place enough emphasis on where people live (Kopytoff 1977; Langness 1964; A. Strathern 1973), or on emic conceptualizations of domestic and social space (Layton 1997; Rodman 1985).

Since my work on family history has focused on the impact of migration on kinship and other demographic phenomena, I can offer students a concrete example of how political economy can shape family life. This segues into an exploration of the rich and burgeoning cross-cultural and historical research dealing with the impact of colonialism, multinationalism, agribusiness, urbanization, development, and nationalist ideology and policy on reproduction, domestic structure, relations of kinship, and family life (S. Barnes 1990; Benería and Stimpson 1987; Borneman 1992; Ginsburg and Rapp 1995; Lockwood 1993; Silverblatt 1980; Warman 1981). Sanday (1990), for example, discusses the preservation of a matrilineal core among the Minangkabau of Indonesia in the face of the successive patriarchal assaults by Islam, the colonial Dutch, and the modern Indonesian state.

Much of this research is closely allied with feminist anthropology, and it is at this point that it is possible to raise recent discussions of the rapprochement between kinship studies and gender studies (Collier and Yanagisako 1987; Diemberger 1993; Feldman-Savelsberg 1995; Goddard 1994; Maynes et al. 1996; Stone 1997; Weismantel 1995; Yanagisako and Delaney 1995). Although Rubin (1975: 169) stressed more than two decades ago that "kinship systems are observable and empirical forms of sex/gender systems," it is only in the last decade that kinship research has "become a key site on which to theorize gender, power, and difference" (Peletz 1995: 367).[9] Not only does a gendered analysis of kinship question the "naturalness" of the family and specific domestic roles, but it also introduces women's subjectivities. Both Abu-Lughod (1993) and Raheja (1996), for example, illustrated the limits of and contradictions inherent in patrilineal descent when seen through women's eyes and heard through women's voices. Feldman-Savelsberg (1995), in her research among the Bangangté of Cameroon, focused on the culinary images that sustain matrilineal ties and hence offer women an alternative to agnatic kinship ideology. Similarly, Lederman (1990) argued that although Mendi women of Papua New Guinea are excluded from clan transactions, they can form *twen* (exchange) relationships and hence build up a powerful basis of support. Lederman suggests that such relationships constitute personhood for both men and women in Mendi society.

Thus, the research linking gender to kinship unfolds into consideration of the connections between kinship on the one hand and personhood and identity (Ostor, Fruzzetti, and Barnett 1982; M. Strathern 1992b) on the other.

Studies of personhood focus on what it means to be human in a particular cultural context. Howell and Melhuus (1993), who have suggested that research on personhood assumed the central place previously occupied by kinship by the mid-1980s, attempt to bring both together with research on gender into a single theoretical framework emphasizing sameness and difference. Hoskins (1990), in some sense, had already operationalized this framework in her discussion of how gender dualism constructs the person and society among the Kodi of eastern Indonesia. The dualistic nature of the person provides the basis for the double descent system whereby each individual claims membership in both a matriclan and a patriclan. Carsten (1995) approached the relationship between kinship and personhood in a slightly different way, illustrating how Malays on the island of Langwawi become persons (kin) by living and consuming together in houses. As part of a challenge to the emphasis that Schneider (1980) placed on kinship as shared substance, Carsten argued instead that "kinship is a process of becoming" and that as a term, it be used to "characterize the relatedness that people act and feel" (1995: 223, 236).

Kinship in a Holistic Context

Each semester that I teach the course on social organization, I usually assign two or three complete ethnographies to supplement our reading of classic and contemporary articles. Generally, each of these ethnographies represents a particular theoretical framework and these can be compared and analyzed to reveal changes, not only in how we as anthropologists have thought about kinship, but also in how we write about it. For example, Witherspoon's (1975) study of the Navajo reflects a symbolic approach emerging out of Geertz's (1966) distinction between patterns of and patterns for behavior. The book is divided into two parts, one focusing on Navajo kinship as a cultural system— "a set of concepts, beliefs and attitudes about solidarity which are embedded in symbols found in culturally defined reproductive processes" (Witherspoon 1975: 13–14)—and the second, emphasizing a social analysis of "real beings, actions, and networks of actions" (Witherspoon 1975: 67). By combining and contrasting these different modes of analysis, Witherspoon is able to deal handily with issues of continuity and change, stability and flexibility.

Witherspoon's approach can be compared with Annette Weiner's (1976) restudy of Trobriand kinship and exchange published at approximately the same time. *Women of Value, Men of Renown* is written from the perspective of feminist anthropology. Women, Weiner argued, are more than "conduits of matrilineal identity. . . . To describe the Trobriands as matrilineal without examining the full consequences of women's actions is as uninformative as what Leach labeled butterfly collecting" (A. Weiner 1976: 16). Weiner suggested that once male and female roles are given equal analytical focus, the multidimensional meanings of kinship, family, and descent are revealed. "It is only by according women value, by refusing to see them as mere pawns exchanged by men or as reproductive objects, that we can offer an answer to the question posed in Schneider's provocative essay 'What Is Kinship All About' " (A. Weiner 1976: 17). Clearly, Weiner took on not only Lévi-Strauss and alliance theory, but also the basic principles of kinship formulated by Fox (1967).

Weiner's approach can then be contrasted with a much more recent ethnography written from both a feminist and a postmodern perspective, Abu-Lughod's *Writing Women's Worlds* (1993). Using a narrative approach, Abu-Lughod focused on the subjective and lived experience of patrilateral parallel-cousin marriage, patrilineal descent, polygyny, reproduction, and honor and shame among Bedouin women in Egypt. "The Awlad 'Ali are pa-trilineal, but reckoning descent, tribal affiliation, and inheritance through the male line does not foreclose women's opportunities or desires to shape their own lives or those of their sons and daughters, or to oppose the decisions of their fathers. . . . Polygyny is an institution oppressive to women in that it causes them pain, but is not necessarily the pleasure for husbands that West-ern fantasies about harems suggest" (Abu-Lughod 1993: 19). In an effort to "write against culture," Abu-Lughod deliberately shuns "ethnographic typifi-cation" and the "generalizing mode of social scientific discourse." The book has no conclusion, something that some students find disconcerting, but they are equally bothered by overly intrusive analytical frameworks. In this latter regard, Lepowsky's *Fruit of the Motherland* (1993), despite its rich ethnogra-phy, has come under the most intense criticism.

Another provocative contrast is provided by two ethnographies of different groups on the island of Madagascar. Bloch's (1971) study of the Merina offered an early example of a historically contextualized and processual approach to kinship analysis. The ethnography also wrestles with many of the issues that were central to debates about descent theory (e.g., the relationship between residence and kinship, or the significance of economic activity to group for-mation and solidarity) and ultimately demonstrates the shortcomings of both descent theory and alliance theory to an understanding of Merina culture and society. Among the Merina, "there are no descent groups of the living, but there is a notion of descent groups in relation to the dead in the tomb" (Bloch 1971: 165). In another insight that was theoretically ahead of its time, Bloch concluded his book with a brief and suggestive mention of the concept of the person, a concept that Astuti (1995) makes central to her study of identity and descent among the Vezo of Madagascar. Although Vezo identity is contingent upon actions in the present, the Vezo are characterized, according to Astuti, by two different types of kinship. One type (*filongoa*) "operates in the present among living people, and one [*raza*] . . . takes effect in the future when people are dead and lie inside the tomb" (1995: 103). The transition from one type to the other occurs at death but is prepared for and anticipated in life and in as-sociation with a significant ritual (*soro*) that determines a person's place of burial. "The transition from *filongoa* to the 'single' *raza*, from life to death, from the present to the future, marks a radical transformation in the nature of the person" (1995: 103). Ultimately, Astuti concluded, kinship is cognatic among the living and agnatic among the dead. This statement offers a complex challenge to our categories of analysis and powerful support for a sensitive and emically-oriented approach to ethnography. Both books do a good job of linking kinship with broader systems of belief and ritual activity.

Finally, because of my particular interests, I sometimes use ethnographies of European societies. These often provide a good illustration of the reconceptualizations that are necessary in order to address particular cultural contexts and remind us, thereby, of the basis of the debate about African models in New Guinea. For example, using Lévi-Strauss's concept of complex structures as a starting point, Bestard-Camps (1991), in his monograph on the Balearic island of Formentera, focused attention on the house, a concept that Lévi-Strauss (1983) also addressed as a specific form of social organization (*sociétés à maison*), and that has recently been the subject of research in diverse ethnographic contexts (Carsten and Hugh-Jones 1995; Kuper 1993; Saul 1991). Bestard-Camps, like Lévi-Strauss, analyzed the house in terms of both descent and alliance. "The house, considered as a descent line, does not form any kind of descent group, given that residence is an element of succession, that only one member of the sibling group is the successor, and that the male line can be supplanted by the female one, and the lineal succession by the lateral. This kind of flexibility under the rigid principle of house continuity is also exemplified in the different modes available to houses for the orchestration of alliances. In their matrimonial strategies it is possible to find close alliances that change remote consanguineous kin into affines, and also alliances outside the limits of consanguinity, but in the realm of homogamy" (Bestard-Camps 1991: 5). In a more holistic fashion, Bestard-Camps's ethnography explored a number of issues that have been raised during the semester: naming practices, household forms, the relationship between property transmission and marriage, and conceptions of identity.

The timeless quality of Bestard-Camps's monograph can be contrasted with Collier's (1997) very recent study of the remaking of Spanish families in the Andalusian community of Los Olivos. Collier, who used a literary device (Benito Pérez Galdós's novel *Doña Perfecta*) to frame her analysis, claimed that her theoretical focus is "the development of modern subjectivity" (1997: 24). Long-term field contact with the people of Los Olivos allowed Collier to document a shift from the duty of social obligations (letting others think for one) to the autonomy of individual desire (thinking for oneself). Romantic love has replaced status in the choice of spouses; partnership has replaced patriarchy as the key value at the heart of marriages; and personal grief rather than respect for the dead is now at the foundation of mourning customs. The concept of self, central to current anthropological thought (Cohen 1994), as well as Gidden's concept of structuration, are at the core of Collier's discussion of transformation and the emergence of "modernity." As Collier noted,

Giddens "observes that all humans are reflexive, in the sense that all people monitor their actions and can produce accounts of their behavior. But only 'modern' people see the self 'as a reflexive project for which the individual is responsible. . . . We are, not what we are, but what we make of ourselves'" (Collier 1997: 25, and Giddens quoted in Collier 1997: 25).

Conclusion

Although kinship may have lost its central place in ethnography and anthropological theory, it remains an important part of human social life throughout the world. It is not hard to convince students of this since they see it all around them in our national political discourse. Indeed, by using examples throughout the semester of how kinship studies have been "repatriated" (again to borrow a phrase from Peletz [1995]), I am able to impress on students the continued value of the conceptual and analytical tools developed during more than a century of anthropological preoccupation with kinship. There is no doubt in my mind, and hopefully not in theirs, that a knowledge of these concepts and of the intellectual debates that have surrounded them makes all of us better anthropologists. Thus, a course on social organization and kinship can and should remain central to our graduate training because in teaching it, one is teaching about some of the fundamental epistemological questions of our discipline: questions about method and theory, about ethnography and analysis, about comparison and reflexivity, about empiricism and interpretivism.

Notes

1. Weston (1995: 89) observes that kinship also disappeared "as a category in advertisements for teaching positions in anthropology." She finds this particularly ironic because it happened just as the debate over new family forms heated up in the United States.

2. A preliminary and brief version of this chapter was published in the January 1998 issue of the *Anthropology Newsletter* published by the American Anthropological Association.

3. For another study of the Nuer that takes history and change into account, see Hutchinson (1985).

4. Similarly, Rosaldo (1988: 77) comments that when he first reached the Ilongots in northern Luzon, Philippines, "they appeared to be 'people without culture'; they lacked the ethnographic staples of the day: lineages, villages, men's houses, elaborate rituals, not to mention matrilateral cross-cousin marriage." Also of importance is Fardon's (1990) edited volume on regional ethnographies.

5. Sahlins's (1989) historical analysis of the border regions of Catalonia in France and Spain offers another good example.

6. Colleen Johnson (1989) explores similar issues, focusing in particular on in-law relationships after divorce and remarriage. More recently, Simpson (1997) has introduced a postmodernist approach in his research on divorce narratives and the representation of family.

7. The underlying question here, similar to that posed with reference to the nature/culture model developed in early feminist anthropology, is the degree to which this is a Western construction.

8. Some of the essays in Maynes, Waltner, Soland, and Strasser (1996) are useful in this regard.

9. Holy (1985) uses the concept of power in his reconsideration of agnatic marriage in the Middle East. The concepts of power and difference are equally important to Atkinson's and Errington's (1990) edited volume on gender in Southeast Asia.

References

Abu-Lughod, Lila. 1993. *Writing Women's Worlds.* Berkeley: University of California Press.

Altorki, Soraya. 1980. Milk-Kinship in Arab Society: An Unexplored Problem in the Ethnology of Marriage. *Ethnology* 19:233–44.

Appadurai, Arjun. 1986. Theory in Anthropology: Center and Periphery. *Comparative Studies in Society and History* 28:356–61.

Astuti, Rita. 1995. *People of the Sea: Identity and Descent Among the Vezo of Madagascar.* Cambridge, U.K.: Cambridge University Press.

Atkinson, Jane Monnig, and Shelly Errington. 1990. *Power and Difference: Gender in Island Southeast Asia.* Stanford: Stanford University Press.

Barnes, J. A. 1954. Class and Committees in a Norwegian Island Parish. *Human Relations* 7:39–58.

———. 1962. African Models in the New Guinea Highlands. *Man* 62:5–9.

———. 1972. Social Networks. *Addison-Wesley Module in Anthropology* 26:1–29.

Barnes, Sandra. 1990. Women, Property, and Power. In *Beyond the Second Sex,* ed. Peggy Sanday and Ruth Goodenough. Philadelphia: University of Pennsylvania Press.

Baumann, Gerd. 1995. Managing a Polyethnic Milieu: Kinship and Interaction in a London Suburb. *Journal of the Royal Anthropological Institute* (N.S.) 1:725–41.

Bell, Sandra, and Simon Coleman, eds. n.d. *The Anthropology of Friendship: Community Beyond Kinship.* London: Berg, forthcoming.

Bernería, Lourdes, and Catherine Stimpson, eds. 1987. *Women, Households, and the Economy.* Brunswick, N.J.: Rutgers University Press.

Berkner, Lutz. 1972. The Stem Family and the Developmental Cycle of the Peasant Household: An Eighteenth-Century Austrian Example. *American Historical Review* 77:398–418.

Bestard-Camps, Joan. 1991. *What's In a Relative? Household and Family in Formentera.* New York: Berg.

Bestor, Theodore. 1985. Tradition and Japanese Social Organization: Institutional Development in a Tokyo Neighborhood. *Ethnology* 24:121–36.

Bledsoe, Caroline. 1993. The Politics of Polygyny in Mende Education and Child Fosterage Transactions. In *Sex and Gender Hierarchies,* ed. Barbara D. Miller. Cambridge, U.K.: Cambridge University Press.

Bledsoe, Caroline, and Uche C. Isiugo-Abanihe. 1989. Strategies of Child Fosterage among Mende "Grannies." In *African Reproduction and Social Organization in Sub-Saharan Africa,* ed. Ron Lesthaegue. Berkeley: University of California Press.

Bloch, Maurice. 1971. *Placing the Dead: Tombs, Ancestral Villages, and Kinship Organization in Madagascar.* Reprint, Prospect Heights, Ill: Waveland Press, 1994.

Boissevain, Jeremy. 1968. The Place of Non-Groups in the Social Sciences. *Man* 3:542–56.

———. 1979. Network Analysis: A Reappraisal. *Current Anthropology* 20:392–94.

Boissevain, Jeremy, and J. Clyde Mitchell, eds. 1973. *Network Analysis.* The Hague: Mouton.

Boon, James A. 1990. Balinese Twins Times Two: Gender, Birth Order, and Household in Indonesia/Indo-Europe. In *Power and Difference: Gender in Island Southeast Asia,* ed. Jane M. Atkinson and Shelley Errington. Stanford: Stanford University Press.

Borneman, John. 1992. *Belonging in the Two Berlins: Kin, State, Nation.* Cambridge, U.K.: Cambridge University Press.

Borofsky, Robert, ed. 1994. *Assessing Cultural Anthropology.* New York: McGraw-Hill.

Bott, Elizabeth. 1957. *Family and Social Network: Roles, Norms and External Relationships in Ordinary Urban Families.* London: Tavistock.

Bourdieu, Pierre. 1977. *Outline of a Theory of Practice.* New York: Cambridge University Press.

Bowden, Ross. 1988. Kwoma Death Payments and Alliance Theory. *Ethnology* 27:271–90.

Brady, Ivan, ed. 1976. *Transactions in Kinship.* Honolulu: University of Hawaii Press.

Brandes, Stanley. 1975. The Structural and Demographic Implications of Nicknames in Navanogal, Spain. *American Ethnologist* 2:139–48.

Breen, Richard. 1982. Naming Practices in Western Ireland. *Man* 17:701–13.

Brettell, Caroline B. 1986. *Men Who Migrate, Women Who Wait: Population and History in a Portuguese Parish.* Princeton, N.J.: Princeton University Press.

———. 1991a. Kinship and Contract: Property Transmission and Family Relations in Portugal. *Comparative Studies in Society and History* 33:443–65.

———. 1991b. Property, Kinship, and Gender: A Mediterranean Perspective. In *The Family in Italy from Antiquity to the Present,* ed. David I. Kertzer and Richard P. Saller. New Haven, Conn.: Yale University Press.

———. 1999. The *Casa* of José Dos Santos Caldas: Family and Household in a Northwestern Portuguese Village, 1850–1993. In *House Life: Space, Place, and Family in Europe,* ed. Donna Birdwell-Pheasant and Denise Lawrence-Zuñiga. Oxford, U.K.: Berg Publishers.

Bringa, Tone. 1995. *Being Muslim the Bosnian Way.* Princeton, N.J.: Princeton University Press.

Brown, Paula. 1987. New Men and Big Men: Emerging Stratification in the Third World: A Case Study in the New Guinea Highlands. *Ethnology* 26:87–106.

Brudner, Lilyan A., and Douglas R. White. 1997. Class, Property and Structural Endogamy: Visualizing Networked Histories. *Theory and Society* 25:132–80.

Campbell, John K. 1963. The Kindred in a Greek Mountain Community. In *Mediterranean Countrymen: Essays in the Social Anthropology of the Mediterranean,* ed. J. Pitt-Rivers. The Hague: Mouton.

Carroll, Vern, ed. 1970. *Adoption in Eastern Oceania.* Honolulu: University of Hawaii Press.

Carsten, Janet. 1991. Children in Between: Fostering and the Process of Kinship on Pulau Langkawi, Malaysia. *Man* 26:425–43.

———. 1995. The Substance of Kinship and the Heat of the Hearth: Feeding, Personhood, and Relatedness Among Malays in Pulau Langkawi. *American Ethnologist* 22:223–41.

Carsten, Janet, and Stephen Hugh-Jones, eds. 1995. *About the House: Lévi-Strauss and Beyond.* Cambridge, U.K.: Cambridge University Press.

Chowning, Ann. 1987. Women Are Our Business: Women, Exchange, and Prestige in Kove. In *Dealing with Inequality: Analyzing Gender Relations in Melanesia and Beyond,* ed. Marilyn Strathern. Cambridge, U.K.: Cambridge University Press.

Cohen, Anthony. 1982. A Sense of Time, A Sense of Place: The Meaning of Close Social Association in Whalsay, Shetland. In *Belonging: Identity and Social Organization in British Rural Cultures,* ed. Anthony Cohen. Manchester, U.K.: Manchester University Press.

———. 1994. Self Consciousness: An Alternative Anthropology of Identity. New York: Routledge.

Collier, Jane Fishburne. 1997. *From Duty to Desire: Remaking Families in a Spanish Village.* Princeton, N.J.: Princeton University Press.

Collier, Jane Fishburne, and Sylvia Junko Yanagisako, eds. 1987. *Gender and Kinship.* Stanford: Stanford University Press.

Combs-Schilling, Elaine. 1985. Family and Friend in a Moroccan Book Town: The Segmentary Debate Reconsidered. *American Ethnologist* 12:659–76.

Cooper, Eugene. 1993. Cousin Marriage in Rural China: More and Less than Generalized Exchange. *American Ethnologist* 20:758–80.

Counts, Dorothy Ayers. 1992. Tamparonga: The Big Women of Kaliai (Papua, New Guinea). In *In Her Prime,* ed. Virginia Kerns and Judith K. Brown. Urbana: University of Illinois Press.

Delaney, Carol. 1995. Father State, Motherland, and the Birth of Modern Turkey. In *Naturalizing Power: Essays in Feminist Cultural Analysis*, ed. Sylvia Yanagisako and Carol Delaney. New York: Routledge.

Di Leonardo, Micaela. 1979. Methodology and Misinterpretation of Women's Status in Kinship Studies; A Case Study of Goodenough and the Definition of Marriage. *American Ethnologist* 6:627–37.

Diemberger, Hildegard. 1993. Blood, Sperm, Soul, and the Mountain: Gender Relations, Kinship and Cosmovision among the Khumbo (N.E. Nepal). In *Gendered Anthropology*, ed. Teresa del Valle. New York: Routledge.

Dresch, Paul. 1984. The Position of Shaykhs among the Northern Tribes of Yemen. *Man* 19:31–49.

———. 1986. The Significance of the Course Events Take in Segmentary Systems. *American Ethnologist* 13:309–24.

———. 1988. Segmentation: Its Roots in Arabia and Its Flowering Elsewhere. *Cultural Anthropology* 3:50–65.

Du Boulay, Juliet. 1984. The Blood: Symbolic Relationships between Descent, Marriage, Incest Prohibitions, and Spiritual Kinship in Greece. *Man* 19:533–56.

Elder, Glen. 1975. Age Differentiation and the Life Course. *Annual Review of Sociology* 1:165–90.

———. 1977. Family History and the Life Course. *Journal of Family History* 2:279–304.

———. 1987. Families and Lives: Some Developments in Life Course Studies. *Journal of Family History* 12:179–99.

Etienne, Mona. 1979. The Case for Social Maternity: Adoption of Children by Urban Baule Women. *Dialectical Anthropology* 4:237–42.

Evans-Pritchard, E. E. 1951. *Kinship and Marriage among the Nuer*. Oxford: Clarendon Press.

Evens, T. M. S. 1989. The Nuer Incest Prohibition and the Nature of Kinship: Alterlogical Reckoning. *Cultural Anthropology* 4:323–46.

Fardon, Richard, ed. 1990. *Localizing Strategies: Regional Traditions in Ethnographic Writing*. Washington, D.C.: Smithsonian Institution Press.

Feil, D. K. 1984. Beyond Patriliny in the New Guinea Highlands. *Man* 19:50–76.

Feldman-Savelsberg, Pamela. 1995. Cooking Inside: Kinship and Gender in Bangangté: Idioms of Marriage and Procreation. *American Ethnologist* 22:483–501.

Fisher, J. L. 1957. The Classification of Residence in Censuses. *American Anthropologist* 60:508–17.

Fox, John W. 1989. On the Rise and Fall of Tulans and Maya Segmentary States. *American Anthropologist* 91:656–89.

Fox, Robin. 1967. *Kinship and Marriage: An Anthropological Perspective*. New York: Penguin.

Franklin, Sarah, and Heléna Ragoné, eds. 1998. *Reproducing Reproduction: Kinship, Power, and Technological Innovation*. Philadelphia: University of Pennsylvania Press.

Fricke, Tom, William G. Axinn, and Arland Thornton. 1993. Marriage, Social Inequality, and Women's Contact with their Natal Families in Alliance Societies: Two Tamang Examples. *American Anthropologist* 95:395–19.

Garrison, Vivian, and Carol I. Weiss. 1979. Dominican Family Networks and the United States Immigration Policy: A Case Study. *International Migration Review* 12:264–83.

Geertz, Clifford. 1966. Religion as a Cultural System. In *Anthropological Approaches to the Study of Religion*, ed. Michael Banton. London: Tavistock.

Giddens, Anthony. 1984. *The Constitution of Society. Introduction to the Theory of Structuration*. Berkeley: University of California Press.

Gilbert, Dennis. 1981. Cognatic Descent Groups in Upper Class Lima. *American Ethnologist* 8:939–58.

Gilmore, David. 1975. Friendship in Fuenmayor: Patterns of Integration in an Atomistic Society. *Ethnology* 14:311–24.

Ginsburg, Faye D., and Rayna Rapp, eds. 1995. *Conceiving the New World Order: The Global Politics of Reproduction*. Berkeley: University of California Press.

Goddard, Victoria A. 1994. From the Mediterranean to Europe: Honour, Kinship, and Gender. In *The Anthropology of Europe: Identities and Boundaries in Conflict*, ed. Victoria Goddard. Oxford: Berg.

Gonzalez, Nancie. 1965. The Consanguineal Household and Matrifocality. *American Anthropologist* 67:1264–80.

———. 1970. Toward a Definition of Matrifocality. In *Afro-American Anthropology: Contemporary Perspectives*, ed. Norman Whitten and John Szwed. New York: Free Press.

Goodenough, Ward. 1956. Residence Rules. *Southwestern Journal of Anthropology* 12:22–37.

———. 1970. *Description and Comparison in Cultural Anthropology*. Cambridge, U.K.: Cambridge University Press.

Goody, Esther N. 1982. *Parenthood and Social Reproduction: Fostering and Occupational Roles in West Africa*. Cambridge, U.K.: Cambridge University Press.

Goody, Jack, ed. 1958. *The Developmental Cycle in Domestic Groups*. Cambridge, U.K.: Cambridge University Press.

Goody, Jack, and S. J. Tambiah. 1973. Bridewealth and Dowry in Africa and Eurasia. In *Bridewealth and Dowry*, ed. Jack Goody and S. J. Tambiah. Cambridge, U.K.: Cambridge University Press.

Goody, Jack, Joan Thirsk, and E. P. Thompson, eds. 1976. *Family and Inheritance: Rural Society in Western Europe, 1200–1800*. Cambridge, U.K.: Cambridge University Press.

Gottlieb, Alma. 1986. Cousin Marriage, Birth Order, and Gender: Alliance Models Among the Beng of Ivory Coast. *Man* 21:697–722.

Gough, Kathleen. 1971. Nuer Kinship: A Reexamination. In *The Translation of Culture*, ed. T. O. Beidelman. London: Tavistock.

Gudeman, Stephen. 1975. Spiritual Relationships and Selecting a Godparent. *Man* 10:221–37.

Gulliver, P. H. 1971. *Neighbors and Networks: The Idiom of Kinship in Social Action among the Ndendeuli of Tanzania*. Berkeley: University of California Press.

Hammel, Eugene A., and Peter Laslett. 1974. Comparing Household Structure over Time and between Cultures. *Comparative Studies in Society and History* 16:73–109.

Hann, C. M. 1998. *Property Relations: Renewing the Anthropological Tradition*. Cambridge: Cambridge University Press.

Hannerz, Ulf. 1992. The Global Ecumene as a Network of Networks. In *Conceptualizing Society*, ed. Adam Kuper. New York: Routledge.

Harrell, Stevan. 1997. *Human Families*. Boulder, Colo.: Westview.

Harrell, Stevan, and Sara A. Dickey. 1985. Dowry Systems in Complex Societies. *Ethnology* 24:105–20.

Harrison, S. 1993. The Commerce of Cultures in Melanesia. *Man* 28:139–58.

Hayden, Corinne. 1995. Gender, Genetics, Generation: Reformulating Biology in Lesbian Kinship. *Cultural Anthropology* 10:41–63.

Herzfeld, Michael. 1982. When Exceptions Define the Rules: Greek Baptismal Names and the Negotiation of Identity. *Journal of Anthropological Research* 38:288–302.

———. 1987. *Anthropology Through the Looking-Glass: Critical Ethnography in the Outline Margins of Europe*. Cambridge, U.K.: Cambridge University Press.

———. 1992. *The Social Production of Indifference: Exploring the Symbolic Roots of Western Bureaucracy*. Oxford: Berg.

Hirschon, Renée. 1984. *Women and Property: Women as Property*. London: Croom and Helm.

Ho, Christine G. T. 1993. The Internationalization of Kinship and the Feminization of Caribbean Migration: The Case of Afro-Trinidadian Immigrants in Los Angeles. *Human Organization* 52:32–40.

Holy, Ladislav. 1985. Power, Agnation, and Marriage in the Middle East. In *Power and Knowledge: Anthropological and Sociological Approaches*. Edinburgh: Scottish Academic Press.

———. 1996. *Anthropological Perspectives on Kinship*. London: Pluto.

Hoskins, Janet. 1990. Doubling Deities, Descent, and Personhood: An Exploration of Kodi Gender Categories. In *Power and Difference: Gender in Island Southeast Asia*, ed. Jane Monnig Atkinson and Shelley Errington. Stanford: Stanford University Press.

Howell, Signe, and Marit Melhuus. 1993. The Study of Kinship, the Study of the Person; A Study of Gender? In *Gendered Anthropology*, ed. Teresa del Valle. New York: Routledge.

Hutchinson, Sharon. 1985. Changing Concepts of Incest among the Nuer. *American Ethnologist* 12:625–41.

Johnson, Colleen. 1989. In-Law Relationships in the American Kinship System: The Impact of Divorce and Remarriage. *American Ethnologist* 16:87–99.

Johnson, Steven L. 1985. Kin and Casinos: Changing Family Networks in Atlantic City. *Current Anthropology* 26:397–99.

Karp, Ivan. 1978. New Guinea Models in the African Savannah. *Africa* 48:1–16.

Karp, Ivan, and Kent Maynard. 1983. Reading The Nuer. *Current Anthropology* 24:481–503.

Keesing, Roger. 1987. African Models in the Malaita Highlands. *Man* 22:431–52.

Kelly, Raymond. 1985. *The Nuer Conquest: The Structure and Development of an Expansionist System.* Ann Arbor: University of Michigan Press.

Kennedy, Robinette. 1986. Women's Friendships on Crete. In *Gender and Power in Rural Greece*, ed. Jill Dubisch. Princeton, N.J.: Princeton University Press.

Kertzer, David I. 1984. *Family Life in Central Italy, 1880–1910: Sharecropping, Wage Labor, and Coresidence.* New Brunswick, N.J.: Rutgers University Press.

———. 1991. Household History and Sociological Theory. *Annual Review of Sociology* 17:155–79.

Kopytoff, Ivan. 1977. Matrilineality, Residence, and Residential Zones. *American Ethnologist* 4: 539–58.

Kuper, Adam. 1982. Lineage Theory: A Critical Retrospect. *Annual Review of Anthropology* 11:71–95.

———. 1993. The "House" and Zulu Political Structure in the Nineteenth Century. *Journal of African History* 34:469–87.

LaFontaine, Jean S. 1973. Descent in New Guinea: An Africanist View. In *The Character of Kinship*, ed. J. R. Goody. Cambridge, U.K.: Cambridge University Press.

———. 1988. Child Sexual Abuse and the Incest Taboo. Practical Problems and Theoretical Insights. *Man* 23:1–18.

———. 1990. *Child Sexual Abuse.* Cambridge: Polity.

Langness, L. L. 1964. Some Problems in the Conceptualization of Highlands Social Structure. *American Anthropologist* 66 (4, part 2): 162–82.

Layton, Robert. 1997. Representing and Translating People's Place in the Landscape of Northern Australia. In *After Writing Culture: Epistemology and Praxis in Contemporary Anthropology*, ed. Allison James, Jenny Hockey, and Andrew Dawson. New York: Routledge.

Lederman, Rena. 1990. Contested Order: Gender and Society in the Southern New Guinea Highlands. In *Beyond the Second Sex: New Directions in the Anthropology of Gender*, ed. Peggy Reeves Sanday and Ruth Goodenough. Philadelphia: University of Pennsylvania Press.

Lepowsky, Maria. 1993. *Fruit of the Motherland: Gender in an Egalitarian Society.* New York: Columbia University Press.

Lévi-Strauss, Claude. 1969. *The Elementary Structures of Kinship.* Boston: Beacon.

———. 1983. Histoire et Ethnologie. *Annales* 38:1217–31.

Lockwood, Victoria. 1993. *Tahitian Transformation: Gender and Capitalist Development in a Rural Society.* Boulder, Colo.: Reiner.

Lomnitz, Larissa, and Marisol Pérez-Lizaur. 1984. Dynastic Growth and Survival Strategies: The Solidarity of Mexican Grand-Families. In *Kinship Ideology and Practice in Latin America*, ed. Raymond T. Smith. Durham: University of North Carolina Press.

Marcus, George, and P. D. Hall. 1992. *Lives in Trust: The Fortunes of Dynastic Families in Late Twentieth-Century America.* Boulder, Colo.: Westview.

Marshall, Mac. 1977. The Nature of Nurture. *American Ethnologist* 4:643–62.

Massey, Douglas, Rafael Alarcon, Jorge Durand, and Humberto Gonzalez. 1987. *Return to Aztlan: The Social Process of International Migration from Western Mexico.* Berkeley: University of California Press.

Maynard, Kent. 1988. On Protestants and Pastoralists: The Segmentary Nature of Socio-Cultural Organization. *Man* 23:101–17.

Maynes, Mary Jo, Ann Waltner, Birgitte Soland, and Ulrike Strasser, eds. 1996. *Gender, Kinship, Power: A Comparative and Interdisciplinary History.* New York: Routledge.

McKinnon, Susan. 1995. American Kinship/American Incest: Asymmetries in a Scientific Discourse. In *Naturalizing Power: Essays in Feminist Cultural Analysis*, ed. Sylvia Yanagisako and Carol Delaney. New York: Routledge.

Mintz, Sidney, and Eric Wolf. 1950. An Analysis of Ritual Co-Parenthood *(Compadrazgo). Southwestern Journal of Anthropology* 6:341–68.

Mitchell, J. Clyde. 1971. *Social Networks in Urban Situations.* Manchester, U.K.: Manchester University Press.

———. 1974. Social Networks. *Annual Review of Anthropology* 3:279–99.

Modell, Judith. 1994. *Kinship with Strangers: Adoption and Interpretation of Kinship in American Culture.* Berkeley: University of California Press.

Munson, Henry, Jr. 1989. On the Irrelevance of the Segmentary Lineage Model in the Moroccan Rif. *American Anthropologist* 91:386–400.

———. 1993. Rethinking Gellner's Segmentary Analysis of Morocco's Ait Atta. *Man* 28:267–80.

Neville, Gwen. 1987. *Kinship and Pilgrimage: Rituals of Reunion in American Culture.* New York: Oxford University Press.

Nutini, Hugo G., and Betty Bell. 1980. *Ritual Kinship: The Structure and Historical Development of the Compadrazgo System in Rural Tlaxcala.* Princeton, N.J.: Princeton University Press.

O'Connor, Mary I. 1990. Women's Networks and the Social Needs of Mexican Immigrants. *Urban Anthropology* 19:81–98.

Okamura, Jonathan. 1983. Filipino Hometown Associations in Hawaii. *Ethnology* 22:341–53.

Ortner, Sherry B. 1984. Theory in Anthropology since the Sixties. *Comparative Studies in Society and History* 26:126–66.

Ostor, Akos, Lina Fruzzetti, and Steve Barnett, eds. 1982. *Concepts of Person; Kinship, Caste and Marriage in India.* Cambridge, Mass.: Harvard University Press.

Paine, Robert. 1969. In Search of Friendship: An Exploratory Analysis in Middle-Class Culture. *Man* 4:505–24.

Peletz, Michael G. 1995. Kinship Studies in Late Twentieth-Century Anthropology. *Annual Review of Anthropology* 24:343–72.

Pina-Cabral, João de. 1984. Nicknames and the Experience of Community. *Man* 19:148–56.

———. 1994. Personal Identity and Ethnic Ambiguity: Naming Practices among the Eurasians of Macao. *Social Anthropology* 2:115–32.

Ragoné, Heléna. 1994. *Surrogate Motherhood: Conception in the Heart.* Boulder, Colo.: Westview.

———. 1996. Chasing the Blood Tie: Surrogate Mothers, Adoptive Mothers, and Fathers. *American Ethnologist* 23:352–65.

Raheja, Gloria Goodwin. 1996. The Limits of Patriliny: Kinship, Gender, and Women's Speech Practices in Rural North India. In *Gender, Kinship, Power: A Comparative and Interdisciplinary History*, ed. Mary Jo Maynes, Ann Waltner, Birgitte Soland, and Ulrike Strasser. New York: Routledge.

Rivière, P. G. 1993. The Amerindianization of Descent and Affinity. *L'Homme* 33:507–16.

Rodman, Margaret C. 1985. Contemporary Custom: Redefining Domestic Space in Langana, Vanuatu. *Ethnology* 24:269–79.

Rosaldo, Renato. 1988. Ideology, Place, and People without Culture. *Cultural Anthropology* 3:77–87.

Rubin, Gayle. 1975. The Traffic in Women: Notes on the Political Economy of Sex. In *Towards an Anthropology of Women*, ed. Rayna Rapp Reiter. New York: Monthly Review Press.

Rubinstein, Hymie. 1983. Caribbean Family and Household Organization: Some Conceptual Clarification. *Journal of Comparative Family Studies* 14:283–98.

Sahlins, Marshall. 1961. The Segmentary Lineage: An Organization of Predatory Expansion. *American Anthropologist* 80:53–70.

———. 1963. Poor Man, Rich Man, Big Man, Chief. *Comparative Studies in Society and History* 5:285–303.

Sahlins, Peter. 1989. *Boundaries: The Making of France and Spain in the Pyrenees.* Berkeley: University of California Press.
Sanday, Peggy Reeves. 1990. Androcentric and Matrifocal Representation in Minangkabau Ideology. In *Beyond the Second Sex: New Directions in the Anthropology of Gender,* ed. Peggy Reeves Sanday and Ruth Goodenough. Philadelphia: University of Pennsylvania Press.
Sandstrom, Alan. 1996. Center and Periphery in the Social Organization of Contemporary Nabuas of Mexico. *Ethnology* 35:161–80.
Sanjek, Roger. 1978. A Network Method and Its Uses in Urban Anthropology. *Human Organization* 37:257–68.
Saul, M. 1991. The Bobo "House" and the Uses of Categories of Descent. *Africa* 61:71–97.
Schildkrout, Enid. 1973. The Fostering of Children in Urban Ghana: Problems of Ethnographic Analysis in a Multicultural Context. *Urban Anthropology* 2:48–73.
Schneider, David M. 1969. Kinship, Nationality, and Religion in American Culture: Toward a Definition of Kinship. In *Forms of Symbolic Action,* ed. R. F. Spencer. Proceedings of the 1969 Annual Meeting of the American Ethnological Society. Seattle: University of Washington Press.
———. 1980. *American Kinship: A Cultural Account.* 2d ed. Chicago: University of Chicago Press.
———. 1984. *A Critique of the Study of Kinship.* Ann Arbor: University of Michigan Press.
Schweizer, Thomas, and Douglas R. White. 1998. *Kinship, Networks, and Exchange.* Cambridge, U.K.: Cambridge University Press.
Scott, John. 1991. Networks of Corporate Power: A Comparative Assessment. *Annual Review of Sociology* 17:181–203.
Shapiro, Warren. 1988. Ritual Kinship, Ritual Incorporation, and the Denial of Death. *Man* 23:275–97.
Silverblatt, Irene. 1980. Andean Women under Spanish Rule. In *Women and Colonization: Anthropological Perspectives,* ed. Mona Etienne and Eleanor Leacock. New York: Praeger.
Simpson, Bob. 1994. Bringing the "Unclear" Family into Focus: Divorce and Re-Marriage in Contemporary Britain. *Man* 29:829–51.
———. 1997. Representations and the Re-Presentation of Family: An Analysis of Divorce Narratives. In *After Writing Culture: Epistemology and Praxis in Contemporary Anthropology,* ed. Allison James, Jenny Hockey, and Andrew Dawson. New York: Routledge.
Smith, Raymond T. 1973. The Matrifocal Family. In *The Character of Kinship,* ed. Jack Goody. Cambridge, U.K.: Cambridge University Press.
Stone, Linda. 1997. *Kinship and Gender: An Introduction.* Boulder, Colo.: Westview.
Strathern, Andrew. 1973. Kinship, Descent and Locality: Some New Guinea Examples. In *The Character of Kinship,* ed. J. R. Goody. Cambridge, U.K.: Cambridge University Press.
Strathern, Marilyn. 1992a. *After Nature: English Kinship in the Late Twentieth Century.* Cambridge, U.K.: Cambridge University Press.
———. 1992b. *Reproducing the Future: Essays on Anthropology, Kinship, and the New Reproductive Technologies.* Manchester, U.K.: University of Manchester Press.
———. 1993. A Question of Context. In *Technologies of Procreation: Kinship in the Age of Assisted Conception,* ed. J. S. Edwards, et al. Manchester, U.K.: University of Manchester Press.
Uhl, Sarah. 1991. Forbidden Friends: Cultural Veils of Female Friendship in Andalusia. *American Ethnologist* 18:90–105.
Verdon, Michel. 1980. Shaking Off the Domestic Yoke. *Comparative Studies in Society and History* 22:109–32.
———. 1982. Where Have All Their Lineages Gone? Cattle and Descent among the Nuer. *American Anthropologist* 84:566–79.
———. 1983. Segmentation among the Tiv: A Reappraisal. *American Ethnologist* 10:290–302.
Waltner, Ann.1996. Kinship between the Lines: The Patriline, the Concubine, and the Adopted Son in Late Imperial China. In *Gender, Kinship, Power: A Comparative and Interdisciplinary History,* ed. Mary Jo Maynes, Ann Waltner, Birgitte Soland, and Ulrike Strasser. New York: Routledge.
Warman, Arturo. 1981. *We Come to Object: The Peasants of Morelos and the National State.* Baltimore: Johns Hopkins University Press.

Weinberg, Daniela. 1976. Bands and Clans: Political Functions of Voluntary Associations in the Swiss Alps. *American Ethnologist* 3:175–89.

Weiner, Annette. 1976. *Women of Value, Men of Renown: New Perspectives in Trobriand Exchange.* Austin: University of Texas Press.

Weiner, J. F. 1982. Substance, Siblingship, and Exchange: Aspects of Social Structure in New Guinea. *Social Analysis* 11:3–34.

Weismantel, Mary. 1995. Making Kin: Kinship Theory and Zumbagua Adoption. *American Ethnologist* 22:685–709.

Weston, Kath. 1992. *Families We Choose: Lesbians, Gays, Kinship.* New York: Columbia University Press.

———. 1995. Forever Is a Long Time: Romancing the Real in Gay Kinship Ideology. In *Naturalizing Power: Essays in Feminist Cultural Analysis,* ed. Sylvia Yanagisako and Carol Delaney. New York: Routledge.

Williams, Brackette. 1995. Classification Systems Revisited: Kinship, Caste, Race, and Nationality as the Flow of Blood and the Spread of Rights. In *Naturalizing Power: Essays in Feminist Cultural Analysis,* ed. Sylvia Yanagisako and Carol Delaney. New York: Routledge.

Witherspoon, Gary. 1975. *Navajo Kinship and Marriage.* Chicago: University of Chicago Press.

Wolf, Eric. 1966. Kinship, Friendship, and Patron–Client Relations in Complex Societies. In *The Social Anthropology of Complex Societies,* ed. Michael Banton. London: Tavistock.

Yanagisako, Sylvia. 1977. Women Centered Kin Networks in Urban Bilateral Kinship. *American Ethnologist* 4:207–26.

———. 1979. Family and Household: The Analysis of Domestic Groups. *Annual Review of Anthropology* 8:161–205.

Yanagisako, Sylvia, and Carol Delany, eds. 1995. *Naturalizing Power: Essays in Feminist Cultural Analysis.* New York: Routledge.

Zavella, Patricia. 1985. Abnormal Intimacy: The Varying Work Networks of Chicana Cannery Workers. *Feminist Studies* 11:541–55.

Zimmer, Catherine, and Howard Aldrich. 1987. Resource Mobilization through Ethnic Networks: Kinship and Friendship Ties of Shopkeepers in England. *Sociological Perspectives* 30:422–45.

Zook, Nancy, and Rachel Hallenback. 1987. Lesbian Co-Parenting: Creating Connections. In *Politics of the Heart: A Lesbian Parenting Anthology,* ed. Sandra Pollack and Jeanne Vaughn. Ithaca, N.Y.: Firebrand.

Chapter Four

Ties That Bond: The Role of Kinship in Primate Societies

Joan B. Silk

As anyone who has survived high school biology knows, offspring in diploid species obtain half of their genetic material from each of their parents. The laws of probability determine the likelihood that individuals who are descended from a common ancestor (kin) will share a given allele. This simple process has profound effects on the evolution of morphological traits as well as on the evolution of social behavior. Genetic relatedness, or kinship, provides the main vehicle for the evolution of altruism through the process of kin selection (Hamilton 1964). Individuals who give alarm calls, share food, tolerate conspecifics at feeding sites, cooperate in intergroup encounters, groom other group members, or defend companions against attack are altruists because their actions reduce their own fitness and enhance the fitness of others.

Primates provide ample evidence of the importance of kinship in social life. For example, female galagos forage alone at night, but spend their days resting with their daughters who occupy adjacent home ranges (Bearder 1987). Male siamangs carry their offspring for much of the day, allowing their mates to forage unencumbered (Chivers 1974; Palombit 1996). Infant rhesus macaques are defended against attack from other group members by their mothers and other close kin (Berman 1980, 1983a, 1983b, 1983c). Female gorillas are more tolerant of their own offspring when they are feeding than they are of unrelated group members (Stewart and Harcourt 1987). Male bonobos spend much of their time with their mothers, even after they reach adulthood (Nishida and Hiraiwa-Hasegawa 1987; Furuichi 1989). This compendium could be continued, filling many pages.

The goal of this chapter is to examine how kinship is woven into the fabric of social life in primate groups. I will begin by describing the evolutionary forces that shape the evolution of altruistic behavior. The theory of kin selection provides an explanation for how evolution can favor behaviors that are costly to the actor but beneficial to the recipient. To fulfill predictions derived from kin selection theory, primates must be able to distinguish kin from nonkin. Thus, the next step is to examine what primates know about kinship. Researchers working in the field and in laboratory settings provide intriguing evidence that primates can and do distinguish relatives from nonrelatives. The final step is to consider how kinship shapes social organization, structures social behavior, and influences the lives of individuals in primate groups. I will focus on one well-studied set of Old World primate species (macaques, baboons, and vervets). Although these species may not be representative of the primate order as a whole (Strier 1994), they nonetheless provide a comprehensive lesson about how kin selection influences social life.

How Kinship Shapes the Evolution of Behavior

Kinship plays a central role in primates' social lives because genetic relatedness is an important element in the evolution of social behavior. Natural selection is generally expected to favor behaviors that enhance the relative fitness of individuals, and much of the behavior that we see in nature follows this logic. Thus, animals forage efficiently for food, compete effectively for access to mates, and flee swiftly from predators. Evolutionary theory tells us that individuals who perform these tasks successfully are likely to leave more descendants than their conspecifics, and the traits that enable them to succeed in these tasks will therefore become more common in the population over time.

However, when we observe the behavior of primates and other animals, we see a variety of behaviors that are difficult to account for in these terms. For example, male chimpanzees form coalitions against members of other communities (Goodall et al. 1979; Nishida et al. 1985), vervet monkeys give alarm calls when they detect predators (Struhsaker 1967; Seyfarth et al. 1980), callitrichids donate insect prey to juveniles (Brown and Mack 1978; Price and Feistner 1993), and many monkeys spend substantial parts of every day grooming other group members (Gouzoules and Gouzoules 1987). These behaviors seem to enhance the fitness of recipients at the expense of the actors, and thereby confound the logic of evolution by natural selection. The evolution of altruistic behaviors like these presents a major challenge to evolutionary theory.

Hamilton (1964) was the first to provide a solution to this puzzle. He realized that relatives share some of their genetic material because they have a common ancestor. Offspring in diploid species, for example, obtain half of their genetic material from each of their parents. If individuals behave altruistically toward their relatives, then they have some chance of conferring benefits upon individuals who carry copies of their own genes. The likelihood of this happening is based upon the genetic relationship between the actor and the recipient. Hamilton also realized that the adaptive value of altruistic acts would depend on the costs of the act to the donor and the beneficial effects of the act on the recipient. The magnitude of these effects will depend upon the kind of behavior that is performed and the characteristics of the individuals involved in the interaction. Thus, it might be less costly for a monkey to give an alarm call to a distant predator than to join in an attack on a powerful group member. Similarly, when a male baboon defends an infant against a potentially infanticidal immigrant male (Palombit et al. 1997), the incremental positive effect on the infant's fitness may be greater than the incremental negative effect on the protective male's fitness.

Hamilton demonstrated that altruistic behaviors will be favored by selection if the costs of performing the behavior are less than the benefits discounted by the coefficient of relatedness between actor and recipient. The coefficient of relatedness, r, is the average probability that two individuals acquire the same allele through descent from a common ancestor. This principle, which is generally called Hamilton's Rule, is stated as:

$$rb > c$$

where

r = the average coefficient of relatedness between the actor and the recipients
b = the sum of the fitness benefits to all individuals affected by the behavior
c = the fitness cost to the individual performing the behavior

Two basic insights can be derived from Hamilton's Rule. First, it is clear that when $r = 0$, this inequality cannot be satisfied. This means that altruism (via kin selection) will be restricted to kin ($r > 0$).[1] Second, costly altruism will be limited to close kin, as the conditions for Hamilton's Rule become progressively more difficult to satisfy as costs rise. For example, when $r = 1/2$, as it is between parents and offspring and full siblings, the benefits must exceed just twice the costs in order for the inequality to be satisfied. When $r = 1/8$, the value for cousins, the benefits must exceed eight times the costs.

Knowledge of Kin Relationships

In order to distribute altruistic acts selectively to their genetic relatives, animals must have some mechanism for distinguishing kin from nonkin, or close kin from distant kin. Kin recognition takes a variety of forms in the animal kingdom (Pfennig and Sherman 1995). Sea squirts are able to recognize others who carry the same allele on the hypervariable histocompatability locus, and house mice use olfactory cues to detect kinship. Some animals learn who their relatives are during the course of development, drawing cues about kinship from patterns of association and interactions.

Primates do not have an innate ability to identify their relatives, even their own offspring (Gouzoules and Gouzoules 1987; Walters 1987). The clearest evidence of this comes from a set of laboratory experiments in which juvenile pigtail macaques were presented with unfamiliar kin and unfamiliar nonkin (Fredrickson and Sackett 1984). The subjects showed no consistent preference for their relatives, suggesting that they had no innate ability to discriminate kin from nonkin. It is possible, of course, that the monkeys were *able* to discriminate between kin and nonkin, but showed no particular affinity for unfamiliar kin. This interpretation is suspect, however, because in most naturalistic settings, macaques show clear tendencies to interact selectively with their relatives (Gouzoules and Gouzoules 1987).

Apparently, even mothers must learn who their own infants are. Mothers' inability to recognize their own infants at birth enables managers of captive colonies to cross-foster newborn infants (Bernstein 1991). Foster mothers routinely accept these strange infants, even if they are not the same sex or precise ages as their own infants. Female macaques are even willing to rear infants of other macaque species (Owren et al. 1993).

We generally assume that primates learn who their relatives are through their early experiences and associations. Infants may learn to recognize their mothers (and sometimes their fathers) through their intimate association early in life (Bernstein 1988, 1991; Tomasello and Call 1997). However, we do not know precisely when this knowledge is acquired, what perceptual cues are used to identify kin, or how this information is coded cognitively.

Although we do not know exactly how primates learn who their relatives are, there is little doubt that they can recognize maternal kin. When vervet monkey mothers hear the tape recorded calls of their own infants played from a hidden speaker, they look toward the source of the call, suggesting that they recognize their own offspring's voices (Cheney and Seyfarth 1980). Primatologists have also amassed a considerable body of evidence that indicates that primates can and do discriminate between kin and nonkin in their day-to-day lives (reviewed in Dugatkin 1997; Gray 1985; Gouzoules and Gouzoules 1987). Many of the behaviors that primates direct selectively to their kin fulfill the biological definition of altruism: the benefits to the recipient exceed the costs to the actor. For example:

- Female primates routinely nurse their own offspring, but do not often nurse other females' offspring (Packer et al. 1992).
- Primates selectively support their relatives when they are involved in agonistic conflicts, and take the greatest risks on behalf of their closest relatives (reviewed by Gouzoules and Gouzoules 1987).
- Primates are generally more tolerant of kin than nonkin at feeding sites (Kawai 1958; Stewart and Harcourt 1987). While food sharing is rare, it is more common among kin than nonkin (Brown and Mack 1978; Goodall 1968; McGrew 1975; Nishida and Turner 1996; Silk 1978, 1979; Starin 1978).
- Primates groom kin at higher rates than nonkin (reviewed by Dugatkin 1997; Gouzoules and Gouzoules 1987).

Limits to Kinship Knowledge

Although primates distinguish between kin and nonkin in many contexts, there seem to be limits on the extent of their genealogical knowledge. Macaques groom and support close kin more than distant kin, but they groom and support distant kin at the same rates as nonkin (Chapais et al. 1997; Kaplan 1978; Kapsalis and Berman 1996; Kurland 1977; Massey 1977). On Cayo Santiago, where rhesus macaques live in large social groups, females treat monkeys related by less than 0.125 much like they treat nonkin, suggesting that this is the threshold for identifying kin (Kapalis and Berman 1996).

Monkeys' failure to distinguish distant kin from nonkin may mean that they classify only close kin as relatives. Sherman (1980, 1981) has suggested that natural selection should favor the ability to distinguish categories of kin that individuals typically encounter in nature. The limits of kin knowledge have been studied in very large provisioned groups that contain diffuse networks of kin. In natural groups, matrilines are typically smaller. Thus, selection may not have favored the ability to recognize distant kin because they were seldom encountered in nature. If Sherman's hypothesis is correct, then we might expect the extent of kinship knowledge to vary across species that form groups of different size and composition in nature.

It is also possible that primates classify distant relatives as kin, but treat them much like nonkin because altruism toward distant kin does not satisfy Hamilton's Rule. If this is true, then we might expect the kinship threshold to vary for different behaviors. All other things being equal, the kinship threshold should be higher for behaviors that involve high costs to the actor than for behaviors that involve little cost to the actor.

In nonmonogamous species, primates do not seem to recognize their paternal kin. Several studies have shown that infants interact preferentially with males who are likely to be their own fathers (Stein 1984; Smuts 1985; Berenstain et al. 1981), but only because their mothers show preferences for associating with former mating partners. In species in which a single male monopolizes access to receptive females, preferential associations between age mates might be expected to occur because they are likely to be paternal half-siblings (Altmann 1979).

Paternal kinship may play a less salient role than maternal kinship in most primate societies because there is nearly always some degree of uncertainty about paternity. Even in pair-bonded species, like gibbons and callicebus monkeys, females sometimes mate with males from outside their groups (Mason 1966; Palombit 1994; Reichard 1995). In some species that form one-male groups, such as patas and blue monkeys, incursions by nonresident males may occur during the mating season (Tsingalia and Rowell 1984; Cords 1987; Struhsaker 1977). In multimale species, male rank is often correlated with reproductive success, but the association is far from perfect.

Another factor that may limit the importance of paternal kinship is that in many primate species (see below), males disperse from their natal groups at

puberty while females are philopatric. While females live with several generations of maternal kin, males spend most of their lives among nonrelatives. Paternal kinship may play a more prominent role when males are the philopatric
sex, as in chimpanzees and spider monkeys.

Knowledge of Other's Kinship Relationships

In addition to knowing something about their own relationships to others,
primates know something about the kinship relationships between other
group members, what are sometimes called third-party kinship relationships.
In a series of elegant laboratory experiments, Dasser (1988a, 1988b) tested the
kinship knowledge of longtailed macaques who lived in a large social group.
Dasser trained two young females to choose photographs of one mother–
offspring pair from their group over photographs of pairs of unrelated monkeys from their group. After they had mastered this task, the females were
asked to choose between pictures of *other* mother–offspring pairs from their
group and pairs of unrelated individuals. They were also asked to match photographs of familiar infants with photographs of their mothers. The monkeys
mastered these two tasks successfully. They also mastered a similar set of experiments that tested their knowledge of sibling relationships. Thus, these
macaques seemed to have some understanding of the nature of mother–
offspring and sibling relationships.

The playback experiment conducted by Cheney and Seyfarth (1980) described above also provided evidence that vervets recognize other monkeys'
mother–infant relationships. When Seyfarth and Cheney played infant's tape
recorded calls to their mothers, females who happened to be nearby looked directly at the infant's mother, suggesting that they knew that there was a special
relationship between them.

Knowledge of third-party kinship relationships may underlie certain behavioral patterns that we see in primate groups. For example, female
macaques do not harass immature offspring of higher-ranking females when
they are near their mothers. This phenomenon, which was first recognized by
researchers studying free-ranging Japanese macaques (Kawai 1958; Kawamura
1958), suggests that macaques understand the relationship between mothers
and their offspring.[2] After fights, primates sometimes redirect aggression toward individuals who were not involved in the original confrontation. Vervet
monkeys selectively redirect aggression toward the kin of their former opponents (Cheney and Seyfarth 1989). For vervets to target their former opponent's kin, they may need to know something about their kinship relationships, or at least their patterns of association. Finally, former opponents
sometimes interact affiliatively immediately after conflicts have ended, a phenomenon which is known as "reconciliation." Reconciliation is sometimes directed toward kin of former opponents, rather than to opponents themselves

(Cheney and Seyfarth 1989; Das et al. 1997; Judge 1991; York and Rowell 1988). Again, knowledge of third-party kinship relationships may be involved in these peaceful post-conflict events.

The Ecology of Kinship Bonds in Primates

While there is a considerable amount of evidence that primates can and do recognize their own relatives and may even recognize other individual's relatives, there is considerable variation in how kinship influences primates' lives. The role of kinship in the daily lives of animals depends on the demographic composition of the groups in which they live. Kin selection will only be an important force in the evolution of social behavior if animals find themselves in situations where they have an opportunity to fulfill the predictions of Hamilton's Rule. At a minimum, kin must be available. The number, availability, and degree of relatedness among kin will depend on how groups are constructed in nature.

In most nonmonogamous primate species, members of one sex disperse from their natal groups at puberty, while members of the other sex remain in their natal groups throughout their lives. In the majority of primate species, females are the philopatric sex (Pusey and Packer 1987), although there are some species in which females disperse (e.g., red colobus monkeys and chimpanzees) and others in which members of both sexes leave their natal groups (e.g., howlers and gibbons).

The primary function of dispersal is to prevent inbreeding (Pusey and Packer 1987; Pusey and Wolf 1996), but inbreeding avoidance does not necessarily favor male dispersal over female dispersal.[3] The prevalence of female philopatry among nonhuman primates is usually linked to females' need to maintain access to food resources, which, in turn, makes it advantageous to live among close kin. Wrangham (1980, 1987) pointed out that female reproductive success is limited by access to nutritional resources, while male reproductive success is mainly limited by access to fertile and receptive females. He also observed that many primates rely heavily on fruit, a resource that is patchily distributed in time and space and often occurs in areas that are large enough to feed a number of individuals. He suggested that sociality may have evolved among primates because groups of females were more successful in competitive encounters than solitary females. Thus, groups were favored because of the selective advantages derived from establishing permanent alliances with other females. Kin selection theory suggests that the most reliable allies will be close kin. Thus, Wrangham argued that females benefited from forming long-term alliances with closely related females. He called these "female-bonded kin groups."

Wrangham's model has been criticized by van Schaik and his colleagues who argue that predation pressure provided the primary selective advantage for group living (van Schaik and van Hooff 1983; van Hooff and van Schaik, 1992; Sterck et al. 1997). Primates in groups were safer from predators because they were able to detect danger sooner, were less likely to become targets for attack, and could deter predators with counterattacks more effectively. Although primates may have been safer from predators when they lived in social groups, they may have encountered more intense competition from group members over access to food when they lived in social groups. If food was limited and clumped, it would have been profitable for females to form alliances in intragroup encounters (Isbell 1991). Again, these conditions favored the formation of kin-based coalitions because kin made the most reliable allies.

These models of the evolution of sociality among primates converge in one important way. They both emphasize the importance of stable alliances among close female kin. If females routinely left their natal groups, kin-based alliances would not be possible, so female philopatry was favored by natural selection in many species.[4]

Matrilineal Societies

The importance of strong kin ties among females is most clearly documented among contemporary Old World monkeys (Gouzoules and Gouzoules 1987). In these species, maternal kinship underlies a suite of features, including female philopatry, well-differentiated relationships among females, matrilineal social networks, and stable and linear matrilineal dominance hierarchies. This constellation of characteristics apparently evolved in the common ancestor of contemporary Old World monkey species and has been conserved subsequently in descendant species, even though they have radiated into diverse ecological niches throughout Africa and Asia (Di Fiore and Rendall 1994; Rendall and Di Fiore 1995). The conservatism of these features suggests that ecology has little influence on social organization and behavior in extant species. However, there may be some variation in these features that reflects adaptation to local conditions. Thus, differences in the distribution of food resources at different sites in Africa have been linked to the nature of social relationships among female baboons (Barton et al. 1996), and variation in group size among longtailed macaques has been linked to the presence of predators (van Schaik and van Noordwijk 1985).

Much of what we know about the role of kinship and the nature of social relationships in Old World monkey groups comes from observations of the members of just three genera: the savannah baboons, macaques, and vervet monkeys. These are the species for which we have the most extensive genealogical data, the most detailed information about behavioral interactions, and the most complete information about female reproductive histories.

In macaques, baboons, and vervets, females form close and enduring social relationships. Grooming, which provides one means to assess the quality of social relationships, is not evenly distributed among potential partners.[5] Some pairs of females groom at higher rates than others, and in some groups, not all pairs of females groom one another.

The distribution of grooming may reflect the social and ecological conditions in which females live (Dunbar 1991, 1992). Females' daily schedules, or activity budgets, must accommodate females' need to find enough food to meet their nutritional needs, to travel from their sleeping sites to the sites where they feed and drink during the course of the day, to attend to their offspring, and to maintain social relationships. Ecological conditions that influence the abundance and distribution of food determine how much time females must devote to feeding and traveling and how much time they can afford to devote to other less pressing activities. When females live in small groups, they may have enough time to groom all other group members. As group size increases, this becomes progressively more difficult. Across primate species, group size is positively correlated with the amount of time that females spend grooming (Dunbar 1991), but there is an upper limit on the amount of time that they spend. In large groups, females must (a) reduce the amount of time spent grooming each of their partners, or (b) limit their grooming to a subset of available partners (Henzi et al. 1997). In several species of monkeys, females appear to adopt the latter strategy. For example, in a group of savannah baboons that contained nineteen adult females, each female groomed on average only eight of the other eighteen females in the group. Moreover, females devoted the majority of their grooming to an even smaller number of partners; nine of the nineteen females in the group devoted more than half of their grooming to a single partner (Silk et al. 1999).

When females do form strong and selective attachments, they often favor maternal kin. High rates of grooming and other forms of affiliative interactions among close kin are widely documented among monkeys, baboons, and vervets (reviewed by Dugatkin 1997; Gouzoules and Gouzoules 1987; Silk 1987).

Matrilineal bonds have a profound impact on females' lives, extending well beyond their grooming partnerships. In many Old World primate species, females intervene in ongoing disputes, providing support for the perpetrator or defending the victim of aggression. Kin play a key role in these coalitions. Females are generally more likely to support kin than nonkin (Berman 1983a, 1983b, 1983c; Chapais 1983; Cheney 1983; Datta 1983a, 1983b; Kaplan 1977, 1978; Kurland 1977; Massey 1977; Silk 1982). Females are also more likely to support their relatives against opponents who rank higher than themselves than they are to support nonrelatives in the same situation (Chapais 1983; Chapais et al. 1991; Cheney 1983; Hunte and Horrocks 1987; Kurland 1977; Netto and van Hooff 1986; Pereira 1989; Silk et al. 1981; Walters 1980; Watanabe 1979). Since allies run some risk of being threatened, chased, attacked, or injured when they intervene against higher-ranking monkeys, females are evidently willing to take greater risks on behalf of kin than on behalf of nonkin.

Nepotistic support has a direct impact on the acquisition of dominance rank (see Chapais 1992 for a detailed analysis of this process). During infancy, infants are protected and supported by their mothers and close female kin when they are threatened by other group members, particularly females who rank lower than their own mothers (Berman 1980; Datta 1983a; Cheney 1977; de Waal 1977; Horrocks and Hunte 1983; Johnson 1987; Lee 1983a, 1983b; Lee and Oliver 1979; Paul and Kuester 1987; Pereira 1989; Walters 1980). As they grow older, young juveniles receive support when they challenge peers whose mothers rank lower than their own mothers and when they challenge adults who are subordinate to their own mothers. Initially, juveniles can defeat older and larger juveniles only when their own mothers are nearby (Datta 1983a, 1983b; Horrocks and Hunte 1983; Walters 1980). Eventually, immatures are able to defeat all group members who are subordinate to their own mothers, even when their mothers are not in the vicinity. Since juveniles are able to defeat everyone that their own mothers can defeat (but not their mothers themselves), offspring acquire ranks just below their mothers.

Chapais has conducted a series of experiments that were designed to examine the role of kin-based alliances on rank acquisition in a group of captive Japanese macaques (reviewed in Chapais 1992). This group was composed of three adult females who each had three immature daughters. In one series of experiments (Chapais 1988), a subgroup was formed that was composed of the three mothers (A, B, and C) and their two-year-old daughters (A2, B2, and C2). In the original group and in the experimental subgroup, A outranked B, and B outranked C. Chapais removed A and B from the subgroup, leaving their daughters as well as C and her daughter C2. In this situation, C outranked A2 and B2, and C2 quickly rose in rank over A2 and B2 as well. When C was replaced by B, B and B2 became the highest-ranking pair. When B was replaced by A, A and A2 were able to regain their original rank. Chapais's experimental studies clearly demonstrate that the presence of related allies influences the acquisition of dominance rank.

The same process, repeated over generations and across families, generates corporate matrilineal dominance hierarchies. Thus, daughters acquire ranks below their mothers who, in turn, occupy ranks below their own mothers.[6] This means that all members of the same matriline occupy contiguous ranks. Moreover, all members of a given matriline rank above or below all the members of other matrilines. Matrilineal dominance hierarchies have now been documented in at least seven species of macaques, baboons, and vervet monkeys (Chapais 1992).

The matrilineal dominance hierarchies that characterize macaque, baboon, and vervet groups have three striking properties. They are transitive, linear, and very stable. In these species, virtually all encounters between a particular pair of females have a predictable outcome—the higher-ranking female wins. One researcher observed more than 2,000 dominance encounters among thirty-one adult female baboons over a one-year period (Smuts 1985). In less than 1 percent of these interactions, the lower-ranking female defeated her higher-ranking opponent. Isbell and Pruetz (1998) reported no reversals among female vervet monkeys in a study that spanned four years. This pattern is also quite typical of other groups of baboons, macaques, and vervets. Since higher-ranking females can regularly defeat lower-ranking females, dominance relationships are transitive. This means that if female A can defeat female B, and female B can defeat female C, then female A can always defeat female C. When all trios are transitive, a linear dominance hierarchy is formed (Chase 1980).

Dominance hierarchies in these species are also very stable over time (Bramblett et al. 1982; Hausfater et al. 1982; Isbell and Pruetz 1998; Samuels et al. 1987; Silk 1988). For example, researchers have documented dominance relationships among female baboons over several decades in Amboseli, Kenya. For more than ten years, dominance relationships were altered only by the death and maturation of group members (Hausfater et al. 1982). Even though dominance hierarchies are sometimes disrupted by radical upheavals (e.g., Ehardt and Bernstein 1986; Samuels et al. 1987; Samuels and Henrickson 1983), long periods of stability are common.

Kinship may contribute to the linearity and stability of dominance relationships among females. A female may be reluctant to challenge a higher-ranking female if she knows that her opponent's relatives will come to her aid. Even if females do not receive support in every encounter, the presence of potential allies may serve as an effective deterrent against challenges. Moreover, the corporate matrilineal structure of primate dominance hierarchies may dampen temporal variation in individual fighting ability and power. Thus, when a female is ill or injured, her ability to physically dominate her opponents may be impaired. However, a single female's weakness may have a small effect upon the collective strength of an entire matriline.

Female dominance rank has important fitness consequences for females. In some species, high-ranking females mature at earlier ages, give birth to healthier infants, and have shorter interbirth intervals than low-ranking females do (reviewed by Silk 1987; Harcourt 1987). Statistically significant associations between dominance rank and all reproductive parameters are not found in every group of macaques, baboons, or vervets (e.g., Altmann et al. 1988; Cheney et al. 1988; Gouzoules et al. 1982; Packer et al. 1995). However, the evidence shows that for most females in most groups, high rank confers reproductive advantages.

The relationship between dominance rank and reproductive success may also contribute to the stability of dominance hierarchies over time. The power of a matrilineage is likely to be related to its size because larger lineages are able to muster more allies than smaller lineages. If this is the case, then differential reproductive success among females of different ranks will perpetuate power differences among matrilines. All other things being equal, high-ranking lineages are likely to become larger, more powerful, and to reproduce more successfully over time, while low-ranking lineages are likely to become smaller, less powerful, and reproduce less successfully.

Beyond Matrilineal Groups

Female macaques, baboons, and vervets provide a tutorial in how kin selection shapes social behavior and influences social structure. But these species constitute a relatively small range of the total variation in primate social structure (Strier 1994) and are derived from only one shallow branch of the primate phylogenetic tree. A complete analysis of the role of kinship would encompass the whole range of variation that we see in nature. However, we know much more about the terrestrial Old World monkeys than we do about most other primates, and detailed information about the role of kinship in other species is often unavailable. What we do know suggests that "In any system in which females live in permanent groups there will always be a tendency for animals to associate with their relatives" (Stewart and Harcourt 1987).

Consider, for example, the great apes, who are our closest living relatives. Female philopatry does not characterize any of the extant great apes (orangutans, gorillas, and chimpanzees). The patterns of relationships among individuals in these species are much more variable than among macaques, baboons, and vervets. Despite this variability, there is clear evidence that nepotism plays an important role in all of the great apes.

Adult orangutans are largely solitary. Males spend most of their time alone, while females travel and interact mainly with their own immature offspring (van Schaik and van Hooff 1996). There is no evidence that females form affiliative relationships with one another or establish differentiated social bonds (van Schaik and van Hooff 1996). However, at some sites, some females' ranges overlap extensively, while other females' ranges overlap very little. Researchers suspect that females who share much of their home ranges are close kin (Galdikas 1988; van Schaik and van Hooff 1996).

In mountain gorilla groups, both males and females typically emigrate from their natal groups (Stewart and Harcourt 1987), limiting opportunities for nepotism. Nonetheless, matrilineal kinship ties create bonds among female gorillas. Adult female mountain gorillas spend more time resting and feeding near their relatives than near nonrelatives, and are more likely to groom and support kin than nonkin (Harcourt and Stewart 1987, 1989; Stewart and Harcourt 1987; Watts 1991, 1994, 1996). Although detailed information about female dispersal is quite limited, there is some indication that dispersing females often join groups that contain females who formerly belonged to their natal group. Sometimes females, who are likely to be sisters, transfer together (Stewart and Harcourt 1987).

In chimpanzees, females usually leave their natal groups when they reach sexual maturity, while males are philopatric (Nishida and Hosaka 1998). At

Gombe, not all females emigrate permanently, and some females maintain close bonds with their adolescent and adult daughters (Goodall 1986). "The close-knit family circle at the heart of a female's web of relationships provides her, as she gets older, with companionship, grooming, play, and—most important—support during agonistic interactions with other community members" (Goodall 1986: 159).

Among chimpanzees, males have more opportunities for nepotism than females do because they remain in their natal groups. Males form strong bonds with one another. At Gombe, males spend much of their time in the company of other males, and affiliative interactions among males are common. Males travel together, rest together, groom one another, and support one another in agonistic contests. Several males have successfully supported (maternal) brothers in their efforts to challenge higher-ranking males.

Both maternal and paternal kin ties may underlie sociality among male chimpanzees. At Gombe, genetic analyses have shown that males are more closely related to one another on average than are females (Morin et al. 1994). The average degree of relatedness among males is about the same as that of half-siblings (≈ 0.25). However, preliminary reports from the Taï forest in Côte d'Ivoire suggest that cooperation among males may not be contingent on close kinship. Genetic analyses of paternity in one group of chimpanzees indicate that approximately half the infants were sired by males from outside the community (Gagneux et al. 1997, 1999). In this population, cooperative activities, such as hunting, may be favored because individuals benefit directly from coordinating their actions and collaborating (Boesch 1994).

Male philopatry also characterizes bonobos (sometimes known as pygmy chimpanzees; White 1996). Nonetheless, adult females groom one another at higher rates than they groom males or than males groom each other (White 1996), which seems to suggest that maternal kinship is not the basis for sociality among females. On the other hand, females spend a good deal of time with adult males, who are likely to be their own sons (Furiuchi 1989; Muroyama and Sugiyama 1996; White 1996). The dominance rank of adult males is influenced by their mothers' presence, although it is not clear if mothers intervene actively on their sons' behalf (Furiuchi 1989; Ihobe 1992).

Although we can detect the effects of kinship on behavior in chimpanzees, gorillas, and orangutans, the extent of nepotism is limited compared to the matrilineal macaques, baboons, and vervets.[7] Smuts (1995) has suggested that female dispersal in great apes has limited the ability of females to form effective alliances and made females more vulnerable to male aggression, dominance, sexual coercion, and infanticide. In addition to having weaker alliances with other females, female chimpanzees and orangutans also spend much of their time alone, further reducing their ability to defend themselves against males. Female bonobos, who do form close bonds with other females and spend much of their time together, are not subject to aggression and sexual coercion by males (Kano 1992).

Conclusion

The basic conclusion that emerges from the literature is that nepotism is a fundamental feature of primate social life. Kinship may have a more systematic impact on the structure of macaques, baboons, and vervets than it does on other primate species, although this is not yet clear. However, whenever relatives live together, kinship exerts a powerful influence on the pattern of social interactions among individuals. Genetic relatedness is a primary ingredient in the cooperative and altruistic interactions that sustain sociality in nonhuman primate groups.

When a chapter like this one is included in an edited volume that is principally concerned with humans, there is an implicit obligation to consider what the data on nonhuman primates tell us about human evolution. However, we know much more about the biological, ecological, and demographic processes that shape the evolution of behavior in nonhuman primates than we do about the processes that shape the behavior of contemporary humans. The capacity for culture alters the evolution of human behavior in complex ways (e.g., Boyd and Richerson 1985), undermining our confidence in simple analogies between nonhuman primates and ourselves. The challenge is not just to enumerate similarities and differences between nonhuman primates and modern humans, but to explain the processes that have maintained behavioral traits that we share with other primates and the processes that have transformed the behavioral traits that differentiate humans from other primate species. Knowledge of the primate record provides a valuable empirical baseline for this exercise.

Kinship provides one example of continuities and discontinuities between humans and other primates. There are no human societies in which biological kinship is entirely irrelevant, but there are many human societies in which kinship is not the primary organizing principle regulating cooperative activity and social institutions (Richerson and Boyd 1998; Richerson and Boyd 1999). Nepotism and reciprocity underlie what Richerson and Boyd (1999) called our "ancient social instincts," while cultural evolution has created additional forces that differentiate human societies from the societies of other primates, enabling human societies to become larger, more stratified, and more complex than those of any other primates. Nonetheless, biological kinship remains an important element at the core of every human society, creating bonds, defining obligations, and sustaining altruism. These bonds have very deep roots in the primate order.

Notes

1. Kin selection is not the only evolutionary mechanism that generates altruism. Reciprocal altruism, in which altruistic acts are exchanged and costs and benefits are balanced over time, provides another mechanism for the evolution of altruistic behavior (Trivers 1971; Axelrod and

Hamilton 1981). In order for reciprocal altruism to favor altruism, individuals must (1) have the opportunity to interact repeatedly, (2) be able to monitor benefits given and received, and (3) make altruism contingent on reciprocation. The conditions for the evolution of reciprocal altruism are thus more stringent than the conditions for kin selection, and nepotism seems to play a more important role in nature than reciprocity does.

2. Caution about attacking offspring of higher-ranking females is warranted because macaque females often defend their infants from attack from other group members.

3. Some researchers contend that dispersal may not have evolved primarily to prevent inbreeding. They suggest that dispersal may enhance individual reproductive opportunities (Moore 1984; Moore and Ali 1984). The relationship between dispersal and inbreeding avoidance is supported by a considerable body of evidence. In a variety of primate species, the offspring of inbred matings are less likely to survive than the offspring of outbred matings (Alberts and Altmann 1995; Bulger and Hamilton 1988; Packer 1979; Ralls and Ballou 1982). Moreover, male tenure in social groups is sometimes linked to the life history of females; in some species males are likely to leave groups before their daughters mature (Henzi and Lucas 1980).

4. The great apes deviate from the pattern of philopatry and male dispersal. Among all of the great ape species, most females emigrate from their natal groups. Gorilla and bonobo females spend much of their time with other females, but frugivorous chimpanzees and orangutans spend much of their time alone or with their offspring. The ecological basis of female dispersal among great apes is not fully understood.

5. Social relationships cannot be measured directly, so primatologists rely upon indirect measures, such as the pattern and frequency of affiliative interactions. Grooming is assumed to be an appropriate proxy measure of the quality of social bonds for two reasons. First, it is the most common form of affiliative behavior in most nonhuman primate species. Second, grooming seems to have become a mechanism for "servicing" social bonds (Dunbar 1991; Seyfarth 1977) in Old World primate species.

6. In provisioned macaque populations, sisters are ranked in inverse order of their ages. Chapais and Shulman (1980) have suggested that this ranking reflects females' reproductive value, which is a measure of future reproductive potential. According to this model, mothers support their younger daughters when they challenge their older sisters because their younger daughters have higher reproductive value than their older daughters. However, younger sister ascendancy is limited to provisioned populations (Hill and Okasayu 1996), suggesting that differences in ecological conditions in captivity and in the wild may contribute to this pattern (Isbell and Pruetz 1998).

7. New findings contradict the accepted consensus that primates have no innate kin recognition mechanism. Using genetic analysis to identify paternal kin, Smith (2000) has found that female baboons in Amboseli, Kenya, associate and interact with paternal half-siblings at higher rates than with unrelated females. Her analyses indicate that this pattern is not explained simply by the fact that half-siblings tend to be close in age and females preferentially associate with agemates. Thus, we must reevaluate the conclusion that primates cannot recognize their paternal kin.

References

Alberts, Susan C., and Jeanne Altmann. 1995. Balancing Costs and Opportunities: Dispersal in Male Baboons. *American Naturalist* 145:279–306.

Altmann, Jeanne. 1979. Age Cohorts As Paternal Sibships. *Behavioral Ecology and Sociobiology* 6:161–69.

Altmann, Jeanne, Glenn Hausfater, and Stuart A. Altmann. 1988. Determinants of Reproductive Success in Savannah Baboons, *Papio cynocephalus*. In *Reproductive Success*, ed. Timothy H. Clutton-Brock. Chicago: University of Chicago Press.

Axelrod, Robert, and William D. Hamilton. 1981. The Evolution of Cooperation. *Science* 211:1390–96.

Barton, Robert A., Richard W. Byrne, and Andrew Whiten. 1996. Ecology, Feeding Competition, and Social Structure in Baboons. *Behavioral Ecology and Sociobiology* 38:321–29.

Bearder, Simon K. 1987. Lorises, Bushbabies, and Tarsiers: Diverse Societies in Solitary Foragers. In *Primate Societies*, ed. Barbara B. Smuts, Dorothy L. Cheney, Robert M. Seyfarth, Richard W. Wrangham, Thomas T. Struhsaker. Chicago: University of Chicago Press.

Berenstain, Leo, Peter S. Rodman, and David G. Smith. 1981. Social Relationships between Fathers and Offspring in a Captive Group of Rhesus Monkeys (*Macaca mulatta*). *Animal Behaviour* 29:1057–63.

Berman, Carol M. 1980. Early Agonistic Experience and Rank Acquisition among Free-Ranging Infant Rhesus Monkeys. *International Journal of Primatology* 1:53–70.

———. 1983a. Matriline Differences and Infant Development. In *Primate Social Relationships: An Integrated Approach*, ed. R. A. Hinde. Sunderland, Mass.: Sinauer Associates.

———. 1983b. Early Differences in Relationships between Infants and Other Group Members Based on the Mother's Status: Their Possible Relationship to Peer-Peer Rank Acquisition. In *Primate Social Relationships: An Integrated Approach*, ed. R. A. Hinde. Sunderland, Mass.: Sinauer Associates.

———. 1983c. Influence of Close Female Relations on Peer-Peer Rank Acquisition. In *Primate Social Relationships: An Integrated Approach*, ed. R. A. Hinde. Sunderland, Mass.: Sinauer Associates.

Bernstein, Irwin S. 1988. Kin Recognition in Animals. *Behavior Genetics* 18:511–24.

———. 1991. The Correlation between Kinship and Behavior in Non-Human Primates. In *Kin Recognition*, ed. Peter G. Hepper. Cambridge, U.K.: Cambridge University Press.

Boesch, Christophe. 1994. Cooperative Hunting in Wild Chimpanzees. *Animal Behaviour* 48:653–67.

Boyd, Robert, and Peter J. Richerson. 1985. *Culture and the Evolutionary Process.* Chicago: University of Chicago Press.

Bramblett, Claude A., Sharon S. Bramblett, Dava A. Bishop, Anthony M. Coelho Jr. 1982. Longitudinal Stability in Adult Hierarchies among Vervet Monkeys (*Cercopithecus aethiops*). *American Journal of Primatology* 2:10–19.

Brown, Kaye and David S. Mack. 1978. Food Sharing among Captive *Leontopithecus rosalia*. *Folia Primatologica* 29:268–90.

Bulger, John, and William J. Hamilton III. 1988. Inbreeding and Reproductive Success in a Natural Chacma Baboon (*Papio ursinus*) Troop. *International Journal of Primatology* 8:635–50.

Chapais, Bernard. 1983. Dominance, Relatedness, and the Structure of Female Relationships in Rhesus Monkeys. In *Primate Social Relationships: an Integrated Approach*, ed. R. A. Hinde. Sunderland, Mass.: Sinauer Associates.

———. 1988. Experimental Matrilineal Inheritance of Rank in Female Japanese Macaques (*Macaca fuscata*). *Animal Behaviour* 36:1025–37.

———. 1992. The Role of Alliances in Social Inheritance of Rank among Female Primates. In *Coalitions and Alliances in Humans and other Animals*, ed. Andrew H. Harcourt and Frans B. M. de Waal. New York: Oxford University Press.

Chapais, Bernard, and Steven Shulman. 1980. An Evolutionary Model of Female Dominance in Primates. *Journal of Theoretical Biology* 82:47–89.

Chapais, Bernard, Michelle Girard, and Ginette Primi. 1991. Non-Kin Alliances, and the Stability of Matrilineal Dominance Relation in Japanese Macaques. *Animal Behaviour* 41:481–91.

Chapais, Bernard, Carole Gauthier, Jean Prud'homme, and Paul Vasey. 1997. Relatedness Threshold for Nepotism in Japanese Macaques. *Animal Behaviour* 53:1089–101.

Chase, Ivan D. 1980. Social Process and Hierarchy Formation in Small Groups: A Comparative Perspective. *American Sociological Review* 45:905–24.

Cheney, Dorothy L. 1977. The Acquisition of Rank and the Development of Reciprocal Alliances among Free-Ranging Immature Baboons. *Behavioral Ecology and Sociobiology* 2:203–18.

———. 1983. Extrafamilial Alliances among Vervet Monkeys. In *Primate Social Relationships: An Integrated Approach*, ed. R. A. Hinde. Sunderland, Mass.: Sinauer Associates.

———. 1986. The Recognition of Social Alliances by Vervet Monkeys. *Animal Behaviour* 34:1722–31.

Cheney, Dorothy L., and Robert M. Seyfarth. 1980. Vocal Recognition in Free-Ranging Vervet Monkeys. *Animal Behaviour* 28:362–67.

———. 1989. Redirected Aggression and Reconciliation among Vervet Monkeys, *Cercopithecus aethiops*. *Animal Behaviour* 110:258–75.

Cheney, Dorothy L., Robert M. Seyfarth, Sandy J. Andelman, and Phyllis C. Lee. 1988. Reproductive Success in Vervet Monkeys. In *Reproductive Success*, ed. Timothy H. Clutton-Brock. Chicago: University of Chicago Press.

Chivers, David J. 1974. The Siamang in Malaya. In *Contributions to Primatology*. Vol. 4. Basel: S. Karger.

Cords, Marina. 1987. Forest Guenons and Patas Monkeys: Male-Male Competition in One-Male Groups. In *Primate Societies*, ed. Barbara B. Smuts, Dorothy L. Cheney, Robert M. Seyfarth, Richard W. Wrangham, and Thomas T. Struhsaker. Chicago: University of Chicago Press.

Das, Marjolijn, Zsuzsa Penke, and Jan A. R. A. M. van Hooff. 1997. Affiliation between Aggressors and Third Parties Following Conflicts in Long-Tailed Macaques (*Macaca fasicularis*). *International Journal of Primatology* 18:159–81.

Dasser, Verena. 1988a. Mapping Social Concepts in Monkeys. In *Machiavellian Intelligence. Social Expertise and the Evolution of Intellect in Monkeys, Apes, and Humans*, ed. Richard W. Byrne and Andrew Whiten. New York: Oxford University Press.

———. 1988b. A Social Concept in Java Monkeys. *Animal Behaviour* 36:225–30.

Datta, Saroj B. 1983a. Relative Power and the Acquisition of Rank. In *Primate Social Relationships: An Integrated Approach*, ed. R. A. Hinde. Sunderland, Mass.: Sinauer Associates.

———. 1983b. Relative Power and the Maintenance of Dominance. In *Primate Social Relationships: An Integrated Approach*, ed. R. A. Hinde. Sunderland, Mass.: Sinauer Associates.

Di Fiore, Anthony, and Drew Rendall. 1994. Evolution of Social Organization: A Reappraisal for Primates by Using Phylogenetic Methods. In *Proceedings of the National Academy of Sciences of the United States of America* 91:9941–45.

Dugatkin, Lee Alan. 1997. *Cooperation among Animals*. New York: Oxford University Press.

Dunbar, Robin I. M. 1991. The Functional Significance of Social Grooming in Primates. *Folia Primatologica* 57:121–31.

———. 1992. Time: A Hidden Constraint on the Behavior Ecology of Baboons. *Behavioral Ecology and Sociobiology* 31:35–49.

Ehardt, Carolyn, and Irwin S. Bernstein. 1986. Matrilineal Overthrows in Rhesus Monkey Groups. *International Journal of Primatology* 7:157–81.

Fredrickson, W. T., and G. P. Sackett. 1984. Kin Preferences in Primates (*Macaca nemestrina*): Relatedness or Familiarity? *Journal of Comparative Psychology* 98:29–34.

Furiuchi, T. 1989. Social Interactions and the Life History of Female *Pan paniscus* in Wamba, Zaïre. *International Journal of Primatology* 10:173–97.

Gagneux, Pascne, David S. Woodruff, and Christophe Boesch. 1997. Furtive Mating in Female Chimpanzees. *Nature* 387:358–59.

———. 1999. Female Reproductive Strategies, Paternity, and Community Structure in Wild West African Chimpanzees. *Animal Behaviour* 57:19–32.

Galdikas, Biruté M. F. 1988. Orangutan Diet, Range, and Activity at Tanjung Putting, Central Borneo. *International Journal of Primatology* 9:1–35.

Goodall, Jane. 1968. The Behavior of Free-Living Chimpanzees in the Gombe Stream Reserve. *Animal Behaviour Monographs* 1:165–311.

———. 1986. *The Chimpanzees of Gombe: Patterns of Behavior*. Cambridge, Mass.: Belknap.

Goodall, Jane, Adriano Bandoro, Emilie Bergmann, Curt Busse, Halali Matama, Esilom Mpongo, Anne Pierce, and David Riss. 1979. Intercommunity Interactions in the Chimpanzee Population of the Gombe National Park. In *The Great Apes*, ed. David A. Hamburg and Elizabeth R. McCown. Menlo Park, Calif.: Benjamin Cummings.

Gouzoules, Harold, Sarah Gouzoules, and Linda Fedigan. 1982. Behavioural Dominance and Reproductive Success in Female Japanese Monkeys (*Macaca fuscata*). *Animal Behaviour* 30:1138–51.

Gouzoules, Sarah, and Harold Gouzoules. 1987. Kinship. In *Primate Societies*, ed. Barbara B. Smuts, Dorothy L. Cheney, Robert M. Seyfarth, Richard W. Wrangham, Thomas T. Struhsaker. Chicago: University of Chicago Press.

Gray, J. Patrick. 1985. *Primate Sociobiology*. New Haven, Conn.: Human Relations Area Files (HRAF) Press.

Hamilton, William D. 1964. The Genetical Evolution of Social Behavior. *Journal of Theoretical Biology* 7:1–51.

Harcourt, Andrew H. 1987. Dominance and Fertility among Female Primates. *Journal of Zoology, London* 213:471–87.

Harcourt, Andrew H., and Kelly J. Stewart. 1987. The Influence of Help in Contests on Dominance Rank in Primates: Hints from Gorillas. *Animal Behaviour* 35:182–90.

———. 1989. Functions of Alliances in Contests in Wild Gorilla Groups. *Animal Behaviour* 109:176–90.

Hausfater, Glenn, Jeanne Altmann, and Stuart Altmann. 1982. Long-Term Consistency of Dominance Relations among Female Baboons (*Papio cynocephalus*). *Science* 217:752–55.

Henzi, S. Peter, and J. W. Lucas. 1980. Observations on the Inter-Troop Movement of Adult Vervet Monkeys (*Cercopithecus aethiops*). *Folia Primatologica* 33:220–35.

Henzi, S. Peter, John E. Lycett, and Tony Weingrill. 1997. Cohort Size and the Allocation of Social Effort by Female Mountain Baboons. *Animal Behaviour* 54:1235–43.

Hill, David A., and Naobi Okayasu. 1996. Determinants of Dominance among Female Macaques: Nepotism, Demography, and Danger. In *Evolution and Ecology of Macaque Societies*, ed. J. E. Fa and D. G. Lindburg. Cambridge, U.K.: Cambridge University Press.

Hooff, Jan A.R. A. M van, and Carel P. van Schaik. 1992. Cooperation in Competition: The Ecology of Primate Bonds. In *Coalitions and Alliances in Humans and Other Animals*, ed. Andrew H. Harcourt and Frans B. M. de Waal. New York: Oxford University Press.

Horrocks, Julia, and Wayne Hunte. 1983. Maternal Rank and Offspring Rank in Vervet Monkeys: An Appraisal of the Mechanisms of Acquisition. *Animal Behaviour* 31:772–82.

Hunte, Wayne, and Julia Horrocks. 1987. Kin and Non-Kin Interventions in the Aggressive Disputes of Vervet Monkeys. *Behaviorial Ecology and Sociobiology* 20:257–63.

Ihobe, Hiroshi. 1992. Male–Male Relationships among Wild Bonobos (*Pan paniscus*) at Wamba, Republic of Zaïre. *Primates* 33:163–79.

Isbell, Lynn A. 1991. Contest and Scramble Competition: Patterns of Female Aggression and Ranging Behaviour among Primates. *Behavioral Ecology* 2:143–55.

Isbell, Lynn A., and Jill D. Pruetz. 1998. Differences between Vervets (*Cercopithecus aethiops*) and Patas Monkeys (*Erythrocebus patas*) in Agonistic Interactions between Adult Females. *International Journal of Primatology* 19:837–55.

Johnson, Julie A. 1987. Dominance Rank in Olive Baboons, *Papio anubis:* The Influence of Gender, Size, Maternal Rank, and Orphaning. *Animal Behaviour* 35:1694–708.

Judge, P.G. 1991. Dyadic and Triadic Reconciliation in Pigtail Macaques (*Macaca nemestrina*). *American Journal of Primatology* 23:225–37.

Kano, Takayoshi. 1992. *The Last Ape: Pygmy Chimpanzee Behavior and Ecology*. Stanford: Stanford University Press.

Kaplan, Jay R. 1977. Patterns of Fight Interference in Free-Ranging Rhesus Monkeys. *American Journal of Physical Anthropology* 47:279–88.

———. 1978. Fight Interference and Altruism in Rhesus Monkeys. *American Journal of Physical Anthropology* 49:241–49.

Kapsalis, Ellen, and Carol M. Berman. 1996. Models of Affiliative Relationships among Free-Ranging Rhesus Monkeys (*Macaca mulatta*) I. Criteria for Kinship. *Animal Behaviour* 133:1201–34.

Kawai, Masao. 1958. On the System of Social Ranks in a Natural Troop of Japanese Monkeys: (1) Basic Rank and Dependent Rank. *Primates* 1–2:111–30.

Kawamura, Shunzo. 1958. Matriarchal Social Ranks in the Minoo-B Troop: A Study of the Rank System of Japanese Monkeys. *Primates* 1–2:149–56.

Kurland, Jeffrey A. 1977. Kin Selection in the Japanese Monkey. In *Contributions to Primatology*. Vol. 12. Basel: S. Karger.

Lee, Phyllis C. 1983a. Context-Specific Unpredictability in Dominance Interactions. In *Primate So-cial Relationships: An Integrated Approach*, ed. R. A. Hinde. Sunderland, Mass.: Sinauer Associates.
———. 1983b. Effects of the Loss of the Mother on Social Development. In *Primate Social Rela-tionships: An Integrated Approach*, ed. R. A. Hinde. Sunderland, Mass.: Sinauer Associates.
Lee, Phyllis C., and Juliet I. Oliver. 1979. Competition, Dominance, and the Acquisition of Rank in Juvenile Yellow Baboons (*Papio cynocephalus*). *Animal Behaviour* 27:576–85.
Mason, William A. 1966. Social Organization of the South American Monkey, *Callicebus mol-loch*: A Preliminary Report. *Tulane Studies in Zoology* 13:23–28.
Massey, Adrianne. 1977. Agonistic Aids and Kinship in a Group of Pig-Tail Macaques. *Behavioral Ecology and Sociobiology* 2:31–40.
McGrew, William C. 1975. Patterns of Plant Food Sharing by Wild Chimpanzees. In *Contempo-rary Primatology: Proceedings of the Fifth Congress of the International Primatological Society*, ed. M. Kawai, S. Kondo, and A. Ehara. Basel: S. Karger.
Moore, James. 1984. Female Transfer in Primates. *International Journal of Primatology* 5:537–89.
Moore, James, and Rauf Ali. 1984. Are Dispersal and Inbreeding Avoidance Related? *Animal Be-haviour* 32: 94–112.
Morin, Phillip, James J. Moore, Ranajit Chakraborty, Li Jin, Jane Goodall, and David S. Woodruff. 1994. Kin Selection, Social Structure, Gene Flow, and the Evolution of Chim-panzees. *Science* 265:1193–32.
Moxon, E. Richard, and Christopher Wills. 1999. DNA Microsatellites: Agents of Evolution? *Sci-entific American* 280, no. 1:94–99.
Muroyama, Yasuyuki, and Yukimaru Sugiyama. 1996. Grooming Relationships in Two Species of Chimpanzees. In *Chimpanzee Cultures*, ed. Richard W. Wrangham, William C. McGrew, Frans B. M. de Waal, and Paul G. Heltne. Cambridge, Mass.: Harvard University Press.
Netto, William J., and Jan A. R. A. M. van Hooff. 1986. Conflict Interference and the Develop-ment of Dominance Relationships in Immature *Macaca fasicularis*. In *Primate Ontogeny, Cog-nition, and Social Behavior*, ed. James G. Else and Phyllis C. Lee. Cambridge, U.K.: Cambridge University Press.
Nishida, Toshisada, and Mariko Hiraiwa-Hasegawa. 1987. Chimpanzees and Bonobos: Cooper-ative Relationships among Males. In *Primate Societies*, ed. Barbara B. Smuts, Dorothy L. Che-ney, Robert M. Seyfarth, Richard W. Wrangham, and Thomas T. Struhsaker. Chicago: Univer-sity of Chicago Press.
Nishida, Toshisada, and Linda A. Turner. 1996. Food Transfer between Mother and Infant Chim-panzees of the Mahale Mountains National Park, Tanzania. *International Journal of Primatol-ogy* 17:947–68.
Nishida, Toshisada, Mariko Hiraiwa-Hasegawa, and Yukio Takahata. 1985. Group Extinction and Female Transfer in Wild Chimpanzees in the Mahale Mountains. *Zeitschrift der Tierpsy-chologie* 67:284–301.
Nishida, Toshisada, and Kazuhiko Hosaka. 1998. Coalition Strategies among Adult Male Chim-panzees of the Mahale Mountains, Tanzania. In *Great Ape Societies*, ed. William C. McGrew, Linda F. Marchant, and Toshisada Nishida. Cambridge, U.K.: Cambridge University Press.
Owren, Michael J., Jacqueline A. Dieter, Robert M. Seyfarth, and Dorothy L. Cheney. 1993. Vo-calizations of Rhesus (*Macaca mulatta*) and Japanese (*M. fuscata*) Macaques Cross-Fostered between Species Show Evidence of Only Limited Modification. *Developmental Psychobiology* 26:389–406.
Packer, Craig. 1979. Inter-Troop Transfer and Inbreeding Avoidance in *Papio anubis*. *Animal Be-haviour* 27:1–36.
Packer, Craig, Susan Lewis, and Anne Pusey. 1992. A Comparative Analysis of Non-Offspring Nursing. *Animal Behaviour* 43:265–81.
Packer, Craig, D. Anthony Collins, A. Sindimwo, and Jane Goodall. 1995. Reproductive Con-straints on Aggressive Competition in Female Baboons. *Nature* 373:60–63.
Paul, Andreas, and Jutta Kuester. 1987. Dominance, Kinship, and Reproductive Value in Female Barbary Macaques (*Macaca sylvanus*) at Affenberg Salem. *Behavioural Ecology and Sociobiol-ogy* 21:323–31.

Palombit, Ryne A. 1996. Pair Bonds in Monogamous Apes: A Comparison of the Siamang *Hylobates syndactylus* and the White-Handed Gibbon *Hylobates lar*. *Animal Behaviour* 133:321–56.

Palombit, Ryne A., Robert M. Seyfarth, and Dorothy L. Cheney. 1997. The Adaptive Value of "Friendships" to Female Baboons: Experimental and Observational Evidence. *Animal Behaviour* 54:599–614.

Pereira, Michael E. 1989. Agonistic Interactions of Juvenile Savannah Baboons II. Agonistic Support and Rank Acquisition. *Ethology* 80:152–71.

Pfennig, David W. and Paul W. Sherman. 1995. Kin Recognition. *Scientific American* 272 (6): 98–103.

Price, Elunded C., and Anna T. Feistner. 1993. Food Sharing in Lion Tamarins: Tests of Three Hypotheses. *American Journal of Primatology* 31:211–21.

Pusey, Anne E., and Craig Packer. 1987. Dispersal and Philopatry. In *Primate Societies*, ed. Barbara B. Smuts, Dorothy L. Cheney, Robert M. Seyfarth, Richard W. Wrangham, and Thomas T. Struhsaker. Chicago: University of Chicago Press.

Pusey, Anne, and Marisa Wolf. 1996. Inbreeding Avoidance in Animals. *Trends in Evolution and Ecology (TREE)* 11:201–6.

Ralls, Katherine, and Jonathan Ballou. 1982. Effect of Inbreeding on Infant Mortality in Captive Primates. *International Journal of Primatology* 3:491–505.

Reichard, Ulrich. 1995. Extra-Pair Copulations in a Monogamous Gibbon (*Hylobates lar*). *Ethology* 100:99–112.

Rendall, Drew, and Anthony Di Fiore. 1995. The Road Less Traveled: Phylogenetic Perspectives in Primatology. *Evolutionary Anthropology* 4:43–52.

Richerson, Peter J., and Robert Boyd. 1998. The Evolution of Human Ultrasociality. In *Indoctrinability, Ideology, and Warfare*, ed. Irenäus Eibl-Eibesfeldt and Frank Kemp. Providence, R.I.: Berghahn.

———. 1999. The Evolutionary Dynamics of a Crude Superorganism. *Human Nature* 10:252–89.

Samuels, Amy, and Roy V. Henrickson. 1983. Outbreak of Severe Aggression in Captive *Macaca mulatta*. *American Journal of Primatology* 5:277–81.

Samuels, Amy, Joan B. Silk, and Jeanne Altmann. 1987. Continuity and Change in Dominance Relations among Female Baboons. *Animal Behaviour* 35: 785–93.

Schaik, Carel P. van, and Jan A. R. A. M. van Hooff. 1983. On the Ultimate Causes of Primate Social Systems. *Animal Behaviour* 85:91–117.

———. 1996. Toward an Understanding of the Orangutan's Social System. In *Great Ape Societies*, ed. William C. McGrew, Linda F. Marchant, and Toshisada Nishida. Cambridge, U.K.: Cambridge University Press.

Schaik, Carel P. van, and Maria A. van Noordwijk. 1985. Evolutionary Effect of the Absence of Felids on the Social Organization of the Macaques on the Island of Simeulue (*Macaca fasicularis fusca*, Miller 1903). *Folia Primatologica* 44:138–47.

Seyfarth, Robert M. 1977. A Model of Social Grooming among Adult Female Monkeys. *Journal of Theoretical Biology* 65:671–98.

Seyfarth, Robert M., Dorothy L. Cheney, and Peter Marler. 1980. Vervet Monkey Alarm Calls: Semantic Communication in a Free-Ranging Primate. *Animal Behaviour* 28:1070–94.

Sherman, Paul W. 1980. The Limits of Group Squirrel Nepotism. In *Sociobiology: Beyond Nature/Nurture*, ed. George W. Barlow and James Silverberg. Boulder, Colo.: Westview.

———. 1981. Kinship, Demography, and Belding's Ground Squirrel Nepotism. *Behavioral Ecology and Sociobiology* 8:251–60.

Silk, Joan B. 1978. Patterns of Food Sharing among Mother and Infant Chimpanzees at Gombe National Park, Tanzania. *Folia Primatologica* 29:129–41.

———. 1979. Feeding, Foraging, and Food Sharing of Immature Chimpanzees. *Folia Primatologica* 31:123–42.

———. 1982. Altruism among Adult Female Bonnet Macaques: Explanation and Analysis of Patterns of Grooming and Coalition Formation. *Animal Behaviour* 79:162–87.

———. 1987. Social Behavior in Evolutionary Perspective. In *Primate Societies*, ed. Barbara B. Smuts, Dorothy L. Cheney, Robert M. Seyfarth, Richard W. Wrangham, and Thomas T. Struhsaker. Chicago: University of Chicago Press.

———. 1988. Maternal Investment in Captive Bonnet Macaques (*Macaca radiata*). *The American Naturalist* 132:1–19.

Silk, Joan B., Amy Samuels, and Peter S. Rodman. 1981. The Influence of Kinship, Rank, and Sex upon Affiliation and Aggression among Adult Females and Immature Bonnet Macaques (*Macaca radiata*). *Animal Behaviour* 78:112–37.

Silk, Joan B., Robert M. Seyfarth, and Dorothy L. Cheney. 1999. The Structure of Social Relationships among Female Savanna Baboons. *Animal Behaviour* 136:679–703.

Smith, Kerri L. 2000. Paternal Kin Matter: The Distribution of Social Behavior among Wild Adult Female Baboons. Ph.D. dissertation. University of Chicago.

Smuts, Barbara Boardman. 1985. *Sex and Friendship in Baboons*. Hawthorne, N.Y.: Aldine de Gruyter.

———. 1995. The Evolutionary Origins of Patriarchy. *Human Nature* 6:1–32.

Starin, E. D. 1978. Food Transfer by Wild Titi Monkeys (*Callicebus torquatus torquatus*). *Folia Primatologica* 30:145–51.

Stein, David M. 1984. *The Sociobiology of Infant and Adult Male Baboons*. Norwood, N.J.: Ablex.

Sterck, Elizabeth H. M., David P. Watts, and Carel P. van Schaik. 1997. The Evolution of Female Social Relationships in Nonhuman Primates. *Behavioral Ecology and Sociobiology* 41:291–309.

Stewart, Kelly J., and A. H. Harcourt. 1987. Gorillas: Variation in Female Relationships. In *Primate Societies*, ed. Barbara B. Smuts, Dorothy L. Cheney, Robert M. Seyfarth, Richard W. Wrangham, and Thomas T. Struhsaker. Chicago: University of Chicago Press.

Strier, Karen B. 1994. Myth of the Typical Primate. *Yearbook of Physical Anthropology* 37:233–71.

Struhsaker, Thomas T. 1967. Auditory Communication among Vervet Monkeys (*Cercopithecus aethiops*). In *Social Communication among Primates*, ed. S. A. Altmann. Chicago: University of Chicago Press.

———. 1977. Infanticide and Social Organization in the Redtail Monkey (*Cercopithecus ascanius schmidti*) in the Kibale Forest, Uganda. *Zeitschrift Für Tierpsychologie* 45:75–84.

Tomasello, Michael J., and Josep Call. 1997. *Primate Cognition*. New York: Oxford University Press.

Trivers, Robert L. 1971. The Evolution of Reciprocal Altruism. *Quarterly Review of Biology* 46:35–57.

Tsingalia, H. M., and Thelma E. Rowell. 1984. The Behaviour of Adult Male Blue Monkeys. *Zeitschrift Für Tierpsychologie* 64:253–68.

de Waal, Frans B. M. 1977. The Organization of Agonistic Relations within Two Captive Groups of Java-Monkeys (*Macaca fasicularis*). *Zeitschrift Für Tierpsychologie* 44:225–82.

Walters, Jeffrey R. 1980. Interventions and the Development of Dominance Relationships in Female Baboons. *Folia Primatologica* 34:61–89.

———. 1987. Kin Recognition in Nonhuman Primates. In *Kin Recognition in Animals*, ed. D. J. C. Fletcher and C. D. Michener. New York: Wiley.

Watanabe, Kunio. 1979. Alliance Formation in a Free-Ranging Troop of Japanese Macaques. *Primates* 20:459–74.

Watts, David P. 1991. Harassment of Immigrant Female Mountain Gorillas by Resident Females. *Ethology* 89:135–53.

———. 1994. Social Relationships of Resident and Immigrant Female Mountain Gorillas, II: Relatedness, Residence, and Relationships between Females. *American Journal of Primatology* 32:13–30.

———. 1996. Comparative Socio-Ecology of Gorillas. In *Great Ape Societies*, ed. William C. McGrew, Linda F. Marchant, and Toshisada Nishida. Cambridge, U.K.: Cambridge University Press.

White, Frances J. 1996. Comparative Socio-Ecology of *Pan paniscus*. In *Great Ape Societies*, ed. William C. McGrew, Linda F. Marchant, and Toshisada Nishida. Cambridge, U.K.: Cambridge University Press.

Wrangham, Richard W. 1980. An Ecological Model of Female-Bonded Primate Groups. *Animal Behaviour* 75:262–300.

———. 1987. Evolution of Social Structure. In *Primate Societies*, ed. Barbara B. Smuts, Dorothy L. Cheney, Robert M. Seyfarth, Richard W. Wrangham, and Thomas T. Struhsaker. Chicago: University of Chicago Press.

York, Alison D., and Thelma E. Rowell. 1988. Reconciliation Following Aggression in Patas Monkeys, *Erythrocebus patas*. *Animal Behaviour* 36:502–9.

Chapter Five

Neoevolutionary Approaches to Human Kinship

Barry S. Hewlett

This chapter aims to introduce readers to neoevolutionary theories and what they have contributed to the study of human kinship. This is a relatively new and controversial theoretical orientation and has few proponents within cultural anthropology. I hope to demonstrate that the few researchers using this theoretical orientation have made substantial contributions to our understanding of human kinship.

A broad rather than narrow conceptualization of kinship is used in this chapter, which means topics such as the family, descent, and marriage will be discussed. The chapter focuses on kinship topics that are often discussed in introductory cultural anthropology textbooks in the hope that the ideas might be incorporated into anthropology courses. There are many other interesting and viable topics in kinship studies (e.g., fictive and ritual kinship), several of which are included in this book, but they are not considered here because of limited space. Also, while kinship is "cultural" in the sense that it is symbolic and transmitted nongenetically from generation to generation, this does not mean kinship is purely cultural; to the contrary, this chapter aims to demonstrate how natural and sexual selection influence the nature and shape of kinship.

What Is "Neo" Evolutionary Theory?

Most biological anthropologists think of themselves as evolutionary and even many cultural anthropologists feel they take an evolutionary approach to culture when they discuss bands, tribes, chiefdoms, and so forth. Keesing (1975) titled the first chapter of his book on kinship "Kinship in Evolutionary Perspective," but he does not use any of the neoevolutionary theories discussed in this chapter. Most neoevolutionary researchers think of themselves as simply "evolutionary," but "neo" is used in this chapter to identify researchers who use a particular set of relatively recent contributions to Darwin's theories of natural and sexual selection.

Before describing some of the neoevolutionary theories, it is important to discuss a few basic concepts that are common to this theoretical orientation. First, the unit of natural selection and the focus of neoevolutionary studies is the individual rather than the group. Humans live in groups and have cultural practices and beliefs because the group enhances the survival and reproductive fitness of individuals. Second, neoevolutionists are interested in ultimate rather than proximate kinds of explanations. Ultimate explanations focus on how particular kin relationships enhance the reproductive fitness of individuals, while proximate explanations focus on social, psychological, hormonal, or cultural factors. They are different kinds of explanations and they are not necessarily contradictory or mutually exclusive. A cultural anthropologist may explain male violence against women as a result of patriarchal social structures, or a biopsychologist may explain it as a result of higher levels of male testosterone. A neoevolutionist, on the other hand, would be interested in explaining *why* particular male-dominated structures exist or *why* testosterone evolved to increase male violence, and how did the structures or hormones increase an individual's reproductive fitness. They are different levels of explanation and are not necessarily contrary to one another.

Kin Selection/Inclusive Fitness

According to Darwin (1859), the measure of "fitness" in natural and sexual selection was the number of offspring an individual left behind. Hamilton (1964) expanded this concept and indicated that an individual's genes existed beyond self and offspring. An individual can enhance his or her reproductive fitness by helping any individual that shares genes with him or her (nieces, nephews, cousins). The degree of help/altruism one provides to another is predicted to be linked to the degree of genetic relatedness. Several examples of kin selection are provided in chapter 4 of this book.

Parental Investment

Darwin (1859) explained the horns, antlers, and bright feathers in particular species as the result of sexual selection rather than natural selection. Natural selection explained how individuals adapted to a particular natural and social environment, while sexual selection explained competition among members of one sex for access to members of the opposite sex. The large elk antlers were the result of males competing among themselves for access to females. Trivers (1972) expanded on sexual selection by pointing out the importance of differential levels of parental investment (PI). In species in which one sex invests more than the other in offspring, this sex will become a limiting resource, and members of the other sex (males, in most birds and mammals) will compete among themselves for access to the first (usually females). Parental investment is defined as anything a parent provides to offspring that increases the offspring's chances of reproductive success at the cost of limiting the parent's ability to invest in future offspring (i.e., this includes anything from teaching, providing, protecting, or caregiving to providing inheritance and social-emotional support to a spouse). Greater female parental investment results in higher reproductive variance among males than females (number of offspring). Greater male reproductive variance means that males successful in competition will have many offspring, while males that are not as successful may not have any offspring. Females, of course, compete among themselves, which leads to reproductive variance as well, but because of differential parental investment, the variability in reproductive success is predicted to be less than that of males (i.e., most females will have offspring). In species with greater female investment, female choice is predicted to guide the course of male evolution through the selection of certain males.

Sex Ratio

Sex ratio theory is an extension of parental investment theory. Trivers and Willard (1973) pointed out that because males are more variable than females in their reproductive success, parents in good environments are predicted to vary the sex ratio of their offspring in favor of males so as to maximize the number of offspring in the third generation. Parents in poor environments are expected to want more females, since males are likely to leave no offspring.

Reciprocal Altruism

Darwin's theory focused on blood relatives, while recent theoretical contributions by Axelrod (1984) and others (e.g., Trivers 1971) indicated reciprocal relationships with nongenetically related individuals can lead to increased reproductive success. This is commonly referred to as tit-for-tat theory or "I'll scratch your back if you scratch mine." Two conditions are necessary for reciprocal altruism to take place: (1) high likelihood that you will be able to recognize and see the individual again (i.e., he or she lives next door, is a roommate, or works with you), and (2) expectation that benefits will exceed costs over time. Friendships, alliances, and cooperatives are just a few examples of reciprocal altruism and are especially common in contemporary stratified societies.

Life History

Life history theory (LHT) is also a recent extension of Darwinian theory. One commonly used model (Williams 1966; Hirshfield and Tinkle 1975)

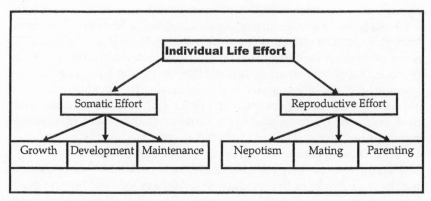

Figure 5.1   Trade-Offs in Life History Theory

identifies two conceptually distinct categories—somatic and reproductive effort—that an individual engages in if she or he is to be biologically successful
(see figure 5.1). Somatic effort refers to the risks and costs involved to ensure
the physical survival of the individual—having shelter, protection from predators and conspecifics, obtaining food, keeping healthy, and so forth. Reproductive effort has to do with getting copies of one's self into subsequent generations. It is divided into three broad categories—parental effort (rearing
children), mating effort (attracting, keeping, and guarding a spouse), and
nepotistic effort (helping relatives besides one's own children). Life history
theorists focus on identifying the trade-offs (costs, benefits) of these various
activities. The two primary trade-offs LHT tries to evaluate are (1) whether to
have offspring now or in the future, and (2) whether to have many offspring
with minimal investment or have few offspring with substantial investment
(i.e., quality versus quantity of offspring). Most of the human research has focused on trade-offs between mating and parenting efforts (Hewlett 1992).

Finally, it is important to remember that all of the above neoevolutionary
theories were developed to explain cross-species behaviors; they are not an-
thropocentric. All three of the theoretical styles described in the next section
employ the theories mentioned above.

Diversity within Neoevolutionary Thought

Table 5.1 summarizes some of the theoretical diversity within neoevolutionary
thought (modified from Smith 2000). In the early 1980s, clear differences developed between neoevolutionary researchers. Napoleon Chagnon, Eric Smith,
Kristen Hawkes, Monique Borgerhoff Mulder, Kim Hill, and Magdi Hurtado
were conducting quantitative behavioral field studies with foragers, pastoralists, and horticulturalists and demonstrated that many aspects of cultural life—
kinship, family, and subsistence systems—were fitness maximizing activities.

Table 5.1   Diversity of Neoevolutionary Approaches

	Evolutionary Psychology	Behavioral (Evolutionary) Ecology	Dual Transmission
Tries to explain	Psychological predispositions, human universals	Behavioral strategies, reproductive trade-offs in different environments	Cultural diversity, cultural change, gene-culture interactions
Key constraints	Cognitive mechanisms of modules, genetic	Ecological, material	Cultural mechanisms, information
Time for adaptive change to take place	Long-term (genetic)	Short-term (phenotypic)	Varies by mechanism (cultural)
Contemporary adaptiveness	Low	High	Varies by mechanism
Primary methods	Survey, interviews in Euroamerican cultures	Field observations in small scale cultures	Mathematical modeling
View of culture	Culture is the manufactured product of evolved psychological mechanisms	Culture always adaptive, no power to co-direct genetic evolution	Culture can drive or co-direct genetic evolution
Kinship systems	Based on specific genetically-based human universals (e.g. kin selection)	Kinship systems maximize reproductive fitness of individuals in particular environments	Conservative cultural mechanisms influence the current distribution of kinship systems

NOTE: MODIFIED VERSION OF SMITH (2000).

Don Symons, Martin Daly, Margo Wilson, John Tooby, and Leda Cosmides, on the other hand, were working with contemporary complex societies (often with college undergrads using pencil and paper questionnaires) and were critical of the "fitness maximizing" researchers because the research did not contribute to a better understanding of human nature and cognition. Demonstrating that a particular cultural behavior increased reproductive success was not important to this group. They wanted to identify universal modules or mechanisms of mind that were selected for in the Environment of Evolutionary Adaptation (EEA), that is, the Paleolithic hunting-gathering environment of evolutionary adaptation. This group eventually became known as evolutionary psychologists (EPs) and distinguished themselves from behavioral ecologists (BEs) who viewed the mind as a general-purpose fitness maximizing organism. This split was occurring while I was a graduate student at the University of California, Santa Barbara, and Symons (an early EP) would conduct seminars on "Why I Am Not a Sociobiologist" to distinguish his interests from those of Smith, Hawkes, and other BEs. It is interesting that Chagnon, one of the first BEs, had an office right across the hall from Symons, and he thought Chagnon's work was consistent with EP—see Symons (1992) for his critique of BEs.

The term "sociobiology" has been dropped from use in most evolutionary studies. For instance, the journal of the Evolution and Human Behavior Society recently changed its name from *Ethology and Sociobiology* to *Evolution and Human Behavior*. There were several reasons for the change: (1) the term evolutionary biology existed before sociobiology so there was no need for a new term, (2) sociobiology focused on hard-wired aspects of behavior, while many neoevolutionists (BEs) viewed human behavior as flexible and adaptive to different environments, and (3) sociobiology generated negative images (e.g., tomato- and egg-throwing at Irv DeVore and other "sociobiologists" at American Anthropological Association meetings in 1977).

The dual transmission theorists (DTs) are the smallest group of researchers and are primarily geneticists or biological anthropologists (Cavalli Sforza and Feldman 1981; Boyd and Richerson 1985; Durham 1992). While they are referred to as dual (gene-culture) transmission theorists, most of their work has focused on the nature of culture and its impact on genes. Because they have background in population genetics, they realize that particular mechanisms of genetic transmission can lead to genetic maladaptation (e.g., mechanisms of Mendelian genetics produce maladaptive genotypes). For instance, if parents in West Africa are heterozygous for the sickle-cell trait, they have a 25 percent chance of producing an offspring that is homozygous for the sickle-cell trait, which leads to death at an early age. If genetic mechanisms can produce maladaptation, it seems reasonable to hypothesize that cultural mechanisms could produce maladaptive patterns as well. Consequently, most of the DTs' research has focused on identifying cultural transmission mechanisms and how they shaped the distribution and diversity of cultural beliefs and practices. Their use of genetic analogies has led them to call culture beliefs and practices "memes."

In order to better understand the stylistic differences, a brief description of how each style views polyandry may be useful. Polyandry occurs in the highlands of Tibet and Nepal where arable farming land is limited. One woman marries brothers, in part, so the arable land is not divided between brothers and each brother takes on a different economic task—farming, herding, or trading. BEs have demonstrated that brothers with equal access to their wife in common do not show a loss of reproductive fitness when compared to a single brother marrying monogamously (Crook and Crook 1988). EPs argue that while polyandry might be adaptive in the contemporary environment, there is no adaptive design to polyandry that was selected for in the EEA. It is not an adaptive mechanism of the mind that has gone through tens of thousands of years of selection. From an

EP point of view, the results of the BE study do not provide insight into human nature. DTs, on the other hand, would point out that there are other similar highland environments where one does not find polyandry so it is important to examine the history and transmission mechanisms of this belief (meme).

Table 5.1 demonstrates that there is disagreement between groups as to what is important to study and how or where to conduct an evolutionary study. But each style offers alternative and not necessarily contradictory insights into human behavior.

Neoevolutionary Contributions to the Study of Human Kinship

Behavioral Ecology

This group of neoevolutionary anthropologists view kinship systems as mechanisms individuals utilize to adapt to a variety of demographic, social, and natural environments. Early studies focused on male reproductive strategies. For instance, Hartung (1976) hypothesized that in societies where wealth (e.g., land, cattle, and the like) can be accumulated, males are likely to transmit it to sons rather than to daughters because there is greater reproductive variance in males than in females (see PI theory). Sons can have many more children than daughters, so the return on patrilineal inheritance is greater than matrilineal or bilateral inheritance. Even in the more complex societies with bilateral descent, the bulk of the productive property, such as land, money, and livestock, tended to be inherited by males rather than females. Inheritance of the throne, the family business, farm, or trade is often by males. In today's environment where a quality education is central to future fitness, there is often greater investment in sons rather than daughters, especially in developing countries such as Africa and Asia.

Matrilineal inheritance on the other hand (Hartung 1985) is hypothesized to be linked to social environments where paternity uncertainty is high. Extramarital affairs and divorce are common in these societies, which hypothetically leads men to invest in their sister's children, the sister's son in particular, where he is sure he is investing in his inclusive fitness rather than in his own children where paternity may not be clear.

Unilineal descent is also linked to exogamy (i.e., to marry outside of the clan or lineage), prescriptive cross-cousin marriage, and bride wealth. Van den Berghe (1983) and Fox (1967) hypothesized that this pattern of marrying close relatives (cousins) outside of one's own clan (cross-cousins) was part of a male strategy to develop larger, stable, and powerful political and military groups. This is consistent with other anthropological hypotheses about the origin of unilineal descent groups (Service 1966), but it is interesting from an evolutionary perspective because it is a system that combines a pattern of kin selection (i.e., marrying cousins) with reciprocal altruism (alliances with nonkin in the clan) that is quite distinct from that among most hunter-gatherers. Most hunter-gatherers are bilateral, usually want individuals to marry far away, disapprove of all cousin marriages, and do not have cross-cutting alliances that tie people together outside of the band. Genetic studies support that different patterns such as inbreeding (i.e., average degree of relatedness) is greater in unilineal horticultural societies than it is among bilateral hunting and gathering societies (MacDonald and Hewlett 1999).

Bride wealth and polygyny are also associated with social environments where wealth can be accumulated. Once humans domesticated plants and animals and could develop a surplus, the first forms of investment of this wealth were reproductive. Men and their male kinsmen sought to control the reproductive power of women since women are the ultimate scarce resource for men (van den Berhe 1983). Two types of polygyny are described by BEs: mate control and resource control (Flinn and Low 1986). The first type occurs in environments where material resources are rather evenly distributed between community members, human population densities are low, and it does not take much time or energy to make a living. The Yanomamo and some hunter-gatherers, such as Australian Aborigines, are examples of this type of polygyny; differential male resources are not important except where males exert considerable effort to control their mates and their male competition. This type of polygyny is commonly portrayed in cartoons where a caveman drags off a woman by her hair and uses a large club to fend off other men. But the most common type of polygyny in the ethnographic record is called resource-control polygyny. This is where resources critical to female reproductive fitness can be monopolized by males and there is differential resource holding power of males (Emlen and Oring 1977). Borgerhoff Mulder (1990) found that East African Kipsigis women were much more likely to select men with large plots of land, suggesting that female choice contributes to polygyny, and several other studies have shown that throughout human history, men who controlled vast sources of wealth often acquired a large number of mates (Betzig 1992). Borgerhoff Mulder (1988) also found that men's families paid higher bride wealth for younger and heavier women and lower bride wealth for women who had previously given birth to children.

Dowry, on the other hand, occurs in highly stratified societies with socially imposed monogamy (and a few highly stratified polygynous societies) and has been viewed as a form of female-female competition for high status males (Gaulin and Boster 1990). Dowry is a means of passing property to one's daughters before death and is thus an investment in the fitness of daughters. Cashdan (1996) also pointed out that females in these societies are also highly dependent upon male investment (i.e., men are important providers) and that greater independence of women would discourage dowry payment. Dickemann (1979) examined stratified societies in Europe and Asia and found hypergamous (women marrying up in class/status) dowry common in middle to upper class/castes along with greater parental investment in sons rather than daughters (e.g., greater likelihood of female infanticide), while bride wealth and greater investment in daughters was common in lower class/castes. This is consistent with the predictions of the Trivers-Willard sex ratio theory described above.

Smuts (1994) has suggested that patriarchy is especially pronounced in humans because of accumulation of wealth and stratification. Once domestication took place, males tended to control the resources that females needed to survive. Stratification enabled powerful males to dominate other males, which meant less interference when the dominant males coerced and controlled females. She points out that the human patriarchal system elaborated on mammalian and higher primate patterns where males and females have different reproductive interests, females tend to choose males who control resources, and males are philopatric (patrilocal).

While many kinship, family, and descent patterns may be adaptive, neoevolutionists are quick to point out that it is necessary to examine kinship systems from an individual's perspective—how they actually work on the ground. Patrilineal descent and cross-cousin marriage may be preferred but this does not mean everyone plays by the rules. Chagnon (1988), an early and controversial proponent of neoevolutionary approaches to kinship, went to great lengths to point out how humans are rule-breakers more than they are rule-makers. Individuals manipulate systems to their own reproductive advantage and environmental situations. He found that: (1) Yanomamo men manipulate their kinship terminologies for female kin in ways to create more potential mates (i.e., they reclassified individuals so they would have more cross-cousins to marry), (2) females that were redefined as wives (cross-cousins) were primarily women in a younger generation and therefore had greater reproductive value, and (3) subadult males tended to reclassify females into the mother category, which was probably important for their reproductive fitness.

Most of the above described studies focus on male reproductive strategies or how male reproductive variance influences kinship structures. Recent work has given more attention to female reproductive strategies. Hawkes's grandmother and show-off hypotheses are important contributions to kinship studies because they question many of the assumptions of the "hunting hypothesis" (Hawkes et al. 2000). This hypothesis suggests that many aspects of human social organization (patrilocality, sharing, monogamy, nuclear family) were consequences of male big game hunting. Males hunted big game to provide for the nuclear family; from a life history perspective, they were investing energy into parental effort (see figure 5.1). The research by Hawkes et al. suggests that fathers/males hunt large game animals to show off to females rather than actually provide for the nuclear family. Among most hunter-gatherers, prey that are widely shared with others are usually asynchronously acquired, provide large amounts of meat, and are associated with high risk of failure. Male hunters who target these widely shared game animals do not gain by providing more for themselves or their family, but by gaining favorable attention or increased mating opportunities. The hunter's family receives little of the meat acquired because it is shared with everyone else in camp. Consequently, women, grandmothers in particular, are hypothesized to be crucial providers for young children rather than the fathers. The fathers' big game hunting is a mating effort rather than a parenting effort. This leads to a dramatically different view of human social organization where matrilocality and female provisioning are central, and the nuclear family and monogamy are not as important.

Discussions of father–child relationships are central to kinship studies in anthropology because they hypothetically demonstrate the importance of culture over biology in understanding kinship systems. Malinowski (1913) was one of the first to make a distinction in two types of fathers among Australian Aborigines—social (pater) and biological (genitor). The social/legal father is the man who is believed by members of his community to have impregnated the child's mother or to have contributed in some other way to the being of the child, while the biological father is the genetic father. The genetic father is also often socially recognized and a person through whom the child may claim kinship with other people. Social fathers are common in many cultures around the world—Australian Aboriginal, Aché, Bari, Nuer, Toda, Nayar, Nyimba, Mehinaku, Trobriand Islanders, and Andaman Islanders, to mention some of the better-known cultures. The social father can be the man who paid the bride wealth, the father who lives and sleeps with the mother, or the man the mother identifies as a legal father.

What is the role of social fathers? Hypotheses from cultural anthropologists are generally consistent with evolutionary theory in that social fathers exist because it is not always clear who the biological father is, while mothers are always certain. This has led kinship specialists to state that the mother and her dependent children are the basic unit of all kinship systems (Fox 1967; Fortes 1958). But recent cross-cultural and cross-species studies by Hrdy (1999) suggest that social fatherhood is a female reproductive strategy. It is a way to confuse paternity so that a few men feel like they have some connection to the child. This increases male investment in the mother and her offspring, therefore enhancing the mother's reproductive fitness. Hrdy predicted that the many fathers strategy is especially likely in environments where resources necessary for survival are scarce or highly variable (e.g., particular natural environments, lower socioeconomic contexts). From Hrdy's perspective, polyandry (i.e., women mating with several men) is much more common than is recognized in anthropology textbooks.

This is just a sampling of studies from an evolutionary ecology perspective. Flinn and Low (1986) discussed the reproductive advantages of different marriage systems and kinship terminologies in different socioecologies, Betzig's (1989) cross-cultural study of divorce indicated that the reasons for divorce are consistent with evolutionary theory (e.g., adultery, infertility, lack of resources), and Borgerhoff Mulder (1990) described the environmental contexts of polygyny.

Evolutionary Psychology

EPs have not paid particular attention to kinship systems. Many are psychologists who conduct research with Euro-American populations, so they have no training in traditional interest kinship systems. EPs are also more interested in describing universal patterns rather than cultural diversity in topics such as kinship and the family. EPs would argue that many of the patterns of BEs described in the previous section are consequences of evolved mechanisms that have shaped culture. These evolved mechanisms include: (1) the ability to identify kin, (2) males' ability to evaluate paternity, (3) males' ability for sexual jealousy, (4) child–caregiver attachment, (5) females' ability to extract male investment (either honestly or through deception), (6) female desire for males with resources, and (7) male desire for young females with high reproductive value. EPs view these as evolved mechanisms because the men or women who had these abilities or characteristics left more of their genes behind in the EEA than those without these features. Therefore, matrilineal descent is based upon males' evolved algorithm to determine that whenever they are unlikely to be the fathers, it is better to invest in sisters' children. Hrdy's (1999) many fathers hypothesis is based upon the assumption that females have evolved mechanisms to obtain male parental investment. Another interesting study by Hagen (in press) identifies another mechanism by which females try to extract male investment—postpartum depression (PPD). His study suggests that the degree of PPD is linked to the degree of father investment (or lack thereof). The depression is a signal that if the father does not start to invest more (providing, caregiving, and socially-emotionally supporting the mother) the mother is going to withdraw her investment in his child.

From an EP perspective, it is important to identify and understand these evolved mechanisms if one wants to understand kinship systems. There are no genes for unilineal descent or different kinship terminologies, but there are evolved mechanisms that contribute to observed cultural patterns.

Dual Transmission

BEs try to demonstrate that kinship and marriage structures, such as patrilineal inheritance and polyandry, are adaptive in particular environments, while DTs try to understand how mechanisms of transmission might lead to coevolution or independent patterning of kinship structures. For instance, if polyandry is adaptive to a highland environment, why is it not found in the highlands of the New World (Bourguignon and Greenbaum 1973)? Many times a statistical relationship can be found between two variables because most of the cases exist in one area of the world. DTs are interested in explaining the distribution of kinship and other structures across the landscape and trying to determine whether they are adaptive to particular environments or whether they are the consequence of other, culturally-specific processes.

Each DT theorist has identified and mathematically modeled several cultural transmission mechanisms, but to demonstrate the contributions of DTs to kinship studies, we will limit our review to those modeled by Cavalli Sforza and Feldman (table 5.2). Cultural transmission from parent to child is called vertical and is the closest to biological transmission; like biological transmission, it is highly conservative and may maintain the status quo, including all the individual variation in existence. With this mode of transmission there is little difficulty accepting an innovation at the individual level; children imitate and are especially receptive, but the innovation will be very slow to spread to others in the population unless other modes of transmission are employed along with parent-to-child transmission. This type of transmission is common to most small-scale cultures (Hewlett and Cavalli Sforza 1988).

A more typically "cultural" mode of transmission is horizontal or contagious, in which transmission is between any two individuals irrespective of their relationship. This is very similar to the transmission of infectious diseases. The spread can be fast if contacts with the transmitters and transmittee are frequent. If transmission is one to many, communication is highly efficient, and if acceptance follows, cultural change may be very rapid. In many-to-one transmission, every recipient is assumed to be influenced by many transmitters, and all transmitters act in concert so that the influence is reciprocally reinforced. Consequently, change in the frequency of a belief or practice over time and space should be slow, and variation within the population low. This mode of transmission tends to generate the highest uniformity within the group.

In order to understand how the first two mechanisms influence cultural diversity, we conducted a study of 49 beliefs and practices in 277 African cultures (Gugliemino et al. 1995). The beliefs and practices included everything

Table 5.2   Mechanisms of Cultural Transmission

	Vertical	Horizontal	One-to-many	Concerted or many-to-one
Transmitter	Parent(s)	Unrelated	Teacher, leader, media	Older members of social group
Transmittee	Child	Unrelated	Pupils, citizens, audience	Younger members of social group
Acceptance of innovation	Intermediate difficulty	Easy	Easy	Difficult
Variation between individuals within a culture	High	Can be high	Low	Very low
Culture change	Slow	Can be rapid	Most rapid	Most conservative

NOTE: MODIFIED FROM HEWLETT AND CAVALLI SFORZA (1988).

from subsistence and settlement patterns to kinship and family patterns. We wanted to understand whether each belief or practice was the result of adaptation to a particular environment, "cultural" diffusion, or "demic" diffusion. Cultural diffusion means the practice or belief diffused from neighboring cultures with the same belief or practice, while demic diffusion means the people moved into a new area and conserved particular aspects of their culture. Vertical transmission hypothetically leads to conservation of culture in demic diffusion. Horizontal transmission, on the other hand, is the mechanism by which cultural diffusion takes place. Linguistic affiliation was used as a measure of demic diffusion, and we developed a clustering index to evaluate how many neighbors had the same belief. The study demonstrated that kinship and family beliefs and practices in Africa had little to do with adaptations to the natural environment or cultural diffusion. Most features of kinship and family were better explained by linguistic affiliation and vertical transmission. Other aspects of culture, house construction for instance, were more influenced by the natural environment, whereas religious beliefs were more likely the result of cultural diffusion and horizontal transmission.

We are conducting further studies to evaluate the coevolution of genes, culture, and language in Africa and the Americas, and preliminary data suggest that kinship and family beliefs and practices tend to be conserved along with genes. In other words, aspects of kinship and family tend to be highly conserved, similar to genes, and their distribution across the landscape does not appear to be linked to adaptations to particular natural environments. This supports Kroeber's (1952) proposition that kinship has more to due with style and play and the creative inclinations of humans rather than with the constraints and practical aspects of daily living.

The data imply that the current distribution of kinship and family patterns is due to demic diffusion and conservative cultural transmission. This is supported by a nonevolutionary study of kinship by Burton et al. (1996) where he uses a sophisticated analysis of kinship and family patterns to describe culture areas. His kinship culture areas fit very nicely with the world's language and genetic distance trees (Jones 1999). He systematically generates two key dimensions of variability in family and kinship—a matricentric–patricentric continuum and a bilateral–unilineal continuum. For instance, Africa is strongly unilineal, but relatively egalitarian on the gender dimension, whereas the middle Old World (North Africa, the Middle East, South and Central Asia and most of China) is unilineal but patricentric. The distribution of the various culture areas of kinship are linked to the movements and expansions of dominant peoples (i.e., demic diffusion and vertical transmission) throughout history (e.g., Bantu expansion).

DTs vary on the hypothesized strength of links between culture and genes. Durham (1992), like the BEs, believes that most of culture is adaptive and that cultural practices enhance reproductive fitness. Culture is most likely to be maladaptive when it is imposed in stratified societies. Boyd and Richerson

(1984) and Cavalli Sforza and Feldman (1981), on the other hand, described several distinct mechanisms of cultural transmission that lead to culture taking a direction of its own.

Summary of Major Contributions

1. Neoevolutionary theory provides new and provocative views of kinship and the family: Hrdy's (1999) research indicates that polyandry is more common than previously estimated and questions many aspects of "natural" mother love; Smuts (1994) explains the neoevolutionary origins of human patriarchy; and Hawkes (1991) questions the provider role of males as being central to the evolution of the human family.

2. Neoevolutionary theory provides a new view of women in kinship studies. Women have a biology to build upon (Fisher 2000) rather than fight against. For some reason or another, biology in kinship studies was perceived as limiting or constraining when, in fact, it enables us to do so much.

3. Neoevolutionary approaches are consistent with theoretical developments in anthropological studies of kinship. First, neoevolutionary theories are consistent with current studies of kinship that emphasize the importance of gender/sex in shaping kinship relations (Stone 1997). EPs and PI theory indicate males and females should have distinct reproductive interests and evolved mechanisms of the mind, while a DT study demonstrated the importance of sex/gender in kinship in defining culture areas of the world that are consistent with genetic and linguistic categories of the world. Second, neoevolutionary emphasis on how individuals manipulate their environments or "culture" for their own interests is consistent with "practice" and "agency" theories (Bourdieu 1977, Giddens 1979) where individuals also actively manipulate their cultural environments.

4. Culture is alive and well in neoevolutionary ("biological") thought. All neoevolutionary styles (EPs, BEs, and DTs) view culture and biology as mutually constituted. BEs view individuals in culture more like practice theorists, while DTs tend to view culture more like Kroeber (1952) and Boas (1938) where culture can take a course of its own and many aspects of kinship systems may have to do with play and "style" rather than with adaptations to particular natural environments.

Evolutionary theory is in a good position to revitalize kinship studies. It is a coherent theory that can generate testable hypotheses. One can focus on universal features of kinship or culturally and historically specific patterns. The abundant criticisms of kinship studies in anthropology were warranted and useful (Schneider 1984; Holy 1996), but they led to the demise of research in this area because they did not offer viable alternative paradigms, other than that kinship systems needed to be studied on their own terms (i.e., from the people's perspective). While important, this view did not help to interpret and explain cultural diversity, and it is impossible to obtain funding to conduct descriptive studies. It is clear that kinship is important for all peoples in all parts of the world. Neoevolutionists would also support cultural critiques of kinship that suggest kinship needs to be more broadly defined in anthropology to include topics such as ritual and "fictive" kin.

References

Axelrod, Robert. 1984. *The Evolution of Cooperation.* New York: Basic.
Betzig, Laura. 1989. Causes of Conjugal Dissolution: A Cross-Cultural Study. *Current Anthropology* 30:654–75.

———. 1992. Roman Polygyny. *Ethology and Sociobiology* 13:309–49.

Boas, Franz. 1938. *General Anthropology.* Boston: Heath.

Borgerhoff Mulder, Monique. 1988. Kipsigis Bridewealth Payments. In *Human Reproductive Behavior: A Darwinian Perspective,* ed. Laura Betzig, Monique Borgerhoff Mulder, and Paul Turke. Cambridge,U.K.: Cambridge University Press.

———. 1990. Kipsigis Women's Preferences for Wealthy Men: Evidence for Female Choice in Mammals? *Behavioral Ecology and Sociobiology* 27:255–64.

Bourdieu, Pierre. 1977. *Outline of a Theory of Practice.* Cambridge, U.K.: Cambridge University Press.

Bourguignon, Erika, and Lenora S. Greenbaum. 1973. *Diversity and Homogeneity in World Societies.* New Haven, Conn.: Human Relations Area Files (HRAF) Press.

Boyd, Robert, and Peter I. Richerson. 1985. *Culture and the Evolutionary Process.* Chicago: University of Chicago Press.

Burton, Michael L., C. C. Moore, J. W. M. Whiting, and A. K. Romney. 1996. Regions Based on Social Structure. *Current Anthropology* 37:87–123.

Cashdan, Elizabeth. 1996. Women's Mating Strategies. *Evolutionary Anthropology* 5:134–43.

Cavalli Sforza, Luca L., and Marcus W. Feldman. 1981. *Cultural Transmission and Evolution: A Quantitative Approach.* Princeton, N.J.: Princeton University Press.

Chagnon, Napoleon. 1988. Male Yanamamo Manipulation of Kinship Classifications of Female Kin for Reproductive Advantage. In *Human Reproductive Behavior,* ed. Laura Betzig, Monique Borgerhoff Mulder, and Paul Turke. Cambridge, U.K.: Cambridge University Press.

Crook, John H., and Stamati J. Crook. 1988. Tibetan Polyandry: Problems of Adaptation and Fitness. In *Human Reproductive Behavior,* ed. Laura Betzig, Monique Borgerhoff Mulder, and Paul Turke. Cambridge, U.K.: Cambridge University Press.

Darwin, Charles R. 1859. *On the Origin of Species.* New York: Random House.

Dickemann, Mildred. 1979. Female Infanticide, Reproductive Strategies and Social Stratification: A Preliminary Model. In *Evolutionary Biology and Human Social Behavior,* ed. Napoleon Chagnon and William Irons. Pacific Grove, Calif.: Duxbury.

Durham, William H. 1992. *Coevolution: Genes, Culture, and Human Diversity.* Stanford, Calif.: Stanford University Press.

Emlen, Steven T. and L. W. Oring. 1977. Ecology, Sexual Selection and Evolution of Mating Systems. *Science* 197:215–23.

Fisher, Helen. 2000. *The First Sex: The Natural Talents of Women and How They Are Changing the World.* New York: Ballantine.

Flinn, Mark V., and Bobbi S. Low. 1986. Resource Distribution, Social Competition, and Mating Patterns in Human Societies. In *Ecological Aspects of Social Evolution,* ed. D. I. Rubenstein and R.W. Wrangham. Princeton, N.J.: Princeton University Press.

Fortes, Meyer. 1958. Introduction to *The Developmental Cycle in Domestic Groups.* Cambridge,U.K.: Cambridge University Press.

Fox, Robin. 1967. *Kinship and Marriage: An Anthropological Perspective.* New York: Penguin.

Gaulin, Steven J. C., and James S. Boster. 1990. Dowry as Female Competition. *American Anthropologist* 93:994–1005.

Giddens, Anthony. 1979. *Central Problems in Social Theory: Action, Structure, and Contradiction in Social Analysis.* Berkeley: University of California Press.

Gugliemino, C. Rosalba, Barry S. Hewlett, C. Viganotti, and Luca L. Cavalli Sforza. 1995. Mechanics of Sociocultural Transmission and Models of Culture Change. *Proceedings of the National Academy of Sciences* 92:7585–89.

Hagen, Edward H. n.d. The Functions of Postpartum Depression. *Evolution and Human Behavior.* In press.

Hamilton, William D. 1964. The Genetical Evolution of Social Behavior. *Journal of Theoretical Biology* 7:1–52.

Hartung, John. 1976. On Natural Selection and Inheritance of Wealth. *Current Anthropology* 17:607–22.

———. 1985. Matrilineal Inheritance: New Theory and Analysis. *Brain and Behavioral Sciences* 8:661–88.

Hawkes, Kristen, James F. O'Connell, Nicholas Blurton Jones, J. Alvarex, and Eric L. Charnov. 2000. The Grandmother Hypothesis and Human Evolution. In *Adaptation and Human Behavior: An Anthropological Perspective*, ed. Lee Cronk, Napoleon A. Chagnon, and William Irons. New York: Aldine.

Hewlett, Barry S., ed. 1992. *Father–Child Relations: Cultural and Biosocial Contexts.* Hawthorne, N.Y.: Aldine de Gruyter.

Hewlett, Barry S., and Luca L. Cavalli Sforza. 1988. Cultural Transmission among Aka Pygmies. *American Anthropologist* 88:922–34.

Hirschfield, Michael F., and Donald Tinkle. 1975. Natural Selection and the Evolution of Reproductive Effort. *Proceedings of the National Academy of Sciences* 72:2227–31.

Holy, Ladislav. 1996. *Anthropological Perspectives on Kinship.* London: Pluto.

Hrdy, Sarah. 1999. *Mother Nature: A History of Mothers, Infants, and Natural Selection.* New York: Pantheon.

Jones, Douglas. 1999. The Emergence of Culture Areas. Paper presented at the annual meeting of the Evolution and Human Behavior Society, Salt Lake City, Utah.

Keesing, Roger M. 1975. *Kin Groups and Social Structure.* Austin, Tex.: Holt, Rinehart and Winston.

Kroeber, Alfred L. 1952. *The Nature of Culture.* Chicago: University of Chicago Press.

Malinowski, Bronislaw. 1913. *The Family among Australian Aborigines.* London: Hodder & Stoughton.

MacDonald, Douglas H., and Barry S. Hewlett. 1999. Reproductive Interests and Forager Mobility. *Current Anthropology* 40:501–23.

Schneider, David M. 1984. *A Critique of the Study of Kinship.* Ann Arbor: University of Michigan Press.

Service, Elman R. 1966. *Primitive Social Organization.* New York: Random House.

Smith, Eric A. 2000. Three Styles in the Evolutionary Study of Human Behavior. In *Adaptation and Human Behavior*, ed. Lee Cronk, Napoleon Chagnon, and William Irons. Hawthorne, N.Y.: Aldine de Gruyter.

Smuts, Barbara. 1994. The Evolutionary Origins of Patriarchy. *Human Nature* 6:1–32.

Stone, Linda. 1997. *Kinship and Gender: An Introduction.* Boulder, Colo.: Westview.

Symons, Donald. 1992. On the Use and Misuse of Darwinism in the Study of Human Behavior. In *The Adapted Mind*, ed. Jerome H. Barkow, Leda Cosmides, and John Tooby. New York: Oxford University Press.

Trivers, Robert L. 1971. The Evolution of Reciprocal Altruism. *Quarterly Review of Biology* 46:35–37.

———. 1972. Parental Investment and Sexual Selection. In *Sexual Selection and the Descent of Man*, ed. Bernard Campbell. Hawthorne, N.Y.: Aldine de Gruyter.

Trivers, Robert L., and Dan E. Willard. 1973. Natural Selection of Parental Ability to Vary the Sex Ratio of Offspring. *Science* 179:90–92.

Van den Berghe, Pierre L. 1983. *Human Family Systems.* New York: Elsevier.

Williams, George C. 1966. Natural Selection, the Costs of Reproduction, and a Refinement of Lack's Principle. *American Naturalist* 100:687–90.

Chapter Six

Schneider Revisited: Sharing and Ratification in the Construction of Kinship

Kathey-Lee Galvin

What is kinship? How are people "related" to one another? Is kinship entirely constructed within separate cultural groups, or do some aspects of kinship translate across cultures? These questions, and others like them, have occupied anthropologists for decades. Kinship as a domain of study lost some of its academic luster during the heyday of a deconstructionist movement that promoted the abandonment of kinship in anthropology, largely because "kinship" was considered to be based on ethnocentric Western conceptions of biological procreation (Schneider 1984; Collier and Yanagisako 1987). At the turn of the century, we see a resurgence of inquiry into the nature of kin relationships. This recent research differs from much earlier work in that it refuses to take for granted the underlying assumption of the biological basis of kinship, but at the same time, this new research does not follow the call to abandon or dismantle kinship in anthropology. The result is a study of kinship from new anthropological vantage points. Examples that I explore here include, first, Weismantel's (1995) arguments for food as a basis for forms of indigenous kinship in an Ecuadorian parish of Zumbagua; second, Parish's (1994) analysis of Newar kinship and marriage ties through "polluted" food; and finally, Carsten's (1995) view of Langkawi processes of kinship building through food, space, and time. Based on this recent research, this chapter suggests that not only is kinship a valid field of study, but also that some bases for the cultural construction of kinship may be universal.

This chapter analyzes these works in reference to Schneider's classic *American Kinship: A Cultural Account* (1980), in which he delved into Euro-American constructs of kinship, and his later book *A Critique of the Study of Kinship* (1984), where he questioned the validity of the field of kinship studies. The three cases I discuss have some common factors that, I suggest, can be generalized to include other systems of kinship construction. Through an analysis of these cases, I demonstrate how a modified model of Schneider's American kinship can be applied cross-culturally, thus challenging his belief that there is no such thing as kinship, or that kinship might only exist in European or American culture (Schneider 1984).

The crux of Schneider's (1984) argument was that anthropologists had founded the domain of "kinship" on the notions of human reproduction and the biologically defined relatedness of their own Euro-American culture. Human reproduction and notions of biological relatedness cannot be presumed to elsewhere structure people's social relationships, and Schneider himself very clearly doubted that they do so. His criticism was sweeping, covering not only anthropologists, who, like Scheffler (1973), explicitly referred to human reproduction in their definitions of kinship, but to all anthropologists, who, since Morgan, explicitly or implicitly grounded kinship in biological relations even when they described cases of "kinship" locally formulated in some other terms. Schneider concluded that "kinship" as conceived in anthropology could not be meaningfully studied cross-culturally.

Some anthropologists agreed with Schneider and called for the abandonment of kinship as a distinct domain of study (Collier and Yanagisako 1987). Others, such as Scheffler (1991), rejected Schneider's critique and have continued to argue that kinship can be cross-culturally defined in terms of reproduction. Scheffler, discussing Schneider's work, wrote, "in other words, relationship by birth is a criterion (*even a sufficient condition*) for inclusion in various categories ethnographically described as kin categories (otherwise why describe them as kin categories to begin with?)" (1991: 365, emphasis in original).

Still others have attempted to reformulate "kinship" in other ways, retaining its usefulness as a cross-cultural category of investigation, or its potential designation as a human universal. Cucciari (1981) posited that all human kinship systems entail a concept of "consubstantiation," which can either be procreative or nurturing. More recently, Carsten (1995) redefined "kinship" as "relatedness." However, the first reformulation does not remove "biology" from the core of kinship, since, by his own admission, Cucciari's "nurturing" kinship rests on an underlying idea of procreation. Carsten's "relatedness" has been criticized as too broad to make kinship distinctive from other social relationships (Holy 1996; see also Stone, introduction, this book). My model is like Cucciari's in that it considers "biological" properties as but one type of "shared substance," but does not posit other types of sharing as falling back on notions of procreation. Like Carsten, I formulate "kinship" in a very broad sense, but my model attempts to tie the concept down to specific "orders" underlying its construction.

Calls for the dismantlement of kinship draw from Schneider's work on American kinship, which exposed the culturally specific notions of kinship as shared biogenetic substance. But this early work and the model of American kinship that he described also contain the seeds from which reformulation of kinship can grow. Schneider's American model is obviously too specific for application cross-culturally (indeed, it is built on American cultural ideas of "nature" and "law"), but can be reformulated as a cross-culturally valid model for the study of kinship. Toward this end, I revisit Schneider's original analysis.

American Kinship

American Kinship: A Cultural Account (1980) was a benchmark in the history of kinship studies. In this study, Schneider deconstructed the assumptions that underlay American middle-class conceptions of relatedness and used these to discuss the popular ideals of what comprised American families in the 1960s. Schneider's two orders, the Order of Nature and the Order of Law, and their resulting three classes (in Nature, in Law, and by Blood, see fig. 6.1) were discerning and retain some legitimacy.[1]

Schneider (1980: 27) asserted that kin relationships that draw from the Order of Nature are perceived as based on human biological reproduction that results in the transmission of biogenetic substance from parents to children. Thus "[t]wo blood relatives are 'related' by the fact that they share in some degree the stuff of a particular heredity" (1980: 24). He then further elaborated the importance of "blood" and biogenetics to American kinship relationships (1980: 23–24). In American kinship, paternal and maternal relationships are considered fixed and irrevocable through the medium of blood.

Schneider's second order of American kin relations is the Order of Law (1980: 29). This order, in contrast to Nature, is "imposed by man and consists of rules and regulations, customs and traditions" (1980: 27) such as those found in marriage. Schneider refers to the obligations and privileges deriving from the Order of Law as a "code for conduct." In American culture, Schneider said, there are two further divisions based upon the marriage of individuals. The persons entering the contract of marriage, or spouses, constitute the "closest" set of Order-of-Law kin relationships. The persons related to each spouse are then included in an additional subset (1980: 22–23). Marriage contracts between individuals determine the resultant kin obligations (codes for conduct) of persons who are related "by Blood" to the spouses. Some mem-

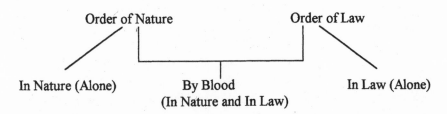

Figure 6.1 Schneider's Model of American Kinship

bers of Euro-American culture have kin relationships based solely on the Order of Law. Members of this group include all those members of a kin network who have no "shared biogenetic substance" with a specified ego; for example, all "in-law" relatives and spouses.

Schneider maintained that the Order of Law and the Order of Nature worked separately and together to order American kinship, producing three classes of kin—(1) those related in Nature, (2) those related in Law, and (3) those related "by Blood," or both in Nature and in Law (1980: 27–28). Thus Schneider viewed American kinship as based in biological reproduction, socio-legal institutions, or a combination of both.

Schneider's class "by Blood" represents the class most highly valued in American culture. Schneider wrote, "Substance has the highest value, code for conduct less value, but the two together (i.e., the 'blood relatives') have the highest value of all" (1980: 63). This type of kin relationship is the "closest" (especially parent–child and sibling bonds) and most publicly binding relationship. It is jurally soluble in the sense that a child can be disinherited, but "to those directly concerned, as to all others who know the facts, the two remain parent and child or sibling to each other" (1980: 24).

Schneider's "in Law" class is the most fluid of the classes. Because American perceptions of "nature" play no direct part in this construction, "in Law" ties are ties that can be unknotted. Laws are acknowledged as created by members of a society, whereas "nature" is considered beyond the realm of such constructions. Even though this class is titled "in Law" it contains some institutional relationships that are not strictly so. The idea of "common law spouse" is an illustration of social ratification that is not immediately dependent on the performance of rites and legal rituals, but is dependent upon the passage of time and adherence to a code for conduct.

Of the class "in Nature," Schneider wrote that it "contains the natural or illegitimate child, the genitor or genetrix who is not the adoptive father or mother, and so on" (1980: 28). Members of this class are anomalous because they do not conform to the highly valued biogenetics-ratified-by-law category. In order to make these persons "legitimate" members of a kin group, special procedures of legal adoption must be followed. The child who is then adopted has an "in Law" relationship with the people who raise it, which circumvents, but does not replace, the "in Nature alone" relationship with its biological parents.

Biologized Kinship

According to Schneider, earlier scholars had considered biological relationships as the universal bedrock of kin structures, but *American Kinship* had exposed such a biologized view of kinship as a feature of Euro-American culture. By 1984, Schneider was convinced that the assumption that reproduction is at the core of kin relationships was not valid cross-culturally:

So kinship is defined by social scientists and anthropologists in particular, as having to do with reproduction because reproduction is viewable as a distinct and vitally important feature of social life. Its distinctness, its vital nature, are given in the analyst's experience of his own culture—they are demonstrable and self-evident—and his not unreasonable assumption is that if we are that way, and if all people are people . . . then all people must hold reproduction in as high value as we do. It is considered to be, after all, as vital a feature of social life as it is of human life itself. But the question is, is this really true of all people? I am not convinced that it is. (1984: 194)

It may seem odd to those raised in European-derived societies that some cultures give little or no weight to human reproduction in their constructions of kinship. But any introductory anthropology course may recount the case of the Nayar where paternity is established by the giving of gifts to the midwife by any of a mater's socially ratified sexual partners. In the Nayar case, human reproduction does produce a mother–child relationship, but the paternal role is established by the socially-ratified custom of gift giving (Gough 1961). So in the case of the Nayar, it can be argued, human reproduction is the process from which relatedness is drawn, but only for the mother and infant; "fatherhood" is the result of legitimized ongoing sexual and social relations and gifts to midwives. Stated another way that draws from Schneider, the mother–infant relationship is based in "nature," whereas the father-infant relationship is a result of a "code for conduct."

It is important to note that even in American culture (and as pointed out by Schneider [1980]), shared biogenetic substance alone does not define a kin relationship with full obligations and advantages. The kin class of "in Nature" includes the marginalized, illegitimate "natural child." That is, shared biogenetic substance is insufficient for membership in the most highly valued relationships when not ratified by cultural actions such as marriage of the parents or the entering of parental names on a birth certificate. Today, another kind of marginalized or slippery kinship in America is designated with the term "deadbeat dad." Deadbeat dads have a "by Blood" relationship with their children that they try to un-ratify, whereas ex-wives and legal authorities seek to keep the relationship ratified.

Schneider's work is most remembered, however, for his drawing attention to the biogenetic basis of American kinship constructions and, second, his calling into question that any biological, let alone biogenetic, conceptions are universal in the construction of kinship. One positive result of Schneider's critique is that anthropologists have approached "kinship" with greater caution and with greater sensitivity to the imposition of Western "biological" biases. While not abandoning "kinship," some contemporary researchers have produced more emic-oriented descriptions and analyses of it. Their work has effectively decentered biology in kinship as the following examples show.

Biology Decentered

The forms of kinship discussed here share a common thread with Schneider's American kinship: in one form or another, all of these relatedness systems are based on the sharing of various substances. In some cases, this substance is concrete and able to be tangibly transferred between parties. In two of the studies, the shared substance is less a concrete material than a cultural invest-ment in the substance. In the final case, while "blood" is one of the kinship-constructing media, its kinship-bestowing properties are not based on biolog-ical aspects of human reproduction.

Weismantel, Food, and Los Andinos

Weismantel's (1995) work with the parishioners of Zumbagua in Ecuador illustrates a form of kinship constructed through the act of sharing sustenance and time. Weismantel noted that in a period of her absence from the field, Zumbaguan kinship groups had somehow transformed into new kinship con-glomerations. A previously childless woman appeared to have become the "mother" of a young girl who had earlier been designated the "daughter" of another woman (1995: 688). This small clue led to Weismantel's challenge to previous thinking about kinship.

Her thesis centered on the idea that the medium of food created a form of kinship unrecognizable to Euro-American kinship taxonomies but that was legitimate to Zumbaguans. Providing sustenance to a person enacted and en-abled a kin relationship that was binding. The responsibility to provide suste-nance, shouldered willingly by the provider, creates a bond of relatedness.[2] Also pertinent to Weismantel's analysis is the idea that time, or temporality, is equally important to the construction of these relationships.

The central illustration offered by Weismantel to support her ideas is the case of Iza and his son. When an urban health worker visiting the parish chastised Iza for his openness about the "adoption" of his son in front of the child, Iza protested, "I *am* going to be his father. Aren't I feeding him right now?" (Weis-mantel 1995: 690). Later, Iza explained to Weismantel how this relationship was built, "He was an orphan, poor boy, so I brought him here to live with me as my son. Where he was living there wasn't enough to eat" (1995: 690). It is unclear whether the child was an orphan because of the lack of food at his previous abode or because of a lack of living parents, but it is clear that food has become a medium that transfuses the boy with relatedness from the food-provider.

Weismantel has demonstrated a nonbiological form of kinship practiced by a specific parish in Andean Ecuador. This case supports Schneider's (1984) ar-guments in that not only is it a case of kinship not based on procreation, but it is also a case that is not modeled on or does not fall back on a procreative model. Thus, it is something other than Cucciari's (1981) "nurturing kinship," which has a notion of procreation behind it, and by which adoptions would be seen as relationships "like" or "as if" those based on procreation.

One aspect of Weismantel's analysis deserves further probing. This is the term "adoption" and its ties to Euro-American kinship. *Webster's* defines "adopt" as "2. to take and rear *the child of other parents* as one's own child, specifically by a formal legal act . . . to take or receive into any kind of new relationship" (1996: 28, emphasis added). Through this definition, the idea of "adopt" is implicitly laden with culturally bound notions of biological reproduction as the central relationship in a person's life. But Zumbaguan adoption *replaces* biological ties between participants: this undermines Weismantel's arguments by semantically making Zumbaguan practices similar to Schneider's American "in Nature" class. The Zumbagua do not *relinquish* biological children of couples; Zumbaguan "adoption" does not privilege biological reproduction and so does not need to negotiate its existence. Referring to Zumbaguan kinship construction practices as "adoption" lessens the ability of the Zumbaguan case to challenge classical forms of kinship in anthropology. Although Weismantel provides a convincing case for nonbiological kin relatedness, she retains the culturally loaded terminology of Euro-American culture to elaborate something considerably different. One of Schneider's students, Carroll, voiced some of these same concerns about the assumptions underlying Euro-American concepts of "adoption" in Eastern Oceania and viewed adoption as an area "pregnant" with possibilities for kinship theory (1970: 3–15).

Parish, Pollution, and the Newar

Steven M. Parish provides us with a different case that has some similarities to Weismantel's yet has some subtle differences. In *Moral Knowing in a Hindu Sacred City* (1994), Parish devotes a considerable amount of space to the Newar concept of *cipa*, or pollution, and how, over time, it transfuses a bride with kinship in her marital household. Here again, the shared substances are food and time; yet in the instance of food, it is the pollution of the family that inhabits the food, rather than the food itself that bestows kinship (1994: 149–51).

In contrast to "adoptive" relationships constructed in Zumbagua, the relationships described by Parish are constructed primarily through marriage. Where Weismantel was concerned mainly with vertical parent–child lines, Parish is concerned with horizontal relationships between "in-marrying" daughters-in-law and their affinal relatives. Through the completion of marriage rites, the bride's natal ties are superseded and the long process of assimilation into her new family begins (1994: 140). Her responsibilities toward the creation of relatedness ties are then twofold: she must be incorporated into her spouse's family through the absorption of patrilineal *cipa*, and second, she must contribute toward the creation of progeny.

One way in which a bride constructs kinship with her spouse's family is through the ingestion of enough food to sufficiently absorb the family's pollution and so displace her own natal *cipa*. New brides are considered the most polluted and threatening of all family members. In the logic of Newar culture, these women have not yet ingested and assimilated enough family *cipa* to be fully related to other members (1994: 154). The ingestion of *cipa* must take place over time; transfusing a new bride takes patience and appetite. In addition, those with higher status in the household are likely to refuse food "contaminated" by lower members of the household in order to *"not incorporate the nature of others"* (Parish 1994: 152, emphasis added). The other way that a bride becomes a member of her affinal kin group is to produce children. This is both a social and biological issue for a new bride. Her role is to reproduce the patrilineage and yet, in Newar thinking, she is not the main biological contributor to an infant. An informant elaborates:

> You don't have to say that the mother gives blood—she has blood, she doesn't have to give blood. The only one who gives anything is the father. The mother has the blood, the man gives seed to the blood. The blood and the seed are mixed. . . . The field is the mother's womb. After the seed has been planted in the field, the mother gives birth. . . . Blood is only soil. The man's semen—this is the real person. . . . Seed is more important than blood. . . . From the man's seed knowledge and intellect develop. From the woman's body only flesh develops. (1994: 146–47)

So biological reproduction does occupy an important position in creating Newar kinship relationships, yet this only holds true for the genitor. Note that a woman is effectively removed from the sharing of important substance by marginalizing her biogenetic contribution to the reproduction of human beings. She is essentially relegated to the role of hostess much in the same way that Delaney discusses the views of procreation in monotheistic world religions (1991). For a Newar, the arrival of an infant through a woman's birth canal is insufficient for her to be fully related to the infant. An infant becomes related to the woman (and her field) through the ingestion of her *cipa* through breast milk, another form of food and caregiving (Parish 1994: 48). *Cipa* transfuses a newborn with relatedness to the woman who shares her breast milk.

The "seed" givers of a household, men, on the other hand, are vested in the lineage concerns of substance sharing: for the patriline, the newborn family member is fully incorporated from conception. The seed is already infused with the pollution of the pater's descent group. The childbearer, on the other hand, must manufacture a relationship with the fetus after birth. One could say that women must "cultivate" relationships with the offspring of their bodies through the sharing of breast milk (food) over time.

For the "field" members of Newar society (women), the fact of biological reproduction has real significance only in relation to the future substance sharing that the lactating mother can provide for newborn members of the patriline. Her continued presence over time in her affinal home can be construed as social ratification. We will return to the importance of time to the creation of nonbiogenetic relatedness constructions after exploring the next case.

Carsten and Malay Models of Kinship-Building

Carsten analyzed Malay culture and the processes involved in building relatedness in opposition to the idea that kinship as a domain of study should be abandoned. Her book *The Heat of the Hearth* (1997) represents a successful attempt to investigate a non-European based culture despite the limitations of herself as a culturally defined Euro-American social scientist. Her intent was to "rescue kinship from its post-Schneiderian demise" (1997: 224) and to provide a model for investigating other cultures through means that do not rely upon the biological/social dichotomy (1997: 224–25). Here again, food has kin-constructing properties; but in Carsten's Malay case, that is expanded in space and time.

Carsten sees the Malay hearth as a medium for building Malay kin relationships, especially parent–child and sibling relationships. The hearth is where kin group members are reproduced; a household womb, one might say. It is the hearth where Malay women create feelings of relatedness with others through the sharing of sustenance. In this case, the sharing is constructed through the tangible aspects of food and the intangible aspects of "hearth." Men in this Langkawi world reside by the hearth through the largess of women; a womanless hearth, notes Carsten, is not to be occupied (1997: 226). Shared sustenance can take the form of milk for infants, created through the blood of the mother, or it can be other forms of food shared with other frequenters of the hearth: usually this food is rice (1997: 227–28). Significantly, breast milk shared with non-hearth children has the ability to instantly create incest taboos between any and all children who have shared the same breast (1997: 227–28). The Malay way of building kin relationships involves time, and as Carsten wrote, "is a process of becoming" (1997: 126).

Men do play some role in the creation of Langkawi kin relationships: Carsten's informants do share with the Newar some beliefs about conception and the seed of the father, but the differences are more striking. A Malay man leaves a seed in the womb of a woman. The woman's blood becomes a fetus if it mixes with the seed of the male. The Malay woman's blood, in contrast to that of the Newar woman, is not a passive field lacking any contribution toward the creation of the fetus. The Newar woman's blood was a "field" where the "agent" of the male created a life. By contrast, the blood of a Malay woman has agency and also acts as creator (Carsten 1997: 230–32).

Carsten explains the Malay attitudes about blood and substance: "Ideas about blood, however, do not imply that the substance is given at birth and remains ever after constant. In fact, substance, like blood, has a fluid quality. . . . It is continuously produced from *food which is eaten*" and "Milk itself is produced from blood and is a kind of blood. As a bodily substance it has a particular significance. First, it increases the degree of shared substance and the strength of emotions . . . the consumption of the same milk can actually create shared substance between otherwise unrelated people" (1997:127 emphasis added).

The creation of fetuses within the womb mirrors what will later take place in the hearth. Carsten offers that the practice of "heating" a woman's body after childbirth is similar to the process of heating food at the household hearth. After childbirth, large rocks that have been "cooked in the hearth" are placed periodically on her stomach (1997: 116–17).

Carsten attempts to view Malay "kinship" as an indigenous construction that may or may not rely upon recognition of biological human processes as foundational. She resists the temptation to see Malay kinship as essentially like Euro-kinship, given that in the Malay case, an infant is born and has siblings, a woman tends the offspring of her body, and so on.

New Orders

I will now describe a modified model of kinship based on the works of Weismantel, Parish, and Carsten, and synthesized with Schneider's presentation of American kinship. A precedent for expanding Schneider's American model beyond its borders has been set by some of Schneider's own students. Thus, while Schneider did not believe that "kinship" as conceived in anthropology was a cross-culturally valid domain, many of his students did describe kinship systems in a way that recalled elements of Schneider's American model of kinship. For example, Inden and Nicholas (1977) analyzed principles of shared caste (as substance) and codes for conduct in rural Bengali kinship systems. This and other examples led Kuper (1999: 158) to note that "the greatest irony is what happened to Schneider's model of American kinship. His students transported it to the furthest reaches of the globe, where it appeared that the natives also had 'kinship systems' predicated on a combination of ideas of 'common substance' and 'blood,' which constituted a 'person' as a 'relative'" (see also Scheffler 1991: 377ff).

The cases discussed in the previous section suggest that Schneider was correct in his belief that a biologized model of kinship, as he described it, is not cross-culturally applicable. But these contemporary kinship researchers have also found ways to explore and describe kinship systems. They accomplish this by illustrating other ways that people create "kinship" amongst themselves. Yet they all appear to have in common the idea that substance sharing, of life-giving or life-sustaining properties, is necessary in one form or another to forge bonds of kinship. All three use food as a medium between persons through which relatedness is constructed. These bonds of constructed kinship additionally require social acknowledgment or ratification.

These ideas are central to the new model of kinship that I propose for the cross-cultural study of kinship systems. Schneider's American framework needs simple expansion to accomplish this aim. The two new orders can be called the Order of Sharing and the Order of Ratification. The Order of Sharing is derived, of course, from Schneider's Order of Nature, and the Order of Ratification is drawn from the Order of Law (see fig. 6.2).

The Order of Sharing

The Order of Sharing operates on an obvious principle. Whether it is a "natural" biological process, such as the commingling of DNA, or regularly feeding a child, it appears that kinship is constructed through substance sharing. The three cases in the preceding section illustrate different types of substance sharing that can be further elaborated into types.

The first type of substance sharing is based on the sharing of food. Food can be thought of in two ways, as sustenance and as conduit. In the Zumbaguan case, food is life sustaining and creates kin relationships because it represents the willingness of the sharers to further subdivide and share family resources and subsistence. Food, in the case of the Zumbaguans, is precious *as* food. The ingestion of the food provides a tangible connection between potential "relatives."

Over time, Weismantel noted, the fed becomes like the feeders. "Those who eat together in the same household share the same flesh in a quite literal sense: they are made of the same stuff" (1995: 695). Weismantel writes that Iza's boy will at some point visually appear to be a member of the family when he "has eaten so many meals with them that his whole body is made of the same flesh as theirs that the bond will be unquestioned. . . . Eventually, he will look like them, smell like them, laugh and gesture like them: when people look at him they will see an Iza" (1995: 695). The sharing of food with the boy is an act of creation and bonding, and the consumption of food over time acts on family bodies in a physiological process that is a part of kinship constructions.

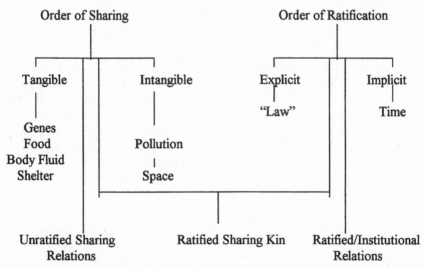

Figure 6.2   Cross-Cultural Kinship Model

Another type of sharing is food as conduit. This type falls into shared intangibles. The Parish study moves away from the tangible qualities of food toward its less physical and more culturally constructed properties ("pollution"). Food is the medium that transfers Newar pollution from a family or person to another individual. In the case of Malay kinship, the sharing of food is inextricably bound to the space where it is consumed. Similar to Newar pollution, this food is more than sustenance and can be considered food as conduit.

Another type of shared substance described in this chapter is the sharing of body fluids. This type of sharing is most similar to the American biogenetic type of sharing but has obvious distinctions. Breast milk, which can also be included in the food-as-sustenance type of substance sharing, can also forge kinship bonds in slightly different ways. For the Newar, it is the avenue through which a woman can infuse an infant with her own *cipa*. The sharing of breast milk is as necessary to the mother–child kinship bond as is the woman's ingestion over time of her affinal relatives' *cipa* to her kinship bond with them. The infant's body is of her body, but its personhood is the patriline's. For the Langkawi, breast milk alters the composition of infants' bodies so immediately and irrevocably that it has the power to forge incest taboos between those who share the breast, even if they do so only once.

"Blood" also has kinship forging properties. For the Newar, blood is merely a "field," but for the Langkawi, female blood is the stuff of life. A Malay woman's blood becomes a person when it mixes with the fluid of a man.

The other type of sharing is the sharing of shelter. Like food, shelter is sometimes no more complex than its physical characteristics, and at other times, is represented by more intangible properties of space. Although in the Langkawi group, rice, as food, is both conduit and sustenance, it also takes on kin constructing qualities from the hearth. Rice eaten where one lives forges bonds between those who partake of it. The space where food is shared is as vested with the ability to create relatedness as other substances.

The intangible aspects in the Order of Sharing often transgress the boundaries in much the same way that food can serve both as sustenance and as conduit. Shelter, when conceived of as a house having physical properties such as a roof or barriers to intruders such as walls, belongs to the tangible class of sharing. Inden and Nicholas noted that Bengali relationships are conceived of in reference to shared body substances and shared space of the house, "Persons who live together in the same house . . . form a solidarity unit. However, their relationship is defined not by sharing bodily substance but by sharing a house" (1977: 7). But they also see food as a product of the space of the "hearth" (1977: 18). Sax made a similar statement concerning the people of Garwhal, "persons who have no 'place' or . . . move from one place to another, are devalued" (1991: 74). Yet conversely, Sax also explained the view of the Gharwal Himalayan village as concurrent with "numerous Indian philosophic traditions that represent place or 'space' as itself a substance distinguished from other substances not only by its non-materiality but also by its active, 'containing' function" (1991: 72).

The Order of Ratification

The Order of Ratification is very close to but broader than Schneider's American Order of Law. It refers to processes that legitimize relationships through social convention (which might be codified in written language and law) rather than the sharing of substances. Forms of ratification can be explicit or implicit. Explicit ratification may include marriage and court judgments. Schneider's idea of "highest value" American kinship, for example, is based on the jurally explicit ratification of presumed DNA relationships.

The one form of implicit ratification easily seen in the cases discussed here is the passage of *time*. All three of the groups in this chapter ratify kinship through the construct of time. The Zumbagua case of "adoption" is not an instantaneous construction. Weismantel discussed how the shared food acted to create similar bodies over time. In the case of the Newar, time is an essential ingredient for a bride's full assimilation into her affinal family. She becomes an official member at the conclusion of marriage rites, or explicit ratification, yet remains suspect and not entirely acceptable until enough time has passed for enough affinal *cipa* to be absorbed. A bride cannot simply sit down and eat food enough to make herself a fully integrated member of her affinal group. Among the Langkawi, kinship is ratified through time at a woman's hearth and family members are discouraged from eating elsewhere. However, breast milk is such a potent kinship medium that those who share it create instant bonds so powerful they preclude future sexual contact.

Sometimes implicit and explicit forms of ratification overlap. In the case of American common law spouses, when enough time has passed and certain behaviors have been maintained, the implicit form becomes explicit and entitles, or burdens, the couple with legal obligations and rights.

New Classes

Drawing a parallel with Schneider's model, mine would logically produce classes of (1) in Sharing alone, (2) Ratified sharing, and (3) in Ratification alone. Schneider's American natural child and Malay breast-milk "siblings" might fall into "in Sharing alone"; the other relationships reviewed earlier are all "Ratified Sharing"; and of course, American spousal and in-law relationships would be "in Ratification alone."

While not arguing for a rigorous distinction between these classes, I suggest that viewing kinship in terms of these divisions does help to make cross-cultural comparisons while avoiding ethnocentric impositions. Thus, for example, adoption in the United States is "in Ratification alone." What

Weismantel labeled "adoption" in Ecuador is by contrast "Ratified Sharing," the construction of kinship through sharing (of food) ratified by time. Thus its meaning to the people of Zumbagua is more comparable to Ratified Sharing relations in the United States (e.g., parent–child relations based on biogenetic sharing and ratified through marriage of the parents, rearing of the children, and so on) than to adoption in the United States. Similarly, the relation between a Newar woman and her in-laws appears qualitatively different from that of an American woman to hers. In the former, the relationship draws both from the Order of Sharing (*cipa*, or pollution) and from Ratification (marriage to the husband), whereas in the latter case, the relation is in Ratification alone.

Conclusion

We have seen an evolution in the recent history of kinship studies. David Schneider rightly claimed that Western cultural conceptions of kinship as biologically based had rendered "kinship" unfit for cross-cultural comparison. But we have also observed how more recent studies benefit from the points made by Schneider and yet go on to analyze non-Western systems of kinship. The three cases presented in this chapter represent a new way of investigating kinship in other cultures, a way that does not take biological bases of kinship for granted. Weismantel, Parish, and Carsten delineate systems and frameworks of kinship that depend upon the sharing of different types of substances, "biological" and other.

I have shown that it is possible to modify Schneider's model of American kinship to incorporate a broader conception of kinship as shared substance, often ratified by other means. This model is based on the expansion of Schneider's two orders. The Order of Nature becomes the Order of Sharing to accommodate other tangibles such as nonbiogenetic shared substances as well as intangibles in the form of space. Substances may include, but are not limited to, food, shelter, and body fluids. Biogenetic substances remain a part of this new model. The second Schneiderian order, the Order of Law, becomes the Order of Ratification and includes social institutions and more abstract and less explicit constructions of legitimacy, such as time.

Schneider's work has served as the focal point for many debates about kinship, its validity, the foundations of possible human universals, and the notion that no such thing as kinship exists. Schneider's early deconstruction of American kinship and his later disassembling of the domain of kinship studies led him to a discerning argument for abandoning kinship. Recent researchers have described kinship of other cultures and I have analyzed their work using some of Schneider's basic principles of American kinship. These principles can in turn be used to reformulate Schneider's American kinship model into one that may represent a cultural universal.

Some who have followed Schneider (e.g., Collier and Yanagisako 1987) have moved away from the idea of cross-cultural comparison and have urged that each culture be approached emically on its own terms. I would argue instead that while the Schneiderians have exposed Western biases in anthropological kinship and demonstrated the value of emic approaches to "kinship," it does not follow that on another level etic concepts and cross-culturally valid models cannot be developed.

Notes

I am grateful to Linda Stone, Nancy P. McKee, Jeannette-Marie Mageo, John H. Bodley, John Patton, and Barry S. Hewlett for their comments on earlier drafts.

1. Schneider maintained that there really was only one basic model of American kinship, but he later (1980: 122) acknowledged that American kinship perhaps showed greater variation than his model presumed.

2. For her more extensive treatment of ideas attached to food in the Andes see Weismantel 1988.

References

Carroll, Vern, ed. 1970. *Adoption in Eastern Oceania*. Honolulu, University of Hawaii Press.

Carsten, Janet. 1997. *The Heat of the Hearth: The Process of Kinship in a Malay Fishing Community*. Oxford: Clarendon Press.

Collier, Jane Fishburne, and Sylvia Junko Yanagisako. 1987. Introduction to *Gender and Kinship: Toward a Unified Analysis*, ed. Jane Fishburne Collier and Sylvia Junko Yanagisako. Stanford: Stanford University Press.

Cucciari, Salvatore. 1981. The Gender Revolution and the Transition from Bisexual Horde to Patrilocal Band: The Origins of Gender Hierarchy. In *Sexual Meanings: The Cultural Construction of Gender and Sexualtiy*, ed. Sherry B. Ortner and Harriet Whitehead. Cambridge, U.K.: Cambridge University Press.

Delaney, Carol. 1991. *The Seed and the Soil: Gender and Cosmology in Turkish Village Society*. Berkeley: University of California Press.

Gough, Kathleen. 1961. Nayar: Central Kerala. In *Matrilineal Kinship*, ed. David M. Schneider and Kathleen Gough. Berkeley: University of California Press.

Holy, Ladislav. 1996. *Anthropological Perspectives on Kinship*. London: Pluto.

Inden, Ronald B., and Ralph W. Nicholas. 1977. *Kinship in Bengali Culture*. Chicago: University of Chicago Press.

Kuper, Adam. 1999. *Culture: The Anthropologists' Account*. Cambridge, Mass.: Harvard University Press.

Parish, Steven M. 1994. *Moral Knowing in a Hindu Sacred City*. New York: Columbia University Press.

Sax, William S. 1991. *Mountain Goddess: Gender and Politics in a Himalayan Pilgrimage*. New York: Oxford University Press.

Scheffler, Harold W. 1973. Kinship, Decent, and Alliance. In *Handbook of Social and Cultural Anthropology*, ed. John J. Honigmann. Chicago: Rand McNally.

———. 1991. Sexism and Naturalism in the Study of Kinship. In *Gender at the Crossroads of Knowledge*, ed. Micaela di Leonardo. Berkeley: University of California Press.

Schneider, David M. 1980. Reprint. *American Kinship: A Cultural Account*. 2d ed. Chicago: University of Chicago Press. Original edition, Englewood Cliffs, N.J.: Prentice-Hall, 1968.

———. 1984. *A Critique of the Study of Kinship*. Ann Arbor: University of Michigan Press.

Webster's New Universal Unabridged Dictionary, s.v. "adoption."

———. 1988. *Food, Gender, and Poverty in the Ecuadorian Andes*. Prospect Heights, Ill.: Waveland Press.

Weismantel, Mary J. 1995. Making Kin: Kinship Theory and Zumbagua Adoptions. *American Ethnologist* 22, no. 4:685–709.

Chapter Seven

Bound by Blood? New Meanings of Kinship and Individuality in Discourses of Genetic Counseling

Lynn Åkesson

For more than two years, I have been working on an interdisciplinary research project on the subject of genetics and culture in modern-day Sweden.[1] My work has focused on genetic counseling sessions and on interviews conducted outside hospitals with people who have sought genetic counseling. Not surprisingly, family relations and kinship have been an important component in these conversations. What is surprising is the great variety in people's attitudes to kinship and blood ties. In this chapter, I discuss these experiences in a wider context. To begin with, I draw attention to the interpretative situation that genetic counseling involves. From this concrete situation, the chapter goes on to consider how genetic investigations of kinship may be made more complicated in the future, particularly as a result of new reproductive techniques.

But genetic counseling means more than just charting biological affinities. When genetic diseases arise, the family is mobilized, for better or worse, in a completely different way than in the case of other diseases, which are, so to speak, the patient's private matter. The consequences of genetic counseling for individuals and their families are discussed in the section "Kinship as Practice." To put today's conditions into perspective, there is another section in which I examine kinship in the light of history. I then return the discussion to the present-day situation and two basic features of modern kinship thinking: individuality and variation. Finally, I consider how increased genetic knowledge can give a new and dangerous meaning to the concepts of kinship and blood ties.

Genetic Counseling

A refugee couple from Yemen came to the genetic counseling clinic at Lund University Hospital in Sweden. The woman was pregnant, and something had evidently gone wrong with previous pregnancies, which made the antenatal care staff suspect a hereditary illness. The couple could not speak Swedish or English, so an interpreter handled the communication between them and the doctor, a clinical geneticist. During the conversation, it emerged that the couple had previously had two boys who both died before reaching the age of one. One of them had died while they were in Italy. The couple had a letter from an Italian doctor with them, or perhaps, rather, a medical certificate, indicating a recessive hereditary disease: Werdnig-Hoffman's syndrome.[2]

The geneticist explained that, for a child to acquire the disease, both parents had to have a genetic predisposition without necessarily having the disease themselves. But if the child received the gene from both parents, then the fatal disease was inevitable. By the workings of genetic mathematics, this means that in every pregnancy there is a 25 percent risk that the child will have the deadly disease, a 50 percent chance that the child will have the gene but still be healthy, and a 25 percent chance that the child will be healthy, without any predisposition to the disease.

The doctor drew chromosomes and explained inheritance patterns. The interpreter translated and the couple nodded. The drawings before their eyes spread out over the paper. The explanation for what had taken the lives of their two boys was inside themselves. The doctor asked about the couple's family members, who appeared to be scattered, refugees in different parts of Europe. But the husband and wife were cousins, which increased the concentration of morbid genes. In this particular case, it proved to be possible to perform a prenatal diagnosis to determine at an early stage whether the fetus was sick, and if so, terminate the pregnancy. It is difficult to describe the couple's relief at this possibility. They could be spared the experience of seeing yet another one of their babies die.[3]

This situation was packed with cultural meaning in many ways. The couple's roots in a marital tradition from a different part of the world prompted a quick and immediate geographical comparison. In a way, the refugee couple also represented a repetition of history. Not very long ago, people in Sweden likewise married within a limited range as regards geography and kinship (Gaunt 1983; Hanssen 1977).

A conversation conducted via an interpreter helps to clarify the layers of interpretation that any conversation with a genetic counselor involves, even when the people on either side of the desk speak the same language. The doctor's explanation of chromosomes, genetic traits, and how they are passed on by inheritance requires a translation from mathematics/genetics to language. A good doctor can communicate these physical facts, which to many people are abstract and not expressed in ordinary everyday language. Patients must nevertheless interpret and translate medical and genetic facts into their own everyday world, apply them to their own and their relatives' lives and bodies. This means that questions such as "Do I have the same disease as my sister? What risk do my children run of getting my father's disease even though I am healthy?" are asked in countless variants (cf. Sachs 1998a). It is also difficult to handle knowledge that says that the threat to the child is in the mother's or father's own genes. Many parents and even grandparents are tormented by guilt about the heritage that they pass on. In one interview, when a woman with a hereditary illness was asked whether her parents felt any guilt, she exclaimed:

> They do! They certainly do. They think that your children shouldn't get sick before you do yourself. Children should not have difficulties in walking [one of her symptoms] and managing by themselves.[4] It's supposed to be the other way around. Children should be helping their parents. When everything's normal. So, they certainly feel guilty!

It also happens that spouses whose child has a genetic disease accuse each other of being "the guilty party," harboring the alien evil. It can be difficult to translate the doctor's objective argument that no one can be guilty of this, or responsible for the strained relations in the family that can result from disease and death.

In the situation with the refugee couple, further components are added to the translation problem. It is not only a matter of conveying information from one language to another, via an interpreter, but also of translating between cultures. The Swedish reality has to be interpreted and translated into experiences gained in a different cultural context. A counseling situation that requires a professional interpreter emphasizes the fact that every conversation of this kind involves translations and personal interpretations. It is easier to overlook this when cultural consensus appears to prevail and when the language, at least superficially, is the same.[5]

Kinship Investigations on New Terms

Charting kinship relations is an important part of genetic examinations. On the basis of the data provided by the person or persons consulting genetic clinics, the doctor draws pedigrees.[6] Kinship relations are important for the classification of the disease: is it due to an individual mutation, or does it run in the family? Oral accounts of family history can be supplemented with blood and tissue samples from relatives who volunteer to provide them, combined with an examination of the medical records of both living and deceased relatives.

In the situation with the refugee couple from Yemen, the investigation was complicated by the fact that the family was dispersed far outside Sweden. Moreover, there were no medical records available to document the deaths of the two boys. The documentation principles of Swedish hospitals, which make it easy to go back to old medical records of patients and their relatives, could not be applied in this case.

Not just geographical and cultural factors but also genetic ones can complicate future investigations of kinship. Modern reproduction technology has made a multitude of new kinship constellations possible. Stone (1997) summed up some of those that have arisen as a result of insemination, in-vitro fertilization, embryo adoption, frozen embryos, and frozen eggs or sperm. It is technically possible, for example, to give birth to one's own twin, to one's uncle or aunt, to one's own grandchild or niece/nephew. Yet another method, surrogate motherhood, entails other complications; for example, in disputes between genetic parents and the surrogate mother about who has the greatest right to the child (cf. Ragoné 1994). It must be underlined, however, that several of these techniques, which have been discussed in detail from a Swedish perspective by Lundin (1997), are not permitted in Sweden, at least not yet. This applies to embryo adoption, surrogate motherhood, and egg donation.[7] But the technical potential exists, involving a challenge to traditional kinship terminology. Snowden et al. (1983: 34) showed that at least ten different terms may be needed to clarify such seemingly self-evident concepts as "mother" and "father." One can thus speak of "genetic mother," "carrying mother," "nurturing mother," and "complete mother," the latter a designation for a woman who combines genetic, carrying, and nurturing motherhood. But there are even more terms for motherhood, such as "genetic/carrying mother," "genetic/nurturing mother," and "carrying/nurturing mother." There is less variety for fatherhood terms, since fathers do not give birth to children, but one can speak of "genetic father," "nurturing father," and "complete father" (Stone 1997).

The term "genetic mother" can now be differentiated even more. In the *International Herald Tribune*, 10–11 October 1998, an article under the headline "New Fertility Technique Shakes Ethical Ground, Experiments Combine Genes from Two Women" described how doctors in New York "for the first time have transferred genes from an infertile woman's egg into another egg, fertilized it with sperm, and placed the resulting embryo in the womb in the hope of growing a baby." The main mass of DNA (the nucleus) was removed from the infertile woman's egg and placed in a healthy donor's egg, from which the nucleus had already been removed. However, there were still mito-chondrial genes remaining in the cytoplasm of the donor's egg that could not be removed. The cytoplasm of the donor's egg was essential for the entire donation, since the infertile woman's cytoplasm did not function properly. Her DNA was therefore moved to a favorable donor environment.

This means that every child resulting from this procedure will inevitably have two genetic mothers. But proportions are important to bear in mind: there are approximately 80,000 genes in a nucleus, compared to about 50 in the mitochondrial DNA. What this means in medical and biological terms is uncertain. Mitochondrial genes are not considered to be so important for a person's appearance or behavior. If they mutate, however, they are known to cause various inherited diseases.

What it means on the cultural level to have two genetic mothers is even more unclear. It will, of course, be more difficult for geneticists to establish kinship in such circumstances. For the individual child and its family, it raises questions about what bloodline and kinship really mean. When the classifications that we are used to thinking with become invalid, we are faced with existential and ontological insecurity—until a new categorization restores order and meaning.

Kinship as Practice

Genetic counselors usually say that, unlike other diseases, hereditary diseases are not just about a simple relation between doctor and patient. In hereditary diseases, the family is involved in a way that can entail many problems. A person's need to obtain genetic information from relatives can clash with demands of personal integrity from individual relatives (cf. Hermerén and Kristoffersson 2000). Among my informants, there is a broad spectrum, from families in which the disease has led to increased cohesion and communication, even between distant relatives, to frozen or collapsed relations between close relatives, such as between siblings or parents and children.

Strong feelings of either cohesion or avoidance presuppose interest and commitment as regards the family. In some families, however, there is little interest in the common inheritance. For instance, a young man with a serious muscular disease gets support from his wife and friends, but no one in his biological family is particularly interested.[8] In an interview, he wonders why this is so:

> The divorce, maybe. My parents are divorced. But they haven't devoted very much time to any of their children, really. They're career people, both of them. So I have had to look after myself. But they really should have helped me when I was small. And worked hard with it. Because I had this handicap. But they've never got very involved in everyday things. I don't think they have a clue. Well, they know that I've had samples taken and that it's a muscular disease. They know it's hereditary. But what they weren't told twenty years ago, they don't know.

Genetic counseling thus also shows the social and cultural implications of kinship. In the counseling situation, and even more in subsequent interviews, the cultural management of biological kinship is exemplified. In these conversations, the picture of the practice-oriented kin is painted, and this is not identical to the biological-genetic picture.[9] In kinship as practice, nearness and distance are created on other premises than biological ones. It may depend on who you like, with whom you find it easy to communicate or socialize, or from whom you can benefit most.

Yet it is striking how often this practice of kinship is motivated by arguments about physical similarity. In families with a number of siblings, some of them perceive themselves as similar, and the similarities are often sorted and grouped according to the different branches of the family. A child may feel a greater affinity to the mother's or the father's side of the family. Statements pointing in this direction are very common: "they're all tall (thin, fat, dark-haired, blond) on my father's side, and me and my sister are the same. But my brother. . . ." With fundamental beliefs like this, it may be difficult to accept genetic information to the effect that a hereditary predisposition to disease, concealed inside the body and invisible to the naked eye, can also be inherited from the side of the family that one does not superficially resemble.

One patient who has received a detailed explanation of the mechanisms of heredity at the genetic clinic, and who must know that genes from both the mother and the father are required, nevertheless thinks in terms of just one branch of the family. To him, the disease is found in those who take after his father's side:

> The second oldest one, there's nothing wrong with her, she doesn't look like the other two of us. She's like mother's side, whereas my brother and me are like our father's side. For he's very small-boned too, for a man. And then my grandmother on my father's side, she's the same. I suppose I'm like her. In looks and that.

It is not uncommon for certain relatives to be "sorted out" in accordance with intricate systems of obligations and perceived nearness or distance. This can mean that they are excluded from information and discussion about diseases in the family. Others are perhaps given too much information against their will, from a member of the family who feels a duty to spread the knowledge to reluctant relatives.

> I see clearly the problems he will have. But he shuts his eyes to it. I'm the type that looks after other people. So they [the health care staff] told me not to care about him, that he really has to manage it himself. He is an adult, after all. I should concentrate on myself. So I don't bring up the matter with him. He has to take the responsibility for it himself. He's been given the information.

It happens, for example, in Huntington's chorea families, that to avoid seeing the same symptoms as those in their sick parents, people break off all contacts with the rest of the family (Kristoffersson 2000). They do not want to be similar, do not want to be related, and they are reticent regarding the biological facts whose relevance they do not really deny at another level.

Historical Kinship Practices

The new reproduction technology certainly brings opportunities to construct blood ties in ways that have never before been biologically possible. But kinship is above all a cultural category, and it is in this function that it has had its greatest significance. In Sweden and in the Western world generally, social kinship has overshadowed biological kinship until recent times. Today we notice an increased focus on biological ties between people, partly at the expense of social ties (cf. Nelkin and Lindee 1995). This focus leads adoptive children to seek their biological roots and prompts childless people to try to use technology to have a child with a biological link with at least one parent (Lundin 1997).

To obtain a perspective on today's situation, on the fears and expectations generated by biotechnology, it may be worth bearing in mind that our contemporary Western obsession with "genuine" blood ties is a new phenomenon. This is shown, for example, in the fact that relatives by marriage were ascribed the same status as blood kin until relatively recent times. In England, it was illegal for a man to marry his dead wife's sister well into the twentieth century. And in Sweden, it was punishable to have sexual intercourse with one's sister-in-law or brother-in-law throughout the nineteenth century. Social kinship thus equated a spouse's siblings with his or her own, thereby imposing the same restrictions that applied to incest between blood relatives.[10] The same applied to stepparents and parents-in-law: they were regarded, to use modern language, as real, biological parents (Gaunt 1983: 236ff). Priority was assigned to social parenthood. The person who brought up a child was also the true parent.

It is against this background that we must interpret the exchange of children between relatives in the old days in Sweden. It was not uncommon for children to grow up with their aunts and uncles, or with grandparents. This did not only occur in cases where the biological parents were dead. Other reasons, whether economic or social, motivated these family constructions (cf. Lundin 1997: 24ff). The practice of placing children with relatives could have consequences for kinship terminology. I have heard stories of Swedish families from the first half of the twentieth century in which the youngest of a large family of children, who happened to be of the same age as their nieces and nephews, were adopted into the family of an older sibling. This meant that one of the siblings in the family was not only an uncle or aunt in the biological sense but also a brother or sister in the social sense.

Families in the past could thus contain kinship relations in a way that leads our thoughts to what can now be accomplished by modern reproductive technology. Today's potential to give birth to one's sibling or grandchild undeniably has certain similarities to yesterday's possibility of bringing up a sibling or a grandchild. And the terms "genetic," "nurturing," or "complete" father or mother had the same validity then that they have now. But there are at least two important differences, one biological and one cultural. In the past, the carrying mother could not be separated from the genetic mother, just as a woman could not give birth to a sibling or a grandchild. Moreover, people do not appear to have felt any need to make a linguistic distinction between different kinds of fathers and mothers, or between biological and nonbiological siblings. Nurture took precedence over biology.

But kinship is not just terminology and genealogical descent. As I have pointed out previously, the practice of kinship is also a matter of relations. And relations between kinfolk have changed radically. Historian Gaunt (1983:267) argues that people today not only have a larger number of living relatives but also have closer contacts with them than ever before. The ethnologist Hanssen (1978) came to the same conclusion in his work on the inhabitants of the suburb of Vällingby in Stockholm, Sweden. When the dependence upon neighbors decreases, the contacts between relatives increases, even if the latter live far apart. Relatives call on the phone, visit each other by car on weekends, or use vacations to visit relatives who live too far away for a weekend trip. In present social commentary, however, modern people are often considered to have neither geographic nor kinship roots. This rhetoric lacks validity on a closer historical and contemporary examination. Nevertheless, many people want to believe that contact between kin was more frequent and relations between kin were better than they are today. The fact that modern people live a greater distance away from their kin is often a sign of broken cohesion between relatives. But that distance, as well as kinship, is not an absolute category may be illustrated with an example from nineteenth-century rural Skåne in the south of Sweden: "A thresher in Vallby in the 1890s had not seen his parents in Stiby—five kilometers away—for two years. When he went to call on them, he found that they had moved to Östra Nöbbelöv without his knowledge" (Hanssen 1976: 53).

The kindred as a unifying factor and the interest in genealogy were, for a long time, chiefly a concern of the prosperous stratum of society. Nonetheless, it was often the family that was mobilized in times of crisis, even among the poorest. A good example can be found in the autobiographical novel *Angela's Ashes* (McCourt 1996), which is set in the 1930s and 1940s. An impoverished Irish family receives assistance from relatives to leave the United States and return to Ireland. In the end, the grandmother, against her will and despite extreme poverty, has to look after her daughter, son-in-law, and all the dirty, hungry children. But she has no emotional interest. The commitment that she summons up is occasioned by duty, and relations between the members of the family are harsh and brutal.

With these historical examples I have tried to illustrate that today's discussion of blood ties and kinship is often conducted in contrast to a very recent historical reality. Without belittling the incredible potential of biotechnology to intervene in and change basic biological conditions, a broader historical and geographical comparison can give important perspectives on the infinite variation contained within the category we call kinship.

Individuality and Variation

From what has been said so far, it should be clear that kinship is a multifaceted concept. It is at the intersection of nature and culture and can thus be defined in many different ways and given different meanings in terms of geography, history, and personal strategy. To distinguish fundamental features in the way present-day people think about kinship, it may be fruitful to refer to what Strathern has said in numerous studies illuminating kinship systems in the Western world and elsewhere. Here I will proceed from her reasoning in *After Nature* (1992). In our Western way of thinking about ourselves as biological beings, reproduction is viewed as a guarantee of some of the qualities that have high cultural value, namely, individuality and variation. According to Strathern, individuality and variation are two of the three cornerstones on which the modern Western idea of kinship rests. The third cornerstone is the seemingly simple fact that two individuals equally engender another. That is how we think, but it is not how everybody thinks. In other parts of the world, the cornerstones of kinship may look different. This is why a non-Western man who came for genetic counseling at the hospital in Lund felt very relieved when discussing a hereditary disease. His grandmother had the disease, but he did not consider himself to be related to his grandmother. The bloodline, in his way of constructing kinship, was a male affair only.

According to our way of looking at it, every human being is born as a new, unique individual. The child receives its biological inheritance from the mother as much as from the father, in a bilateral kinship system, but the genetic mix of the child is completely new and unique to that one child. In this way, reproduction guarantees individuality. The newborn person is a distinct individual. And the special position of the individual is culturally guaranteed; for example, in legislative and political contexts. Our society, at least ideally, consists of independent individuals, each with their own responsibility and their own personal appearance.

The importance of personal distinction may be exemplified by the ambivalence about something as common as twins. In some cases, twins have even been killed. In Turner's (1969) classical text about the Ndembu people in Africa, newborn twins were placed in the river. They were young hippopotamuses, it was said, so they were being restored to their rightful element. Human beings have just one child at a time. Anything else was by definition inhuman. Although we have not resorted to such drastic methods, we in Europe have also ascribed a special status to twins, especially identical twins. Even until recently, people associated them with special characteristics, or explained their birth as the result of something that had happened to the mother during the pregnancy (cf. Tillhagen 1983). Identical twins are examples of spontaneous or natural cloning, which thwart our desire to be able to distinguish one person from another. Identical or almost identical people create confusion in our cultural classification.

Individuals produce individuals by means of sexual reproduction, to return to Strathern's discussion. This guarantees human diversity. With biotechnology, however, these cornerstones of kinship are threatened by several technological specialties, not the least of which is the new reproductive technology.

Moreover, with cloning it becomes technically possible to create individuals without variation and variation without individuality. In the first case, we are dealing with duplicates, making identical individuals. This reduces the diversity in a society. In the second case, it is a question of hybrids or monsters, in reality transgenetic cloning or the mixture of human and animal embryos. In this way we get diversity, but none of these beings can be called individuals.

Cloning humans, like mixing embryos, is not permitted anywhere in the world at the moment of writing. But the technique has its advocates. Some people believe that if there is a serious shortage of donated organs for transplantation, cloning could be a way to produce one's own biological "spare parts."[11] The technology exists, and the fears for what it can lead to can be seen in the horrific visions produced by popular culture. Films such as *The Boys from Brazil* and *Jurassic Park* are just two well-known examples of a large genre dealing with the fear of what can happen in the future (cf. Ideland 1997; Nelkin and Lindee 1995; Åkesson 1998). The message is that dangerous forces are unleashed if traditional sexual reproduction is bypassed with the aid of technology.[12] Then both individuality and variation are threatened and one's personal family tree is lost in a diffuse prehistory with a multitude of unknown ancestors.

Bound by Blood, and by the Alien Inside

Blood has long been the popular metaphor for biological kinship. We say that blood is thicker than water. Having something in the blood means having certain innate, inherited properties (Jones 1996). Added to this idea of the significance of blood is also the insight that it is valuable that new blood is brought into the family. Knowledge of the problems that can arise from reproduction between individuals who are too closely related is nothing new. People have long been able to observe the effects of inbreeding among domestic animals, or of marriages between close relatives in the royal houses and aristocratic families of Europe, with the increased frequency of disease among the offspring. "Inbreeding," or marriage between close relatives, was often used as a pejorative epithet when people wanted to sling mud at the inhabitants of the neighboring village, or at the rich people in one's own village. When interviewed by an ethnological fieldworker in the village of Sturup in Skåne in the 1970s, a small farmer reflected on the problems of inbreeding:

> Some people got married within the family, second cousins. There was too much marrying kinsfolk, too much inbreeding. Many of them went crazy. They married inside the family so that the money wouldn't go out of it. But it didn't help them very much when they went crazy anyway. (Åkesson 1985: 378)

At the same time, such marriages, for example, between cousins, have positive qualities on a cultural level, particularly in the form of economic security, which is reinforced by alliances between relatives. In Scandinavia, marriage between cousins has been practiced in the nobility and among landowning farmers, partly for this reason (Gaunt 1977, 1983). Moreover, it could happen that people in a village made a strategic choice to emphasize how closely they were related, even though they were not actually blood relatives to any greater extent than people in other villages. The claim to be related was used to unite them against the outside world. Other people's scornful talk of inbreeding and degeneration was the price they had to pay for the strong sense of village community (Åkesson 1985: 378ff; Strathern 1981).

But sex between closely related people, such as parents and children, is strictly taboo, with few exceptions. The old Swedish word for incest, *blodskam* or "blood-shame," shows us that behind the concept lies the idea that such relations lead to tainted blood, to disease, and degeneration. Fresh blood from outside is needed to guarantee the variation represented by the unique individuals. Yet many people are afraid of the diversity resulting from the admixture of fresh blood, or genetic material (cf. Rose 1994). New blood is all right, but blood that is too foreign can set other ideas in motion, racism, for example. Knowledge of the advantages of genetic mixture may find it difficult to compete with the tenacious cultural structures that make anything alien suspect (Hanssen 1977: 74ff; Åkesson 1985: 379ff).

Attitudes to and treatment of "the alien" have a powerful cultural charge (Douglas 1966; Turner 1969). It is often easier to handle something alien and divergent when it can be incorporated into a cultural classification system and named (Åkesson 1991). Traditionally, the alien has been outside us, categorized in terms of visible deviation or obvious criteria such as skin color, sex, or geographic origin.[13] With the expansion of modern genetics and gene technology, such categories become far too crude. The alien, nameless, and dangerous Other can just as easily be something invisible inside us, an integral part of our kin and of our own interior. Blood literally binds us together, and the familiar security of kinship can conceal the unknown and the alien.

Notes

1. The research project "Genetics, Gene Technology, and Everyday Ethics" is financed by the Bank of Sweden Tercentenary Foundation. The research group includes, besides myself, Susanne Lundin, who has also contributed to this book, Malin Ideland, and Cecilia Fredriksson, all from the Department of European Ethnology, Lund University; Ingrid Frykman, Department of Genetics, Lund University; and senior consultant Ulf Kristoffersson, Lund University Hospital. I am grateful to Ulf Kristoffersson for arranging the contacts between the patients and me. I also wish to thank him, Ingrid Frykman, and Susanne Lundin for constructive criticism of this chapter. For a discussion of what kind of knowledge can be produced in an interdisciplinary context, see Åkesson (2000), Lundin and Åkesson (1999a), and Lundin and Åkesson (1999b).

2. The disease is described by Marteau and Richards (1996:39): "Werdnig-Hoffman's syndrome (spinal muscular atrophy, type 1; severe infantile spinal muscular atrophy) is a degenerative disease of the horn cells of the spinal cord that leads to a progressive loss of control of

muscle movement. Symptoms of muscular weakness are usually present at birth or soon after-wards and death is inevitable within the first two years. The disease is recessively inherited. Pre-natal diagnosis using linkage methods became available in 1991."

3. Selecting fetuses, using modern medical technology to choose which should live and which should not, is a controversial issue. In the case with the refugees discussed in this text, the choice is fairly easy. Few people would object to the use of prenatal diagnosis and abortion to terminate a pregnancy that can only have one result: that the child will die a painful death in its two first years. In other cases, abortion is far from self-evident.

4. Werner's syndrome.

5. Anthropologist Lisbeth Sachs has devoted several studies to the problem of genetic trans-lation and the difficulty of assimilating genetic information and assessing one's own risk of be-coming ill. Her works concern both immigrants and native-born Swedes. For references in Eng-lish see, for example, Sachs 1996, 1997, 1998b.

6. The family trees that genetic counselors draw are surprisingly like those used in anthro-pology. Both use a circle for women, and the fact that men are represented by a square in genet-ics as opposed to a triangle in anthropology is no obstacle to immediate understanding. Geneti-cists draw the same kind of diagonal stroke over the symbols of the deceased, supplemented with information about cause of death, to clarify any heredity in the history of morbidity. Although the geneticist and the anthropologist are looking for different things in people's genealogy, they both perceive kinship a priori as significant for the individual (Lundin and Åkesson 1999a; cf. also Sachs 1998a).

7. It may be pointed out that Sweden adopts an extremely restrictive attitude toward repro-duction technology compared with many other countries in the Western world. It thus happens that Swedish citizens go abroad to get treatment that is not available in Sweden. In-vitro fertil-ization, for example, is offered only to people living in stable heterosexual pair relationships, with the women being under the age of 45. For a detailed discussion see Lundin (1997).

8. Kugelberg-Welander's syndrome, spinal muscular atrophy type III.

9. In a similar way, ethnologist Stefan Beck (2000) shows the discrepancy between the bio-logical and social kin in his interesting work on cystic fibroses in Cyprus.

10. The Swedish language allows for greater differentiation of kinship than many other Eu-ropean languages. The paternal and maternal lines are specified in the words for grandfather (*morfar* and *farfar*, literally "mother's father" and "father's father"), grandmother (*mormor* and *farmor*), uncle (*morbror* and *farbror*), and aunt (*moster* and *faster*). Cousins are not distinguished in this way, however. Interestingly, relatives by marriage are designated by the same terms as par-ents' siblings. Your mother's brother's wife is called *moster* although she is not literally your "mother's sister." Social kinship becomes biological in this terminology.

11. I have discussed the shortage of organs for transplantation in studies of attitudes to dead bodies in modern Sweden (Åkesson 1996, 1997). Lundin examines present-day attempts to solve the same problem through xenotransplantation, that is, the use of animal transplants with human DNA (Lundin 1999; see also Papagaroufali 1997).

12. The potential of modern reproduction technology to spawn criminal activity is explored in novels such as *The Genesis Code* (Case 1997) and *Blue Genes* (McDermid 1997).

13. A hundred years ago in Sweden, even people from the neighboring parish, from little more than ten miles away, were regarded as strangers and could be treated with chilly suspicion (Hanssen 1977: 139ff).

References

Åkesson, Lynn. 1985. Veta sitt värde. In *Modärna tider: Vision och vardag i folkhemmet*, ed. Jonas Frykman and Orvar Löfgren. Lund: Liber Förlag.
———. 1991. *De ovanligas betydelse*. Stockholm: Carlssons.

———. 1996. The Message of Dead Bodies. In *Bodytime: On the Interaction of Body, Identity, and Society*, ed. Susanne Lundin and Lynn Åkesson. Lund: Lund University Press.

———. 1997. *Mellan levande och döda: Föreställningar om kropp och ritual.* Stockholm: Natur och Kultur.

———. 1998. Cloning—Crowning Glory of Creation? In *Aspects of Gene Technology: Report from an IVA Seminar Series 1997–1998.* Stockholm: Royal Swedish Academy of Engineering Sciences (IVA).

———. 2000. Does Gene Technology Call for a Gene Ethnology? On the Goals of Knowledge and the Use of Concepts in Interdisciplinary Research. In *Natur und Kultur*, ed. Rolf-Wilhelm Brednich, Annette Schneider, and Ute Werner. Göttingen: Deutsche Gesellschaft für Volkskunde, in press.

Beck, Stefan. 2000. Natur, Kultur und Reflexible Köper. Humangenetische Prozesse und Diskurse als Gegenstand Volkskundlicher Forschung. In *Natur und Kultur*, ed. Rolf-Wilhelm Brednich, Annette Schneider, and Ute Werner. Göttingen: Deutsche Gesellschaft für Volkskunde, in press.

Case, John F. 1997. *The Genesis Code.* New York: Ballantine.

Douglas, Mary. 1966. *Purity and Danger: An Analysis of the Concept of Pollution and Taboo.* London: Routledge & Kegan Paul.

Gaunt, David. 1977. Preindustrial Economy and Population Structure. *Scandinavian Journal of History* 183–210.

———. 1983. *Familjeliv i norden.* Stockholm: Gidlunds.

Hanssen Börje. 1976. Hushållens sammansättning i österlenska byar under 300 år. *RIG 1976*, no. 2:33–60.

———. 1977. *Österlen: Allmoge, köpstafolk och kultursammanhang vid slutet av 1700-talet i sydöstra Skåne.* Stockholm: Gidlunds.

———. 1978. *Familj, hushåll, släkt.* Stockholm: Gidlunds.

Hermerén, Göran, and Ulf Kristoffersson. 2000. Genetics and Ethics—Attitudes among Swedish Clinical Geneticists. In *Genetics, Ethics, and Society in Worldwide Perspective*, ed. Dorothy Wertz and J. C. Fletcher, in press.

Ideland, Malin. 1997. Understanding Gene Technology through Narratives. In *Gene Technology and the Public: An Interdisciplinary Perspective*, ed. Susanne Lundin and Malin Ideland. Lund: Nordic Academic Press.

Jones, Steve. 1996. *In the Blood: God, Genes, and Destiny.* London: HarperCollins.

Kristoffersson, Ulf. 2000. Sjukdom, Arv och ärftlighet—vad säger vårt arv om sjukdomsrisker och hur får vi veta något? In *Arvets Kultur: Essäer om Genetik och Samhälle*, ed. Susanne Lundin and Lynn Åkesson. Lund: Nordic Academic Press.

Lundin, Susanne. 1997. *Guldägget. Föräldraskap i biomedicinens tid.* Lund: Historiska Media.

———. 1999. The Boundless Body: Cultural Perspectives on Xenotransplantation. *Ethnos* 64, no. 1:5–31.

Lundin, Susanne, and Lynn Åkesson. 1999a. GenEtnologi. Om trärvetenskapens vedermödor och belöningar. *Kulturella perspektiv* 2:22–32.

———. 1999b. *Amalgamations: Fusing Technology and Culture.* Lund: Nordic Academic Press.

Marteau, Teresa, and Martin Richards. 1996. *The Troubled Helix: Social and Psychological Implications of the New Human Genetics.* Cambridge, U.K.: Cambridge University Press.

McCourt, Frank. 1996. *Angela's Ashes.* New York: Scribners.

McDermid, Val. 1997. *Blue Genes.* New York: Scribners.

Nelkin, Dorothy, and Susan Lindee. 1995. *The DNA Mystique: The Gene as a Cultural Icon.* New York: Freeman.

Papagaroufali, Elina. 1997. Human and Animal Gene Transfers. In *Gene Technology and the Public: An Interdisciplinary Perspective*, ed. Susanne Lundin and Malin Ideland. Lund: Nordic Academic Press.

Ragoné, Heléna. 1994. *Surrogate Motherhood: Conception in the Heart.* Boulder, Colo.: Westview.

Rose, Hillary. 1994. *Love, Power, and Knowledge: Towards a Feminist Transformation of the Sciences.* Cambridge: Polity.

Sachs, Lisbeth. 1996. Causality, Responsibility, and Blame—Core Issues in the Cultural Construction and Subtext of Prevention. *Sociology of Health and Illness* 18, no. 5:632–52.

———. 1997. The Diagnosis of Risk: Implications for the Quality of Life. In *Cancer, AIDS and the Quality of Life*, ed. J. A. Levy et al. New York: Plenum Press.

———. 1998a. *Att leva med risk: Fem kvinnor, gentester och kunskapens frukter.* Stockholm: Gidlunds.

———. 1998b. The Visualization of the Invisible Body. In *Identities in Pain*, ed. Jonas Frykman, Nadia Seremetakes, and Susanne Ewert. Lund: Nordic Academic Press.

Snowden, Robert, G. D. Mitchell, and E. M. Snowden. 1983. *Artificial Reproduction.* London: Allen and Unwin.

Stone, Linda. 1997. *Kinship and Gender: An Introduction.* Boulder, Colo.: Westview.

Strathern, Marilyn. 1981. *Kinship at the Core. An Anthropology of Elmdon, a Village in Northwest Essex in the Nineteen-Sixties.* Cambridge, U.K.: Cambridge University Press.

———. 1992. *After Nature: English Kinship in the Late Twentieth Century.* Cambridge, U.K.: Cambridge University Press.

Tillhagen, Carl-Herman. 1983. *Barnet i folktron: Tillblivelse, födelse och fostran.* Stockholm: LTs förlag.

Turner, Victor. 1969. *The Ritual Process: Structure and Anti Structure.* Ithaca, N.Y.: Cornell University Press.

Chapter Eight

The Threatened Sperm: Parenthood in the Age of Biomedicine

Susanne Lundin

M ats twists in his chair, trying to find a comfortable position without waking the slumbering baby in his lap. Three months ago he became a father, to Gustav. He and his wife Eva are no longer just a couple but are now what they call a real family. It is possibly this feeling of security in belonging to an accepted social unit that enables Mats to speak openly about the complicated feelings that childlessness awakened in him.

Mats and Eva had tried to have a child for a little more than a year before they suspected that something might be amiss and sought medical help. At the Women's Clinic in Sweden they were told not to worry as "these things sometimes took a bit of time." The months passed by and they became more and more convinced that there was something wrong with Eva. Over the next few months, she was examined a number of times until, with the aid of keyhole surgery, the doctor was finally able to confirm that there was no physical defect. Mats became the center of attention after this, and tests soon showed that he had poor-quality sperm, not good enough to produce children. Shortly afterward, Mats and Eva were offered treatment at the Women's Clinic.

In Sweden, about 250,000 couples are involuntarily childless. This is a situation that often leads to complicated feelings about everything from the meaning of parenthood to the relation between sexuality and reproduction. Those women and men who do not want to accept a life without children can now choose among several forms of artificial reproduction. In 1978, the first so-called test-tube baby was born in England, and in Sweden, the first was in 1982. Since then, about 7,000 Swedish children have come into being by such methods. In vitro fertilization (IVF) is the medical umbrella term for all treatments whereby conception takes place outside the body. Assisted fertilization refers to methods by which conception takes place in the woman's body—for example, microinjection where sperm with reduced quality is transferred into the egg with a pipette. It was such artificial insemination (Intracytoplasmic Sperm Injection, or ICSI) that was offered to Mats and Eva. With the aid of technology, parenthood can thus be realized. But the possibilities offered by technology are—as we will see—not without complications.

The starting point for this article is the interplay between medical technology and people's longing for parenthood. In the early 1990s, at the start of my research on reproductive technology, I was confronted by a world of high-tech equipment and medical records, doctors, diagnoses, and medical management, side by side with childless couples uncertain of their own self-identity but full of hope about parenthood. This was certainly a specific sociocultural arena, and, simultaneously, a scene of action for numerous questions of burning interest to society.

It immediately became apparent that the medical procedure was only one part of the treatment carried out at the clinics. Of at least equal importance, although difficult to nail down, were those cultural actions, the guiding principles whereby the actual sexual roles, the optimal body, and the real family were created (see Rapp 1993; Strathern 1992; Franklin 1993; Ragoné 1994; Rose 1994; Stone 1997).

The basis for this discussion consists of interviews with childless couples.[1] The focus is thus on couples, which says more about the Swedish law than about social reality. Childlessness is certainly not only a problem for married women and men. When Swedish statistics report data on childless people, they also contain a large dark figure including all those individuals who have not been registered by inquiries into infertility, namely, single people as well as homosexual and lesbian couples. Sweden is, as I have discussed elsewhere (Lundin 1996, 1997b), the most restrictive country in the Western world as regards artificial conception. Moreover, only heterosexual couples receive treatment.[2]

In the following, we will meet some of these women and men, and follow their encounters with the medical world. The clinic is the first step in the treatment program that will, as they hope, result in parenthood. At the same time, they enter into another journey where their innermost preconceptions about parenthood and identity clash with cultural and medical practice. They not only undergo medical treatment, but also an identity- and gender-forming process.

Could It Be the Man's Fault?

Within gender analysis, a relational approach prevails, that is, the knowledge that society always ought to be observed against a background of social and gender-based conditions (Jordanova 1989; Butler 1990; Showalter 1992).[3] A common link in the last decade's feminist critique has been to describe women's situation in a world interpreted primarily through male values. Less attention has been paid to those contexts where women's skills are prioritized and men's experiences are more hidden (Uddenberg 1982; Frykman 1991). The following discussion examines this perspective—a focus on male identity and fatherhood in relation to motherhood—against a background of specifically Swedish experiences. This brings us back to Mats and Eva.

When Mats was informed about his malformed sperm, almost two years had passed from the couple's first contact with a doctor. One can, of course, ask why the fertility tests concentrated primarily on Eva. Even Mats and Eva had concluded that "it was her there was something wrong with." Obviously the experts and the couple themselves had considered infertility a mainly female problem. This supposition can be considered remarkable given the history of sperm donation since the 1920s.[4] It is also a routine measure today to ask the man for a sperm sample. The medical profession is also highly competent in treating both female and male infertility, and the increasingly common process of microinjection is one example of this.

One can thus state that the medical competence exists that should have stopped the one-sided examination and the delayed treatment. But medical theory and actual routines are two different things. Even though Mats and Eva's case took place a few years ago, before microinjection became a standard method of treatment, their experiences are not unique, but shared by many other childless couples. This situation raises the question of if the examination of the couple's infertility was not only guided by the relevant medical knowledge but also by cultural and gender-specific values, from an uncritical "conviction that," as Mats said, "it just can't be anything to do with the man." Eva was also convinced that such a thought process exists, and she expressed how this presumption affected not only the clinic's position but also her own and Mats's reactions as follows:

> Nobody, absolutely nobody said anything indicating that there could be something wrong with Mats. We finally realized that this could be the case and Mats gave some sperm samples in the summer of 1989. The results showed that 90% were malformed. This of course created new roles for us both. Mats was totally shattered because it was him who had the problem, my reaction was to be angry with the gynecologist who had never even mentioned such a possibility.

Mats himself said that it was like being "struck by lightning, just think, I could only produce powerless sperm, I wasn't a real man anymore." Involuntary childlessness usually leads to mutual sorrow due to the perception of a future life without children, being unlike a family that fulfills a "natural place" in society. It becomes clear that childlessness also awakens other very specific questions about female and male identity, as seen in the couple's reaction on hearing that Eva was healthy. Their mutual relationship was altered at once. Suddenly, it was not Eva's womb and her sadness about missing out on motherhood that was most important, but Mats's infertility, or more to the point, his weak sperm, which he increasingly came to associate with both reduced fertility and atrophied sexuality.

Other men relate similar experiences. Jan, who eventually became a father through insemination in Finland, says, that "even though I had tried to prepare myself for the worst it was almost as if someone had turned off the sun. I felt worthless in bed and just plain unmanly." For both these men, the information pertaining to useless sperm meant that they did not feel themselves to be adequate men. It is clear that their sperm symbolizes more than just reproductive material, which gives us reason to look more closely at the relationship between semen, fertility, and the desire to be a "real man" (cf. Beck and Beck-Gernsheim 1995).

Gender and Biology

The modern Western link between egg and sperm, between male sexuality and identity, is by no means a universal figure of thought. Old folk myths, as for example among the Yenga Tale in Africa, give us a hint of a conceptual world in which children come about solely by the agency of women (see Neely 1984). The Western concept of Mother Earth is also a metaphor based on an interpretation of reproduction that differs from today's knowledge. It presents an organic image in which nature is identified with an autonomous female fertility, very like that of the Yenga Tale.[5]

The mechanistic world view of the fifteenth century in Europe resulted in the growth of new value systems that denied "Mother Earth," as well as women in general, her dominant and life-giving role. Instead, the concept of female unpredictability was put forward, of chaos that had to be controlled by male rationality (Merchant 1989). The following centuries saw the transformation of nature into a controllable and profit-making resource, at the same time that women's bodies increasingly became objects for man's desire and vessels for the fruits of his body.[6]

Now we should not be misled into thinking that men and women in the past were perceived as being sexually similar, let alone equally valuable for reproduction. The female orgasm was not considered less important than the male's release of semen; even in the face of the emerging image of female passivity contra male dynamism, this analysis stayed alive until the age of the Enlightenment.

This ideological reorientation resulted in consequences for sexual functions as well as for views of reproduction. Women and men assumed increasingly more opposed positions that resulted in the woman's passive role being complemented by the male's mission to conquer (Johannisson 1994; Laqueur 1994). One might have assumed that the discovery of the woman's egg in the nineteenth century ought to have corrected ideas about propagation. In reality, a scientific legitimacy was created for society based on gender separation; the egg became the symbol for the woman's stupidity and compliance, whilst the sperm distinguished itself as the warrior of desire.

In her classic study *The Woman in the Body*, Martin (1987) showed how specific conceptions prevail in medicine that can, for example, foster the image of a passive egg into which target-conscious sperm drill. Martin raised the issue of whether the egg is not, in fact, powerfully pulling small insecure sperm toward it, or whether the male and female parts of reproduction are involved in equal measure. Most descriptions of the process are firmly based on a form of gender construction in which women are passive beings as opposed to the active role played by men. But the strength of these values can also be confirmed by medicine's seeming biological objectivity. The message is clear, women's subordination to male superiority has a genetic base.

The insight that scientific facts are culturally impregnated has had a tremendous impact. On the basis of these epistemological premises, feminist scholars besides Martin have shown how, for example, the medical world is steered by patriarchal patterns of thought (cf. Haraway 1997; Jordanova 1989). This is a phenomenon that has been called the Male Gaze, by which it is seen to be the man's task to engender children, and the woman's duty to "hatch" the fertilized eggs. These images leave no room whatsoever for male imperfection; ultimately, this means that male infertility is culturally unacceptable.

There are many scientific theories as to how male supremacy is reproduced. If these theories are tested, it becomes evident that old patriarchal norms permeate our world view. A striking example is the investigation of Mats and Eva. This clearly shows that, although new interpretations of reproduction have had an impact on the medical world, health care is still influenced by a diffuse assumption that childlessness cannot be due to a male defect. At the same time, empirical studies, such as my own, show that theories of the Male Gaze are sometimes too one-sided (cf. also Jay 1993). They concentrate too often on the formation of female subordination. But the tenacious patriarchal ideas do not just produce images of women. As we will see, special images of men also arise, images that are not always radiating dictatorial powers, but sometimes even vulnerability.

In the Female Arena

Inspired by Martin's discourse analysis, I plunged into the specialist medical literature. The aim of my close scrutiny of gynecological texts was to find a link between ideology and practice, between scientific descriptions and gender construction. I soon noted that terms such as passive eggs and active sperm did not occur in textbooks on gynecology and obstetrics.[7] Furthermore, it turned out that the description of the egg in the passive voice as *being fertilized* had its grammatical counterpart in descriptions of sperm *being deposited* in the vagina during intercourse. It was thus difficult to find a gender-determined way of thinking about reproduction in the experts' own texts.

These terms explicitly support the view that conception occurs in cooperation between egg and sperm. Indeed, as one doctor said, "today everyone knows that it is actually the egg that attracts the sperm to it."

But although old ideas about male activity and female passivity are no longer found in gynecological texts, they occur instead in a more elusive way in the encounter between doctor and patient. Examples can be found in the medical information aimed at childless parents. In *Hjälp till graviditet* ("Assistance to Pregnancy") the reader is told that fertilization takes place in the Fallopian tube, "to which the sperm *have swum*," whereas "the egg cell *is transported* to the uterus" (Sundström 1992, italics mine).

What patients encounter while reading these texts, and what I observed them encountering at the clinics, indicated that there was a gap here between theory and practice, between the experts' doctrines and what happens in everyday hospital work. It is in the interplay between these different modes of thought that certain images of the man emerge, images that differ a great deal from the standard cultural profile of the man. Listen, for example, to how a midwife at an IVF clinic describes male patients:

> The man usually comes wandering in slightly behind and can be a bit arrogant. They don't look you in the eye when you talk to them. You can see they just want to disappear, and of course, having totally worthless sperm samples isn't easy. Then he just puts all the blame on himself. You feel really sorry for them, there's so much asked of them. But the girls, they're really positive and talk a lot while the man is very quiet. But then when the baby's born something clicks! He's most often the one who holds the baby, he really feels that he is someone again.

The midwife accurately recreates the atmosphere that marks men's and women's ways of dealing with the sensitive situation prevailing in the IVF clinic, a situation in which the man above all is part of a very special context. My male informants often express the feeling of helplessness provoked by the inability to produce children, an impotence that shows itself on many levels, not least in the waiting room. There is often a highly charged atmosphere here, as well as a very special interpretative template, which leads one's thoughts to the Male Gaze, but which should rather be described in terms of a Female Gaze.

Other health care staff also note the image of inequality that occurs among the couples, that the men stay a few paces behind their partners as they enter the reception area. Later, in the waiting room, they often sit "waiting, looking a bit sullen like these men often do," says a nurse. Sometimes the man's behavior causes wonder, but more commonly, the reaction among staff is that of criticism. It would be easy to interpret the situation at the clinic in the same way as the midwife above did, that is, as representative of natural male/female behavior, but if we are to bypass these stereotyped descriptions of gender roles, of contact-seeking women and quiet men, then it is important to develop a broader context.

In the Western world, pregnancy and the examinations associated with it are matters between the mother and the doctor. This institutionalization of giving birth has often resulted in a complicated relation between the individual and the health care apparatus, not least in terms of medical competence being represented by a male doctor with a female patient. In the medical arena, the father has been a figure in the background, seldom seen. His participation in the pregnancy has normally been limited to sexual intercourse, and in latter years, visits to the ultrasound tests and his presence in the delivery room. With assisted fertilization, the situation becomes totally altered. Male participation is removed to a clinical environment that is, in addition, a typically female arena, an arena that is charged not only with women's most special and intimate experiences, but also with these patients' vulnerability. For a childless man to find himself in an area dominated by women and in a subordinate position, he can easily experience aroused feelings of alienation and insecurity (cf. Hagström 1996).

This becomes all the more clear when one realizes that the man's presence, unlike the woman's, is for one clinical necessity only. When the woman is asked into a room, it can be for an interview, a blood test, or a gynecological examination. The male's participation, however, is limited to those occasions when he fills a lab glass with sperm or urine, regardless of whether it is he or the woman who is infertile. It is, after all, the woman who is the center of attention and who is to give birth to the baby. A male informant considered that "as a man you aren't worth much when you go in, it's all about her." Mats said, "I got there, gave my sperm and left; there wasn't really much else I could do." These men are forced to wait passively without any chance to become part of the chain of events, of reproduction.

The Threatened Sperm

Many analyses report the displeasure women may experience during gynecological examinations (Jordanova 1989). The men I met at the clinic were certainly not put in such physically vulnerable situations, but they experienced an awkward social exposure connected with the production (and examination) of their sperm. One man told me of the time he was to give sperm. With mug in hand, he was shown into the toilet, and he was then to turn off a light outside the room when he was finished. "I stood there knowing that everybody knew exactly what I was up to in there, everybody! It was terrible!"

Being brought, even temporarily, into the middle of this women's world after sitting on the perimeter is not easy for these men. This is apparent in the waiting room and even more so when confronted with the laboratory staff. One man told me about his humiliation when offered a microscope with which to observe his own sperm. "They wanted me to see for myself that there were only a few that functioned and that the others were slow; it didn't feel too good to see those poor slow ones that couldn't get in anywhere. It was like a big failure, because you know what they say," he added with a little embarrassed laugh, "that's where your manliness is" (cf. Petchesky 1987; Turkle 1996).[8]

This man knows that his sperm have to move fast to be able to make the connection with the egg. His "slow sperm" are deviants from the so-called norm. Normality is thus explained in both medical and colloquial terminology by the use of terms denoting competitiveness such as "spermal competition," "sperm rivalry," or "hurdle-racing" (Lundin 1997a).[9] These terms cause discomfort in many male patients, and this is not solely based on biological grounds—that their sperm is not wholly healthy—but also on uneasiness about the links between competition, battle, and manliness. The listless sperm serve to confirm not only an impaired bodily function, they also question the patient's manliness and identity. It was precisely this physical evidence of unmanliness that my informant observed through the microscopes.

When the man leaves a sperm sample and feels all the stares, a complex picture of masculinity is actualized. This concerns both those men who are the cause of a couple's childlessness and those men who donate sperm for fertilization. It is here that we can recognize the notion that male sexuality is a precondition for a child's inception. Without ejaculation and the release of semen, there is no sperm, and without sperm, there is no child. It is in this unavoidable connection between sexuality and the production of a child that the image of manhood is shaped. Here lies the physically obligatory connection between sexuality and masculinity, a construction that allows the sexual release to become a confirmation of male competence.

However, the lifeless sperm shows with great clarity how fragile this constructed connection is, how infertility leads to "a feeling of worthlessness in bed," as Mats says, and being "unmanly in every way." Poor semen not only destroys a future as a father, it penetrates the core of self-identity by calling into question the man's sexual prowess, his manliness. Such vulnerability is, as we have seen, contrary to what our culture usually associates with men in the image of the powerful life-giving man and the receptive woman. Parallel to this analysis that uncovers the fundamentals of patriarchal Western culture are the issues of male power and dominance. The possession of power often has a downside: the need for constant reaffirmation creates an anxiety over the loss of control. From this perspective, one can understand that many men—when they are placed in a kind of feminine subordinate situation at the IVF reception area, and are scrutinized by both the Male Gaze and the Female Gaze—create for themselves a shield of thorny silence. They can also feel helplessness or panic when their sperm is analyzed, their potency and power being called into question.

Constructing Parenthood

The link between reproduction and gender identity is different for men and women. Women's and men's infertility have always been painful, but women have, in addition to that, been the center of attention for a thorough treatment program. Their wombs have often been described as wells that can all too easily dry up. In the Swedish peasant society of the nineteenth century, childlessness was defined in the first instance as a woman's problem. The childless wife was a *gallko* ("a barren cow"), who brought misfortune on the marriage. Metaphors like this clearly suggest the female area of responsibility, which is to give birth to and bring up children.

If we listen to Eva's view of the absent pregnancy, when the childlessness was still assumed to be due to her, it is clear that she felt threatened not only as a person but also as a woman. The difference between Eva and her husband, and this is a frequently recurring pattern among other involuntarily childless couples, is that Eva's low self-esteem is not primarily related to her own sexuality but is associated with not being able to be a mother and with not being able to "have anyone to love who is a part of myself."

Eva and other women talk about how important it is to have an outlet for this feeling of sorrow, not having a child to take care of. This desire to "care for" is described by these women as an instinctive part of womanhood, as primeval as reproduction itself. In a woman's world, whether it be at the workplace or with relatives and friends, there is, as my informants as well as many studies point out, a great deal that revolves around the family (cf. Uddenberg 1982; Wirtberg 1992). Here, in contrast to how most men behave with each other, it is communication about children and family that is the entrance ticket to the social network. Not being able to offer any shared experiences, talk about the baby's colic, or exchange advice about the best diapers, draws attention to these women's biological and sociological exclusion (cf. Hagström 1996). Infertility becomes not only a hindrance to the production of a child but also to identification with a typical woman's role. Many childless women therefore experience life in a vacuum, leaving them socially paralyzed. Many, nevertheless, attempt to break out of this isolation by talking to their mothers, close friends, or other women in the same situation.

Men, however, often choose to remain silent about their infertility.[10] Near relatives may be informed, workmates less often. This silence grows out of cultural constructions that link fatherhood with sexuality, or to use another male informant's words, being childless is "being a failed stallion."

A Child That Looks Like Me

When Mats and Eva received the news that their childlessness was due to malformed sperm, they were forced into a whole new plan of action. Until this point, their thoughts had revolved around hormone therapy and even touched upon insemination. Eva had even pondered adoption, which is a real alternative for infertile women in Sweden, where the law forbids egg donation.[11]

Adoption had never been a viable alternative for Mats, however. From the moment when their involuntary childlessness became reality, his thoughts had hovered around the hope of a biological child against all the odds. This dream crashed with the news of Mats's poor sperm quality. No matter which strategy they chose, adoption or sperm donation, he would be cut off from the genetic links to any future child.

Mats and Eva's thoughts concerning the biological and social aspects of parenthood remind us how other childless couples view these issues. One usually finds a feeling of doubt about adoption, regardless of who is the cause of the childlessness. Lars, for example, thought this way: even though his wife's prospects of pregnancy aided by IVF were minimal, he favored this biomedical method as the only possible alternative. Another man, Gösta, who together with his wife was in treatment at the same Women's Clinic as Mats and Eva, stated how important it was to "first have something of your own," before even considering adoption.

It is probable that this yearning for a biological child originates from a general problem that is attached to the father's role in Western culture (cf. Stone 1997). In contrast to motherhood, fatherhood is characterized by an insecurity, a feeling of being slightly left out at the beginning because of the strong connection between mother and child. The father has always been surrounded by a certain biological uncertainty—to which various forms of paternity suits in the past and in the modern world bear witness.[12] It could be this insecurity that often leads men to prefer biomedical treatment. With the aid of technology, it is possible, as a childless man points out, "to be part of the symbiosis; I mean, the conception outside the body gives us [his wife and himself] the same experience." Further, for the first time in history it is now possible, with DNA profiles, to establish with almost total certainty who the father of a child is. This technique allows examination of genetic profiles in order to remove any doubt about family relationships.[13] Fatherhood can also be verified in even more concrete terms, says one doctor, "when the IVF couple go to the laboratory and see with their own eyes how sperm and egg join together. It's a bit strange that it is only through childlessness, when your body has left you up the creek, that you actually get a chance to grasp conception."

This is perhaps why so many childless men prefer assisted fertilization to adoption. It is clearly important for many men to receive confirmation of the physical kinship with the child. "A child of my own who looks like me" strengthens the connection between genetic reproduction and fatherhood, between biology and identity. Gösta, mentioned above, says that he wants to have something of his own, "but now I can consider adoption because I've got the evidence that we can have children ourselves."[14]

Sensitive Women and Rational Men

In both yesterday's and today's traditional women's role in the Western world, there is an inherent expectation of a natural caring mentality. This gender-distinct principle consequently affects the way our life is organized. As I have discussed above, this is a cultural construction linking reproduction with, on the one hand, female social competence and, on the other hand, male sexual competence.

These norms obviously do not prevent those childless women whose experiences I have discussed here (or their partners) from dreaming of a biological child. This wish is often described as a purely physical desire for a pregnant body, breasts heavy with milk, and fetal movements under the skin. The soon-to-be middle-aged Sigbritt describes with great insight this desire as a yearning to be taken away, "from the flat-breasted, officious, briefcase-carrying bureaucrats to the association of the wise and experienced, those who know."

But even in the face of such a powerful yearning for a motherhood firmly based upon the body, it is still possible to conjure up a more all-embracing feeling of parenthood. Many women maintain that they have a natural capacity to take care of children, their own and other women's. One woman told me that she would look after "any child who looked scared in the playground." Her husband, however, "would probably find it hard to take a direct liking to another child."

Where children are concerned, this natural empathy of women and instinctive doubtfulness of men is often expressed. Statements such as "women find it easier to look after other children because they're so sensitive" are paralleled by the idea that "men are more rational."

Many of today's notions about innate womanly and "real" manly characteristics are based upon a view of humanity that entails a clear division between body and intellect, between nature and culture. The human body is a well-known and commonly used metaphor for collective structures, an image in which the "head" is given the superior role, while the rest of the "body" is of necessary, although lesser, relevance.[15] This metaphor enables the description of the family organization and the consequent gender-specific values that infuse our culture. This is a question of a tacit cultural understanding whereby male attributes are welded to the intellectual productive sphere and women to the caring and reproductive functions (cf. Corea 1988). The family thus appears as an organic unit guided by the male head.

The genetically programmed "sensitive" woman and the reflective man surveying the prospects of parenthood manifest this dualistic value pattern. From this perspective it becomes easier to understand why my informants see the man's craving for a child of his own in terms of rationality; that is, that the reluctance about adoption is described as an intellectual act, not as an emotional expression of longing for a genetic link to the child.

This idea lets men give prominence to the importance of "having our own child" while their wives can feel that "the biological umbilical cord is strong but that adoption also creates an umbilical cord." Within the framework of this thought process, women can maintain their femininity in a variety of ways; biological motherhood can be replaced with that of social motherhood, which is inherent in adoption.[16] On the basis of their socially creative gender possibilities, all women thus possess the ability to participate in that association that Sigbritt mentions above, belonging "to those who know."

If we leave the discursive level, however, it becomes clear that the gender-determined ideas do not always correspond to my informants' everyday practice. Here we find instead men who are victims of their longing and need for a child of their own, and women who view adoption as a way to give a needy child a family and themselves a mother's role. The idea of sensitive women and rational men thereby has its counterpart in matter-of-fact women and emotional men.

Anachronistic Genetic Ideals

Today we live in a society that demands equality between the sexes in a way that is completely different from anything in the past. And even if there are justifiably many people who point out the lack of impact that these demands have had on society, there is a great difference between the late twentieth century and conditions in the previous century. Shared custody of children after divorce, shared parental benefits, common parental training courses, and diverse economic measures are only a few Swedish examples. Expectancy of equality even exists within people's love lives; this wish for mutual sensuality and passion reflects a specific state of affairs in modern society.

Spouses today work in different fields, in contrast to the previous century's agricultural society where husband and wife were held together by farming and other shared activities. When togetherness in work no longer plays the most important part in a relationship, then other links are required, such as love. However, the late twentieth century has not only resulted in a break from the framework of the family economy, but also a liberation from the necessary connection between reproduction and sexuality. As contraception allows sexuality without children, one can see that assisted fertilization allows children without sex. Giddens (1993) called this relation "plastic sexuality," and argued that the transformation of the love life also should be seen in the light of women's battles for equality; it thus holds the potential for emancipation.[17]

His reasoning is useful for understanding the importance placed on fertility, sexuality, and romance today; an intimacy is created here of a kind that was previously unseen, as is an emotional togetherness requiring care and attention. It is in this mutual project that the couple finds confirmation—when the man becomes a man and the woman emerges as a woman. It is a relationship in which both partners' needs are to be satisfied. Previous notions about passive women are being replaced with a new focus on both partners' common pleasure. A romantic institution such as this undoubtedly creates a situation of mutual dependency, in which each partner needs to see certain aspects of his or her own identity reflected in the other. Special requirements are demanded here, not least of all from the man. What was once his right to sexual discharge has been reshaped to an expectation of satisfying the woman's sexual desires and thereby sealing the romance.

An analysis of modern love and plastic sexuality provides us with a perspective from which to view the situation prevailing at IVF clinics. It is evident that present-day perceptions of men and women to a certain extent oppose childless people's own daily reality. Today's society is permeated even on a general level by different gender models. Among the many varying notions we have today, alongside those concerning gender equality and emancipation, is the notion that men have deeply rooted urges, impulses that are difficult to control, while women are ascribed a more controlled sexuality which easily turns them into erotic objects (cf. Salomonsson 1998).

The medical arena accentuates this confrontation between tenacious structures and modern ideas about gender equality. Technology's potential to allow women to become pregnant without sexuality may thus reduce women to receptacles, which as we have seen does not necessarily imply their subordination to the male partner. The male's childlessness, however, means that his potency is easily questioned. IVF sets new expectations on sexual competence—demands that, instead of arising from older phallocentric values or modern equality, concern the fact that these men are in demand as sperm producers (cf. Connell 1995). In this context, the concept of semen, and above all life-giving semen, is more than ever a sign of virility. And more than ever, the modern understanding of potency is linked to a noticeable perception of masculinity as being bound to biology.[18]

Earlier presumptions about men and women are thus actualized in the IVF clinic; images out of step with the outside world that is continually changing and developing with new material at hand. This implies that at the same time that childless couples go through IVF, they experience things lying outside the medical treatment. They assimilate something quite different from what one would have assumed. For example, when men look via the microscope into their bodies and see listless sperm, they obtain a medical perspective and a concrete picture of their (reduced) masculinity. This is a learning process that materializes otherwise vague conceptions about body and identity. Thus, in the IVF clinics not only children are produced but also normative ideas about gender and family. The clinic can be the site of remarkable connections between important questions and microprocesses, between cultural patterns and personal identity. The route through the treatment therefore becomes a highly existential journey, a biological and cultural learning process of an unforeseen nature.

Notes

1. My studies of artificial reproduction are largely based on interviews with childless couples and health service staff. The empirical material was collected from 1993 to 1997. The basis for

this chapter is a broad corpus of ethnological research material on reproductive technology (see Lundin 1995, 1996, 1997a, and 1997b). Unless otherwise stated, quotations come from my own interviews.

2. Sweden, Norway, and Germany are restrictive countries in terms of IVF. Traditional IVF is allowed, as is sperm donation. All other forms, for example, egg donation, surrogate mothering, or treatment of single women, are forbidden.

3. Foucault's discourse analysis and Derrida's deconstructionism have been important sources of inspiration as a starting point but are also open to question (Foucault 1973, 1981; Derrida 1986).

4. The first child by insemination was born in Germany in 1834. Today, there are various methods for depositing the sperm directly in the egg, such as Subzonal Insertion (SUZI), Partial Zonal Dissection (PZD), and Intracytoplasmic Sperm Injection (ICSI). Assisted fertilization nowadays involves men as well, to a large extent. At certain Swedish clinics, about 59 percent of the patients are men.

5. Compare also the situation in present-day cultures, for example, Sachs's (1993) discussion of the Singhalese outlook, according to which reproductive responsibility is not primarily ascribed to the individual's biological characteristics but is sought in the social environment. Similar causes could be cited in preindustrial Swedish peasant society; a woman's childlessness could be caused by someone putting the evil eye on her.

6. Laqueur (1994) discusses the links between reproduction and sexuality. He points out that the nineteenth century saw a growing scientific zeal to scrutinize human biology, interpreting women's sexuality as being of no significance for conception, while men's importance was stressed, with their potency playing a crucial role.

7. Nor were there any words that could lead the reader's thoughts to the reverse of the female ideal, the destroyer who lures and devours the man.

8. Petchesky (1987) observes how different optical equipment is presented as objective data (see also Turkle 1996).

9. Fighting terminology is also prevalent in the media (see Ideland 1997; Lakoff and Johnson 1980).

10. The State's public investigations use the following terms: "Insemination has until now been carried out behind closed doors, the aim being that no outsiders should be able to find out that insemination has taken place. Reproduction through insemination has obviously been seen as embarrassing to a certain extent. Due to this approach parents involved with insemination have been unable to discuss the process with anyone outside the clinic." SOU 1983 42:94 (see Wirtberg 1992).

11. According to Swedish law today, egg donation is forbidden but is still under investigation. Insemination with the husband's sperm is allowed, as is sperm donation (see Statens Medicinsk-Etiska Råd 1995).

12. Historian Gillis states that this insecurity leads to specific rituals. In England during the eighteenth century, the man was enjoined to take on the caring parental role, to arrange the birth and look after the baby (Gillis 1992). One could even discuss if this insecurity is something that today's women can suffer from; egg donation and surrogate mothering alter women's preconceived biological functions and can possibly therefore create new motherhood patterns.

13. DNA profiling (according to the English company University Diagnostic Limited in London) is aimed at those who wish to identify their true father or mother, those who are involved in cases of disputed paternity, and those who wish to confirm their family relationships to satisfy immigration requirements (see Marteau and Richards 1996: 254–55). In Sweden, the Department of Forensic Medicine deals with these issues.

14. Many infertile men, for whom sperm donation is an alternative, choose IVF rather than adoption. This form of assisted conception also seems to confirm a sense of belonging and fatherhood. Several men point out that they feel involved, since the wife is pregnant and they can thus follow a biological process. The longing for equality with the child can moreover be better satisfied by IVF than by adoption. Adopted children in Sweden are usually of a different ethnic

origin from their Swedish parents. When choosing sperm donation, the couple can be sure that the donor belongs to the same ethnic group as themselves. This increases the chances of physical similarity between fathers and children (Lundin 1997a).

15. Most systems describe leaders such as statesmen or religious heads whose duty is to control the people; this kind of symbolism is very powerful—the association with the body allowing the metaphor to appear as pure and immovable as the biological prototype (cf. Douglas 1966; Zelizer 1993; Åkesson 1997).

16. As I have pointed out in other contexts in a way similar to this, women who concentrate totally on motherhood through IVF actualize precisely this biological possibility (Lundin 1996). The image of the pregnant and breast-feeding woman is in focus here (see Ragoné 1994).

17. Giddens (1993) discusses the transformation of the love life as a result of women's battles for equality. Plastic sexuality is Giddens's term for decentered sexuality, freed from the needs of reproduction. "It frees sexuality from the rule of the phallus, from overweening importance of male sexual experience" (1993: 2). Giddens's discussion of gender is important but at the same time too harmonizing. As many feministic and gender-oriented studies point out, the phallocentric mental concept is even today one of the most important foundations of Western culture.

18. When we unveil the mechanisms that shape prototypes of men and women, their biological essentialism, it is easy to see just these specific categories and not the dynamic relation that exists in between. In other words, the woman is always given the subordinate role, and the man is exposed to the Female Gaze. An altogether biased gender deconstruction can result in new unequivocal truths whereby gender concepts apply to bygone days or to other societies; that is, that the mental construct of the rational man and the caring woman appears as a historical constant.

References

Åkesson, Lynn. 1997. *Mellan levande och döda. Föreställningar om kropp och ritual.* Stockholm: Natur och Kultur.

Beck, Ulrich, and Elisabeth Beck-Gernsheim. 1995. *The Normal Chaos of Love.* Cambridge, U.K.: Polity.

Butler, Judith. 1990. *Gender Trouble. Feminism and the Subversion of Identity.* London: Routledge & Kegan Paul.

Connell, Robert W. 1995. *Masculinities.* Cambridge, U.K.: Polity.

Corea, Gena. 1988. *The Mother Machine—Reproductive Technologies from Artificial Insemination to Artificial Wombs.* London: Women's Press.

Derrida, Jacques. 1986. *La loi du genre.* Paris: Parages.

Dofs Sundin, Monica. 1995. Den födande mannen—provrörsbefruktning i Hollywood. *Häften för kritiska studier* 4:58–70.

Douglas, Mary. 1966. *Purity and Danger.* London: Routledge & Kegan Paul.

Ernald Netterfors, Sigbritt, and Inger Hallén. 1994. *Barnen som aldrig blev.* Stockholm: Alfabeta.

Fjell, Tove Ingebjorg. 1988. *Fødselens gjenfødelse. Fra teknologi til natur på fødearenaen.* Kristiansand: Høyskoleforlaget.

Foucault, Michel. 1973. *The Birth of the Clinic. An Archeology of Medicine Perception.* London: Tavistock.

———. 1981. *The History of Sexuality. An Introduction.* Vol. 1. New York: Penguin.

Franklin, Sarah. 1993. Making Representations: The Parliamentary Debate on the Human Fertilization and Embryology Act. In *Technologies of Procreation: Kinship in the Age of Assisted Conception,* ed. Jeanette Edwards, Sarah Franklin, Eric Hirsch, Frances Price, and Marilyn Strathern. Manchester, U.K.: Manchester University Press.

Frykman, Jonas. 1991. Pappa kom hem. In *Pappa och jag,* ed. C. J. de Geer. Stockholm: Sesam.

Giddens, Anthony. 1993. *The Transformation of Intimacy. Sexuality, Love, and Eroticism in Modern Societies.* Cambridge, U.K.: Polity.

Gillis, John. 1992. Bringing up Father. Britisk faderidentiteter fra 1750 til i dag. *Den jyske historiker* 58–59:149–76.

Hagström, Charlotte. 1996. Becoming a Father and Establishing Paternity. In *Body Time: On the Interaction of Body, Identity, and Society*, ed. Susanne Lundin and Lynn Åkesson. Lund: Lund University Press.

Haraway, Donna Jeanne. 1997. *Modest Witness @ Second Millennium. Female Man Meets Onco-Mouse: Feminism and Technoscience.* New York: Routledge.

Ideland, Malin. 1997. Kroppssamhället—om genetikens metaforer. *Kulturella Perspektiv* 1:14–24.

Jay, Martin. 1993. *Downcast Eyes: The Denigration of Vision in Twentieth-Century French Thought.* Berkeley: University of California Press.

Johannisson, Karin. 1994. *Den mörka kontinenten. Kvinnan, medicinen och fin de siècle.* Stockholm: Nordstedts.

Jordanova, Ludmilla. 1989. *Sexual Visions: Images of Gender in Science and Medicine between the Eighteenth and Twentieth Centuries.* London: Harvester.

Koch, Lene. 1989. *Ønskebarn. Kvinder & reagensglasbefrugtning.* Charlottenlund: Rosinante.

Lakoff, George, and Mark Johnson. 1980. *Metaphors We Live by.* Chicago: University of Chicago Press.

Laqueur, Thomas. 1994. *Om könens uppkomst. Hur kroppen blev kvinnlig och manlig,* trans. Oejevind Lang. Stockholm/Stehag: Symposion.

Lundin, Susanne. 1995. Längtan efter social och biologisk identitet. *Kvinnovetenskaplig tidskrift* 1:34–42.

———. 1996. Power over the Body. In *Body Time: On the Interaction of Body, Identity, and Society,* ed. Susanne Lundin and Lynn Åkesson. Lund: Lund University Press.

———. 1997a. Visions of the Body. In *Gene Technology and the Public. An Interdisciplinary Perspective,* ed. Susanne Lundin and Malin Ideland. Lund: Nordic Academic Press.

———. 1997b. *Guldägget. Föräldraskap i biomedicinens tid.* Lund: Historiska Media.

Lundgren, Britta, Inger Lövkrona, and Lena Martinsson. 1996. *Åtskilja och förena. Etnologisk forskning om betydelsen av kön.* Stockholm: Carlsson.

Marsiglio, William. 1995. *Fatherhood: Contemporary Theory, Research, and Social Policy.* London: Sage.

Marteau, Theresa, and Martin Richards. 1996. *The Troubled Helix. Social and Psychological Implications of the New Human Genetics.* Cambridge, U.K.: Cambridge University Press.

Martin, Emily. 1987. *The Woman in the Body: A Cultural Analysis of Reproduction.* Boston: Beacon.

Merchant, Carolyn. 1989. *The Death of Nature: Woman, Ecology and the Scientific Revolution.* San Francisco: Harper and Row.

Neely, Barbara. 1984. A Yenga Tale. In *Test-Tube Women: What Future for Motherhood?*, ed. Rita Arditti, Renate Duelli Klein, and Shelley Minden. London: Pandora.

Nordborg, Gudrun. 1991. Läkarmakten över moderskapet. *Retfærd* 52:75–89.

Petchesky, Rose. 1987. The Silent Screen. In *Reproductive Technologies. Gender, Motherhood, and Medicine,* ed. Michelle Stanworth. Cambridge, U.K.: Polity.

Price, Frances. 1993. Beyond Expectation: Clinical Practices and Clinical Concerns. In *Technologies of Procreation. Kinship in the Age of Assisted Conception,* ed. Jeanette Edwards, Sarah Franklin, Eric Hirsch, Frances Price, and Marilyn Strathern. Manchester, U.K.: Manchester University Press.

Ragoné, Heléna. 1994. *Surrogate Motherhood. Conception in the Heart.* Boulder, Colo.: Westview.

Rapp, Rayna. 1993. Accounting for Amniocentesis. In *Knowledge, Power & Practice: The Anthropology of Medicine and Everyday Life,* ed. Shirley Lindenbaum and Margaret Lock. Berkeley: University of California Press.

Rose, Hilary. 1994. *Love, Power, and Knowledge; Toward a Feminist Transformation of Science.* Cambridge, U.K.: Polity.

Sachs, Lisbeth. 1993. Sjukdom, diagnos och terapi: En kamp mellan onda och goda krafter. In *Ondskans etnografi*, ed. Lena Gerholm and Thomas Gerholm. Stockholm: Carlsson Bokfoerlag.

Salomonsson, Karin. 1998. *Fattigdommens besvärjelse*. Lund: Historiska Media.

Showalter, Elaine. 1992. *Sexual Anarchy: Gender and Culture at the Fin de Siècle*. London: Virago.

Statens Medicinsk-Etiska Råd. 1995. *Assisterad befruktning. Synpunkter på vissa frågor i samband med befruktning utanför kroppen*. Stockholm.

Statens Offentlinga Utrednigar. *SOU* 1983:42.

Stone, Linda. 1997. *Kinship and Gender: An Introduction*. Boulder, Colo.: Westview.

Strathern, Marilyn. 1992. *Reproducing the Future. Anthropology, Kinship, and the New Reproduction Technologies*. Manchester, U.K.: Manchester University Press.

Sundström, Per. 1992. *Hjälp till graviditet*. Malmö: Curakliniken.

Turkle, Sherry. 1996. *Life on the Screen. Identity in the Age of the Internet*. London: Weidenfeld and Nicholson.

Uddenberg, Nils. 1982. *Den urholkade fadern. En bok om män och fortplantning*. Stockholm: Wahlström and Widstrand.

Uvnäs-Moberg, Kerstin, and Rigmor Robert. 1996. *Hon & han födda olika*. Stockholm: Bromberg.

Winston, Robert. 1996. *Making Babies: A Personal View of IVF Treatment*. London: BBC Books.

Wirtberg, Ingegerd. 1992. *His and Her Childlessness*. Stockholm: Karolinska Institutet.

Zelizer, Barbie. 1993. From Body as Evidence to the Body of Evidence. In *Bodylore*, ed. Katherine Young. Knoxville: University of Tennessee Press.

Chapter Nine

Mischief on the Margins:
Gender, Primogeniture, and
Cognatic Descent among the Maori

Karen Sinclair

Cognatic descent has puzzled anthropologists for over a century.[1] Accustomed to neat unilineal systems, which often were the bases for both affiliation and residence, cognatic descent presented them with new questions. Were the groups formed corporate in nature? Given the choice of descent through males or females, under what conditions were these groups formed either way? Early researchers also noted a "patrilineal bias" (a preference for patrilocal residence and transmission of property to patrilineal descendants [Stone 1997]) in many cognatic systems. Some scholars then came to view cognatic systems as similar to patrilineal ones, though more "flexible," allowing different residence choices and shifting affiliations so that precarious resources could be better exploited (Keesing 1975). In this view, the idea of descent group recruitment through women emerged as a cognatic system's "second best," though a sometimes useful choice.

Missing from these earlier studies was an understanding of the complex dynamics of cognatic descent within the broader context of social structure. In addition, viewing cognatic systems through a "patrilineal lens" prevented scholars from seeing what is perhaps most interesting about these systems, namely the intersections between kinship and gender. This chapter discusses these intersections and places them within a broader context of social structure among the cognatic Maori of New Zealand in precolonial times.

Before British rule, the Maori were a highly stratified society organized into chiefdoms. Rank was extremely important and superceded gender in that women, though inferior to men of their own rank, were superior to lower-ranking men. Maori cognatic descent groups were internally stratified; the highest-ranking male (the chief) was ideally a man descended from a founding ancestor through a pure line of patrilineal descent and primogeniture, or succession of eldest sons.

Primogeniture was an important principle in indigenous Maori society. Firstborn sons of senior males were simultaneously held in high regard and were responsible for perpetuating descent groups and the larger social system. *Tohi* (birth/initiation) rituals were performed for all new male members of the society but differed according to the rank of the newborn and the social position he was expected to occupy. Through these rituals, status, indeed legitimacy, was bestowed on parents, the descent group, and ultimately upon the Maori social system itself. Firstborn males were initiated into the system through special *tohi* rituals that sanctified them as social beings. By implication, other categories of persons (those who did not undergo these rituals) were perceived as potentially antisocial, in some way threatening the order and coherence of the system.

While Maori cultural ideology exalted the lofty and legitimate position of firstborn males, women and younger brothers nevertheless figure prominently in Maori mythology. In almost all cases, their appearances herald creative, generative, transformative feats, while their positions within the social system were suspect and ambiguous. There is, then, a discrepancy between the cultural dogma (descent ideology) and myth: the most legitimate characters in terms of dogma, that is, eldest sons, have a secure place in and perpetuate the social system, while the socially more marginal are highlighted in the mythology. An examination of this discrepancy leads us into the basic structures of Maori cosmology. There it becomes clear that women and younger brothers are indeed marginal beings eluding classification. Yet their creative and generative powers not only give them prominence in myth, these same powers carry implications for the ways in which cognatic descent groups can be configured. Thus, the danger that women and later-born sons pose is not only a mythological phenomenon; they present real dangers to the social system itself. The *tohi* rituals smooth over the contradictions of Maori society, insisting that order and inevitability will triumph over disorder and contingency.

To elucidate these points, I first briefly describe Maori social structure and the tensions that result between ascription, or the preferred and ritually sanctioned mode of inheritance and descent group replacement, and achievement. From there I turn to the mythology to see how this tension is given expression and I also examine the cosmological structures that emerge. Finally, I investigate the social and cosmological ways through which women and younger brothers threaten a cultural system that so carefully employs ideology and ritual to exclude them. That the cosmos may be used to control and constrain women is certainly not a new insight (see Douglas 1975), but its power over less fortunate (in this case lower-ranking) men has not been examined in any detail. The Maori case provides us with precisely this information, for in this case, an entire cosmological system has as its goal (admittedly one among many) the restriction and limitation of those not born to wield power and authority.

Our knowledge of precolonial Maori social structure is in large part derived from the reports of early missionaries, ethnographers, and government agents; these documents were produced, then, by the very agents of colonial-ism that transformed the society and culture. These sources reflect both a male and a British Victorian bias and therefore fail to recognize or acknowl-edge the importance of women. Indeed, for many years, it appeared to be ax-iomatic that Maori women did not hold power, but were themselves inimical to its presence. Hence, women were banned from unfinished construction sites, while menstruating women were prohibited from any area where food was to be found. It was presumed that men were powerful, while women were simultaneously inefficacious and threatening to the exercise of male potency.[2]

In the past twenty years, there have been new approaches to our under-standing of women and their problematic cultural construction. Buckley and Gottlieb's *Blood Magic* (1988) addressed the complex and intricate relation-ships between power and pollution. For the Maori, Hanson's (1982) work pro-vided an innovative examination of women's restrictions, constraints, and rit-ual efficacy, showing that women have a mixed nature—one that evades classification and that, in itself, merits examination for issues of potency and effectiveness.

Maori Social Structure

Importance and prestige in precolonial Maori society was a direct function of genealogical distinction, which was derived from primogeniture, seniority of descent, male line descent, and genealogical depth (Goldman 1970: 35; see also Hiroa 1962). Primogeniture in the senior line bestowed access to chiefly rank. The firstborn son was known as the *matamua* ("elder," "first," "fore-limb") and was the official chiefly heir in high-ranking families. While the firstborn woman could hold an honorific title (*tapairu*), she was not, except in the rarest of cases, eligible for chiefly office. Moreover, the respect owed to seniority was permanent; all descendants from older brothers retained ge-nealogical ascendancy over descendants of younger brothers. Senior brothers and senior lines were referred to as *tuakana* and controlled titles, while younger brothers and junior lines were called *teina* and were, in Goldman's words, "in permanent subordination" (Goldman 1970: 36).

A separate term designated descent lines made up solely of senior males and their descendants. The term *ure tu*—upright penis—is a striking expres-sion of male sexuality that conferred extraordinarily high status. Yet such a unique designation suggests something out of the ordinary and particularly worthy of deference, reflecting how infrequently a purely male line comprised of eldest sons actually occurs in a cognatic system and what special recogni-tion it commands when it does appear. Goldman (1970: 37) wrote:

> When the Maori designated such an extraordinary line as *ure tu* they were graph-ically depicting the directness of descent in earthly imagery. We recognize as well the religious association of masculine *mana* [ritual power or authority] with the

specific fecundity and vigor that chiefly descent (the bone of the lineage) gives to their descendants. As the erect penis it was singly appropriate for the distinguished line of chiefs to stand apart from all others.

Rank had a religious dimension that was expressed in terms of *mana*. Political authority, prestige, and influence were all a consequence of one's *mana*, which was bestowed by the gods at birth, but secured only after one's birth rituals had been carried out properly.[3] A firstborn, with the advantages of high rank and ceremonial protection in the form of the *tohi* ritual, might appear to have had his future position well secured. However, *mana* was a variable condition, augmented by great deeds and diminished by defeat and disgrace. Thus, while firstborns carried definite advantages, their younger brothers stood to gain an edge by sheer ability. "Numerous examples are recorded of low born individuals achieving high status by virtue of exceptional ability and because 'power vacuums' were constantly occurring in Maori society as results of warfare and historical change" (Jackson 1978: 352; but see also Best 1975 and Firth 1973).

In fact, Jackson (1978: 352) goes so far as to recommend that *mana* obtained from seniority of descent, or ascription, should be analytically distinguished from *mana* based on achievement. Such a distinction is not confined to the kinship system. The tension between genealogical status and individual ability also receives considerable attention in mythology. Interestingly, and I think significantly, the feats of younger brothers share a mythological and social domain with those of women, suggesting that in both social life and in mythology, this pair is able to destabilize the ideal workings of the social system. Specifically, the most famous younger brother is Maui, a culture hero and trickster found throughout the Pacific. Here, I am only concerned with the New Zealand versions of the myths. I use those versions considered to be the most important, namely those that, because they were considered to be sacred, were not designated for a European audience.

Women and Younger Brothers in Mythology

The two creative forces of the Maori mythological world are the linked pair of Maui and Hine Nui Te Po (Great Lady of the Night). Both are mediators, both possess dual natures, both elude the boundaries and classifications that define the Maori cosmos, and perhaps most importantly, both are creators and destroyers.

The exploits of Maui and Hine Nui Te Po need to be understood within the context of the mythology of creation. In one creation myth, after the universe has been given its present form, Tane, the son of the Sky Father and Earth Mother, searches in vain in the sky for a woman who would be his mate. With his father's advice and his mother's guidance, he fashions a woman out of clay, breathes life into her nostrils, and takes her as his wife.

It is of great importance that the female does not originate in the sky but instead is generated from earthly materials. Schwimmer (1966: 17) wrote:

> This tells us a great deal about the Maori world order. We already know that there are two basic opposites in this world order. They first appeared as Sky and Earth, Male and Female, earth being the female. Now we see Tane looking in the sky for the female being he needs. It is not surprising that he cannot find it there; for the female element is on the earth. But in refusing [Tane's request for a women from the sky] Rangi [the Sky Father] gives a new name to earth, namely, "the realm of fate" (*whare o aitua*) while he calls sky the "realm of life" (*whare o te ora*). Thus he allots to the earth those beings that are transitory and subject to death while the sky becomes the realm of the permanent, the undying.

As the myth proceeds, women move away from the world of life and light and become connected to darkness and death. Tane and Hine-ahu-one (Earth Formed Maid) produce a daughter, Hine Titama (the Dawn Maid). In time, she too becomes the wife of Tane. Her shame, when she discovers the truth of her relationship with her father/husband, compels her to move into the world of darkness and to leave behind, forever and for others, the world of life and light. Henceforth she will be known as Hine Nui Te Po, Great Lady of the Night, and her descendants will know death. Mortality has entered the human condition and a woman is its agent.[4]

Several oppositions emerge here that begin to define the Maori cosmos. There is the world of life, found above, associated with a masculine principle. By contrast, the realm of Fate, of death, is found below and is linked to femininity. The underworld, associated with death and darkness, is also the realm of disorder and misfortune. These values are paralleled by and echoed in the spatial orientation of the cosmos so that the heaven, the realm of the sky, the dimension above, carries with it concomitant values of order and rightness. In opposition to this, notions of chaos and defeat are connected to the lower realms. Other lexical associations of darkness suggest decay, rottenness, loss of control (Salmond 1978: 12).

Against this backdrop, Maui and Hine Nui Te Po (henceforth, Hine) are linked from the midpoint to the end of a sequence of five myths that culminates in Hine's triumph over Maui. The first myths, which deal with Maui's creative feats, often at the expense of women (discussed below), occur on earth. The third story represents a transition in which Maui begins his journey on earth but travels to the underworld on a secret mission to discover the whereabouts of his parents. The last two myths take place below, in Hine's domain, and lead to his destruction. The five myths, therefore, display a pattern of two in which the action occurs above, a transition, and two in which Hine and Maui meet below.

The Maui cycle has been examined by Thornton (1987: 77), a classicist who not only sees Homeric parallels, but who is able to penetrate the Maori cosmos through her understanding of the language and the culture. She pointed out that in one version, the Maui cycle is a cosmogonic narrative. Maui's exploits make human life possible by establishing the length of the day, the breadth of the earth, and ultimately humanity's mortality. A trickster, Maui is also an important creator, guiding and forming much of the human landscape. "Through his endeavors society became possible; nature was harnessed and put to the service of man" (Jackson 1978: 353).

However, as both Orbell (1995) and Jackson (1978) have pointed out, Maui, a younger brother, is a miscarriage, a creature that in the Maori cosmos arouses fear and premonitions of danger: such beings have no loyalty to kinship groups, and as we shall see, this is Maui's primary social and metaphysical feature (Orbell 1995). Even before his career begins, Maui resists ready definition: at birth, he is given up for dead, but he survives and is raised throughout his childhood by both gods and humans. He prevails, despite his mother's conviction that he is dead, and is raised by the gods, only to return to his family once he has matured. Maui means left-handed, the neutral (*noa*) as opposed to the ritually marked (*tapu*) side of the body. We see in the lexical associations with Maui a conjunction of younger brothers, *noa*, and left-handedness, instead of the ideals of elder brothers, *tapu*, and right-sidedness that govern the cosmos and social relations.

In his first exploit, Maui steals a human jawbone and harnesses it in the service of mankind. He uses the jawbone to slow the sun (thereby making the day longer)[5] and to fish up New Zealand out of the sea.[6] Jawbone, *kauae* in Maori, refers not only to the left-handed aspect of Maui, but also to social structure, for it is a prefix to *kauaeraro*, which means younger brother, or *kauaemua*, elder brother. In other words, embedded in the myth are allusions to the kinship hierarchy that marks Maori social life. The use of a jawbone in the Maui myth, rather than some other appendage, is significant. For not only does Maui perform a deed that is beyond the scope of most mortals, he does so with a piece of human anatomy that brings us back, through lexical and cosmological meanings, to descent. The lower jawbone represents the strength of the ancestors and recalls the solidity and perpetuity of descent groups.

The other word for jawbone, *paewai*, indicates a person of importance and relies on metaphors of house structure. These images suggest house building, families, and meeting houses (a critical aspect of Maori sociality and ritual life). The lexicon leads us into family life with values of solidity, support, and legitimacy, values that Maui at once reinforces by making social life possible and undermines by his persistent position outside social boundaries and his constant summoning forth of the very forces (achievement, creativity) that challenge the cultural order. With Maui, perpetuity, legitimacy, and solidity are ironically embodied in a *younger* brother, one whose next exploit allows us to see that he is capable and willing to take critical Maori ideals and simultaneously sustain and destabilize them.

Maui's second feat involves the stealing of fire from a very important woman.[7] In one version, this woman is Hine herself. Hine is associated with fire (*hika*, explained below). The fire in this myth, to be given to humanity, is found on Hine's fingertips, her margins, that aspect of her where she begins and ends, where her dual nature is most obvious, and where she is most vulnerable.

In the third myth, Maui tricks his parents by shutting out the dawn, the time when they were to retreat to their underground home. This tactic allows him to follow his parents to their subterranean abode, an act that, of course, now allies Maui through his parents to the underworld. This is a significant transition, for it not only involves Maui's movement between above and below, but it also demonstrates his dual nature.

In the fourth myth, Maui's father, having discovered his son's duplicity, decides to perform the *tohi* rite. This is done in the underworld. At a critical juncture, his father makes a mistake and the ritual is not completed. As a result, Maui is permanently removed from and must remain forever outside the social order.[8] Moreover, during Maui's inauspicious *tohi* ritual, Hine's fiery genitals are seen on the horizon, a deadly omen. The already marginal position of Maui is now given further cosmological expression (Thornton 1987, 1992). Maui is neither natural nor social, having an ambiguous birth status and a failed social initiation. Unlike thoroughly social and socialized beings, Maui is now free to move through the cosmos, emphasizing all the while the strength of ability, of achievement, at the expense of order and ascription (Jackson 1978: 349).

In the fifth myth, Maui is in the underground, the realm of Hine, a goddess with whom he has met up before and with whom he has unique commonalities. The myths have set him up for the final battle, positioning him appropriately and allowing us to know his dual nature. In the hope of assailing and overcoming Hine and thereby eliminating human mortality, Maui's strategy is one of invasion: he will enter the sleeping Hine's vagina and defeat her once and for all.

In Maui's confrontation with Hine (the goddess of death and darkness), we have a return to the original gendered universe that appeared with the separation of the Earth Mother from the Sky Father and the absence in the sky of a suitable mate for Tane: man procreates and woman cuts off life (Thornton 1992). Maui seeks a reverse birth, a journey that will negate the existence of death: by entering through Hine's sexual organs, a successful journey would allow Maui to traverse Hine internally and exit through her mouth. His failure, which is inevitable, leads both to Maui's destruction and the ensured continuation of mortality as part of the human condition.

There is almost no chance that he will survive. The lightning flashes that were apparent during his *tohi* ceremony prove to be fiery blazes emanating from Hine's genitals. If the *tohi* ritual suggests a transition from asocial to social being, Hine herself characterizes the transition between birth and death. And once more, the Maori lexicon leads us to the necessary associations: *hika* means "fire," a definitive connection to Hine. It also suggests the act of love-making, which was traditionally like making fire, done by both a man and a woman. In addition, *hika* summons forth notions of female sexuality and, finally, we arrive at the place we started—lines of descent. Hine and Maui have already met and fought with fire in the second myth. At that point, Maui won. At this juncture, Hine wins. Maui urges the birds (his companions) to be silent as he embarks on his perilous, if somewhat ludicrous, journey. However, the sight of Maui preparing to enter the recumbent goddess proves too much for the birds' restraint. Their laughter awakens Hine who encloses Maui within her body, and in so doing, kills him.

In his entire career, Maui's concerns, despite his outsider status, have been symbolically linked to descent lines. We must also bear in mind that it was the confusion of descent and kinship (the conflation of father and husband) that caused Hine to leave the realm of light and enter darkness. No matter how complex the myths, descent and female reproduction have remained constant themes.

The movement of both Hine and Maui in the marginal arenas of the cosmos is both creative and destructive. Maui is responsible for many of the attributes that make human social life possible, while the underworld provides such distinctly cultural provisions as tattooing, carving, and feather cloaks. Thus, both Maui and Hine merge the cultural and the natural, the human and the divine. In the most profound ways, they are each responsible for life and death, creation and degeneration.

What do these two characters, Maui and Hine, have in common? Why do they, indeed why must they, appear together? These are powerful individuals who, in almost all ways, resist categorization. They do not fit, and it is here that their power is to be located. Indeed, Hine is, as Thornton (1987: 84) points out, a composite monster, the granddaughter of the heavens who is now a dangerous source of death and destruction. Maui and Hine each stand on and represent a threshold, a transformation of being. Note the dual-natured aspect of Hine, a goddess transmogrified into a monster, while Maui himself is an asocial trickster who never completely joins the social order. An ambiguous figure, neither god nor man, raised by human and divine forces, Maui moves in unrestricted ways in domains ordinarily closed to mortals. He resists definition as either human or social.[9] Furthermore, both Hine and Maui employ antisocial essences to social ends: Maui is asocial and yet promotes aspects of life that facilitate human society, while Hine, dangerous and threatening in a way that only women can be, is essential to and defines the human condition, in her role as procreator and as goddess of death.

Hine too is a mediator. For she is a feminine principle signifying simultaneously life and death. In the earlier myth, we followed Tane's search for a woman and learned that mortality and life have a profound connection. Fertility and creativity are to be found along with vulnerability and chaos. Through the myth we discover the simple message: women both give life and take it away; they are life-givers and death-dealers. Maui and Hine are both powerful mediators who, in resisting classification, effect a reconciliation and underscore the chasm between the divine and human, life and death. In the fifth myth, a powerful boundary or threshold, the vagina, separates life and death. On one side of the portal is Maui, celebrant of life and humanity, on the other side lies death and defeat. Similarly spatial dimensions have been maintained: Maui has left the world of light above to attempt to conquer Hine in the depths of darkness. It is fitting that this significant battle is waged on such a powerful boundary. For as women represent life and death, the vagina becomes an important metaphor for describing woman's dual nature: it is at the same time the most sacred and profane part of a woman. This admixture of holiness and pollution is the very essence of the sacred. Female sexual organs are potent then both because of their generative power and because of the danger inherent in their ambiguity. For while the vagina invokes the imagery of life and birth, it bears equally strong intimations of sex and death. Thus, the vagina is referred to as *whare o aitua*, "the house of death, of misfortune" (Biggs 1960: 2). Similarly Johansen (1954: 220) wrote: "In Best's [1975] material it is confirmed that the genitals not only of Hine Nui te Po but of all women have death in them. The genitals of woman are 'killers of man' it says expressly, and they are denoted by words like *rua iti* and *whawhaia* which denote black magic."

An extremely ambiguous symbol, the vagina is powerful precisely because it resists classification. Thus, in death life may be affirmed, as at birth death is implied. Symbolically, women encompass many opposing notions in Maori culture. Their ambiguity is further heightened because they summon forth conventions regarding life and death, fertility and sexuality, creativity and pollution.

It is not surprising then that maleness and ascription are discussed in terms of purity, while femaleness and achievement are "suspect and expressed in terms of impurity and pollution" (Smith 1974: 70), for pollution is an apt metaphor for those aspects of the system that are out of control and most threatening. Indeed, legitimacy is the province solely of the senior male. However, while the ideology suggests that pollution is almost always destructive, Jackson (1978: 354) cautioned us to pay attention to its creative elements: "Travel across boundary lines when subject to intellectual and ritual control serves to regenerate the system and assist differentiation; it does not devastate the system." In the rituals for the firstborn son we see how this is accomplished.

Rituals for Firstborns

Firstborn sons of senior lines went through several rituals, all of which demonstrated not only their importance, but reasserted the fundamental structure of society and of the cosmos. Much of the ritual is designed to separate the male child from the night world of spirit, the danger of contact with blood and the feminine principle. Indeed, the darkness associated with Hine and the female principle, te Po, was conceived as a womb in which new life was generated. Hence, it is the realm not only of endings, but of beginnings. The child is welcomed into the world of light, which contrasts with the world of darkness he has left behind. So too, he moves into life on a journey that makes him more social as it removes him from association with decay and degeneration. The rituals acknowledge that he has crossed a powerful threshold, literally the vagina, metaphysically a boundary between life and death, lightness and darkness. In his chants, the ritual specialist (*tohunga*) recalls the time of the creation of woman. Thus, Best (1975: 23) wrote: "This address to the infant welcomes him as emerging from the sheltered haven of the embryo, as having crossed the threshold formed by Tane when he fashioned the first woman from a portion of the body of the Earth Mother."

The next ritual takes place when the umbilical cord falls off, approximately eight days after birth. Free now of any connection with his mother, the child is submerged in water, a typical Maori ritual of purification. As a male child, he is held by the right hand— representing strength and vitality—and is "called upon to enter into the tapu sphere of influence from the Supreme Being, the realm of light and life and therein acquire all high class knowledge" (Best 1975: 31–32). This ritual confers *tapu* (ritual potency) and *mana* upon the child, who through these rituals has been placed in the hands of the gods. At these rituals, important cultural objects, greenstone ornaments and carved weapons, are laid out on cloaks. The entire ensemble is considered extremely sacred, for it embodies ancestral power, and in many ways manifests cultural achievement. Women, even the mother, are expressly forbidden to sit on the mats.

The final ritual—the *pure* ritual—renders the child brave in war. Here, rituals separate the male child from the night world of spirit (Po), bring him into the human world, and endow him with the characteristics of a warrior. The rituals are the same as those that warriors used to undergo before and after battle. Birth, like warfare, is a kind of human triumph, an appropriation of divine life by mankind (Sahlins 1985).

In making the transition from darkness to light, the child becomes a warrior (or in some cases a cultivator); he leaves the world of women, enters the world of men, and becomes, in short, a social creature. Only the firstborn undergoes these rituals, suggesting that others who have not been separated from the dangerous darkness of the Po, who have not had the gods invoked to give them *mana*, are somehow less than social, less than legitimate.

Women are prohibited from attendance at the more esoteric aspects of the rituals, or at least nineteenth-century observers reported their absence. But their presence was there in other ways, namely, in the cloaks on which the rituals were carried out and that were designed and made exclusively by women. Weiner (1992) indicates that cloaks are women's "inalienable possessions" and as such, are empowered to act as the source of difference and hierarchy.

Once again, social structure and femininity are conjoined. Weiner pointed out that the term *kahu* means "cloak" as well as "the membrane that surrounds the fetus." *Kahukahu* is "the germ of a human being, the spirit of the deceased ancestor, a stillborn infant, and the cloth used by women during menstruation" (Weiner 1992: 50). These associations clearly call up both Hine and Maui and the peculiarities of their status.

Moreover, women's role in reproduction is reechoed in their role in production of cultural valuables (*taonga*). Cloaks represent the power, the *mana*, of a descent group, and these are made and controlled by women. Weiner (1992: 51) wrote: "A possession like a feathered cloak or a jeweled crown can affirm rank, authority, power and even divine rule because it stands symbolically as the representative of a group's historical or mythical origins." Weiner's analysis allows us to see that what is involved in inalienable objects is *mana*, which is clearly procreative power. Power is however, problematic; we know it to be dangerous.[10] Weiner astutely refers to the ethnographic muddle that has resulted from opposing profane, or polluting, female sexuality to effective and potent male sexuality (see also Hanson 1982; Hanson and Hanson 1983; and Shore 1992).[11] It is interesting that pregnancy was seen as the only time in which women were *tapu*, that is, at this time they were no longer ritually neutral, or *noa*. No one ever thought, until recently, to make sense of this exception. What is in fact signified is that pregnancy connotes a more generalized female power, but an ambiguous power, a power that matches and complements the power of Maui, the younger brother. Weiner (1992: 53) wrote: "With the Maori, mana is transferred through rituals to a woman's flax threads that she uses in weaving cloaks. Not only the weaver but the weaving poles are tapu and while working, both the poles and the threads have to be attended to appropriately or [sickness and death can occur]."

These examples show how highly valued women's cosmological potency is and how its transformation into material possessions has the highest value. The relation among women, reproduction, and *mana* is as central to high-ranking women's access to power and authority as it is to high-ranking men's political achievements. With high-ranking women, all things associated with pregnancy and birth are infused with *mana* and, in this state, women are *tapu*.

Weiner goes on to point out that, ritually, weaving is as complex and yields the same transformative results as do the rituals that prepare males for warfare. In fact, the goddess of childbirth and of weaving is the same: Hine-te-iwaiwa. What does this signify? In both cases, weaving and childbirth are direct or indirect indicators of female procreative abilities and women's capacities to mediate life and death.[12]

For, at birth and at death, women and their inalienable possessions, most notably their woven cloaks, occupy prominent positions. Women are the chief mourners, welcoming visitors onto the ceremonial ground and surrounding the body until it is placed in the ground. At the same time, a cloak, woven solely by women, is tied around the coffin. During secondary burials, characteristic of the Maori until at least the nineteenth century, the bones of high-ranking individuals were wrapped in woven cloaks.[13] In these examples, women's domestic productions comprise cosmic signposts. Cloaks, so representative of women's reproductive abilities, appear at all rites of passage, emphasizing the generative potential of women. In reference to the birth rituals, Weiner points out the significance of cloth: the umbilical cord was tied with a specially designated piece of flax, while the cord of a high-ranking infant was cut by a special piece of nephrite whose name recalled specific cloaks.

Weiner, citing Best (1975), emphasized that after birth the child was brought back to a house on the paternal side. This would not necessarily be true in all cases. It seems quite possible that were the couple residing uxorilocally, the infant would be brought back to the mother's house. This suggests that a ritual understood by nineteenth-century ethnographers to ensure patrilineal continuity was in fact far more flexible and far less devoted to male supremacy. This, of course, is not Weiner's concern, but it is mine. The nature of cognatic descent is such that women were as effective as descent group recruiters as were men.

As it turns out, the manufacture and handling of cloaks are important currency in status rivalry and negotiation. The ceremonial exchanges that mark all momentous events in individual lives readily become "an occasion for exchange that takes on political consequences. Junior lines compete with senior lines while the authority invested in a chiefly title can be diminished or expanded depending upon the title-holder's leadership skills" (Weiner 1992: 62). It is here that women's cosmological partners, younger brothers, once more make their appearance. In other words, cloaks provide the template upon which the tensions between junior and senior, achieved and ascribed status are enacted. From our point of view, the tension between ascription and achievement is commingled with the cosmological position of women and younger brothers.

Gender, Mythology, and Social Structure

In Maori mythology, we saw that Hine and Maui each have dual natures. This is hardly surprising, for there is a duality involved in Maori cognatic descent. In representing, at the same time, structure and antistructure, both Hine and Maui are able to demonstrate the double edge involved in Maori descent reckoning.

Nineteenth- and early twentieth-century ethnographers had understood Maori gender ideology as encompassing pollution beliefs about women. In this manner, the presumed patrilineal bias, touted by so many, was complemented by an ideology that limited the participation of women. Hanson (1982) has been more instrumental than almost anyone in forcing a reexamination of these assumptions. I take his position further by analyzing how an ideology that constrained women could be understood in conjunction with cognatic descent and, therefore, with a system of descent in which women were both powerful and threatening. Pollution becomes a metaphor for the problematic nature of women. Where, then, did pollution ideology exist?

Rules limiting women were quite clear. Menstruating or pregnant women were banned from almost all domains in social life. Violations produced striking results: crops failed, birds flew away, and the environment deteriorated with astonishing rapidity. All ritual activities, all construction sites of houses and of boats, were prohibited to women. Johansen (1958: 223) wrote:

> Men were allowed to be spectators at canoe making operations but not so women. For if a woman passes over the place where the canoe is being made, *ka oma nga atua*, the gods will desert the place, for the passing of the female organ over the ground desecrated the tapu of the spot. It was looked upon as a very unfortunate thing for a woman to step over a male child causing it to be stunted. It was also bad form for a woman to step over the body of a man, an act of impertinence.

Younger brothers were also viewed as polluted, while elder brothers were seen as pure. *Mua*, the term applied to elder brothers, refers to the front, to sacred places, while *muri*, a term applied to younger brothers, refers to nonsacred places such as cookhouses. Jean Smith (1974: 70) adds, "The elder and younger brother are also connected with the upper and lower parts of the body; the elder brother could be called *upoko* (head, *ariki*) while in the expression *taamanga kootore* the younger brother is connected with the buttocks."

In effect, a system emerges in which women and younger brothers are allied together against axiomatic male seniority. Connected with senior maleness are values of hierarchy, ascription, and purity, while with younger brothers and females, there are values of social inversion, achievement, and danger. What is significant is not merely that younger brothers and women are seen as pollutants but that they appear so often in Maori conceptions of both degeneration and creativity, with the presence of each reinforcing the actions of the other.

The presumed danger of younger brothers and women derives from their antisocial, marginal status; a system that is based on an ascribed hierarchy of firstborn males is profoundly threatened by the creative feats of women and younger brothers. In mythology, as we have seen, this is especially obvious. Jackson (1978: 349) wrote:

> The contrast between those who are directly concerned with maintaining the status quo (elders) and those who are liberated from the normal constraints of the given order (the clever youngsters) is often expressed as a contrast between the inflexibility or inadequacy of status superiors and the flexibility and cleverness of status inferiors. In other words the folktales elaborate a formal contrast between status position on the one hand and personal capability on the other.

For Jackson, the problem is ultimately one of achievement versus ascription. "The discontinuity between successive generations or between elder and younger siblings is thus one instance of a far more profound problem, namely the problem of achieving continuity or identification between what is socially necessary and what is individually possible" (Jackson 1978: 357).

There can be no doubt that this describes some of the recurrent social tensions faced by the Maori. However, other issues of kinship loom even larger in the perception of women and younger brothers as antisocial menaces to the system. The perceived threats of women and younger brothers are not merely mythological expressions, they represent significant dangers to descent ideology and descent group formation.

There were several levels of Maori social organization. The highest, the *waka*, or canoe, was a loose confederation of tribes with a shared, putative tradition. As an organizing force, it was of little practical consequence. The next level, the tribe, was a descent group in the broadest sense, since membership was based on descent from an ancestor traced through male and female links. The major unit of social organization was the *hapu*. The *hapu* was a cognatic decent group that controlled a territory where most of the members lived together and that regulated land use and production and management of important assets such as canoes and meeting houses (Metge 1990).

Women's importance as reproducers is manifest in the word *hapu*, which not only means subtribe but also "pregnant." In addition, an umbilical cord is buried in the *hapu*'s ground, thereby binding individuals to parcels of *hapu* land. For both the umbilical cord and the ground, the word is the same, *whenua*. The lexicon emphasizes the importance of women as recruiters for the *hapu*.

While lower-ranking lines in the *hapu* tended toward endogamy, the upper ranks preferred marriage outside the group to advance status interests. "The hapu appears to have been a complex type of descent group with a double composition: bilateral or endogamous in its lower ranks, preferentially patrilineal and exogamous in its upper ranks" (Goldman 1970: 52–53). It was precisely at this level of social organization that the contradictions in the system manifested themselves. For despite putative "preferential patrilineality" at the upper levels, the Maori were unequivocally cognatic, tracing descent from both sides. And while women as reproducers were important to the *hapu*, the *hapu* had, by virtue of cognatic descent, uncertain control over high-ranking women's reproduction. A woman born to the *hapu* might reproduce new members for it, but then she might not, as her children could wind up as members of her husband's descent group. An affinal woman might also reproduce new members for the *hapu*, but then again, her children could very well be destined for her natal *hapu*. In mythology, women were both life-givers and death-dealers; in worldly life, women were potentially givers or deprivers of progeny for the *hapu*. For the upper levels of Maori society, women's reproductive power could contribute to or cut off the continuity of the descent group. The end result of women's reproductive power was perpetually ambiguous.

In a like vein, younger brothers could upgrade their rank by leaving their descent group and becoming founders of new *hapu*. There was in fact no reason why they had to fall into line behind their elder brothers and every reason, replete with examples, why competence could overrule seniority. Thus, the integrity of the descent group was threatened in very fundamental ways by that now familiar combination of younger brothers and women. Elder versus younger, men versus women were merely ways of conceptualizing the legitimate and system sustaining versus the antisocial and system threatening. Ultimately, the tension between ascription and achievement can be understood in these terms as well: ascription supports, while achievement undermines the social order.

The ideology of descent and primogeniture asserts that order and certainty can only be realized through a system based on the ascribed prerogatives of firstborn males. Departures are depicted as degenerative and illegitimate. However, the converse is in fact true. The creative, generative characteristics of younger brothers and women that we see in the mythology is reflected again in the actuality of descent group formation. For primogeniture and its consequences yield social reproduction, while descent through women or younger brothers is generative, yielding entirely new social structures. Descent ideology and primogeniture mask but cannot obliterate these contradictions in the system. The truly creative power of women and younger brothers is defined as illegitimate and threatening not because the logic of the system is impregnable, but precisely because the rules that engender it are in fact provisional and arbitrary. The status quo reinforces a system of rank and hierarchy based on seniority, but the mythological and lexical constructions reveal the very real power and potency of women and younger brothers.

Conclusion

Cognatic descent, which permits women to inherit land, to hold chiefly office, and to participate in crucial decisions regarding their natal kin groups, as well as to ensure their perpetuation, was, not surprisingly, enigmatic to colonial British officialdom. For two centuries, it was argued almost without question that there was a patrilineal bias to what was a cognatic system, that the limitations placed on women's ritual position could easily account for the devaluation of women in that most formidable aspect of kinship—descent group recruitment. Here, I argue instead that the uncertain position and disruptive potential of both women and younger brothers in Maori descent group continuity finds expression in both mythology and ritual.

There was, to be sure, a distinction between ritual restrictions and the temporal power of women. But as Linnekin (1988) and Hanson and Hanson

(1983) have demonstrated, arguing that women are opposed to men because women are devoid of *tapu* misses the very essence of females in practical and cosmological configurations. In a similar vein, younger brothers are not quite so devoid of power as proponents of primogeniture would have us believe. Indeed, both women and younger brothers are seen as threats to the social order, and ritual restrictions are used to limit their spheres of action. Women and younger brothers represent what is new, what is generative, what is creative, as opposed to replication and reproduction of the ordinary. In this sense, our rebellious pair is indeed dangerous and threatening, as apparently the Maori realized.

The entire Maui cycle gains its potency by Maui's lack of commitment to the status quo and through his link to powerful women such as Hine. Moreover, his actions take place, especially in the most important versions of the myths (the ones that, because sacred, were not designed for a European audience), in a formulaic movement from above, through a transition, to below. Both Maui and Hine are marginal, resisting classification, eluding ready categorization. And it is here that their power is to be found.

That Maori thought more highly of descent groups whose members were exclusive descendants of senior males is clear in the expression *ure tu*, erect penis. Such lavish, if earthy, praise indicates significant preference. Moreover, it is more than Mary Douglas's notion that power inheres in the ambiguous that has allowed feminists to reexamine the place of women in cosmological systems. The very processes that limit female participation—menstruation, pregnancy, and contact with the dead—are the very crucial building blocks of descent groups. High-ranking women are as effective as their children's fathers in descent group recruitment. Under such conditions, is it really surprising that the very ways through which women form descent groups are constructed as dangers to the larger welfare of the group? To single out high-ranking women would be ineffective; the prohibitions, the mythological depictions of womanhood as menaces must encompass all females. But there can be no denying that women who are genealogically able to defy the system are indeed dangerous and threatening. By the same token, Maui is an exemplar of how brains, ingenuity, and guile can overcome inherited position. While there are attempts to keep younger brothers from usurping the position of their elders, or to ensure that they stay committed to the group and not form one of their own, these measures are only necessary because younger brothers are indeed a danger to the status quo. Given the very real threats that our couplet pose, it is not surprising that ritual and mythology have been used to keep them in their place, to limit the changes they can bring about.

Earlier ethnographers assumed that "simple kinship" systems were neat and free of ideological conflict. They neither looked for nor found contradictions. Now, our gaze has shifted, acknowledging what Louise Lamphere (in this book) has pointed out, that kinship is a transformed subject as the century has ended, "Its center is perhaps in the Euro-American system and the contact of that system with others." But the transformation is not only with kinship, it is with the people with whom we work and with ourselves.

Notes

1. I conducted initial fieldwork with the Maori in 1971–73 with many additional periods of research from 1982 to 2000. These trips have been supported by grants from Eastern Michigan University, Fulbright, the National Science Foundation, and the National Endowment for the Humanities. For my earlier work on Maori gender, see Sinclair 1992, 1993.

2. The position of women within Maori descent groups has been reexamined in the work of Binney et al. (1986), Binney (1988), Metge (1990), Salmond (1991b), and Webster (1975).

3. Salmond (1989: 57), writing about *tapu* and *mana*, has suggested that "the physical experience of mating, reproduction, and growth" provides the basis for a "genealogical description language to account for entities of all kinds . . . and the emergence of the cosmos itself."

4. Tane's duplicity seems not to figure in the mythology. It is Hine's decision to move to the darkness below and her activities there that define her and the dangers to mortals result.

5. In some versions, he gets the jawbone from his grandfather, in others, from his grandmother. In the grandfather version, he finds it in a cave and it is clearly a source of *mana*.

6. This event only occurs in the popular version. In the more esoteric version, it is Papa, the Earth, who appears on Maui's fishhook.

7. In the more popular version of the myth, Maui steals fire from his grandmother (Kahukiwa and Grace 1984, for example). But in the more esoteric version, it is Hine. Since this is more consistent with Maori understandings of both Hine and Maui, I am following that position in the chapter.

8. The more popular version has his father failing to dedicate him to a god. This is the version found in Grey's *Polynesian Mythology* (1965) that differs from Thornton's analysis, which relies on the Te Rangikaheke version in Maori. The Te Rangikaheke version is generally acknowledged as the version of the elite. In the Grey version, the *tohi* ritual takes place earlier in the cycle. Yet it is more suitable here, for it is a rite of passage, occurring at a time of transition.

9. Jackson (1978: 359) indicates that his kinship status is especially problematic. He wrote: "In the Te Rangikaheke portions of the Maui myth Maui mediates between the opposed terms: sons-parents, in the early sections, and culture-nature, in the final section. In this sense, Maui is both acultural and anatural, neither man, nor not man yet both. This is why his origins are said to be human (child of human parents) and nonhuman (protected and raised by the elements). It is not clear that he is really his parent's child and he is also the youngest, which places him furthest from the parental descent line."

10. Weiner (1992) claimed that women's procreative power lies at the root of *mana*'s metaphysical efficacy.

11. Until recently, it was believed that men were *tapu*, a condition that women only approximated when pregnant. Otherwise, women's being was not only ritually neutral (*noa*) but in fact threatening to male *tapu*.

12. Weiner (1992) pointed out as well that the poles used by women to support themselves during delivery were similar to those used for weaving into god sticks, thus cementing the link between birth and weaving.

13. Weiner (1992: 57) wrote: "Best [1975] describes the ritual associated with the reburial of bones and it is exactly like the display of a child after the naming ceremony." Cloaks here provide a link between opposite ends of the life cycle, and in so doing, place women firmly as gatekeepers.

References

Best, Elsdon. 1975. *The Lore of the Whare Kohanga.* Reprint, Wellington: Government Printer.

Biggs, Bruce. 1960. *Maori Marriage.* Auckland: Polynesian Society.

Binney, Judith. 1988. Some Observations on the Status of Maori Women. *Journal of New Zealand History* 23:22–31.

Binney, Judith, Gillian Chaplin, and Craig Wallace. 1986. *Nga Morehu.* Auckland: Oxford University Press.

Buckley, Thomas, and Gottlieb, Alma. 1988. *Blood Magic: The Anthropology of Menstruation.* Berkeley: University of California Press.

Douglas, Mary. 1975. *Implicit Meanings.* London: Routledge & Kegan Paul.

Firth, Raymond. 1973. *Economics of the New Zealand Maori.* Reprint, Wellington: Government Printer.

Goldman, Irving. 1970. *Ancient Polynesian Society.* Chicago: University of Chicago Press.

Grey, Sir George. 1965. *Polynesian Mythology.* Reprint, Auckland: Whitcombe and Tombs.

Hanson, F. Allan. 1982. Female Pollution in Polynesia. *Journal of the Polynesian Society* 91:335–81.

Hanson, F. Allan, and Louise Hanson. 1983. *Counterpoint in Maori Culture.* London: Routledge & Kegan Paul.

Hiroa, Te Rangi. 1962. *The Coming of the Maori.* Wellington: Whitcombe and Tombs.

Howard, Alan, and Robert Borofsky, eds. 1989. *Developments in Polynesian Ethnology.* Honolulu: University of Hawaii Press.

Jackson, Michael. 1978. Ambivalence and the Last Born: Birth Order Position in Convention and Myth. *Man* 13:341–61.

Johansen, J. Prytz. 1954. *The Maori and His Religion in Its Non-Ritualistic Aspects.* Copenhagen: Munksgaard.

———. 1958. *Studies in Maori Rites and Myths.* Copenhagen: Munksgaard.

Kahukiwa, Robin, and Grace, Patricia. 1984. *Wahine Toa: Women of Maori Myth.* Auckland: Collins.

Keesing, Roger. 1975. *Kin Groups and Social Structure.* Fort Worth, Tex.: Holt, Rinehart and Winston.

Linnekin, Jocelyn. 1988. Who Made the Feather Cloaks? A Problem in Hawaiian Gender Relations. *Journal of the Polynesian Society* 97:335–60.

Metge, A. Joan. 1976. *The Maoris of New Zealand.* New York: Routledge & Kegan Paul.

———. 1990. Te Rito o te Harakete: Conceptions of the Whanau. *Journal of the Polynesian Society* 99:55–92.

Orbell, Margaret. 1985. *Hawaiki: A New Approach to Maori Tradition.* Christchurch: University of Canterbury Press.

———. 1995. *The Illustrated Encyclopedia of Maori Myth and Legend.* Christchurch: University of Canterbury Press.

Sahlins, Marshall. 1985. *Islands of History.* Chicago: University of Chicago Press.

Salmond, Anne. 1978. Te Ao Tawhito: A Semantic Approach to the Traditional Maori Cosmos. *Journal of the Polynesian Society* 87:5–28.

———. 1989. Tribal Words, Tribal Worlds. In *Culture, Kin, and Cognition in Oceania,* ed. Mac Marshall and John L. Caughey. American Anthropological Association, Special Publication, number 25.

———. 1991a. *Two Worlds.* Auckland: Viking.

———. 1991b. *Tipuna*—Ancestors: Aspects of Maori Cognatic Descent. In *Man and a Half: Essays in Pacific Anthropology and Ethnobiology in Honour of Ralph Bulmer,* ed. Andrew Pawley. Auckland: Polynesian Society.

———. 1997. *Between Worlds.* Auckland: Viking.

Schwimmer, Erik. 1966. *The World of the Maori.* Auckland: Reed.

Shore, Bradd. 1992. Tapu and Mana. In *Developments in Polynesian Ethnology*, ed. Alan Howard and Robert Borofsky. Honolulu: University of Hawaii Press.

Sinclair, Karen. 1992. Maori Women at Midlife. In *In Her Prime*, ed. Judith Brown and Virginia Kerns. Urbana: University of Illinois Press.

———. 1993. The Price of Innovation: Maori Women and Social Change. In *Balancing Acts: Women and the Process of Social Change*, ed. Patricia Lyons Johnson. Boulder, Colo.: Westview.

Smith, Jean. 1974. *Tapu Removal in Maori Religion*. Auckland: Polynesian Society.

Stone, Linda. 1997. *Kinship and Gender: An Introduction*. Boulder, Colo.: Westview.

Thornton, Agathe. 1987. *Maori Oral Literature As Seen by a Classicist*. Otago: University of Otago Press.

———. 1992. *The Story of Maui by Te Rangikaheke*. Canterbury Maori Studies 5. Christchurch: University of Canterbury Press.

Webster, Steven. 1975. Cognatic Descent Groups and the Contemporary Maori. *Journal of the Polynesian Society* 84:121–52.

Weiner, Annette. 1992. *Inalienable Possession: The Paradox of Keeping-While-Giving*. Berkeley: University of California Press.

Chapter Ten

Power, Control, and the Mother-in-Law Problem: Face-Offs in the American Nuclear Family

Allen S. Ehrlich

A merican society has placed great importance upon the roles and functions embedded within the nuclear family. Even the briefest of visits to a research library provides an abundance of published materials pertaining to subjects on marriage and the family in the United States. Yet, despite all the studies that have been done in this area of scholarship, very little research has been oriented toward the study of in-laws, and virtually no significant body of material has been published specifically on the mother-in-law problem. A recent computer bibliographical search on "mother-in-law" using two different social science data banks yielded a grand total of five pieces of research published on the subject of mother-in-law in American society.[1]

As an anthropologist, I find this a most curious and puzzling phenomenon, given the fact that historically we have created a rather strong negative stereotype of this particular affinal relative. Yet, the nonexistence of a body of research on the subject raises the obvious question, "Indeed, does a mother-in-law problem really exist in American society?" In response to the question, this chapter will argue that not only does the mother-in-law problem exist in American culture, but that a specific form of the problem is dominant. Structurally, it is the dyadic relationship between wife and husband's mother that appears to control the contours of the mother-in-law problem as opposed to the relationship between husband and wife's mother. Like a talented actress, it is the husband's mother who plays the starring role in this "Great American Drama" of family life.

In taking this position, there are three kinds of materials that support the suggested thesis. Initially, it might be noted that while our professional journals have not seen mothers-in-law as a topic of sufficient interest or importance for analysis, the same cannot be said of segments of the popular culture print medium, such as advice columns like "Dear Abby" and "Ann Landers."

Indeed, one finds strong support for the prevalence of the mother-in-law problem in the writings of both columnists. It is interesting to note, that while there have been changes over the years in terms of the kinds of problems written about that reflect attitudinal changes in American society, the flow of letters involving mother-in-law complaints has remained steady. This would seem to indicate that the problematic mother-in-law relationship has not been an ephemeral one. In her last book, Eppie Lederer—alias Ann Landers—commented on the continuity and frequency of in-law problems in our society:

> In 1961 I wrote my first book. . . . In that book, I dealt with the problem that produced the greatest number of letters. Chapter Six . . . was called "Must We Outlaw the In-Law?" Today, many years later, in-law problems still figure prominently. . . . My mail provides daily evidence that the in-law problem is no myth. (Lederer 1978: 643)

However, what is of greater interest are Ann Landers's comments that pinpoint the patterns found in the in-law complaints. First, in comparing mother-in-law complaints with those against fathers-in-law, she estimates that for every letter received about a father-in-law problem, she receives fifty letters dealing with mother-in-law problems (Lederer 1978: 643). Second, when the comparison is made within the general category of in-law, she states that 90 percent of all complaints against in-laws are directed specifically against mothers-in-law (1978: 650). Finally, and most significantly, she notes that of these mother-in-law complaints, fully 80 percent of them focus upon husband's mother as the troublesome relative (1978: 650).[2]

While Abigail Van Buren does not give the kinds of quantitative estimates provided by Ann Landers, nevertheless, her work leaves little doubt about her perception of the mother-in-law relationship. She has described it as being problematic and contentious, a kind of deadly contest between mother-in-law and husband's wife in which "luckily Mrs. Newlywed at least has sex on her side. Otherwise, any fair-minded referee would declare it no contest" (1958: 56).

In trying to put some scholarly clothing onto this body of advice column data, I did eventually come across some shreds and patches of material hidden in the sociological literature on marriage and the family published in the 1950s and 1960s. Studies that had looked at the question of in-law adjustment generally seemed to agree with the patterns suggested by the advice columns. Interestingly, the research indicated that the study of in-law problems again turned out to be primarily the study of the mother-in-law problem (Duvall 1954: 216, 318; Komarovsky 1964: 259–61; Landis and Landis 1963: 333; Thomas 1956: 235; Wallin 1954: 468). Duvall commented in her book, *In-Laws: Pro & Con*, "When men and women are given an opportunity to indicate who in their experience is the most difficult of in-laws, more mention mother-in-law than any other relative by marriage" (1954: 216). Of 992 persons in her sample having in-law difficulties of some kind, almost one out of two respondents (49.5 percent) mentioned mother-in-law as being most problematic (1954: 187).[3]

However, of greater significance is the other pattern found in these works. Two of the studies also allude to the female-female nature of the mother-in-law problem in much the same way that the advice columns suggested. In a study to test for sex differences in attitudes toward in-laws, Wallin not only found that wives more than husbands disliked their mothers-in-law, but that they did so at a ratio of greater than two-to-one (1954: 468). In addition, when Duvall elicited the specific nature of complaints about mothers-in-law, she clearly struck a nerve, which tapped into intensity of feelings along gender lines. The figures in her study tell the whole story: of 1,369 separate mother-in-law complaints, 1,227 of these complaints came from women (1954: 187).[4]

Given the above findings, how can we explain the contours that the mother-in-law problem takes? After all, most marriages produce two mothers-in-law. Why is it that the dyadic link between wife and mother-in-law in particular is such a point of contention? To explain this phenomenon, we must turn to two other types of cultural materials. My basic approach will involve looking at the cultural notion of the nuclear family as an autonomous social unit and linking that perception with traditional sex role socialization patterns.[5]

In American society, most middle-class individuals play out their lives in two different nuclear families: the family of orientation—the family into which one is born, and the family of procreation—the family one creates through marriage and progeny (see fig. 10.1).

These families are drawn as overlapping for illustrative purposes, but it can be posited that there is a cultural value in American society that really says the overlap ought not to occur. For nuclear family organization in American culture stresses fission rather than coalescence. It calls for fragmentation at each succeeding generation and the emergence of new and independent nuclear

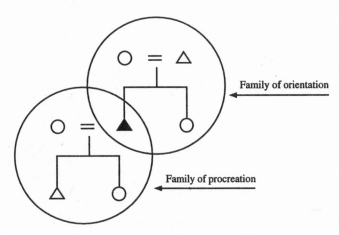

Figure 10.1 Overlapping Families of Orientation and Procreation

families. Initially, I would suggest that when one finds the husband's family of orientation overlapping with his family of procreation, then one of the necessary conditions for the development of the mother-in-law problem exists. This factor when linked to materials on sex-role socialization in our society allows us to begin to understand why the mother-in-law problem generally takes the specific form that it does.

Sex-role socialization materials clearly indicate that women in our society historically have received very different socialization cues from those received by males. Simply put, the major adult roles toward which women traditionally have been socialized in our society have been the roles of "wife" and "mother." All cultures make the distinction between adult and nonadult. In American society, female adulthood traditionally has been defined in terms of (a) marriage, (b) the establishment of a new household, and (c) the bearing and raising of children. Historically, young girls have been socialized to believe that the home will eventually be the focus of their adult activity and, more important, that the home will be the arena of their decision-making. If we correctly understand the social dynamics of family sex roles as traditionally defined by American culture, then the long-standing aphorism "A man's home is his castle" is really topsy-turvy. For it is females who have been socialized to perceive the home as *their* domain. When the implications of these cultural definitions and perceptions are fully grasped, then the most common complaint against mother-in-law becomes readily understandable. Mother-in-law is overwhelmingly seen as a problematic relationship because of the feeling that she interferes or is meddlesome in daughter-in-law's adult domestic domain. Indeed, letters to the advice columns strongly follow this pattern. How else can one explain the types of complaints written about, which I am sure often seem trivial or unimportant to many readers?

DEAR ABBY: In your opinion, whose place is it to bake a birthday cake for a man? His wife's or his mother's? I feel that when a boy becomes a man and takes a wife, that is where his mother's obligation should end and his wife should take over. I have been trying to bake Steve's birthday cake for the last 10 years, but every year when I tell his mother I'd like to bake Steve's cake, she says: "After I'm gone, you'll have the rest of your life to bake Steve his birthday cake, so while I'm here please don't deprive me of that pleasure." Now what am I supposed to do?

BUGGED

While the subject of that letter may appear to be about baking a cake, the real issue is one of power and control. Clearly, the linkage of our nuclear family-oriented kinship system with female sex-role socialization has created a set of conditions wherein the mother-in-law who intrudes into the household matters of her daughter-in-law does so at the high risk of being perceived as an interloper—a challenger in the one area of authority where, traditionally, American culture has led the daughter-in-law to believe she will have power as an adult. Hence, it is posited that criticisms, suggestions, and "help-ful hints" from mother-in-law functionally become kinds of challenges to daughter-in-law's adulthood—challenges to her ability to take care of hus-band, home, and family. The mother-in-law problem when placed within the context of daughter-in-law's home is a problem of power—a struggle involv-ing control and decision-making within a culturally defined female domain.[6]

At this juncture, a very important point must be raised involving the dyadic delineation that has been presented thus far. At the surface level, the mother-in-law problem may well appear to be dyadic; in reality, however, it is triadic in nature. For I am firmly convinced that the crucial causal component of the mother-in-law problem involves husband behavior. In turning to the role of the husband within the kinship web of the mother-in-law problem, our focus shifts to the nature of husband's reaction to wife's complaints. The mother-in-law materials I refer to in this section of my study were collected from 106 people. Of these, there were 84 females and 22 males. In terms of race and so-cioeconomic status, the sample is essentially white and middle class—5 mid-dle-class black females are included in the sample. All 106 people filled out a written questionnaire that emphasized open-ended responses; there were 54 face-to-face or telephone follow-up interviews.[7]

What emerges from the questionnaire and interview materials is that husband reactions follow a particular pattern. Since the mother-in-law problem is essentially one that involves husband's mother, in the best of all worlds he would like to disavow that any such problem exists. Material col-lected from wives with a mother-in-law problem suggest that once the na-ture of the difficulty is made known to husbands, a rather predictable re-sponse occurs. Generally, the way in which husbands attempt to deal with their wives' complaints focuses upon various forms of denial and nonin-volvement. Most men do not want to become enmeshed in the differences between their wives and their mothers and—if given the opportunity—will gladly absent themselves. For the husband feels he is in a no-win situation. Indeed, he perceives *himself* as a victim. He sees himself caught between his wife and his mother, and senses that whatever he does is going to alienate one of them—or in his worst nightmare, possibly both of them! Hence, husbands in this triadic situation most often react to their wives' com-plaints with a variant of the response, "I don't want to get involved"—a phrase loaded with negative affect from the perspective of the wife, as will be shown later.

In collecting the questionnaire data, the following linked questions were asked: (1) "Have you ever attempted to get your husband involved with the prob-lems you are experiencing with your mother-in-law? (____ Yes ____ No)," and (2) "If 'yes' is checked, what was your husband's response and reaction to your request for help?" At first, I was surprised at the number of women who checked "no" as their response to the first question. However, upon conducting some fol-low-up interviews, a most interesting pattern emerged. A number of the women

who were contacted indicated that when they first approached their husbands
about their mother-in-law problems, their husbands' reactions were so negative
that they gave up on any further attempts to work out their problems through
discussion with their spouses. As one woman commented:

> One evening after supper, when I first told my husband that I felt his mother was
> interfering in ways that I didn't like and that I wish he'd talk to her, I was shocked
> by his reaction. He just sat there and stared at me. He didn't say anything, just si-
> lence. I could see he was very angry with me and I could feel his hostility even
> though he wasn't talking. After a couple of minutes of this silent treatment, he
> got up and said some things in his mother's defense. Then he walked into the
> next room, and left me sitting at the kitchen table alone—end of discussion.

For these wives, the subject of the mother-in-law problem was surrounded by
an air of taboo. It was a subject to be avoided; most certainly, something not
to be confronted. One woman's voice spoke for many others when she remarked quite matter of factly, "I was *not allowed* to talk about it. My husband
could not bear to listen to my complaints about his mother."

The research completed thus far leads me to conclude that among husbands
there exists a pattern that might be alluded to as the "silent male" syndrome.[8]
By that, I do not necessarily mean total silence on the part of husbands,
though in some of the instances reported—as those just noted—indeed, it was
just that. Rather, what I would like to propose is that the "silent male" syndrome has as its focus an inability or unwillingness on the part of husbands to
communicate to their mothers the problems that their wives are experiencing. I
would suggest that the silence of the husband is essentially rooted in his desire
to try to get himself into a disengagement mode. However, I would argue that
there are really two versions of the disengagement pattern that are important to
distinguish because of differences in the thrust and bluntness of the message the
husband is sending to his wife.

The first version might be categorized as the "We're all reasonable people
and should be able to work this problem out" response. From the interview
materials, however, it appears that the "we" in "we're" more often than not
does *not* include the husband. Many of the wives indicated that when push
came to shove, a husband saw this position as a suggested discussion between
his "reasonable wife" and his "reasonable mother," while his "reasonable self"
was nowhere in sight. Indeed, in these cases, what the end result of this stance
amounted to was that, whatever the problems were, the wife should be able to
resolve them unilaterally through discussion with her mother-in-law.

Several points might be made here. First, the obvious difficulty with this
problem solving suggestion is that the kind of issues around which the
mother-in-law problem revolves usually are laden with very strong emotional and personal feelings—issues concerning husband, home, children, a
sense of self. Issues that often cannot easily be discussed calmly and ration-
ally, especially between the leading actors in this real-life domestic drama.

Second, we see that this stance is oriented primarily around husband disengagement. It becomes a vehicle by which husbands distance themselves from the mother-in-law problem, receding far into the background of the family setting. In essence, it is a type of "Where's Waldo" tactical maneuver—while husbands are present within the landscape of mother-in-law turmoil, they are very difficult to find. As a side note on this disengagement mode, in two cases, wives commented that their husbands indicated an unwillingness to become involved because—from the husbands' point of view—it was a "women's problem."

The second version of the "silent male" mode of adaptation to the mother-in-law problem might be called the "What's the big deal? You're making a mountain out of a mole hill!" response. This response, I would argue, is loaded with qualitatively different affect from the one discussed earlier. In reacting to wife's complaints about his mother, husband is forcefully showing his wife where his loyalties lie. Indeed, he is taking a very confrontational position on the issue of the mother-in-law problem that—unfortunately for his wife—turns the spotlight on her. In this instance, husband's response accomplishes two things simultaneously. It is not only a classic case of denial, but at the same time, it immediately disengages him from any discussion about his mother. For what husband is really saying to wife is, "My mother's not the problem, you are!" It is a response that embodies a saying from sports that men use all the time, namely, "The best defense is a good offense." This response is both hostile and aggressive with the result that wife is now put in a defensive posture, while at the same time, the object of the projected discussion—husband's mother—disappears from sight.

The negative effect of this response can be a devastating moment of truth in a marriage. For it may portend—in ways not earlier realized by wife—the nature of husband's maternal ties and support for mother.[9] In the collection of mother-in-law materials, wives referring to themselves as being second best to husband's mother was a repeated theme. As one woman pointedly commented about her husband, "At some level, he never could tell his mother he was married and that meant his relationship with her had to change. He never made a choice that she was not the number one woman in his life."

For husbands caught in this familial web of tension, it is as if confrontation with their mothers becomes the equivalent of breaking some genetic nonaggression pact. For these men, silence and inaction appear to be the instruments of power with which they attempt to do damage control on behalf of their mothers. In approaching husbands about problems involving their mothers, wives are essentially seeking some type of support. They are asking for help, and to some degree, it is a testing of spousal loyalty. Rather than support, what they wind up experiencing is spousal alienation. The end result of this second mode of behavior has the same effect as the first. Once again, the burden of the resolution of the mother-in-law problem is placed squarely upon the shoulders of wife *alone*—it is *her problem*.

I think it can be asserted that the various "silent male" responses contain a message to wife that she really does not want to know, namely, that there are strong maternal ties that, in the end, both delimit and supersede husband's loyalties to her.[10] It is this message that I would argue becomes a crucial facet in our understanding of the mother-in-law problem and forces us to come to terms with its triadic nature and structure. Ultimately, where husband's action—or in this instance, inaction—is perceived by wife as being unsupportive, one has the final hot ingredient for cooking up this fiery and steamy kinship stew known as the mother-in-law problem.

Notes

Modified versions of this paper were delivered at the annual meetings of the Popular Culture Association in San Antonio in March 1997, and the American Anthropological Association in Washington, D.C., in November 1997. I should like to thank Karen Ehrlich, Jessica Kross, Marie Richmond-Abbott, Karen Sinclair, and Linda Stone for their collective critical eye and their helpful comments on an earlier draft of this chapter. I also wish to acknowledge a sabbatical leave granted by Eastern Michigan University that gave me the opportunity to turn my attention to writing up some of the mother-in-law research. Finally, I especially want to express my gratitude to David Aberle for the enthusiasm and encouragement he has shown me during several discussions of this kinship study.

1. This void has led to the fairly recent publication of a number of "how to" books on in-law relationships (Arnstein 1985; Averick 1989; Bilofsky and Sacharow 1991; and Strauss 1996). It might be noted that in 1951, a nonprofit educational organization named the Public Affairs Committee felt the need to publish pamphlet No. 174, entitled *How to Be a Good Mother-in-Law and Grandmother* (Neisser 1951).

2. It should be emphasized that this finding is not the result of females writing greater numbers of letters to advice columns than males. In an essay on Ann Landers, Stupple has remarked that, "Lederer and her syndicate are reluctant to provide detailed circulation information but we do know that nearly half of the letters that come in are from males" (1975: 17). Also, Grossvogel makes a similar point in noting that the advice column "has been fed over the years by a fairly even distribution of male and female correspondents, according to Ann Landers—an estimate she has repeated on more than one occasion" (1987: 72).

3. Duvall (1954: 221, 231), Landis and Landis (1963: 333), and Lederer (1978: 644) all found that the second most difficult in-law was sister-in-law, with *husband's* sister filling the problematic kinship role. I cannot help but express the feeling that the Freudian implications of this finding are worthy of a study of its own.

4. There were only two pieces of research I found that did not conform to this pattern. A study by Hoye reported that "females scored [only] slightly higher on the mother-in-law adjustment test than did their husbands" (1971: 43). It should be noted, however, that the conclusions of this study were based on a rather small sample of thirty-nine couples who were all living in a single county in North Carolina. The other contrary finding was in Komarovsky's book, *Blue Collar Marriage*, where she noted that level of education appeared to be a factor among the men with in-law problems. In those blue-collar families where husbands did not finish high school, Komarovsky observed, "The surprising finding . . . is the prevalence of in-law problems among the less-educated husbands. One-third of these men experience strain in relation to their in-laws, the same proportion as that of women with in-law grievances, irrespective of the women's education" (1964: 259). Parenthetically, it might be noted that a later study of working-class families concluded that it was primarily wives who experienced mother-in-law problems (Rubin 1974: 88–89).

5. In the 1950s, a series of articles appeared in the sociological literature that asked the question whether it was men or women who have greater difficulty establishing their independence based upon family and gender role socialization patterns in American society. This discussion, in turn, had theoretical implications for the study of marriage and in-law adjustment patterns (Komarovsky 1950, 1956; Stryker 1955; Thomas 1956; Wallin 1954; Winch 1950, 1951).

6. While there has been some criticism involving the universality of Rosaldo's argument that all societies have organized themselves around a female domestic sphere versus a male public sphere (1974), the analysis of the materials on the mother-in-law problem strongly supports the utility of that opposition in American culture. For an overview of some of the criticisms of the domestic/public opposition along with Rosaldo's response, see "The Use and Abuse of Anthropology: Reflections on Feminism and Cross-Cultural Understanding" (1980).

7. People included in this nonrandom sample primarily fall into the following four categories: (1) students at Eastern Michigan University and Washtenaw Community College, (2) people attending various professional meetings where I have presented papers on my mother-in-law research, (3) friends and their friends, and (4) anthropologists who responded to a call for mother-in-law materials through the "cooperation column" in *Anthropology Newsletter.*

8. In the book *Linked Lives: Adult Daughters and Their Mothers,* Fischer briefly comments on family role behavior, contrasting the silence of married sons with the mediative role of married daughters (1986: 152–53). However, after she makes this point, the silence pattern of sons/husbands is not developed any further, nor is it linked to the presence of the mother-in-law problem.

9. It might be noted here that the husband himself may well not comprehend the depth or the dimensions of this psychodynamic facet of his persona. In the book *The Secrets Men Keep,* Druck suggests that in most instances men are not consciously aware of their own strong maternal ties and feelings. While the focus of the book is on male–male relationships, nonetheless, one finds the following very poignant comments on the son–mother relationship (1985: 167): "Men do not often discuss their unresolved feelings about their mothers. While they play a key part in their relationships with other women, these emotions are often hidden away out of our awareness. Men's deepest feelings toward their mothers remain some of their best-kept secrets, *even from themselves*" (emphasis mine).

10. If one wishes to seek out possible factors underlying the strong maternal ties these husbands exhibit, I think one has to move to the psychological level of analysis. More specifically, one must look to the psychological literature that deals with the subject of early childhood socialization of males and focuses upon issues of the resolution of gender identity and separation that lead to the establishment of ego boundaries. Ever since the publication of the two groundbreaking books *The Reproduction of Mothering* (Chodorow 1978) and *In A Different Voice* (Gilligan 1982), we have become acutely aware of the experiential differences of males and females during the early childhood socialization period. In this literature, one finds a portrayal in which both males and females as infants experience mother as their first and most significant relationship. Yet, in the case of a male, there comes a time in his early childhood when he is expected to separate and give up his identification with the one person to whom he has the strongest ties, the greatest emotional attachment. He must turn away from mother and move towards what she is not—towards maleness. It is a separation filled with pain and differs from the separation process young females experience. Given the above material, it would not seem unreasonable to suggest that in those cases of the mother-in-law problem where husband's maternal ties appear to be stronger than those to wife, we are dealing with instances where the socialization issues of separation and individuation were never satisfactorily resolved. And so these earlier psychological patterns live on. As Rubin has noted, "And long after the conflict between our need for separation and our desire for unity has left center stage, these issues will live inside us to influence the next act" (1983: 52). For those readers who might wish to delve into this area of study involving insights from the object relations school of psychology, a good starting point is the chapter entitled "The Child Within," in the book *Intimate Strangers* (1983: 38–64).

References

Arnstein, Helene S. 1985. *Between Mothers-in-Law and Daughters-in-Law.* New York: Dodd, Mead.

Averick, Leah Shifrin. 1989. *How In-Laws Relate: It's All Relative.* New York: Shapolsky.

Bilofsky, Penny, and Fredda Sacharow. 1991. *In-Laws/Out-Laws.* New York: Copestone.

Chodorow, Nancy. 1978. *The Reproduction of Mothering: Psychoanalysis and the Sociology of Gender.* Berkeley: University of California Press.

Druck, Kenneth M. 1985. *The Secrets Men Keep.* Garden City, N.Y.: Doubleday.

Duvall, Evelyn Mills. 1954. *In-Laws: Pro & Con.* New York: Association Press.

Fischer, Lucy Rose. 1986. *Linked Lives: Adult Daughters and Their Mothers.* New York: Harper and Row.

Gilligan, Carol. 1982. *In a Different Voice.* Cambridge, Mass.: Harvard University Press.

Grossvogel, David I. 1987. *Dear Ann Landers.* New York: Berkley.

Hoye, Doris D. 1971. *Mother-in-Law Adjustment of Young Marrieds.* Ph.D. diss., University of North Carolina, Greensboro.

Komarovsky, Mirra. 1950. Functional Analysis of Sex Roles. *American Sociological Review* 15:508–16.

———. 1956. Continuities in Family Research: A Case Study. *American Journal of Sociology* 63:42–47.

———. 1964. *Blue Collar Marriage.* New York: Random House.

Landis, Judson T., and Mary G. Landis 1963. *Building a Successful Marriage.* 5th ed. Englewood Cliffs, N.J.: Prentice-Hall.

Lederer, Esther Pauline. 1978. *The Ann Landers Encyclopedia, A to Z.* Garden City, N.Y.: Doubleday.

Neisser, Edith G. 1951. *How to Be a Good Mother-in-Law and Grandmother.* New York: Public Affairs Committee.

Rosaldo, Michelle Zimbalist. 1974. Woman, Culture, and Society: A Theoretical Overview. In *Woman, Culture, and Society,* ed. Michelle Zimbalist Rosaldo and Louise Lamphere. Stanford: Stanford University Press.

———. 1980. The Use and Abuse of Anthropology: Reflections on Feminism and Cross-Cultural Understanding. *Signs: Journal of Women in Culture and Society* 5:389–417.

Rubin, Lillian Breslow. 1974. *Worlds of Pain: Life in the Working-Class Family.* New York: Basic.

———. 1983. *Intimate Strangers: Men and Women Together.* New York: Harper and Row.

Strauss, Yvette. 1996. *The Other Mother: How to Be an Almost Perfect Mother-in-Law.* San Luis Obispo, Calif.: Impact.

Stryker, Sheldon. 1955. The Adjustment of Married Offspring to Their Parents. *American Sociological Review* 20:149–54.

Stupple, David. 1975. Ann Landers and Public Moral Advice. *The Peninsular Papers* 1:12–22.

Thomas, John L. 1956. *The American Catholic Family.* Englewood Cliffs, N.J.: Prentice-Hall.

Van Buren, Abigail. 1958. *Dear Abby.* Englewood Cliffs, N.J.: Prentice-Hall.

Wallin, Paul. 1954. Sex Differences in Attitudes to "In-Laws": A Test of a Theory. *American Journal of Sociology* 59:466–69.

Winch, Robert. 1950. Some Data Bearing on the Oedipus Hypothesis. *Journal of Abnormal and Social Psychology* 45:481–89.

———. 1951. Further Data and Observations on the Oedipus Hypothesis. *American Sociological Review* 16:784–95.

Chapter Eleven

Colliding/Colluding Identities: Race, Class, and Gender in Jamaican Family Systems

Lisa M. Anderson-Levy

Growing up in Jamaica, I was surrounded by strong, independent, capable women, most of whom were single. As I reflect on it now, practically all my female role models were not legally married; these were women who had either never been married or were divorced. My mother was a part of the latter group. As I grew up, I received conflicting messages about my role as a woman. On the one hand, there was the notion of the importance of women being autonomous; and on the other, there was the idea that this autonomy was constrained by the various roles women occupy within the context of the family. Thus, even though my mother held a full-time job and was the primary caregiver for my brother and me, in the context of a relationship with a man, she still considered it her (and any woman's) job to ensure that the man's needs were met. Her identity as an independent woman collided with her identity as a woman in a relationship with a man. This is one example of how paradoxical constructions of gender roles produce conflicting identities in the lives of women in Jamaica. Perhaps another example will help to clarify my point.

In December 1996, my partner and I went to Jamaica for three weeks. This was the first time Rob had been to Jamaica and the first time he met my extended family. On the second night after our arrival we went to a family gathering where there was a buffet dinner. Since he was unfamiliar with some of the dishes, I took him around the table and explained what everything was before I rejoined a discussion I had been having with a group of relatives. A few minutes later my mother came up to me and said, "aren't you going to help Rob?" I told her that I had, that I had told him what everything was. She said, "No, I mean aren't you going to fix him a plate?" At first I didn't understand—thinking that he was perfectly capable of getting his own food. Then it dawned on me that serving him was seen by my mother as part of my role as his wife.

I hid my surprise and annoyance as best as I could and explained that I would not serve him, and that he could help himself. I had this same conversation a few minutes later with my grandmother, and then with an aunt. All of these women were surprised by my refusal to serve, or as they said, to "help" Rob. I believe they were particularly surprised because he was a "foreigner," and that this, in combination with his maleness, made it even more imperative that I wait on him. Here, my identities as woman and wife collided as my expectations of these roles clashed with those of my family.

I use the terms collide and collude throughout in order to explicate the complexities of conflicting identities. By referring to my identities as woman and wife as colliding, I mean that even though I consider myself to be an autonomous person capable of doing what I choose when I choose, this "freedom" is curtailed by the intrusion of other aspects of my identity. By colluding, I mean that as these various aspects of my identity smash into each other, they obscure the forces that construct them.[1] Because these identities operate simultaneously, my identity as wife in this instance did not simply conflict with my identity as woman, these identities collided, interpenetrated each other, and in the process, colluded or obscured their mutual relations. There is some violence or force inherent in the use of these terms as these identities crash into each other. Intersecting and overlapping denote an orderliness that I do not believe is always the case in how the various aspects of a person's identity operate. Using the terms collide and collude, rather than intersecting or overlapping to describe the operation of identities in women's lives, allows me to explore the idea that often these identities are not merely in conflict with each other, but that they also inadvertently conceal the relationship among themselves.

This anecdote serves as an entrée into a general discussion about the manner in which various identities collide and collude in the daily lives of Jamaican women in ways that constitute the very category of woman. Drawing on recent feminist critiques and on postcolonial theories of race and class, I demonstrate the significance of using the intersections of race, class, and gender to frame understandings of the construction of heterosexual family units, or households, in Jamaica. I suggest that the intersections of race, class, and gender are not only productive of each other but also of Jamaican family systems. How do these intersections create specific family types/forms among certain social/racial groups? And how do definitions of womanhood vary in ways that constitute the very category—woman—itself? These questions acquire particular significance in a nation where the motto "out of many one people" is challenged and perhaps even subverted by the insidious and all-encompassing effects of racial, social, or gender hierarchy and difference. The Jamaican motto, found on the national coat of arms, was intended to speak to a common cultural bond by virtue of being Jamaican despite racial/color differences.

It would be prudent at this time to locate myself regarding the subject matter of this chapter. I am a Jamaican woman who has lived in the United States for the past twelve years. I spent my first twenty-one years in a Jamaican middle-class, single-parent household. Discussing kinship in Jamaica is personal and, at times, rather difficult because it compels me to confront my own middle-class, and to some extent, skin-color privilege. When I lived in Jamaica, men would often refer to me as a "brown-skin lady." This means that although I am not "light-skinned," there were certain courtesies that were accorded me on the basis of skin color. Additionally, it compels me to examine the extent to which I, and other Jamaicans, have internalized the racism from our colonial past and how this in turn has affected the ways in which we construct kin networks. From time to time throughout this chapter, I will refer to my family or friends and use them as examples to crystallize main points, but their experiences cannot, of course, be extrapolated to the entire population.

That I am choosing to observe and critically assess a group of which I still consider myself a part raises the question or problem of the "native" anthropologist and epistemic privilege. Kirin Narayan (1997) noted that the boundary that has traditionally existed between "native" and "regular" anthropologists is artificial and arbitrary and collapses upon close inspection. Am I a "native" anthropologist even though I have lived in the United States for the past twelve years? And native to whom? To which group? As Narayan observed, there is too much intra- and intergroup heterogeneity to assume that it is possible for anyone to be uniquely qualified to reveal the "inner secrets" of any particular group. The complexities of multiply intersecting axes of identity means that we all shift our group alliances situationally, which further displaces any notion of a "native" expert (K. Narayan 1997). Furthermore, identifying myself as Jamaican puts me in a peculiar position because it also raises the question of whether or not my self-identification is really a rhetorical strategy to claim epistemic privilege. While this is a genuine concern, it is overridden by my belief in the importance of creating a context for the construction of knowledge. All knowledge is produced from a particular location or point of view, and making this apparent is an essential part of responsible scholarship (Haraway 1988).

This chapter situates this discussion within the larger one of kinship studies in the Caribbean. From there, I move into a discussion of the importance of theorizing about race, class, and gender within the context of examining kinship in Jamaica, emphasizing how these categories are productive of each other. I reiterate that although I shall be dealing with race, class, and gender in separate segments of the chapter, this is for explicative ease only and not because I believe that these categories can be disassociated in any real way. On the contrary, my primary objective is to demonstrate the import of theorizing about the intersections of race, class, and gender in Jamaican family systems. In the final two sections, I will show how these intersections operate in different arenas by looking briefly at family systems in two socioeconomic classes, the lower class and the middle class.[2] I will be dealing with two different notions of class. The first is class as a reflection of economic status, which is more in line with how class is perceived in the United States; the second is class based less on economic assets and more on social status.

Kinship in the Caribbean

Kinship studies in the Caribbean have had a long, if difficult, history. Much of this history has to do with how early twentieth-century anthropology in the United States constructed its object of study as distinct and particular, having its own historicity, and sitting outside the purview of white/European experience. The object of study was formulated in response to earlier evolutionary notions of cultural development, which espoused the belief that human cultures are progressive, moving unidirectionally from a more primitive state toward "civilization," then defined as European. This formulation of the object as completely outside or beyond the European experience was an important, if unintentional, rhetorical strategy because, for a period, it effectively excluded certain groups, such as blacks in the United States, from anthropological study.

For several decades, this criterion for the object of study likewise justified the exclusion of West Indian peoples as worthy of academic pursuit, and this framing permitted West Indian peoples to be seen as culturally deficient because their "culture" had been decimated by the devastation of slavery in the Americas.[3] Culture was seen as a homogenous, static, distinct whole that could be fissured and irreparably damaged, instead of as a multiply constituted, fragmented conglomeration that evolves through time and that is capable of adjusting to a variety of circumstances. A growing need to explain the dire social conditions of blacks, brought about by shifts in the political climate, was essential in a reformulation that made it possible for anthropologists to consider Caribbean peoples as significant objects of study.[4] Arising from a legacy of colonialism, nonwhite Caribbean peoples were considered to be "primitive" enough, and in this way, worthy of scholarly inquiry.

The Caribbean area and its peoples eventually came to be seen as deserving of academic pursuit in terms of explaining their social condition, which manifested itself in what early researchers believed was a chaotic or disorganized family type. Consequently, the research was framed to emphasize opposition from a naturalized Western, white, middle-class, male-centered norm.[5] Therefore, despite the tremendous amount of anthropological work on family systems in the Caribbean, and specifically in Jamaica, a large portion of this research framed these groups as "culturally" deficient. The foci of this work in Jamaica sought to explain family systems in terms of inherent dysfunction and/or survivals from an African past.[6] So, for instance, high rates of "illegitimacy" and/or low marriage rates within the lower socioeconomic strata were explained as pathological, due to either an inherent deviance among Jamaicans, particularly women, or as surviving from a chaotic, sexually indiscriminate past (Barrow 1996).

More recent anthropological studies on kinship in Jamaica (see for example, Douglass 1992; Smith 1996, 1988, 1987) have paid significant attention to the ways in which class and race intersect and operate within family systems. However, with the notable exception of Douglass (1992), gender has not been recognized or utilized as an analytic category in conjunction with race and class to construct more textured tapestries of Jamaican lives. This lack has been extensively noted (see Barrow 1996, 1988; Wiltshire-Brodber 1988; Mohammed 1988). It is crucial that race, class, and gender be viewed as productive of each other in order to draw out what this means for the study of kinship within the context of either Jamaica or the Caribbean.

Smith (1996, 1987) has analyzed in some detail how race or color and class operate within and intersect to produce particular phenomena like the dual marriage system. Absent from these analyses is how race, class, and gender continuously produce and reproduce each other, and how these identities are then productive of family systems. Within the context of this discussion, the term "gender" refers almost exclusively to the experiences of women. I use the term self-consciously and am aware that it is problematic to use it in this manner but have chosen to do so in deference to the fact that women (as an analytic category) have largely been ignored in this literature. An additional shortcoming of my discussion is that it refers solely to heterosexual identities and how these are expressed within the context of heterosexual family systems. These identities are dynamic, historically constituted, and are continually negotiated—being made, unmade, and remade. They are constitutive of each other, inextricably linked, and must thus form the basis of studies aiming to understand the subtleties of family systems in Jamaica.

Theorizing Race and Class in Jamaica

Why is it important to theorize about race in an ostensibly black nation? Most Jamaicans would be quick to agree that class is a more cogent category in discussions of inequality, because although we Jamaicans may not view ourselves as racist, we do acknowledge that we make fine distinctions based on class. The problem, however, is that race and class cannot be easily or simply extricated from each other.[7] More importantly, there is no way to talk about family or kin networks in Jamaica without discussing the centrality of both race and class to kinship. Jamaicans, like people everywhere, do not simply live in one dimension, affected singly and in turn by race, class, or gender. These categories or constructs are imbricated in and exert pressures upon the daily existence of Jamaicans in all arenas of life. By this I mean that these axes of identity—race, class, and gender—collide to produce the lived experiences of individuals and groups.

A number of black feminist theorists (notably hooks 1989, 1984; Hill Collins 1997; and Lorde 1984) have written extensively about the importance of critically examining these categories as intersections or layers, rather than individually, which does not reflect the reality in the lives of black people.[8] Black women, for instance, are not women sometimes, black sometimes, or class-associated sometimes. All of these dimensions of identity work in complex ways to create and constitute the daily existence of black women. Recognizing the variety of lived experiences of Jamaican women that results from the collisions of these axes is therefore crucial to any understanding of social systems, such as kin networks, which themselves constitute and perpetuate these axes of identity.

Third World feminists have consistently argued for the importance of theorizing about race and class in addition to gender in any examination of the lived experiences of Third World peoples. I use the term Third World feminist broadly, as Uma Narayan (1997) does, to refer not only to feminists living and working in the contexts of Third World countries but also to include feminists of color within Western contexts. In this regard, black feminist theorist bell hooks contended that "There is much evidence substantiating the reality that race and class identity creates differences in quality of life, [and] social status . . . which are rarely transcended" (hooks 1984: 4). Anticolonialist struggles in the Caribbean, and specifically in Jamaica, focused primarily on drawing attention to the crippling effects of class and race oppression. Trinidadian feminist scholar Wiltshire-Brodber noted that "because race and class mutually reinforced each other . . . [they] also provided a central focus for resistance and change. Class, race, and color thus converged and overlapped" (1988: 144). Race, color, and class collided with each other in the production of identities even as they also obscured the ways in which they were productive of each other in the daily lives of Jamaicans.

As a result of the colonial experience in Jamaica and the Caribbean, the analytic categories of race and class constitute each other in ways that are often taken for granted. Race and class are especially slippery and difficult to define in the Jamaican context precisely because there is so much overlap between the terms and so many layers of meaning within each term. For instance, although this is changing, there has been a national consciousness that holds that people with very dark skin typically are poorer, less educated, and more lacking in personal integrity and morality than those with lighter skin. Conversely, those with lighter skin are typically thought to possess both greater financial resources and moral fortitude (Leo-Rhynie 1997). Similarly, "class" is difficult to pin down. In Jamaica, class is not always associated with material wealth. Within this context, it is possible for a light-skinned, educated, poor woman with a "good family name" to be considered a member of the middle class, whereas the same woman with darker skin would not be as readily viewed as middle class and may be more likely to be considered as a member of a lower class. For the lighter-skinned woman, color, education, and a good name collide to collude her class identity in a way that simply does not occur for the darker-skinned woman.

Even though I use the work produced by American feminists of color, it is important to note that theorizing about race in Jamaica is somewhat different than talking about it in the United States. For instance, the majority of the population in Jamaica is of African descent; hence, racial difference is not simply determined as being "other" than white as it is in the United States.[9] Instead, as noted, the racial hierarchy is such that black people with "lighter" skin are privileged in ways that "darker"-skinned people are not. In most instances, *color* becomes more cogent than *race* per se. In general, classes in Jamaica are divided along racial lines such that the lower socioeconomic strata are composed primarily of descendants of African slaves and indentured East Indian workers. The middle and upper classes, conversely, are typically composed of some of the two groups previously mentioned, as well as Chinese, Portuguese, Syrians, and Lebanese immigrants, and a small Jewish population (Smith 1988).

A comment a friend made to me many years ago serves as a good example of how skin color creates privilege for some segments of the Jamaican populace. In the U.S. construction of race, my friend is a light-skinned black woman, but in Jamaica, she and her family were considered to be "Jamaican white."[10] She moved with her spouse and three children to the United States. After living in Florida for about six months, they returned to Jamaica because, this woman said, in the United States, they were just "another black family" with no special privileges. This was very different than their experience in Jamaica where they were considered to be "Jamaican white" and were able to reap the benefits of that status.

Our colonial legacy and the more recent experience of economic imperialism, in the form of multinational corporations, also complicate discussions about race in Jamaica. To a great extent it is true that the overt kinds of racism evident in the United States, for instance, are not observable in Jamaica. Instead, there is a more covert form of racism apparent in internalized and naturalized beliefs of some members of the populace. Thus, the differences are not as stark as black versus white. Rather, the degrees of blackness are so closely allied with class that they are inextricably linked.

Theorizing Gender in Jamaica

While the prominence of race and class as analytic categories should not be underestimated, it has often been noted by West Indian feminists that, in Caribbean contexts, these categories obscure the significance of gender as a useful, even fundamental, category of analysis. Wiltshire-Brodber noted that the "dominance of race, color and class in Caribbean colonial societies, historically made the issue of gender peripheral to an understanding of power, dominance and change" (1988: 144). Gender has long been placed at the bottom of hierarchies of identity, beneath race and class, and thus ignored. This was primarily because race and class oppression, in the form of slavery and colonial surveillance, were deemed to be more critical obstacles to the freedom of Caribbean, and certainly Jamaican, people (read: men) and were granted more political attention to the detriment of gender.

Against this backdrop, gender as a category of analysis emerges as significant not only because women and men experience the world in different ways, but also because women are central figures in Jamaican family systems (Smith 1996). Despite this centrality, however, anthropological discourses have until very recently ignored women as worthwhile objects of study.[11] A consequence of this is that even when they have been the objects of study, women have been subjected to the kind of sexism that renders them invisible in certain domains (Barrow 1988). Women have been the focus of research in what have typically been described as "female" domains, such as the family and child rearing (Prior 1993). This obscures women's contributions outside these domains with disastrous consequences because of the interconnectedness of various social systems such as economy and kinship. For example, although women fought alongside men during independence movements in the 1960s, their economic condition vis-à-vis men has not improved but has deteriorated. As Jamaican feminist activist Ford-Smith (1997) has noted, women's material conditions have worsened, thereby increasing their economic reliance on men within the context of family systems. It would thus not be possible to conduct a critical analysis of family systems without examining the relationship between gender and the economy in constituting various family forms. This underscores the importance of gender as a meaningful analytic category in the examination of kin networks in Jamaica.

It is also essential to explore the role of colonialism in the construction of gender. The connection between colonialism and race and/or class oppression is seen as more obvious or more tangible than that between colonialism and gender oppression. Colonialism constructs gender in much the same way with one major exception: gender differences and gendered norms and behaviors are persistently viewed as "natural" in the way that race and class differences used to be. Cuales asserted that this naturalization is due in part to "the belief that gender inequalities are not (fully) social but [are] to some extent natural, whereas class oppression is entirely social and due to a system of exploitation" (1988: 120). This conceptualization stems from the notion that women and men are different and that these differences are "natural," that is, biological rather than social. Without going into an in-depth discussion of the essentialism versus equality debate (Schor 1994), one problem with this analysis is that in the same way that "feminine" and "masculine" are socially constructed, the categories "female" and "male" are also socially constructed and their meanings are subject to interpretation.[12]

The hitherto unquestioned "naturalness" of the categories female and male must be scrutinized because an understanding of gender as emanating from these "natural" categories of female and male elides the ways in which colonialism is constitutive of the category "woman" itself. Several feminist scholars, among them Mohanty (1991), argue that rereading the colonizers as white and "masculinized" demonstrates that colonialism had a particular agenda directed not just toward people of color but particularly toward women of color. The colonizers had a vested interest in representing the colonized in ways that fit the colonial agenda; depending on the colonial mission, Third World people were variously constructed as childlike, incapable, or irrational. For example, at varying historical moments, colonized men have been depicted as lazy or effeminate, while women have also been variously constructed as strong and "un-sexual" or as highly sexual (Davis 1983). Mohanty noted that "the British colonial state established a particular form of rule through the bureaucratization of gender . . . in terms of the institution of colonial services" (Mohanty 1991: 16). These discursive constructions of Third World people, particularly women, served to essentialize and victimize them by portraying them as static, as stuck in whatever historical moment is convenient for whomever is describing them. Consequently, it is crucial, within the context of family systems in Jamaica, to examine the constitutive role of colonialism in the construction of not just race and class, but also of gender as an analytic category.

Along with theorizing these axes of identity, it is important to remember that because race, class, and gender are socially constructed, their meanings, indeed their very parameters, vary across time and circumstance and, as such, are fundamentally unstable. I certainly do not want to suggest that I believe Jamaicans, and specifically women, are bound and static in their environment, or unable to initiate and negotiate change. Just the opposite is true. Although there are models of behavior for women and men of varying classes/races/colors, both sexes strategize and maneuver within the family structure in order to get what they want. Women in particular engage in a variety of tactics at their disposal to ensure their own economic survival as well as that of their children. It is important to examine the ways women and men negotiate these strategies, both in the present and historically, in order to understand the emergence of varying family types within specific classes.

Race and Class as Constitutive of Gender

In Jamaica, the concept of femininity is so race/color/class specific that a critical distinction is made between "woman" and "lady," with the former referring to lower-class, poor females, and the latter referring to middle- to upper-class females. A light- to medium-skinned black woman will be referred to as a "brown skin lady" while a dark-skinned woman is almost always, unless she is wealthy, referred to as a "woman." The difference between "woman" and "lady" is viewed as inherent, biological, and as such, is thought to be evident in the female's behavior, public/private decorum, and ways of speaking. "A lady carefully monitors her speech. She must not speak loudly. . . . She does not use vulgar language or patois . . . is seldom seen on the street outside of her car" (Douglass 1992: 245). This is in contrast to a "woman," who goes to "rum bars" with men, plays dominoes, drinks alcohol, dances suggestively, and who must either take the bus or walk wherever she is going. In another vein, a "lady" is often a wife while a "woman" is not afforded the respectability that is associated with marriage (Douglass 1992: 245). The relationship between "woman" and "lady" is complex and is bound by issues of class and race.

These raced and classed notions of gender are also evident in the relations that emerge from a basic mistrust between the sexes. Within Jamaican society, it is expected that men will be unfaithful to their partners—wives, common-law wives, or "baby mothers" (Prior 1993). This type of behavior is expected because of the pervasive stereotype of men as being sexually uncontrollable and insatiable. It is not uncommon for a wealthy or middle-class man to have two separate families; he may be married to one woman, usually of his own class and possibly color, while the other woman is usually from a lower class and her children are illegitimate. While this practice is not overtly encouraged, it is mostly overlooked if the man is discrete (Smith 1987). Most women know about their husband's philandering, but it is certainly not considered sufficient grounds to end a marriage; instead, the behavior is tolerated. Lower-class men may do the same thing although they cannot afford to take care of both families; hence, they may move from woman to woman rather than maintaining two families simultaneously for an extended period of time. Ortmayr contended that these situations exist because "[m]en in Jamaica do not like to take on responsibility" (1996: 253). This observation is simplistic and ignores the economic factors that make this dual-family life on the part of men possible, and even acceptable. Compounding this is a view of multiple children as a sign of male virility: "accumulating children would be public manifestations of his [male] potency—of his masculine social power" (MacCormack and Draper 1987: 146).[13] As I mentioned above, and will explain in more detail below, there are some economic justifications for the representation of men as marginal within the context of the family.

Race and class specific constructions of femininity have served to maintain different kinship systems in lower- and middle-class groups. For example, the differentiation made between "woman" and "lady" is one of the factors that perpetuates the notion that it is acceptable for men to maintain dual families as long as the "other woman" is beneath him in social status. These intersections have also created distinct kinship patterns in both lower and middle/upper classes. In the former, female-centered networks emphasizing consanguineal relations, namely mother/child intergenerational bonds, predominate; while nuclear families that emphasize affinal relations, namely wife/husband relations, dominate in the latter (Harrison 1990).

Additionally, the institution of marriage itself can be seen as productive of the category gender. Marriage in Jamaica has been extensively, though not exhaustively, examined, and I will not attempt to retrace those discussions in any detail (Douglass 1992; Sobo 1993; Smith 1996, 1987, 1986). My primary concern is to demonstrate the importance of including race, class, and gender as analytic categories in conversations about marriage. Very often, marriage has been viewed or analyzed with respect to race and class but not gender; I would argue that marriage is an excellent example of the constitutive power of race and class in terms of gender within the context of kinship in Jamaica. This is because marriage forms are situated within the framework of colonial constructions of womanhood, which not only determine the general form of the marriage itself, but also shape the ways women involved view themselves and their experiences. In this way, the rate of marriage for the population as a whole may be seen as a consequence of, among other things, particular constructions of gender. As the discussion below will demonstrate, particular constructions of femininity play a significant role in determining which women will marry, as well as when and to whom they will get married.

Race, Class, and Gender in Lower-Class Kin Networks

The marriage rate in Jamaica is rather low: in 1984, the rate was 4.6 per 1,000 people, similar to what it was in 1879 (Douglass 1992: 126). In 1988, it was 4.4 per 1,000 people, and the average between 1974 and 1988 was 4.3 per 1,000 people (Sobo 1993: 193). Historically, as a consequence of slavery, the idea of marriage was tied to the notion of being "civilized," with civility being closely connected to Christianity, economic success, and "whiteness." For the lower classes, there was reduced social pressure to marry before starting a family because Jamaican society, and possibly even the people themselves, believed they were somehow less "civilized" and less restricted. This is corroborated by Douglass, who pointed out "[m]arriage itself is defined as civilized behavior and therefore indicative of class; marriage is also defined as white and therefore indicative of color" (1992: 130). Marriage was, and to certain extent still is, something rich people do. As a result, among the lower classes, kin networks tend to be female-centered. The important bond is not between a woman and a man, but between a woman and her children. Consequently, households tend to consist of a woman, her dependent children, and, oftentimes, her mother (Ortmayr 1996: 251). Marriage is not typically an important part of this kin system because there are few economic assets to protect or to pass down through the generations.

Marriage also becomes an option for people who, after living together for several years and having several children, now deem their relationship more economically secure (Prior 1993). Marriage is thus not an economic strategy that is used to any large degree by poor women. Because steady employment is unpredictable, keeping a partner who might not make regular economic contributions for extended periods is not beneficial to poor women. Instead of monogamous marriage, it has made better sense for poor women, over their life spans, to have a series of partners who offer financial support. Thus, in the lower class, a sort of serial monogamy without marriage emerges. People in this group may have children without getting married or even necessarily living together.[14] The pattern could look something like this—a woman involved with a man would deliberately get pregnant with his child in order to ensure that he would continue to make economic contributions to her household. This is a fragile relationship and often will not last for an extended time, at which point the woman may begin the process with another man. In Jamaica, it is not at all unusual for a woman to have two or three children with different fathers. This was the case with a member of my family who has five children. The first two were with different men and the last three were with the same man, whom she later married.

The kinship system that emerged in the lower socioeconomic stratum also reflects the ways in which women and men view each other. Terms in the local dialect or patois both describe and define these relations. For instance, a woman will refer to a man with whom she has a child outside of marriage as her "baby father," and a man in the same type of situation will refer to the woman as his "baby mother." This term does not necessarily indicate a close emotional bond between a woman and man, although it could; it does usually imply an economic bond between the couple. Usually it means that the man is or is supposed to be making a financial contribution to the welfare of the child. Thus, in the lower class, the term "baby father" or "baby mother" connotes higher status because it signifies that there is, at the very least, an economic bond between two people in the form of a child to support. Another component to the rise in status centers on the related increase in social power garnered by women and men in the lower class who have children. For women, childbirth is a mark of social adulthood, while for men, having several children is a mark of virility.[15] It is important to note that in the middle and upper classes this term ("baby mother" or "baby father") is hardly, if ever, used and is considered to be derogatory.

Job scarcity among the poor also plays a significant role in the emergence of this kinship system in the lower class because it leads to economic insecurity, which breeds suspicion between the sexes. Douglass notes that "women question male partners' sincerity about taking financial responsibility and men say they fear that women will try to control their lives if they marry" (1992: 127). This economic insecurity combined with internalized racism have created a situation in Jamaica within the last five or ten years where women have literally altered their bodies, particularly skin color, in order to secure their economic survival. Noticing the value placed on light-skinned women in Jamaica, dark-skinned women among the lower socioeconomic stratum have begun to use a variety of agents, ranging from toothpaste to bleach, to lighten the color of the facial skin. These women hope to make themselves more attractive to men of their own or a higher class who may prefer lighter-skinned women. In this way, a woman's physical appearance becomes the embodiment of her economic strategy. This illustration does not imply that middle-class women do not also engage in this activity. The difference is that class privilege means that their usage of these bleaching agents is private, within their homes. Among women in the lower class, usage is more visible since poverty often means they are denied access to private spaces, such as private rooms or offices, and are instead forced to use public spaces such as market areas or sidewalks. Additionally, they generally use harsher chemicals because they cannot afford less-abrasive products. Although this generalization cannot be extrapolated to an entire class of women, it is important as an illustration of the complexities involved in women's economic strategies, class status, and identity formation within the context of kin networks. This is an example of how racial, social, economic, and gendered identities collide, and in the process, obfuscate the myriad of ways they work together to shape daily life.

Despite all this, it would be erroneous to assume that economic pressures are the only ones at work in the construction of lower-class female–male unions. While it is true that high unemployment and economic instability are vital factors in determining marriage form, marriage itself may be seen as significantly influencing the very ways in which womanhood is constructed in this socioeconomic stratum. By this I mean that very often women in the lower class are constructed as unmarriageable, as not in possession of the qualities necessary to be a "good" wife. "Good wives" are often constructed as being of a certain educational level, one which would allow them to be employed in administrative positions in prestigious companies and not as manual laborers. Related to this is the idea that they would be good arbiters of "high culture" in that they are able to speak "proper" English and are acquainted with "proper" etiquette and able to pass these abilities on to their children. Additionally, a lighter skin color is often included as more desirable in an ideal wife because it is inextricably connected to the other ideals I mentioned above. If the ideal is described as light-skinned, for instance, dark-skinned women are excluded from even considering themselves as potential wives. Women who are constructed as outside the "ideal," which is usually a middle-class ideal, are again excluded from the possibility of seeing themselves as potential wives. It is in this way that marriage may be seen as a site that demonstrates the operation of race and class in the constitution of gender.

Race, Class, and Gender in Middle-Class Kin Networks

The situation is somewhat different among the middle and upper classes, where the predominant and preferred family type is the nuclear family, which presupposes that a woman's first allegiance is to her husband and then to her children. In this group, marriage is fairly important for economic and moral reasons. For the very wealthy, class endogamy is the product of economic interests: it is important to make a match with someone who is also from a wealthy family in order to maintain control of financial resources. Where they occur, cross-class marriages are closely tied to gender relations; it is mostly women who marry "up" (hypergamously, that is, they marry men who have higher social status). As Douglass noted, "in Jamaican marriages, then, hypergamy coexists with isogamy . . . [b]ut the pattern is clearly organized by gender: Women marry 'up' and men marry 'down' . . . because gender hierarchy is accepted as normal in heterosexual relations" (1992: 136).

As I stated earlier, although marriage itself is a status symbol, there are other social expectations involved as well. These social expectations mean that women of this class are expected not to have children outside of wedlock. Although there are no longer any legal sanctions, there is considerable social shame associated with "illegitimate" children in the middle/upper class.[16] Women in this group consider themselves "above" having children without being married. These women have more to lose by having illegitimate children in the form of social status and access to resources than do women of lower classes. Women in this class who have illegitimate children are less marriageable than their childless counterparts. Abortions are fairly common in this group, in contrast to the poor who cannot afford them. In this group, marriage is a way of declaring independence and the attainment of adulthood, fulfilling much the same function that having a child does in the lower classes (Douglass 1992: 139).

Another integral part of fulfilling social expectations is the influence of Christianity and its impact on the formation of gender identity. As in the United States, women from lower socioeconomic groups are considered to be inherently more sexual, with an uncontrollable sexuality, than women from the middle/upper class. Thus, there is a predominant notion concerning what sort of sexual behavior is "natural" to women and men. Ideally, middle-upper-class women are seen as completely in control of their sexuality: they must tolerate sex in order to please and keep their husbands. "Good Christian women" are similarly perceived to lack an interest and enjoyment in sex, but are supposedly available whenever their husbands "need" it. All men, on the other hand, are perceived as having a wild and uncontrollable sexuality and of having the potential to cheat on their wives. If their wives do not "provide" sex, they are justified in finding it elsewhere. In other words, women are held responsible for reining in the husband's sexual appetite.

The experience of another family member illustrates this point. She was seventeen when she became pregnant. The child's father was from a higher-status, although not a particularly wealthy, family in town, while the mother was from a lower-status family, although they were not poor. The difference in status derived from differences in educational levels and occupations. In the higher-status family, one parent was a schoolteacher and the other a headmaster; while in the lower-status family, one parent was a mason and the other was illiterate. So even though the actual economic levels may have been comparable, these two families were in different social classes as a result of differences in status. In the ensuing scandal, the woman was held responsible for the situation that resulted in her pregnancy because she was unable (or unwilling) to keep her desires and those of her lover in check. The paradox of this situation was that even though the woman was from the lower social class, and therefore susceptible to the stereotype of rampant sexuality, as a woman, she is considered to be more in control of her sexuality than a man, despite her class. Any untoward behavior by men is generally explained or dismissed with the phrase "a man 'im name" (patois for "he's not culpable because he's a man"). This reinforces the perception of male sexuality as inherently uncontrollable, which pervades the entire society and is not class or race specific; the idea of female sexuality, on the other hand, is class and race specific. As Douglass notes, "women are expected to conform not to a single measure of femininity, but to *class-specific* attitudes and behaviors that carry connotations of color" (1992: 243). It is also important to note that as a globalizing U.S. culture gains more of a foothold in Jamaica, these notions of female sexuality are changing. Nevertheless the roots of these attitudes are deep.

Conclusion

The intersections of race, class, and gender in Jamaican kinship are difficult to explicate because they are so interwoven and accepted as a "natural" part of the fabric of society. I was raised to believe that because I grew up in a country where people who "looked" liked me composed the majority of the population, there was no racism; because of my privileged position, I was unable to see the classism until after I had moved to the United States. This way of seeing and being is so insidious that most Jamaicans may not even be conscious of the myriad layers that bind their lives. People in positions of privilege may deny that skin color offers them any advantages, while the underprivileged may deny that they accord greater respect to others based on skin color. All these add to the complexities inherent in any discourse on kinship in Jamaica. Colonization of the island and the early establishment of a racial, social, and gendered hierarchy constructed and continues to be productive of kinship systems today. If we are to understand how these axes of identity operate in the production of kin networks, we must first be cognizant of how they interact with and produce each other. I am not advocating the uncritical use of gender as an analytic category, which simply requires the researcher to add women and stir (Mohammed 1995). Instead, I am espousing critical reconceptualizations of race, class, and gender that pay attention to their mutually constitutive functions and how this is then productive of kinship systems. In other words, in addition to race, class, and gender being productive of each other, as these identities collide, they enter into a dialectical relationship with kin systems, where both are productive of each other.

The kind of analysis that pays attention to multiple axes of identity and how they constitute each other is significant for several reasons. First, this analysis begins with the premise that people are multiply constituted and thus seeks to examine and expose how these various axes of identity are either deliberately or inadvertently obscured through their naturalization in sundry social contexts. It is important to examine how the collision of these identities colludes the inner workings of social relations from even the participants themselves. This approach takes into account the innumerable tactics people employ in order to ensure their survival. Secondly, an awareness of the complexities of social systems, such as kinship, improves comprehension of the mechanisms of social change and provides broader contextualization that may be utilized to effect social change. The aim of this work is not to re-inscribe stereotypes of responsible, hardworking black women in opposition to irresponsible, lazy black men. As Brown et al. (1997) attest, there is as much diversity among men and their familial relations as there is among women in the Caribbean. Rather, my intent has been to focus attention on the importance of seeing, theorizing, and understanding people as influenced by multiple axes of identity. One or another of these may be foregrounded at any one time, but it is the inevitable collision of these identities and the resulting collusion of their various aspects that create the experiences that inform daily life and practice.

Notes

This chapter emerged from a series of long discussions and heated debates with family, peers, and mentors and was made possible because of the incredible patience and encouragement from a number of people to whom I am deeply grateful. They include Linda Stone, Daphne Berdahl, Kathleen Barlow, Jennifer Stampe, Amy Porter, Jen Fox, Jodi Horne, Dawn Rae Davis, Lisa Disch, Keith Vargo, Ragnaheidur Propper, Pamela Anderson, and Robert Levy.

1. The negative connotation of this word is useful here because it gets to the injustice or harm that may occur when the relationship among various aspects of identity is obscured.

2. The term kinship, as argued by Fabian, is loaded with temporal significance and its usage has typically implied a certain "primitiveness." Throughout the chapter, I use the terms kin, kin networks, family, and family systems interchangeably as a way of demystifying or de-exoticizing the term kinship. My fluid usage is an attempt to destabilize or denaturalize this meaning (see Fabian 1983).

3. The construction of this object of study was in reaction to evolutionary theories that espoused a hierarchy of human cultural development (see Szwed 1972). Additionally, Mohammed (1988: 172) noted that "[t]he origins of family studies in the Caribbean are to be found in the polemics among [U.S.] anthropologists of the time."

4. This of course refers to anthropologists educated in the United States. British anthropologists, complicit in the colonial project, had a differing agenda, although with similar results. See note 3 above.

5. A similar situation occurred with blacks in the United States, where their bleak social conditions were blamed on an inherent cultural defect, as evidenced by their family structures compared with the norm (see Barrow 1996).

6. See, for instance, note 5 above.

7. In an interesting discussion about the interconnectedness of race and class, Bakan (1990) noted that "[i]n Jamaican society, racism and class rule are intricately linked, and one cannot be understood without the other . . . [t]he slave origins . . . led to the development of a general correlation between class and race in the society as a whole: the fairer the skin color, the higher the individual's social status."

8. My discussion about how these axes of identity have been theorized necessitates using the work of U.S. feminists of color simply because I have greater access to these works. While I am aware that Caribbean, particularly Jamaican, feminists have theorized about these axes and intend to use some of this work, I have only limited access to many of these studies because they are simply not available in the United States.

9. In 1975, the racial composition of the Jamaican population was described as "91 percent African, 6 percent Mixed, 2 percent East Indian, 0.5 percent Chinese and 0.5 percent White" (Smith 1988).

10. A complete explication of this complex term is outside the scope of this paper. It is used by Jamaicans to denote light-skinned Jamaicans who may not be considered white within a U.S. context but who receive skin color privilege on this basis.

11. It is worthwhile noting here that anthropological discourse also ignored women as producers of knowledge. They ignored women as a category of "knowers," as people who possess special or important knowledge. One of the pioneering methods of theorizing how women's unique social position permits them to create a particular epistemic standpoint can be found in the work of Harstock (1997).

12. For an explication of this see Butler (1990).

13. Davis (1983) discusses the stereotype of black male sexuality, which I do not wish to perpetuate with my portrayal of Jamaican men, however, it is important to point out the connections some men make between having several children and their virility.

14. Prior (1993: 314) observed that "[c]ouples tended to set up visiting relationships whereby the couple did not coreside [and that] [c]hildren . . . may be born from these unions."

15. MacCormack and Draper noted that "for both men and women, perceptions of self-identity and social power are contingent upon the expression of sexual potency which is confirmed by the birth of children" and further that "women's social strength is even more closely identified with the bearing and rearing of children" (1987: 143, 146).

16. Douglass noted that the "Status of Children Act of 1976 sought to diminish the negative legal and institutional effects of illegitimacy for children, but its social and emotional significance remains" (1992: 188).

References

Bakan, Abigail. 1990. *Ideology and Class Conflict in Jamaica: The Politics of Rebellion.* Montreal: McGill-Queen's University Press.

Barrow, Christine. 1988. Anthropology, the Family and Women in the Caribbean. In *Gender in Caribbean Development*, ed. Patricia Mohammed and Catherine Shepherd. Mona, Jamaica: University of the West Indies.

———. 1996. *Family in the Caribbean: Themes and Perspectives.* Kingston, Jamaica: Randle.

Brown, Janet, Arthur Newland, Patricia Anderson, and Barry Chevannes. 1997. Caribbean Fatherhood: Underresearched, Misunderstood. In *Caribbean Families: Diversity Among Ethnic Groups*, ed. Jaipaul Roopnarine and Janet Brown. London: Ablex.

Butler, Judith. 1990. *Gender Trouble: Feminism and the Subversion of Identity.* New York: Routledge.

Cuales, Sonia. 1988. Some Theoretical Considerations on Social Class, Class Consciousness, and Gender Consciousness. In *Gender in Caribbean Development*, ed. Patricia Mohammed and Catherine Shepherd. Mona, Jamaica: University of the West Indies.

Davis, Angela. 1983. *Women, Race, and Class*. New York: Vintage.

Del Valle, Teresa. 1993. *Gendered Anthropology*. London: Routledge.

Douglass, Lisa. 1992. *The Power of Sentiment: Love, Hierarchy, and the Jamaican Family Elite*. San Francisco: Westview.

Fabian, Johannes. 1983. *Time and the Other: How Anthropology Makes Its Object*. New York: Columbia University Press.

Ford-Smith, Honor. 1997. Ring Ding in a Tight Corner: Sistren, Collective Democracy, and the Organization of Cultural Production. In *Feminist Genealogies, Colonial Legacies, Democratic Futures*, ed. M. Jacqui Alexander and Chandra Talpade Mohanty. New York: Routledge.

Haraway, Donna. 1988. Situated Knowledges: The Science Question in Feminism and the Privilege of Partial Perspective. *Feminist Studies* 14, no. 3:575–99.

Harrison, Faye V. 1990. Women in Jamaica's Urban Informal Economy: Insights from a Kingston Slum. In *Third World Women and The Politics of Feminism*, ed. Chandra Talpade Mohanty, Ann Russo, and Lourdes Torres. Bloomington: Indiana University Press.

Harstock, Nancy C. M. 1997. The Feminist Standpoint: Developing the Ground for a Specifically Feminist Historical Materialism. In *Feminist Social Thought: A Reader*, ed. Diana Tiejens Meyers. New York: Routledge.

Hill Collins, Patricia. 1997. Defining Black Feminist Thought. In *The Second Wave: A Reader in Feminist Theory*, ed. Linda Nicholson. New York: Routledge.

hooks, bell. 1984. *Feminist Theory: From Margin to Center*. Boston: South End Press.

———. 1989. *Talking Back: Thinking Feminist, Thinking Black*. Boston: South End Press.

Leo-Rhynie, Elsa A. 1997. Class, Race, and Gender Issues in Child Rearing in the Caribbean. In *Caribbean Families: Diversity Among Ethnic Groups*, ed. Jaipaul L. Roopnarine and Janet Brown. London: Ablex.

Lorde, Audre. 1984. *Sister Outsider: Essays and Speeches*. Freedom, Calif.: Crossing Press.

MacCormack, Carol P., and Alizon Draper. 1987. Social and Cognitive Aspects of Female Sexuality in Jamaica. In *The Cultural Construction of Sexuality*, ed. Pat Caplan. London: Travistock.

Mohammed, Patricia. 1988. The Caribbean Family Revisited. In *Gender in Caribbean Development*, ed. Patricia Mohammed and Catherine Shepherd. Mona, Jamaica: University of the West Indies.

———. 1995. Writing Gender into History: The Negotiation of Gender Relations among Indian Men and Women in Post-Indenture Trinidad Society. In *Engendering History: Caribbean Women in Historical Perspective*, ed. Verene Shepherd, Bridget Brereton, and Barbara Bailey. New York: St. Martin's.

Mohanty, Chandra Talpade. 1991. Under Western Eyes: Feminist Scholarship and Colonial Discourses. In *Third World Women and the Politics of Feminism*, ed. Chandra Talpade Mohanty, Ann Russo, and Lourdes Torres. Bloomington: Indiana University Press.

Narayan, Kirin. 1997. How Native is a "Native" Anthropologist? In *Situated Lives: Gender and Culture in Everyday Life*, ed. Louise Lamphere, Heléna Ragoné, and Patricia Zavella. New York: Routledge.

Narayan, Uma. 1997. *Dislocating Culture: Identities, Traditions, and Third World Feminism*. New York: Routledge.

Ortmayr, Norbert. 1996. Illegitimacy and Low-Wage Economy in Highland Austria and Jamaica. In *Gender, Kinship, Power: A Comparative and Interdisciplinary History*, ed. Mary Jo Maynes, Ann Waltner, Birgitte Soland, and Ulrite Strasser. New York: Routledge.

Prior, Marsha. 1993. Matrifocality, Power, and Gender Relations in Jamaica. In *Gender in Cross-Cultural Perspective*, ed. Caroline B. Brettell and Carolyn F. Sargent. Upper Saddle River, N.J.: Prentice Hall.

Schor, Naomi. 1994. This Essentialism Which Is Not One: Coming to Grips with Irigaray. In *The Essential Difference*, ed. Naomi Schor and Elizabeth Weed. Bloomington: Indiana University Press.

Smith, Raymond T. 1986. *The Matrifocal Family: Power, Pluralism, and Politics.* New York: Routledge.

———. 1987. Hierarchy and the Dual Marriage System in West Indian Society. In *Gender and Kinship: Essays Toward a Unified Analysis*, ed. Jane Fishburne Collier and Sylvia Junko Yanagisako. Stanford: Stanford University Press.

———. 1988. *Kinship and Class in the West Indies: A Genealogical Study of Jamaica and Guyana.* Cambridge, U.K.: Cambridge University Press.

———. 1996. *The Matrifocal Family: Power, Pluralism, and Politics.* New York: Routledge.

Sobo, Elisa Janine. 1993. *One Blood: The Jamaican Body.* Albany, N.Y.: SUNY Press.

Szwed, John. 1972. An American Anthropological Dilemma: The Politics of Afro-American Culture. In *Reinventing Anthropology*, ed. Dell Hymes. New York: Pantheon.

Wiltshire-Brodber, Rosina. 1988. Gender, Race, and Class in the Caribbean. In *Gender in Caribbean Development*, ed. Patricia Mohammed and Catherine Shepherd. Mona, Jamaica: University of the West Indies.

Chapter Twelve

Kin and Gender in Classic Maya Society: A Case Study from Yaxchilán, Mexico

Cynthia Robin

Ancient Maya kings recorded versions of their life histories in hieroglyphic texts and images on buildings and monuments throughout their civic-ceremonial centers. These three media—text, image, and space—worked together to form publicly circulating narratives that combined history, worldview, and personal and political goals, strategies, and agendas (e.g., Ashmore 1986, 1991, 1998; Freidel et al. 1993; Gillespie and Joyce 1997; Joyce 1992, 1993, 1996; Marcus 1992a, 1995; Schele and Freidel 1990). Ordered human relationships, especially kin and gender relations, were important to ancient Maya constructions of power, and establishing these relationships in life narratives was critical to a king's assumption of power. As such, a unified analysis of kinship and gender (*sensu stricto*, Yanagisako and Collier 1987) seems appropriate in the Maya case.

In terms of gender, analysis of imagery on ancient Maya monuments as discourses on the meaning of gender relations reveals a notion of gender complementarity. A complementary gender construct views the female–male pair as the significant unit in society, constructed through the union of different actions undertaken by differently gendered persons (Gillespie and Joyce 1997; Josserand 1993; Joyce 1992, 1993, 1996). The texts on ancient Maya monuments are often studied to elucidate historical facts in the life histories of kings who are usually, but not always, male, presenting us with a male focused view of the past. By contrast, reading texts as discourses on meaning reveals a construction of gender compatible with that presented in associated images. Texts, images, and spatial layouts do not simply recount a univocal pan-Maya ideology. These narratives were authorized by specific people, mostly kings, and occasionally other elites. Reading texts as having authors and audiences allows exploration of different experiences and perceptions of self and society, held by various authors and other actors (e.g., Freidel et al. 1993; Jones 1977; Schele and Freidel 1990; Tate 1992).

Where gender studies focus on illuminating culturally constructed attributes, kinship studies in Maya archaeology often focus on documenting the fit
of Western anthropologically constructed kinship systems (e.g., matrilineal,
patrilineal, cognatic) and ancient Maya data.[1] Debate is still ongoing as to
which system best describes the ancient Maya case (for reviews, see Hopkins
1988; Sharer 1993; Wilk 1988). I follow Sharer's (1993) position that Maya
kinship was not a single system but one that has varied in time and across
space among the Maya. The key to understanding ancient Maya concepts of
kinship, like gender, lies in an examination of the discourses used by the ancient Maya to circulate their narratives (e.g., Gillespie and Joyce 1997;
Josserand 1993; Marcus 1992a). People's life narratives, their actions and decisions in relation to others, and their perceptions of natural and supernatural order were the building blocks of kinship, not idiosyncrasies to be subsumed into a system. Following a brief discussion of debates in kinship studies
leading to the development of a "discourse approach" to kinship (Bourdieu
1977; Schneider 1984; Urban 1996), this chapter uses discourse to analyze
connections between person, kin, and gender in ancient Maya society.

A Discourse Approach to Kinship

As kinship defines the relationships people have with one another, it has been
central to anthropological thought. Changes in kinship studies have often
mirrored changes throughout the larger field of anthropology. Kinship studies in particular, and anthropological studies in general, have turned from
defining culture as an abstract and internally coherent system of rules to understanding culture as historically situated sets of meanings created and conceived by people based upon their knowledge of the interworkings of their
world. This study focuses on kin relations and their meaning as constructed
in ancient Maya discourse. While I do not want to argue that studies of kinship systems and those of kin relations and meaning are or need be mutually
exclusive pursuits (see Stone 1997), studies of kinship as culturally constructed have arisen, in part, from dissatisfactions with the systematic and categorical view of kinship (e.g., Barnes 1971; Bourdieu 1977; Goody 1990; Kelly
1993; Peletz 1995; Schneider 1968, 1984; Urban 1996; Wilk 1988; Yanagisako
and Collier 1987). For example, descent theory (Fortes 1953) grouped societies into two types, those forming descent groups and those not forming descent groups, and divided the former into descent types—unilineal and
nonunilineal or cognatic. However, Western anthropology's descent constructs may not be universally applicable to all groups, and in any case, a concept of "groupness," as either there or not there, is an oversimplification. As
Urban noted (1996: 140–46), group membership may or may not be mutually
exclusive. People may form groups of varying sizes with varying degrees of in-
clusivity and exclusivity. People in the same society may belong to multiple

groups at the same time. Groups may come together in certain situations, with these same groups being nonexistent in other situations.

Furthermore, Stone (1997) reminded us that virtually all societies exhibit bilateral kinship (as opposed to bilateral descent) in the sense that most people "consider that they are related to their mothers and fathers and, through them, to other people" (1997: 60). The common ancient Maya use of the "child of mother" and "child of father" glyphs in royal titles indicates a recognition of bilateral kinship (Joyce 1996). A recognition of bilateral kinship does not necessarily imply that a biological model is the basis for kinship, as this relationship is particular to historical developments in Western society (Schneider 1968, 1984; Yanagisako and Collier 1987; Yanagisako and Delaney 1995). For example, the people of Zumbagua in highland Ecuador (Weismantel 1995) or the Nuyoo from the coastal Oaxaca region of Mexico (Monaghan 1995: 193–97) make kin through nourishment and nurturing—and this nourishment and nurturing is not predicated on a Western procreative model. Similarly, Weber (1978: 356–68) contended that pre-Christian European notions of kinship, specifically the father–mother–child relationship, are not based on the biology of this relationship. He gave, as an example, the Greek term *homogalaktes*, meaning sibling groups, which is defined as persons suckled with the same milk. Thus, what makes kin relatives may not always be a biological relationship, but common maintenance of persons in a household.

Recognized bilateral kinship often muddies clearly demarcated divisions between traditional unilineal descent group types (Stone 1997). In a specifically defined descent system, certain "biases" or "allowances" often result in practical relations that resemble other descent systems. An example from a group traditionally defined as patrilineal is the Nuer. Among the Nuer, when nonpatrilineal kin may join a residence and become real patrilineal members, this descent system could be termed patrilineal with cognatic allowances (Stone 1997: 165). An example from a group traditionally defined as having bilateral descent is the Quechua speakers of Q'ero, Peru. For the Quechua of Q'ero, patrilineal "biases" emerge due to gender relations where the male has a dominant role in political and economic domains, a system that could be termed bilateral with patrilineal biases (Webster 1977: 29). Additionally, variation between groups classified as having the same descent system is often as great a variation as that between different descent systems: traditional descent system labeling may, at times, obscure more behavior than it elucidates (Collier and Yanagisako 1987; Stone 1997). As Goodenough (1956) pointed out some time ago for residence rules, there is greater variability and flexibility in kin systems than systemic anthropological classification allows. Stone (1997) and Wilk (1988), among others, suggested that kinship studies should not focus on debates over *our* terminological distinctions, but ask what the people themselves consider important about their kinship.

Urban (1996: 137–82; see also Bourdieu 1977, and Schneider 1984) questioned general methods developed within anthropology to "find" kinship, abstracting kin terms from language or genealogical charts and studying these as an internally coherent system of rules. Abstracting kin terms from language or kinship charts from social relations assumes that every society has a concept of meaning similar to the way we make dictionaries, where terms, such as kinship terms, can be assigned meaning outside a mode of linguistic and social interaction. The opposite is the case: defining terms, as in dictionary making, is not a universal practice. Dictionaries are only one of many discourses on meaning. Through discourse, meanings of expressions become fixed as they are repeated across time and space, between contemporaries, and through generations. Discourses on meaning can be any public discourse widely circulating in a social group. There is no evidence that pre-Columbian Maya peoples practiced dictionary making, but they did record narratives "written" in linguistic, artistic, and spatial conventions to convey meanings.

The object of a discourse-centered approach to kinship is not construction of a genealogy or abstraction of kin terms followed by definition of the "system" behind them. It is examination of kin terms within the context of people's discourse (Urban 1996: 166). The focus is not to elucidate all the possible kin relations that could be reconstructed based on texts, but to examine the function and meaning of kin terms as actually used in discourse. What role expectations do kin terms imply for kinspeople? Why does a person use a term of kin relation in discourse to refer to another person rather than referring to them by a name or pronoun? Why, when, and where are kin relations active in social life? Discourse analysis provides a means to define kin relations irrespective of our own (Urban 1996: 148).

Ancient Maya Kinship at Yaxchilán

The ancient Maya were one of many peoples who inhabited Mesoamerica, an area encompassed by modern-day Mexico, Belize, Guatemala, El Salvador, and Honduras, prior to Spanish conquest in the sixteenth century. Scholars traditionally define the height of Maya civilization as the Classic period that spans approximately A.D. 250 to 900. The Classic was the period when the ancient Maya flourished in the arts, employed intricate systems of writing, calendrics and astronomy, and constructed large cities, each of which maintained a complex governmental system under the divine rule of a single king. Inhabitants of ancient Maya cities certainly shared many views on society and the world, but it does not seem that they were ever unified as a centralized whole. Classic Maya political organization is considered one of loosely tied polities, changing in size and power through time (Marcus 1992b, 1993). Each polity was associated with a paramount civic-ceremonial center. Yaxchilán was one such center.

Yaxchilán was located along the Usumacinta River in modern-day Chiapas, Mexico (fig. 12.1). Impressive architectural remains and their elaborate carvings

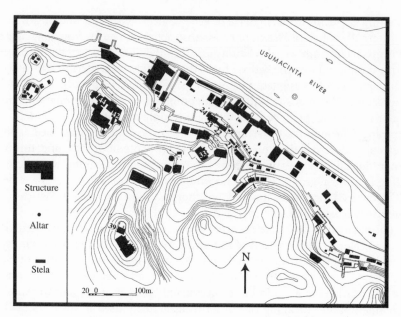

Figure 12.1   Map of Yaxchilán (structures mentioned in text are identified). Drawing by Ian Graham after John Bolles's map of 1931, © President and Fellows of Harvard University, reprinted with permission, Harvard University Press.

have made Yaxchilán a focus of archaeological inquiry since the 1850s (e.g., Maler 1901, 1903; Maudslay 1889–1902; Morley 1937–38; Proskouriakoff 1961, 1963, 1964; summarized in Hammond 1994; Mathews 1988; Sharer 1994). The current analysis of Yaxchilán texts, images, and spaces is indebted to the detailed corpus of recently published architectural, iconographic, and epigraphic studies of Yaxchilán (Bardslay 1987; Josserand and Hopkins 1995; Mathews 1988; Schele 1991; Schele and Grube 1994, 1995; Tate 1992).

At Yaxchilán, carved stone lintels above the doorways of palace/administrative buildings and carved stelae, two-sided, freestanding stone monuments located in open plazas and in front of buildings, provide one of the most complete political histories of a Maya city. Yaxchilán's political history was largely recorded from the perspective of later kings who trace their power to a founder, Ruler 1 (Penis Jaguar),[2] in A.D. 320. Although other information on Yaxchilán's political history was inscribed in texts at other cities (e.g., Bardsley 1987: 3; Mathews 1988: 232, 234; Schele 1982: 226; Schele and Freidel 1990: 304), this chapter addresses only the history that Yaxchilán elites chose to present at Yaxchilán. At Yaxchilán, rulers were listed as numbered successors from Ruler 1 up to Ruler 10 (Lord Skull [II])[3] in A.D. 526. After Ruler 10's reign, the record of successors from Ruler 1 ceased, and no successor was recorded until Ruler 11 (Bird Jaguar [III]), who came to the throne around A.D. 630.[4] Under Rulers 11 to 15, Yaxchilán reached its peak of power and then declined into obscurity. A ten-year hiatus between the death of Ruler 12 (Shield Jaguar [I]), in A.D. 742, and the accession of his son Ruler 13 (Bird Jaguar [IV]), in A.D. 752, is a second gap in Yaxchilán's history. Scholars have long postulated that a power struggle could be a plausible explanation for this gap (Mathews 1988; Proskouriakoff 1963; Schele and Freidel 1990; Sharer 1994; Tate 1992).

Though Yaxchilán texts and images did center on the life histories of male rulers, these rulers also recorded their lives as shared with other female and male kin and nonkin. Twelve of the thirty-four protagonists introduced in Yaxchilán texts were women, who were contemporaries, mothers, or wives of rulers. Yaxchilán art has long been noted for its elaborate portraits, particularly of royal women (Proskouriakoff 1961). Paired male and female actors in texts and images vividly relate how ancient ritual action and military alliances resulted from the interdependence of genders (figs. 12.2a and b). In civic-ceremonial rituals, female figures presented bowls and cloth, and male figures offered scepters, all specifically gendered objects (fig. 12.2a; Gillespie and Joyce 1997). A single offering to the gods was achieved through complementary participants and actions (Joyce 1992, 1993, 1996). Similarly, military and marriage alliances were often depicted as women, contemporaries, or wives offering war implements to rulers (fig. 12.2b; Gillespie and Joyce 1997; Marcus 1983; Schele and Mathews 1991).

Although Yaxchilán rulers did record kin relations with other protagonists, they seldom recorded these as genealogies. It does seem that each of the last

a. Lintel 24   b. Lintel 26

Figure 12.2 Lintels from Structure 23, Yaxchilán: a, Ruler 12 and Lady Xoc perform ritual blood letting; b, Lady Xoc gives Ruler 12 military implements. Drawings by Ian Graham and Eric von Eow, © President and Fellows of Harvard University, reprinted with permission, Harvard University Press.

five kings recorded at Yaxchilán was the son of his predecessor in office, if no other king ruled in the ten-year gap between Rulers 12 and 13 (e.g., Mathews 1988; Schele and Freidel 1990; Sharer 1994). Two rulers, Ruler 10 (Lord Skull [II]) and Ruler 8 (Bird Jaguar [II]), were not sons of previous rulers. Ruler 10 was the son of Ruler 7 (Moon Skull). For less documented rulers, kin relations are unknown, largely because these rulers were recorded solely in succession lists that linked kings to one another by office and deeds, but not by kin relation. These lists neither claimed nor denied that hereditary rule was at the genesis of the links in the succession. As Wilk noted (1988: 142), while a succession might emphasize male links, these links do not necessarily imply that patrilineages were present because the mechanisms of succession may not have been the same as the mechanisms of descent. Additionally, ethnographic research has shown that "father–son" links in kin group organization may result from relations that have no jural basis in kinship, such as situations where males, within a restricted group of families, become dominant in political realms (Webster 1977:29). This may have been the case at Yaxchilán.

Yaxchilán kings had one of two names, Jaguar or Skull. Both Jaguars and Skulls traced their succession equally to the founder, Ruler 1 (Penis Jaguar). However, based on current data, we do not know if all were related to him. Many people at Yaxchilán who used the Jaguar name were related to each other. Similarly, people who used the Skull name were related, suggesting that certain names were used by groups of relatives. These names were often passed from parents to their children. For example, Ruler 12 (Shield Jaguar [I]), was the son of Ruler 11 (Bird Jaguar [III]) and Lady Shield. Ruler 12's name seems to combine that of his parents. In other cases, a child's name may only reflect one or neither parent's name. One marriage was recorded between a Jaguar and a Skull; Ruler 13 (Bird Jaguar [IV]) and Lady Great Skull. Their son did not refer to himself as Skull, but as Shield Jaguar [II], Ruler 14. The son of Ruler 14 (Shield Jaguar [II]) and Lady Bloodletter, did not refer to himself by either his mother's or his father's name, but as Lord Skull [III], Ruler 15. Possibly, the Skull in his name refers to his paternal grandmother, Lady Great Skull, through whom two generations of Yaxchilán rulers before Ruler 15 claimed military assistance. Along similar lines, Mathews (1988: 321) suggested that Ruler 15 took the Skull name as the namesake of previous rulers with the same name, Rulers 6 and 10. Although Lady Great Skull was a local elite, we lack evidence to support a kin relation between her and previous Skull rulers. But certainly, the Skull relatives of Lady Great Skull were powerful during Ruler 15's reign. By taking the name Skull, Ruler 15 may have been choosing to emphasize his kinship and/or succession links to and claim legitimacy from one powerful faction over another. At Yaxchilán, it seems, while names were linked to groups of relatives, they were not passed in singular or systematic ways between people, but may have been chosen to express relations to one's most powerful relatives. As Marcus (1992a) noted, tracing specific linkages may not have been the critical factor in determining power in ancient Maya society, but rather, power was derived from the ability to document linkages to important persons and gods.

The Yaxchilán emblem glyph, the unique glyph naming Yaxchilán, is different from other Classic Maya emblem glyphs because it has two main signs. Main signs are interpreted as naming either (or a combination of) a city, a territory or state ruled by a city, or the rulers of a city (Mathews 1991). Yaxchilán's two main signs may have some relation to the two groups of rulers at Yaxchilán, Skull and Jaguar. The succession of Yaxchilán rulers could be explained as a result of relationships between a restricted group of elite families from which an acceptable ruler could be drawn, coupled with a male-dominated system of rulership.

Text, Image, and Space

Texts and images were situated on lintels, wall stucco reliefs, and stelae located throughout the city. Stelae could be viewed from outside. Lintels and wall stucco reliefs were only observable if one was standing in a doorway or inside a building. Most carvings included both text and image, though a few lintels simply contained text, and a few stelae simply had images on one of their two sides.

An issue in the study of ancient Maya texts and images is: who was their audience? Only elites recorded written histories. We have no evidence that commoners could read and write. It is widely considered that they could not. Are texts stories that are written by elites, about elites, and for elites? Are their messages representative of ideas held only by elites, or of Maya society as a whole?

At Yaxchilán, many texts were recorded on lintels in the doorways of palace/administrative buildings, places where access may have been limited. Who would have gone into these buildings to see the lintels? The majority and largely agrarian populace living outside of cities had a wide range of opportunities to come to cities and interact with their inhabitants at public ceremonies and markets, and as participants in rotating *corvée* services. While the nature of possible restrictions, for example, gender, age, or status, on people's access to Maya civic-ceremonial centers is still unclear, those members of society who did have access had opportunities to view stelae, if not lintels.

As we will see in the Yaxchilán case study, in certain instances, texts and images were recorded in space in such a way that redundant messages were conveyed in text and in image, on lintels and on stelae. When the same message was repeated in various spaces and in both text and image, it seems as though Maya elites were reiterating their messages unambiguously to all their varied audiences (Schele and Freidel 1990). Certain aspects of these public messages were not merely representations of an elite mentality and ideology; they also represented an understanding of the world and a person's place in it that was meaningful though possibly equivocal in meaning to the varied readers (for similar conclusions, see Gillespie and Joyce 1997).

In addition to access issues relating to the location of texts and images on stelae or building lintels, the city of Yaxchilán encompassed three different topographic zones. There could have been distinctive access patterns associated with each zone. Zones included a floodplain, a number of hilltops, and an area of low ridges that lay between the floodplain and the hilltops. Although buildings and stelae were situated in all zones (see fig. 12.1), the buildings and stelae on the floodplain surrounded large, open plazas, and those on the hilltops surrounded smaller, often enclosed, plazas (Mathews 1988: 3). These topographic and organizational distinctions may have been associated with more restricted access to hilltop locations and greater public access to the large open plazas on the floodplain, which were spaces more appropriate for large ceremonies (Bardslay 1987: 2; Schele and Freidel 1990: 277). An imposing building, Structure (Str.) 33, located on the ridge between the floodplain and hilltops, was the center-most architectural feature of the city (Mathews 1988: 3; Morley 1937–38: 551; Tate 1992: 131).

Establishing Kin Terms

A first step in any analysis of kin relations has always been identification of relevant kin terms (e.g., Goodenough 1967). Unfortunately, no anthropologist or linguist has yet found a way to define kin terms in a foreign language without first looking for terms that we recognize as kin terms. What if people define kinship differently or use kin terms that are not recognizable to us? Urban suggested that an essential second step to identification of kin terms in another language is to return those terms to discourse. If we can document the grammatical role of terms we easily identify, we can use grammar as a basis to identify other terms that are used as kin terms, but may not be consistent with our kin vocabulary (1996: 148).

In Yaxchilán texts, one finds the following kin terms that are immediately recognizable within a Western understanding of kin terms: "child of mother," "child of father," "mother of child," and "mother's brother." These terms were structured grammatically as nouns that refer to persons also identified by a proper name and associated royal epithets. Kin terms generally preceded proper name/epithet strings, and were often affixed by the possessive u or y. The relative position of proper names and epithets along the subsequent nominal string was quite variable, and the proper names were usually not preceded by the possessive.

One other term also occurred at the beginning of name/epithet strings and was preceded by the possessive u. This is u-hoy-na, or "precious/holy woman." Some scholars interpret "precious/holy woman" as a kin term referring to "wife" (e.g., Jones and Jones 1995: 12–15), while other scholars suggest "precious/holy woman" is not a kin term but a female royal epithet (e.g., Harris and Stearns 1992: 65). I suggest "precious/holy woman" is a kin term because it acts grammatically like identified kin terms, although I also agree that it should not be interpreted as "wife." Contextually, there is no indication that the women referred to as "precious/holy women" were necessarily wives of the men with whom they were interacting. One term, *y-atan*, which is translated as wife, is infrequently recorded in ancient texts, although it was not used at Yaxchilán. Rosemary Joyce (pers. comm.) suggested "female member of the kin group in the upper generation" as a working gloss for "precious/holy woman," given its contextual association with royal women from upper generations.

Understanding Discourse Structure

Individual buildings and stelae in ancient Maya cities provided the stages for texts and images. Texts grouped on a building often related a single narrative (Josserand 1986, 1993; Reents-Budet 1989). The order in which texts and images were inscribed on buildings and stelae allows us to read narratives as they were sequentially added to the city by different persons (Mathews 1988; Tate 1992). Within these temporal and spatial frames, we can situate kings' claims to power and examine how these related to kin and gender relations.

Ancient elites arranged buildings in meaningful ways throughout Maya cities, and a cultural map of their worldview can be inferred from a city's plan (Ashmore 1991). Further, understanding the formalization and symbolic meaning of architecture in Maya cities can provide insight into personal and political goals, strategies, and agendas (Ashmore 1986, 1989, 1991, 1996, 1998). That is, in ancient and modern Maya cosmology, the world was divided into four quarters intersecting at the cardinal directions. The cardinal directions reflected movement along the sun's path, which, as it was conceived by ancient observers, circled the sky by day and the underworld by night, moving counterclockwise from sunrise in the east, with zenith in the north, sunset in the west, and nadir in the south (e.g., Gossen 1974; Hanks 1990; Joyce 1996; Schele and Freidel 1990; Tate 1992). Along this cycle, north and south also were transposed with up and down. As north was symbolically linked with "up" and "sky," at many ancient cities, it seems that placement of monuments and architecture in a northern position could represent power equal to that of the sun's ascension into the sky (e.g., Ashmore 1991; Coe 1988: 235; Miller 1985: 7–8).

Cardinal directions could be represented as both absolute locations—north, south, east, and west—and as relative locations—up/down, right/left, front/back—which could be conceptual correlates for absolute locations as discussed above. In paired images on stelae, male rulers were often situated to the right or in the upper position in the composition, again perhaps to claim the same power as the rising sun (Joyce 1996: 174–75).

Absolute and relative locations of textual inscriptions and the directional movement of their readers were also an integral part of ancient writing. As texts were inscribed on buildings and stelae, these concrete places provided a meaningful spatial frame of reference for the texts. For writing, as for images and architecture, meaning was not simply invested in what was written or who wrote it, but where it was written. If we remove words and images from space, part of their meaning may be lost.

Although the stories recounted in ancient texts are simple, grammar, style, and associated images are quite expressive (Hanks 1986, 1988; Harris and Stearns 1992; Josserand 1986, 1995; Lounsbury 1980; Reents-Budet 1989). A primary expressive feature of ancient and modern Maya discourse is grammatical parallelism. Grammatically parallel statements are used as a linguistic device to denote an equivalence between statements. Parallel statements may repeat anything from words, phrases, and sentences to entire event sequences. Although an indeterminate number of statements may parallel one another, couplets are most common. By changing one element in each parallel statement, different people, actions, or events are equated. A simple example is parentage statements:

Shield Jaguar, child of mother Lady Shield, child of father Bird Jaguar.

Recording his parentage in a couplet, Shield Jaguar sets up mother and father as positional equivalents. Parallelism is also used to emphasize the main or peak event in a series of events in a narrative by repeating that event (Josserand 1986: 13). Other linguistic devices, such as special affixes called the Posterior Event Indicator and the Anterior Event Indicator, mark main and background events respectively (Josserand 1986: 14–15). Understanding discourse structure in text, image, and space allows the reader to document how persons and actions were related in Maya thought and practice.

Yaxchilán's Discourse Structure

Maler's 1903 and Tate's 1992 analyses of Yaxchilán stelae show a consistent patterning of events associated with the cardinal orientations of stelae. On the east or north sides of stelae, capture and warfare events were usually recorded. When time was recorded for these events, they were earlier than the civic-ceremonial rituals recorded on the west or south side of the same stela (Tate 1992: 98–101, 142).[5] The reading order of texts across buildings parallels that found on stelae.[6]

In addition, gender and kin relations were also co-implicated with this spatial patterning of time and event. Actors involved in the east or north side events tended to be single males, usually the king. Often the king stood alone, but additionally the king's male captives could be depicted or discussed. Where other persons were shown or mentioned with the king in these events, these were usually nonkin relations such as dignitaries from other cities, or male kin not introduced by kin terms in the associated text. The east or north sides of stelae faced into open plazas. As Joyce (1996) noted, front sides of stelae, facing into plazas, were often associated with male rulers at Classic Maya centers.

West- or south-side actors tended to be male/female groups partaking in complementary actions. In the texts recording these complementary actions, often a ruler's parentage was noted, and kin terms identified actors that were

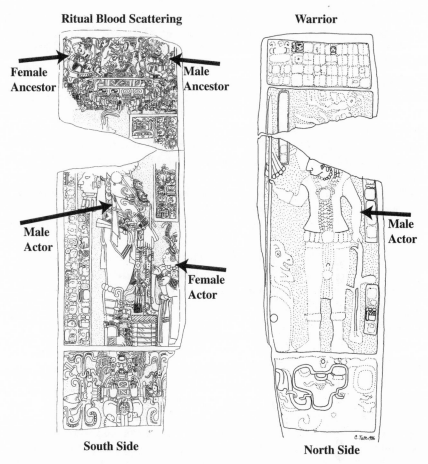

Figure 12.3 Stela Syntax. Stela 1. Adapted from YAXCHILAN: THE DESIGN OF A MAYA CEREMONIAL CITY by Carolyn E. Tate, Copyright © 1992. By Permission of the author and the University of Texas Press.

related. The well-preserved Stela 1 of Ruler 13 is a vivid example of this stelae syntax (fig. 12.3).

On the two-dimensional surface of a building facade or stelae, narratives seem written to progress along the sun's path. The rising points on the sun's path, east and north, and the setting points along the sun's path, west and south, then become positional equivalents in the two-dimensional plane. While readers walked around the two sides of a stela or from doorway to doorway along a building, their spatiotemporal movement mirrored that of the actors in the texts and associated images. This spatiotemporal ordering of texts and people's movement is not surprising, because it is similar to paths and positional equivalencies used by modern Maya ritual narrators (Gossen 1974; Hanks 1988, 1990). Both the content of the narrative and its reading order seem to foster an understanding of the world in which various readers of a narrative and the royal actors within a narrative were mutually involved in a certain spatiotemporal movement. The extraordinary and powerful spatiotemporal movement of royal actors through the particulars of their life narratives were centered within and co-implicated by the similar, but mundane, spatiotemporal bodily movement of the people reading the narratives.

This discourse parallelism provides us with the framework to reconstruct how people, action, and worldview were linked in thought and practice at Yaxchilán (fig. 12.4). People and their actions were understood in relation to the cycle of the sun, where beginnings and endings of a narrative were not endpoints on a linear string, but locations along the cycle. This association of text, image, and space and its inferred cultural meaning will be referred to hereafter as "the discourse structure."

In the discourse structure, events portrayed in the east and north were earlier and background events. Events portrayed in the west and south were central and came later. Single actors (male) and their actions, captures, and royal visits tended to be located in east or north positions equivalent to the rising sun. As Yaxchilán life stories were often authorized by and written about male egos, the arising actions/actors reflected their male perspective. But there are cases, as we will discuss below, where women played the prominent roles in texts. For example, on Stela 35 that centers on Lady Ik Skull, her image appears in the arising north position. Thus, it seems that single women and men could both attain the arising position.

Complementary male/female actors, involved in ritual actions and accessions, tended to be located in west or south positions equivalent to the setting sun. Within this spatiotemporal ordering, the actions of single actors (east and north) resulted from the unified efforts of actors who were legitimized through appropriate kin relations traced intergenerationally through their

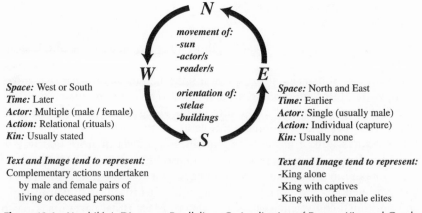

Figure 12.4 Yaxchilán's Discourse Parallelism: Co-Implication of Person, Kin, and Gender in Time and Space

parents and cross-generationally through relations involving male and female pairs, some of whom were husbands and wives (west and south).

Seemingly, individual male, nonkin-related actions arose to the east and north and were legitimized by their inclusion in a web of spatial discourse on complementary kin and gender relations found in the west and south. Over the duration of a particular narrative, the single king presented himself as the unification of the different relations in which he engaged. Here, it seems, individual deeds were essential to legitimizing one's right to occupy an important social role, but these individual deeds were, in themselves, social. This agglomeration of different relationships by the single king is similar to Joyce's (1996) documentation of how single actors could encompass both gender identities by de-emphasizing sexual characteristics and incorporating elements of male and female wardrobes in their image.

In a recent article on ancient Maya gender complementarity, Joyce (1996: 181) argued that the male/female social unit cautions against assuming individualistic motivations as the sole determinants for action. Independent, autonomous action caused by an individual is itself a cultural construct. Other constructs of action highlight relational action, acting in relation to another who is the cause of action. Individual and relational actions do not simply represent a dichotomy. Relational deeds may be essential to formation of individual actions, and individual deeds may be essential to formation of relational actions (Battaglia 1995; Joyce 1996; Kray 1997; Meskell 1999; Strathern 1988). Some scholars look to Classic Maya monuments and their depictions of important personages as symbolic of the rise of individualism (e.g., Tate 1992). However, viewing ancient Maya individual action itself as social, will challenge a notion of a strict individual/social dichotomy.

A number of contemporary and ancient American examples illustrate similar conceptions of action. For example, in contemporary Yucatec Maya ideology, the uniqueness of an individual exists only within networks of social relations (Hanks 1990). The ancient Olmec, like the ancient Maya, are known for their depictions of single rulers, which are often correlated with the rise of a Western form of individualism. As Grove and Gillespie (1992) pointed out, images of Olmec single rulers are depicted as linked to kinspeople and ancestors in various ways. As well, the construction of the Olmec ruler's depiction drew upon corporate stone-quarrying projects. For these reasons, Grove and Gillespie suggested that the sacred power of the individual king and that of the group were not in antithesis, but linked, and variably emphasized in different situations.

Manipulating Discourse Structure: Life Stories of Two Yaxchilán Rulers

In order to understand how Yaxchilán rulers created and manipulated the discourse structure to record their life histories and rhetorically assume power, I examined the narratives of the two most documented kings at Yaxchilán, Rulers 12 and 13. I summarized the main narrative themes and their

spatiotemporal associations in the order in which Rulers 12 and 13 authorized the inscription of narratives throughout their reigns. Reading these narratives in the order of their inscription allows us to understand the ruler's
historical presentation of self. Proposed dates for the inscription of texts and
images are based on the latest recorded date in a single narrative (Mathews
1988: table 1–2, table 10–3; Tate 1992: Chapter 6).[7] According to Roberto
García Moll, the most recent excavator at Yaxchilán, inscription dates may
differ from construction dates of buildings (Mathews 1988: 333–34). Thus,
the inscription date is more important than the building construction date in
understanding the historical presentation of narratives. Although many
building lintels seem to have been carved for particular buildings and remained in them, sometimes lintels and stelae were moved to new locations
by later rulers, as is noted below.

Ruler 12, Shield Jaguar [I]: A.D. 681–752

Ruler 12 was the first Yaxchilán ruler to record extensive life narratives. He
recorded thirty-five events across buildings and stelae; seventeen were captures, and eighteen, including his accession, were civic-ceremonial rituals.
Captures involved male actors and individual actions performed by a king.
Kin terms were never used to identify persons involved in captures. Civic-
ceremonial rituals were performed by male and female actors who were introduced by kin terms on at least the first occasion that their name was mentioned in Ruler 12's life narratives. Introducing each new actor into the narratives with a kin term suggests that kinship had a central structuring role in
legitimizing actors, actions, and the relations between them.

Ruler 12's first three inscriptions (Stelae 19 and 20, and Str. 44 steps III and
IV) reiterate the discourse structure with a predominant focus on his life and
actions. These monuments were situated on one of the city's hilltops. The next
inscription recorded in Ruler 12's reign, Str. 23, was located in the low-lying
expanse of open plazas. It may have been designed by "precious/holy woman"
Lady Xoc, since she was recorded as the artist on Lintel 25 of Str. 23 (Tate
1992: 120) and she was a prominent actor. Through the narrative, she participated in complementary ritual action with Ruler 12 (see fig. 12.2a) and she
envisioned an ancestor. On Lintel 26, Ruler 12 receives military implements
from Lady Xoc, symbolic of the alliance created through their coordinate actions (see fig. 12.2b). There were extensive references to Lady Xoc's natal kin
on Lintel 23. As in many lintel narratives, the narrative of Str. 23 embellishes
complementary action to the near exclusion of individual action.

Subsequently, Ruler 12 added four steps to Str. 44 and changed the focus
of his narratives to his relations with other Jaguar rulers, one of whom was
his father. The events recorded on the steps were largely parallel statements
about captures undertaken by Ruler 12, Ruler 11, and Ruler 9. On each step,
he gave his parentage statement associated with final actions undertaken, a

commemoration of his accession (step V) and of his three captures (steps I, II, and VI). The later pairing of capture records and mention of parentage is unusual.

One final all-textual inscription in the reign of Ruler 12, Lintel 56, recounted the complementary participation of "precious/holy woman," Lady White Serpent, and Ruler 12 in a building dedication. Unfortunately, contextual data for Lintel 56 are unclear. The data may have come from Str. 11, a building that Moll's archaeological data indicate was not built until Ruler 13's reign (Mathews 1988: 336). In this case, the lintel was likely resituated in Str. 11 by the later Ruler 13.

Through historical time, Ruler 12 reiterated the temporal and spatial frames of discourse. Within the course of individual narratives and throughout the course of his life, there was an initial focus on his actions and a later focus on actions undertaken in relation to others. Through time, Ruler 12 linked himself to an extensive social network. In the large open plazas of the city, he placed monuments to his most distant relations. He placed his close natal kin on hilltops overlooking these plazas. As open plazas were plausible locations for large public ceremonies, Ruler 12 seems to have given his distant relations center stage. In his use of kin terms to introduce new actors and his spatial arrangement of inscriptions about his relations, Ruler 12 appears to have created a large inclusive social network of legitimate and related actors that spatially focused on more distant relations.

Possibly too many legitimate actors were created through Ruler 12's encompassing social network. For ten years after he died, no king was definitively recorded. There is some textual evidence now that Lady Xoc had a son, who was named on Str. 23 (Jones and Jones 1992). This son of one of the most elaborately recorded women in Maya history was not to be the next ruler. Power struggles between multiple persons are a plausible explanation for this gap (e.g., Proskouriakoff 1963; Schele and Freidel 1990; Sharer 1994; Tate 1992). Some of the people who may have been involved in this struggle included Lady Xoc and her son, and Lady Ik Skull, the wife of Ruler 12, and her son. Lady Ik Skull's son finally becomes the next king, Ruler 13 and, interestingly, neither were recorded on any of Ruler 12's monuments.

Ruler 13, Bird Jaguar [IV]: A.D. 752– circa 767

Ruler 13 erected more monuments and authorized more inscriptions than any other Yaxchilán king, which led scholars to credit his reign as the height of Yaxchilán's power. Across buildings and stelae, he recorded sixty-three events, including captures (four), accessions (five), civic-ceremonial rituals (forty-three), births (two), deaths (five), and sacrifices carried out by gods (four). Unlike previous rulers, the majority of Ruler 13's texts emphasized relational action and life cycle events over captures. The act of capturing was largely reduced to the captor titles he listed in his nominal phrase. De-emphasizing discussion of male "individual" actions, but linking them directly to his identity as titles in his nominal phrase, he chose to highlight the construction of action through complementary gender and kin relations.

Like other rulers, Ruler 13 manipulated discourse to link actors and their actions within a cultural worldview. Earlier monuments focused on aspects of his life, and later monuments focused on his life as related to the lives of others. Rather than recapitulate the traditional use of the discourse structure, which we explored in Ruler 12's monuments, I will now highlight Ruler 13's novel manipulations of it.

There were two women with the Skull name in Ruler 13's life. One was his mother, Lady Ik Skull, who may be regarded as having higher status because she came from the larger civic-ceremonial center of Calakmul, located in modern-day Campeche, Mexico (e.g., Marcus 1976; Schele and Freidel 1990). The other, his wife, Lady Great Skull, was probably a local elite.

Although actors in Ruler 13's life story were related along many of the same lines as the actors in Ruler 12's life story, Ruler 13 uses kin terms and spatial syntax to reference these people in quite a different manner. Many new actors were initially brought into Ruler 13's narratives without kin term introductions. While Ruler 12 only recorded his parentage statements on monuments situated in hilltop locations, Ruler 13 recorded his parentage on monuments throughout the city. He didn't seem to want anyone to miss his parentage; a program that may have been part of what Schele and Freidel (1990: 285) called Ruler 13's "campaign of legitimization." While Ruler 12 put his monuments to more distant relations in a central, public place by locating them in the city's low-lying areas of open plazas, Ruler 13 placed his nuclear family unit, his wife Lady Great Skull, his son Chel-te (Ruler 14), and himself, in the epicenter of the city in Str. 33. Monuments to more distant affines and nonkin relations were placed throughout the city, radiating from Str. 33 and intermingled with monuments referencing his parentage (Tate 1992: 132). Like Ruler 12, Ruler 13 documented a large group of legitimate political actors, but he also used kin terms and spatial arrangements to indicate that a smaller group within these, his nuclear family, were more central and legitimate than others.

Three initial inscriptions, most likely carved for Ruler 13's accession (Tate 1992: 126), traditionally link the ruler's previous captures to his later accession, legitimized under the joint auspices of his mother and father (Str. 41 steps, Stelae 11 and 12). In Ruler 13's next inscription, on Str. 22, he linked himself to previous rulers by incorporating four old lintels, attributed to Ruler 7 (Moon Skull) and Ruler 10 (Lord Skull [II]) (Mathews 1988: 68–78; Tate 1992: 129). In the lintel of the set carved under the auspices of Ruler 13, the text-only Lintel 21, he recorded parallel ritual actions he and Ruler 7 undertook. Where previous Jaguar rulers connected themselves through parallel captures to previous Jaguar rulers, Ruler 13 connected himself to previous Skull rulers. As noted above, while Ruler 13's wife, Lady Great Skull, was a local elite, we lack evidence to support a kin relation between her and previous Skull rulers. In this monument, Ruler 13 may be emphasizing his relation, through his wife, to previous Skull rulers, or he may simply be establishing himself as their successor.

Stela 35, discovered inside Str. 21 (Mathews 1988: 208; Tate 1992: 197), depicted Ruler 13's mother Lady Ik Skull and recorded her as his mother. Stela 35 was the only one at Yaxchilán where a person was depicted on both sides: Lady Ik Skull was the sole Yaxchilán actor to co-opt representation of east and west in her singular image. Giving his mother a singular image and omitting reference to his father may point to Lady Ik Skull's higher status as a royal from the larger site of Calakmul (e.g., Marcus 1976). It may also indicate the important role she played in assisting Ruler 13 to become king over other contenders, although evidence for this assistance is purely inferential. It is unclear exactly when Stela 35 was inscribed because its latest chronological notation was a reference to Ruler 13 being in the third *katun* of his life (which was 40 to 60 years old [Mathews 1988: 208; Tate 1992: 124]. Thus, the time span for this inscription could span Ruler 13's reign.

Although Lady Ik Skull did not need to share a stage, Ruler 13 certainly had a need to share his stage. Inside Str. 21 was a carving of a throne upon which Ruler 13 is seated with four other people who probably were Lord Great Skull (his wife's brother), Lady Great Skull (his wife), Lady Ix, and Lady Six Tun (precious/holy woman). In sharing the throne, the seemingly individual power of the single king is shown to be contingent on his alliance with others (Tate 1992: 130).

Three subsequent inscriptions on Strs. 24, 1, and 42 focus on Ruler 13's more distant relations. Str. 24, which records the death of important Yaxchilán people, does include his parents' deaths as well as those of more distant kin.

The next monument inscribed, Str. 33, situated Ruler 13's nuclear family, his wife, Lady Great Skull and son Chel-te, Ruler 14, in the center of the city and linked them to supernatural origins recounted on the steps of the building. Rhetorically, Ruler 13 may have been trying to fix his son as a preordained ruler through his paternal and maternal connection to the supernatural. Similarly, Schele and Freidel (1990: 293–305) proposed that Ruler 13's textual references to his son were part of a campaign to secure his succession. Subsequent Strs. 13 and 16 combine references to his parents as well as more distant relations.

Next to be inscribed were Stela 10, located in front of Str. 39, and Str. 10. Stela 10 depicts the traditional east/capture, west/ruler below his parents' motif. However, on the east side of the monument, his parents stood in the image and were recorded in the text that depicted and documented one of his captives. This unusual occurrence of images of and statements about parents in the east may have been a rhetorical attempt to imply that his captive taking was not simply legitimized through appropriate kin relations but was preordained based upon his specific parentage. Again, Ruler 13 seems to focus on his parentage and legitimacy. In a final inscription on Str. 2, Ruler 13 recorded his relations with his wife's family who had given him military assistance.

Throughout his life, Ruler 13 was very interested in manipulating discussions of kinship so that they would focus on his parents and his nuclear family. He placed references to his parents throughout the city and prominently recorded his nuclear family in the center of the city, thus giving them the most legitimacy. While at one level, proliferation of inscriptions and monuments by Ruler 13 may be a sign of a successful reign, Tate argued that this proliferation may also be the product of an insecure reign. Far more legitimate political actors were discussed in narrative and shown sharing the throne of the single king (1992: 123). Likewise, Ruler 13's rhetorical attempts to secure his son's rule may not be the sign of ultimate success of the Jaguar group. These may be attempts to control increasing factionalized and fragmented political relations among an ever-growing number of legitimate elites who may have had valid political claims. In the subsequent history of Yaxchilán, we know the result of Ruler 13's reign: Yaxchilán did not become a stronger or more powerful city but became, instead, a city in decline. After two subsequent rulers, the construction of political monuments would come to an end as they did at other Maya cities during the ninth and tenth centuries A.D.

Conclusion

Ancient Maya kings recorded versions of their life histories in text, image, and space throughout their civic-ceremonial centers. Reading these texts as discourses on meaning provides a way to understand how ancient Maya authors and audiences understood ordered human relationships. As we saw at Yaxchilán, kin and gender relations were important to ancient Maya constructions of power. Establishing appropriate kin and gender relations was critical to a king's assumption of power. In fact, each new ruler's discursive representations of kin and gender relations took as its model the discursive representations made by previous rulers. Through historical time, a discourse parallelism unfolds, which new rulers manipulated to describe their life stories. As each new generation of rulers modeled his representations on those of previous generations, each selectively assimilated the words and representations of others into his own experiences, a process that indeed exemplifies the making of culture (Bakhtin 1981; Urban 1991).

Over at least three hundred years, the kings of Yaxchilán developed, employed, and manipulated an elaborate syntax that incorporated space, image, and text as a three-part discourse. The significance of the discourse was related to its formalized spatial location on monuments. Publicly, kings proclaimed certain aspects of their messages over and over again through time and space, in ways that literate and illiterate residents and visitors alike could comprehend. Just as the sun always rose in the east and set in the west in an ever repeating cycle, actors and their actions were held in balance with cultural notions of the world. In the north and east, seemingly individual actions of males, such as capturing enemies and partaking in royal visits, arose out of a web of appropriate complementary gender and kin relations between children and their parents, husbands and wives, men and women. Maternal and paternal, natal and affinal, and nonkin relations were encompassed by the single king and provided legitimacy for his actions. While individual deeds were essential to the king's right to occupy his important social role, these actions were only appropriate if they were enmeshed in a web of complementary kin and gender relations.

Kinship is far more than a system that is constructed exterior to people's lives and then imposed on them. Kinship refers to relations that people actually have, role expectations that they come to associate with these relationships, and the traditional and novel ways that actors manipulate them. The ancient Maya did not look at kinship and divide it into systems and subsystems that would govern the transmission of office or transmission of membership. Rather, their social reality of kin relations was created through publicly circulating discourse. Through historical time, a discourse structure linking people, action, and worldview was developed and manipulated. This discourse structure provided a constraint on the use of kinship and kin terms in public narratives that would have simultaneously provided a constraint on the social reality of kin relations. In public discourse, complementary kin relations passed from mothers and fathers, were created anew between men and women, husbands and wives, and were central to setting appropriate action.

Far from univocal, the specifically authorized narratives of Yaxchilán's history represented and incorporated the personal experiences of different people and related those experiences to an author's understanding of the world. Although texts were primarily authorized by kings and most vividly represented their perspectives, the voices of the many others—other genders, other kin, other legitimate political factions—can be recognized, if not completely understood.

Notes

I gratefully acknowledge the support of all those who have helped me revise and polish this chapter. Linda Stone's advice and editing helped me pull together the final version. Wendy Ashmore and Sue Kent initially put me in touch with Linda Stone. Robert Sharer, Rosemary Joyce, Greg Urban, Susan Gillespie, John Harris, Katheryn Josserand, Nicholas Hopkins, and Gloria Robin provided invaluable information and assistance. Other readers, whose comments on earlier versions are reflected in this chapter, are Christopher Jones, Norman Hammond, and Edward Robin. I thank Mark Schwartz for creating the figures in this chapter. Any errors are my own.

1. See Bardslay 1987; Beals 1932; Coe 1965; Edmonson 1979; Eggan 1934; Fox and Justeson 1986; Gillespie and Joyce 1997; Haviland 1967, 1968, 1973, 1977, 1985; Hopkins 1988; Jones and Jones 1992; Jones et al. 1990; Josserand 1993; Joyce 1981; Marcus 1983; Mathews 1988; McAnany 1995; Nutini 1961; Proskouriakoff 1961; Roys 1939, 1940; Schele and Freidel 1990; Sharer 1993; Tate 1992; Thompson 1982; Wilk 1988.

2. "Nicknames" of Yaxchilán rulers are used throughout this essay to lessen the number of foreign terms for readers unfamiliar with Mayan languages. "Nicknames" are English translations of rulers' names. For example, Ruler 1 is named *Yat-Balam* ("Penis Jaguar").

3. As some Yaxchilán rulers had the same name, roman numerals are placed in parentheses after rulers' names to distinguish between distinct rulers with the same name (e.g., Lord Skull [I], Lord Skull [II]).

4. The Mayan date recorded for a capture undertaken by a ruler named Knot Eye Jaguar on step I of Str. 44 has multiple correlations in the Julian calendar because it was recorded as a calendar round date, a cycle of time that repeats every 52 years. The November 30, A.D. 512, correlation would indicate that the Knot Eye Jaguar mentioned here was the same person as Ruler 9, Knot Eye Jaguar (Mathews 1988: 161). The November 17, A.D. 564, correlation would indicate that this Knot Eye Jaguar was a second ruler named Knot Eye Jaguar [II] who would have reigned between the Yaxchilán rulers I have enumerated here as Rulers 10 and 11 (Tate 1992: 258).

5. Even though some texts and images at Yaxchilán are either eroded or broken with missing pieces, regular patterning is quite consistent across uneroded monuments and monument segments (Tate 1992: 98).

6. Nine out of twelve buildings containing narratives authorized by a single king follow this spatial syntax. Although events recorded in Mayan texts do not necessarily follow a linear time frame, they comprise a series of temporally related events that were written to tell a story in a particular order (Josserand 1986: 13). It is this ordered story that need not follow a temporally sequential order, that begins in the east or north and ends in the west or south.

7. The only disagreement in Mathews's (1988) and Tate's (1992) reconstruction of inscription order relevant to the current discussion is their ordering of Str. 1, 33, and 42 inscriptions. Mathews (1988: table 10–3) argued that Str. 1 and 42 inscriptions date to May 5, A.D. 755, the latest date recorded in each narrative, and Str. 33 inscriptions date to April 4, A.D. 757, the latest date recorded there. Tate argues that the inscriptions on all three buildings were completed for an event happening in April 4, A.D. 757, for two reasons, (1) the three inscriptions are stylistically similar (1992: 131), and (2) April 4, A.D. 757, was a *katun* ending, the ending of a twenty-year period in the Maya calendar that would have been a significant temporal event likely marked by ceremony that may have included the dedication of buildings and inscriptions (1992: 117). Here, I have followed Mathews's ordering because it is based on the single narrative (building) framework and I feel that timing of ancient ceremonies and associated building and inscription dedications is not well understood.

References

Ashmore, Wendy. 1986. Petén Cosmology in the Maya Southeast: An Analysis of Architecture and Settlement Patterns at Classic Quirigá. In *The Southeast Maya Periphery*, ed. Patricia A. Urban and Edward M. Schortman. Austin: University of Texas Press.

———. 1989. Construction and Cosmology: Politics and Ideology in Lowland Maya Settlement Patterns. In *Word and Image in Maya Culture: Explorations in Language, Writing, and Representation*, ed. William F. Hanks and Don S. Rice. Salt Lake City: University of Utah Press.

———. 1991. Site-Planning Principles and Concepts of Directionality among the Ancient Maya. *Latin American Antiquity* 2:199–226.

———. 1996. Authority and Assertion: Ancient Maya Politics and the Upper Belize Valley. Paper presented at the 95th Annual Meeting of the American Anthropological Association, San Francisco.

———. 1998. Monumentos políticos: Sitio, asentamiento, y paisaje alrededor de Xunantunich, Belice. In *Anatomía de una civilización. Aproximaciones interdisciplinarias a la cultura Maya*, ed. Andrés Cuidad Ruíz, Yolanda Fernández Marquínez, José Miguel García Campillo, Mª. Josefa Iglesias Ponce de León, Alfonso Lacadena García-Gallo, and Luis T. Sanz Castro. Madrid: Sociedad Española de Estudios Mayas.

Bakhtin, Mikhail M. 1981. The *Dialogic Imagination: Four Essays*. Austin: University of Texas Press.

Bardslay, Sandra. 1987. Inaugural Art of Bird Jaguar IV: Rewriting History at Yaxchilán. Master's thesis, University of British Columbia.

Barnes, John A. 1971. *Three Styles in the Study of Kinship*. Berkeley: University of California Press.

Battaglia, Debbora, ed. 1995. *Rhetorics of Self-Making*. Berkeley: University of California Press.

Beals, Ralph L. 1932. Unilateral Organization in Mexico. *American Anthropologist* 34:467–75.

Bourdieu, Pierre. 1977. *Outline of a Theory of Practice*. Cambridge, U.K.: Cambridge University Press.

Coe, Michael D. 1965. A Model of Ancient Community Structure in the Maya Lowlands. *Southwestern Journal of Anthropology* 21:97–114.

———. 1988. Ideology of the Maya Tomb. In *Maya Iconography*, ed. Elizabeth P. Benson and Gillett G. Griffin. Princeton, N.J.: Princeton University Press.

Collier, Jane, and Sylvia Yanagisako. 1987. Introduction to *Gender and Kinship: Essays Towards a Unified Analysis*, ed. Jane Collier and Sylvia J. Yanagisako. Stanford: Stanford University Press.

Edmonson, Munro S. 1979. Some Postclassic Questions about the Classic Maya. *Estudios de cultura Maya* 12:157–78.

Eggan, Fred. 1934. The Maya Kinship System and Cross-Cousin Marriage. *American Anthropologist* 36:188–202.

Fortes, Meyer. 1953. The Structure of Unilineal Descent Groups. *American Anthropologist* 55:25–39.

Fox, James, and John S. Justeson. 1986. Classic Maya Dynastic Alliance and Succession. In *Supplement to the Handbook of Middle American Indians*. Vol. 4, *Ethnohistory*, ed. Victoria R. Bricker and Ronald M. Spores. Austin: University of Texas Press.

Freidel, David A., Linda Schele, and Joy Parker. 1993. *Maya Cosmos: Three Thousand Years on the Shaman's Path*. New York: Morrow.

Gillespie, Susan D., and Rosemary A. Joyce. 1997. Gendered Goods: The Symbolism of Maya Hierarchical Exchange Relations. In *Women in Prehistory: North America and Mesoamerica*, ed. Cheryl Claassen and Rosemary A. Joyce. Philadelphia: University of Pennsylvania Press.

Goodenough, Ward. 1956. Residence Rules. *Southwest Journal of Anthropology* 12, no. 1:22–37.

———. 1967. Componential Analysis: Kinship Studies in Cultural Anthropology Are Producing a New Tool for Semantic Analysis. *Science* 156:1203–9.

Goody, Jack. 1990. *The Oriental, the Ancient, and the Primitive: Systems of Marriage and the Family in the Pre-Industrial Societies of Eurasia*. Cambridge, U.K.: Cambridge University Press.

Gossen, Gary H. 1974. *Chamulas in the World of the Sun: Time and Space in the Maya Oral Tradition*. Cambridge, Mass.: Harvard University Press.

Grove, David C., and Susan D. Gillespie. 1992. Ideology and Evolution at the Pre-State Level: Formative Period Mesoamerica. In *Ideology and Pre-Columbian Civilizations*, ed. Arthur A. Demarest and Geoffry W. Conrad. Santa Fe, N.Mex.: School of American Research Press.

Hammond, Norman. 1994. *Ancient Maya Civilization*. New Brunswick, N.J.: Rutgers University Press.

Hanks, William F. 1986. Authenticity and Ambivalence in the Text: A Colonial Maya Case. *American Ethnologist* 14, no. 4:64–88.

———. 1988. Grammar, Style, and Meaning in a Maya Manuscript. *International Journal of American Linguistics* 54, no. 3:331–65.

———. 1990. *Referential Practice: Language and Lived Space among the Maya*. Chicago: University of Chicago Press.

Harris, John F., and Stephen K. Stearns. 1992. *Understanding Maya Inscriptions: A Hieroglyph Handbook*. Philadelphia: University Museum, University of Pennsylvania.

Haviland, William A. 1967. Stature at Tikal, Guatemala. *Expedition* 7:14–23.

———. 1968. Ancient Lowland Maya Social Organization. *Middle American Research Institute, Tulane University* 26:93–117.

———. 1973. Rules of Descent in Sixteenth Century Yucatán. *Estudios de cultura Maya* 8:217–26.

———. 1977. Dynastic Genealogies from Tikal, Guatemala. *American Antiquity* 42:61–67.

———. 1985. Population and Social Dynamics: The Dynasties and Social Structure of Tikal. *Expedition* 27:34–41.

Hopkins, Nicholas A. 1988. Classic Maya Kinship Systems: Epigraphic and Ethnographic Evidence for Patrilineality. *Estudios de cultura Maya* 17:87–121.

Jones, Christopher. 1977. Inauguration Dates of Three Late Classic Rulers of Tikal, Guatemala. *American Antiquity* 42, no. 1:28–60.

Jones, Tom, and Carolyn Jones. 1992. The Xok-Balam Connection Revisited: A Reexamination of the Text. In *U Mut Maya IV*, ed. Tom Jones and Carolyn Jones. Arcata, Calif. Photocopy.

———. 1995. Maya Hieroglyphic Workbook. Prepared for the 1995 Weekend Workshops on Maya Hieroglyphic Writing at Humboldt State University, Arcata, Calif.

Jones, Tom, Carolyn Tate, and Randa Marhenke. 1990. Blood Cousins: The Xok-Balam Connection at Yaxchilán. In *U Mut Maya III*, ed. Tom Jones and Carolyn Jones. Arcata, Calif. Photocopy.

Josserand, J. Kathryn. 1986. The Narrative Structure of Hieroglyphic Texts at Palenque. In *Sixth Palenque Round Table, 1986,* ed. Virginia M. Fields. Norman: University of Oklahoma Press.

———. 1993. Women in Classic Maya Hieroglyphic Texts. Paper presented at the 92nd Annual Meeting of the American Anthropological Association in Washington, D.C.

———. 1995. Participant Tracking in Maya Hieroglyphic Texts: Who Was That Masked Man? *Journal of Linguistic Anthropology* 5, no. 1:65–89.

Josserand, J. Kathryn, and Nicholas Hopkins. 1995. The Inscriptions of Yaxchilán: A Short Course on Maya Hieroglyphic Writing Featuring the Inscriptions of Yaxchilán. Prepared for Jaguar Tours in Tallahassee, Fla. Photocopy.

Joyce, Rosemary A. 1981. Classic Maya Kinship and Descent: An Alternative Suggestion. *Journal of the Steward Anthropological Society* 13, no. 1:45–57.

———. 1992. Images of Gender and Labor Organization in Classic Maya Society. In *Exploring Gender through Archaeology: Selected Papers from the 1991 Boone Conference,* ed. Cheryl Claassen. Monographs in World Archaeology 11. Madison, Wis.: Prehistory Press.

———. 1993. Women's Work: Images of Production and Reproduction in Pre-Hispanic Southern Central America. *Current Anthropology* 34, no. 3:255–74.

———. 1996. The Construction of Gender in Classic Maya Monuments. In *Gender and Archaeology,* ed. Rita P. Wright. Philadelphia: University of Pennsylvania Press.

Kelly, Raymond C. 1993. *Constructing Inequality: The Fabrication of a Hierarchy of Virtue Among the Etoro.* Ann Arbor: University of Michigan Press.

Kray, Christine. 1997. Worship in Body and Spirit: Practice, Self, and Religious Sensibility in Yucatán. Ph.D. diss., University of Pennsylvania.

Lounsbury, Floyd G. 1980. Some Problems in the Interpretation of the Mythological Portion of the Hieroglyphic Text at the Temple of the Cross at Palenque. In *Third Palenque Roundtable, 1978,* pt. 2, ed. Merle G. Robertson. Austin: University of Texas Press.

Maler, Teobert. 1901. *Researches in the Central Portion of the Usumatsintla Valley: Reports of Explorations for the Museum, 1898–1900.* Peabody Museum of Archaeology and Ethnology, Memoir 2, no. 1. Harvard University.

———. 1903. *Researches in the Central Portion of the Usumatsintla Valley: Reports of Explorations for the Museum.* Peabody Museum of Archaeology and Ethnology, Memoir 2, no. 2. Harvard University.

Marcus, Joyce. 1976. *Emblem and State in the Classic Maya Lowlands: An Epigraphic Approach to Territorial Organization.* Washington, D.C.: Dumbarton Oaks.

———. 1983. Lowland Maya Archaeology at the Crossroads. *American Antiquity* 48:454–88.

———. 1992a. *Mesoamerican Writing Systems: Propaganda, Myth, and History in Four Ancient Civilizations.* Princeton, N.J.: Princeton University Press.

———. 1992b. Dynamic Cycles in Mesoamerican States. *National Geographic Research and Exploration* 8, no. 4:392–411.

———. 1993. Ancient Maya Political Organization. In *Lowland Maya Civilization in the Eighth Century A.D.,* ed. Jeremy A. Sabloff and John S. Henderson. Washington, D.C.: Dumbarton Oaks.

———. 1995. Maya Hieroglyphs: History or Propaganda? In *Research Frontiers in Anthropology,* ed. Carol R. Ember, Melvin Ember, and Peter Peregrine. Upper Saddle River, N.J.: Prentice Hall.

Mathews, Peter. 1988. The Sculpture of Yaxchilán. Ph.D. diss., New Haven, Conn.: Yale University.

———. 1991. Classic Maya Emblem Glyphs. In *Classic Maya Political History,* ed. T. Patrick Culbert, School of American Research. Cambridge, U.K.: Cambridge University Press.

Maudslay, Alfred P. 1889–1902. *Biología Centrali-Americana: Archaeology.* 5 vols. London: Porter and Dulau.

McAnany, Patricia. 1995. *Living with the Ancestors: Kinship and Kingship in Ancient Maya Society.* Austin: University of Texas Press.

Meskell, Lynn. 1999. *Archaeologies of Social Life: Age, Sex, Class et cetera in Ancient Egypt.* Oxford, U.K.: Blackwell.

Miller, Mary E. 1985. Tikal, Guatemala: A Rationale for the Placement of the Funerary Pyramids. *Expedition* 27, no. 3:6–15.

Monaghan, John. 1995. *The Covenants with Earth and Rain: Exchange, Sacrifice, and Revelation in Mixtec Sociality.* Norman: University of Oklahoma Press.

Morley, Sylvanus G. 1937–1938. *The Inscriptions of Petén.* 5 vols. Washington, D. C.: Carnegie Institution of Washington, Publication 437.

Nutini, Hugo G. 1961. Clan Organization in a Nahuatl Speaking Village in the State of Tlaxcala, Mexico. *American Antiquity* 63:62–78.

Peletz, Michael G. 1995. Kinship Studies in Late Twentieth-Century Anthropology. *Annual Review of Anthropology* 24:343–72.

Proskouriakoff, Tatiana. 1961. Portraits of Women in Maya Art. In *Essays in Pre-Columbian Art and Archaeology,* ed. Samuel K. Lothrop. Cambridge, Mass.: Harvard University Press.

———. 1963. Historical Data in the Inscriptions of Yaxchilán, Part I, the Reign of Shield-Jaguar. *Estudios de cultura Maya* 3:149–67.

———. 1964. Historical Data in the Inscriptions of Yaxchilán, Part II, the Reigns of Bird Jaguar and his Successors. *Estudios de cultura Maya* 4:177–202.

Reents-Budet, Dorie. 1989. Narrative in Classic Maya Art. In *Word and Image in Maya Culture: Explorations in Language, Writing, and Representation,* ed. William F. Hanks and Don S. Rice. Salt Lake City: University of Utah Press.

Roys, Ralph L. 1939. *The Titles of Ebtun.* Washington, D.C.: Carnegie Institution of Washington, Publication 505.

———. 1940. *Personal Names of the Maya of Yucatán.* Washington, D.C.: Carnegie Institution of Washington, Publication 523, Contribution 31.

Schele, Linda. 1982. *Maya Glyphs: The Verbs.* Austin: University of Texas Press.

———. 1991. Notebook for the Fifteenth Hieroglyphic Workshop at Texas. Institute of Latin American Studies at University of Texas in Austin.

Schele, Linda, and David A. Freidel. 1990. *A Forest of Kings.* New York: Morrow.

Schele, Linda, and Nikolai Grube. 1994. Notebook for the Eighteenth Maya Hieroglyphic Workshop at Texas. Institute of Latin American Studies at University of Texas in Austin.

———. 1995. Notebook for the Nineteenth Maya Hieroglyphic Workshop at Texas. Institute of Latin American Studies at University of Texas in Austin.

Schele, Linda, and Peter Mathews. 1991. Royal Visits and Other Intersite Relationships among the Classic Maya. In *Classic Maya Political History,* ed. T. Patrick Culbert, School of American Research. Cambridge, U.K.: Cambridge University Press.

Schneider, David M. 1968. *American Kinship: A Cultural Account.* Englewood Cliffs, N.J.: Prentice Hall.

———. 1984. *A Critique of the Study of Kinship.* Ann Arbor: University of Michigan Press.

Sharer, Robert. 1993. The Social Organization of Late Classic Maya: Problems of Definitions and Approaches. In *Lowland Maya Civilization in the Eighth Century A.D.,* ed. Jeremy A. Sabloff and John S. Henderson. Washington, D.C.: Dumbarton Oaks.

———. 1994. *The Ancient Maya.* Stanford: Stanford University Press.

Stone, Linda. 1997. *Kinship and Gender: An Introduction.* Boulder, Colo.: Westview.

Strathern, Marilyn. 1988. *The Gender of the Gift.* Berkeley: University of California Press.

Tate, Carolyn. 1992. *Yaxchilán: The Design of a Maya Ceremonial City.* Austin: University of Texas Press.

Thompson, Philip C. 1982. Dynastic Marriage and Succession at Tikal. *Estudios de cultura Maya* 14:261–87.

Urban, Greg. 1991. *A Discourse-Centered Approach to Culture: Native South American Myths and Rituals.* Austin: University of Texas Press.

———. 1996. *Metaphysical Community: The Interplay of the Senses and the Intellect.* Austin: University of Texas Press.

Weber, Max. 1978. *Economy and Society.* Berkeley: University of California Press.

Webster, Steven S. 1977. Kinship and Affinity in a Native Quechua Community. In *Andean Kinship and Marriage,* ed. Ralph Bolton and Enrique Mayer. Washington, D.C.: American Anthropological Association, Publication 7.

Weismantel, Mary. 1995. Making Kin: Kinship Theory and Zumbagua Adoptions. *American Ethnologist* 22, no. 4:685–709.

Wilk, Richard R. 1988. Maya Household Organization: Evidence and Analogies. In *Household and Community in the Mesoamerican Past,* ed. Richard R. Wilk and Wendy Ashmore. Albuquerque: University of New Mexico Press.

Yanagisako, Sylvia J., and Jane Collier. 1987. Toward a Unified Analysis of Gender and Kinship. In *Gender and Kinship: Essays Toward a Unified Analysis,* ed. Jane Collier and Sylvia J. Yanagisako. Stanford: Stanford University Press.

Yanagisako, Sylvia J., and Carol L. Delaney. 1995. Naturalizing Power. In *Naturalizing Power: Essays in Feminist Cultural Analysis,* ed. Sylvia J. Yanagisako and Carol L. Delaney. New York: Routledge.

Chapter Thirteen

Parenting from Separate Households:
A Cultural Perspective

David Jacobson, Joan H. Liem, and Robert S. Weiss

In the United States, many parents live in separate households although they share responsibility for raising their still immature children. Most such couples have come to this arrangement after a time of marriage and living together; others have never married, although they once lived together; and still others never have lived together at all (cf. Bray and Depner 1993). It is much more likely now than in any earlier generation that parent couples not living together will attempt to share parental responsibilities rather than permitting one parent (usually the mother) to carry these responsibilities alone. Much of this has come about as a result of changes in beliefs about the needs of children for access to both parents and about the abilities of fathers as well as mothers to care for children (Buchanan, Maccoby, and Dornbusch 1996; Maccoby and Mnookin 1992).

Whatever the reasons for this arrangement, parenting from separate households presents problems for parents and children. The problems include challenges to assumptions about families and households and changes in the logistics of domestic life. The first entails beliefs about roles, relationships, and resources; the second deals with the demands of deploying those resources. In this chapter, we examine the ways in which two-household families experience these problems.

We base our discussion on interviews with parents and interviews and projective tests with children in twelve families, in each of which the parents were attempting to raise the children from separate households. The families were identified from listings of divorces in Massachusetts court records. We selected couples who were within two years of their divorce decrees and who had at least one child aged six to eleven. The parents ranged in age from the late twenties to the early forties. Eleven of the families were Caucasian; one was African American.

In each family, we conducted qualitative interviews with both parents and with one, two, or three children. (The youngest child we interviewed in any of our families was five.) We also collected projective test material from the children. Two of us (Jacobson and Weiss) divided the interviewing of the fathers between us. A third member of the research team (Liem) interviewed all of the mothers. An advanced graduate student in clinical psychology interviewed the children. Most interviews took place in families' homes, although a few, at the request of informants, were conducted at the interviewers' university offices.

Interviews were taped and transcribed. The transcripts were analyzed using the techniques of issue-oriented analysis (cf. Weiss 1994). Interview materials were coded into fairly inclusive categories (e.g., "boundary issues"). Some coded categories had already been developed during the data collection stage, through discussions and exchange of memoranda among the members of the research team. Materials within code categories were summarized and interpreted. Draft reports were exchanged among researchers for discussion, interpretation, and revision.

A Cultural Perspective

Whatever else it is, parenting from separate households is a cultural problem. It is a cultural problem because many of the difficulties entailed in two-household parenting derive not from the attributes of the persons involved but rather from socially defined ideas and ideals about families, households, and the relationships within and between them. The effort to parent from separate households is constrained by people's cultural ideas about what constitutes a family, about what it means to be a parent, about relationships between parents and between parents and children, about relationships within and between households, and about the management of resources.

Although diversity characterizes marital and domestic arrangements in the United States (Del Carmen and Virgo 1993), it has been suggested that middle-class Americans subscribe to a set of beliefs that constitute what may be called the "standard model" of families and households (Skolnick 1991). In this model, the family is nuclear, neolocal, and coresidential. That is, upon marriage, a husband and wife are expected to establish a household of their own and that household will contain only nuclear family members. Others may reside in a household, but that situation is seen as exceptional and one that is to be avoided when possible. When children reach adulthood, they are expected to live independently in other households. Moreover, spouses typically pool resources and share household and parental tasks (although resource management and the division of labor are variable). In this model, the members of the family/household are entitled to one another's attention and affection. Upon divorce, ex-spouses should dissolve their combined household and move apart and establish (or join) separate households. Although cooperation in post-divorce parenting may be an ideal, ex-spouses are expected to be independent agents, neither pooling resources nor sharing domestic rights and duties.

That these ideas are cultural is evident when they are seen in comparative perspective. People in other cultures hold quite different assumptions about households and families (cf. Bohannan 1971). For example, in societies with unilineal descent groups, the functional domestic unit is not the freestanding nuclear family but rather the larger kin group within which it is contained. The descent group is the unit of resource management and it is the group in which various tasks, including those of parenting, are shared. That is, parental responsibilities are distributed across different individuals in the same descent group, a pattern reflected in the extension of kin categories (e.g., "mother," "father") to group members other than biological parents. Moreover, it is assumed that members of such descent groups will reside together, either in multigenerational households and/or in neighboring houses, which, although physically separate, are conceptualized as a single social unit.

The Ashanti of West Africa illustrate the role of cultural beliefs in the organization of familial and household relationships (cf. Abu 1983; Clark 1989; Fortes 1949, 1950, 1969). Among the Ashanti, parenting from separate households is customary. Traditionally a woman was expected to live with her husband when her children were young, but to live with her kinsmen (e.g., mother, brothers and sisters, and other matrilateral relatives) when her children were old enough to begin to participate in the activities of the matrilineal descent group. Consequently, husbands and wives would live, for a significant period of their marriage, in separate households. When mother and children moved to reside with members of their descent group, children typically shuttled back and forth between parental households. In this duolocal system, husbands and wives were not expected to coreside or share resources, although both were expected to take active roles as fathers and mothers. In this regard, the Ashanti have had a pattern of co-parenting from separate households. Such co-parenting worked because the parents were autonomous agents and household boundaries were permeable, with children moving freely back and forth between them.

The difference between the models of the Ashanti and middle-class Americans underscores the role of cultural beliefs and expectations regarding the ease or difficulty in parenting from separate households. It also pinpoints the source of a salient problem associated with the American family: the issue of defining (and, after divorce, renegotiating) boundaries. In American single household families, there are often problems regarding how resources such as earned income, space, and material possessions are to be shared. Couples in which both spouses work must negotiate the extent to which the income of each is accessible to the other. Some have separate bank accounts and pool money from their separate accounts only for what they agree are shared expenditures. Space in single household families is not always entirely shared.

The husband may have his den, workshop, or office, which is considered distinct from the shared household, and the wife may have her own spaces. There are various assumptions about what goes on in the shared household with the "sharedness" often less than complete. Indeed, when people move from a single household to a two-household situation, it is sometimes with the expectation of resolving issues of control over finances and space.

However, in two-household parenting arrangements, people often discover that despite having established separate households, struggles continue over what is to be shared and not shared. These struggles now focus on the accessibility of each parent's household to the other parent's entrance and use: to telephone calls and visits with the children in which the other parent comes into the home and spends time there. They also take the form of renegotiating responsibilities for the continued financial support of children. In single household families, there seems to be an underlying assumption that, whatever the emphasis on separateness, resources ultimately are pooled and that all family members have relatively easy access to what is defined as family space. In two-household families, the operating assumption appears to be what's mine is mine and what's yours is yours. Under these circumstances, there is a necessity to clearly define boundaries. The need to establish these boundaries in moving from a single household to a two-household arrangement seems inescapable. On the physical level, negotiations must go on regarding access to each other's physical space, especially as it is used for child care. On the economic level, decisions must be made about who pays for what child-related costs. And, on the emotional level, boundaries must be established around those ideas and feelings that are to be shared between ex-spouses and those that are not.

Differences among the couples attempting to parent from the separate households we studied reflect the extent to which they continue to hold the assumptions of the standard model of the American middle class or have changed their beliefs to bring them into accord with their changed situations. Although we cannot generalize from our set of informants, their experiences suggest the following hypotheses. Where people define household boundaries as permeable, there is less difficulty in co-parenting from separate households; where people assume role flexibility (i.e., the division and distribution of parental tasks across persons), there is less difficulty in co-parenting from separate households. In short, we posit an inverse relationship between household boundary permeability and parental role flexibility on the one hand, and the difficulty of post-divorce parenting on the other.

In this study, we define "difficulty in co-parenting" in terms of several related aspects (or dimensions) of interaction. In our view, the most important criterion is the level of conflict between parents and their ability to manage it. Other criteria are the ability to distinguish between co-parental and ex-spousal relationships, the capacity to function jointly as parental authorities, and the involvement of children in the parental relationship. On the basis of these criteria, we differentiate between couples who demonstrate more or less difficulty in co-parenting. In less difficult cases, conflict between parents was infrequent, and when it did occur, they were able to resolve or manage it; parents shared information about their children and made decisions together with respect to them; and they supported one another's parenting efforts. In more difficult cases, parents demonstrated an inability to interact without conflict and an inability to resolve or manage the conflict when it began; they did not share information or decision-making regarding their children; and they undermined one another's attempts to parent. (For a fuller discussion of the classification of co-parenting types, see Howard 1996.)

Household Boundaries and Parental Relationships

Among the parents we interviewed, the permeability of household boundaries ranged from those that were relatively "closed" to those that were relatively "open." In some cases, people were deeply concerned about their ex-spouses having access to their households. Some mothers changed the locks on their doors and threatened to take out restraining orders. Others told the children to meet their fathers outside because they were no longer welcome inside the family home. In still others, fathers retained keys to the family home, spent time with the children in it, and had more or less comfortable access to the refrigerator as well as other family space.)

At the closed end of the continuum, one woman's comments illustrate the tension surrounding the issue of establishing boundaries.

> [My ex-husband] was coming inside to pick up the boys. I haven't wanted him to come inside the house, but he stores a lot of stuff downstairs and he was supposed to have gotten it out a couple of months ago. It's a mess down there. I was having some work done, and I said, please come and clean up, and he never did it. I found out a few times about him being here, so I just need to figure out something. . . . I don't trust him. He is just going to take what he wants. So there's a big mess. When he comes in, he is not respectful of my stuff. One day he came, and I asked him to please call me forty-five minutes [before] he was leaving, so I could be here because it takes him [that long] to get here. . . . He didn't call and he got here and I wasn't here and so he broke into the bulkhead and pulled it all apart. And now animals can get in there and he won't fix it.

This problem is also evident in the comments of a father, describing the tensions between him and his ex-wife on his access to her house.

> [My ex-wife] had a lot of bad feelings about that [his coming into the house]. [T]here was a period where I still had things in the house and she felt that I was coming into the house when I shouldn't. . . . [My daughter] would forget something in the house. She would have a key. I'd tell her [I'd] go into the house and get it and [my ex] would get mad at me. She said she was going to get injunctions

234234   *Part 5, Chapter 13: Jacobson, Liem, Weiss*

against me so I'd never come in the house. You know . . . threatening me with an
injunction for breaking into the house.

At the other end of the spectrum, the boundaries between households
were looser and family members entered and exited as though they were still
a single unit. One father described his access to the house he used to share
with his wife:

> I usually pick [the children] up on Friday nights. I usually see them maybe
> once during the week. [My ex-wife] works one night a week so I go over there
> and see 'em. [W]e jointly own the house, so I'll do work for her if she has some
> major repairs or something to do around the house. [I]t's like we're married,
> but we're not married. . . . I could go and see the kids or do [things] with the
> kids any time, and there's no problem. It's a very loose type structure as far as
> going back and forth and seeing the kids. It's not as strict [as the situation with
> my ex-wife's] friends who are divorced. I mean most of them throw out the
> husband and that's it. They don't want any part of them, they don't want them
> near the house, they don't want anything to do with them. [Our situation] is
> not like that.

The permeable end of the continuum is also evident in the case of a couple,
who, although divorced and living in separate households, exchanged services
and support across residential boundaries. The father described the arrangement this way:

> Although we're independent, I'll call her occasionally. I'll be in the middle of
> cooking and I'll lose the recipe card and can't remember [if] I'm supposed to
> bake it for thirty or forty minutes, I'll call her up. How long do I bake it for? And
> she calls me if her car doesn't sound right, that kind of stuff.

They also adjust their domestic routines to accommodate one another's
schedules.

> I just call up a day or two ahead of time and say I'm going to come and grab the
> kids, and I take them for a couple of days at a time . . . and she'll call and say can
> you watch the kids for four or five hours. She'll drop them off at my house or I'll
> go and pick them up. If I unexpectedly get a day off from work I can call her up
> and take the kids for a couple of hours. It's not a problem. It's very, very flexible
> that way.

Moreover, they keep one another informed about their children when residing with the other parent.

> If one of the kids gets a hangnail, you know, if it's really really minor, you know, we
> don't call the other parent. But if it's something serious we'll call . . . if one of the kids
> gets sick we call. . . . For example, when my youngest one broke his arm, I happened
> to be working. He had broke his arm playing at her house. Before she left for the
> hospital she called me and says, hey, Tommy broke his arm. I'm taking him to the

hospital. She told me what hospital she was going to. And she called me later and let me know how things worked out. As it turned out I was lucky enough [to get] another guy come in and cover for me on my job. So I went up and I met her at the hospital and it worked out. You know, he [the son] was all upset and crying and whatnot. When I got there and started talking to him, you know, he calmed down.

They also cooperate in dealing with common problems, as the mother indicated in the following remarks.

We do talk about the kids. Tommy had trouble with school, we both decided it was best that maybe [he] see a psychiatrist. Everything is basically discussed . . . and it's very open . . . any problems with the kids. I've had situations here where Tommy just got so out of control and I, I'm losing it, and I will call him [her ex-husband] and say hey, could you maybe talk to him. We had situations arise . . . me seeing somebody, and Tommy felt threatened. So, he sat down with both of us, and we talked to him and explained that we're still friends, we can't live together but that doesn't mean that we don't care about them. We tried to really let the kids know that even though we're not together, we're still together for them and we very much work as a team.

In between these end points, there are situations in which household boundaries are relatively impermeable, but in which there is flexibility in the exercise of parental roles. For example, in one family, ex-spouses manage their households independently and do not depend on one another for domestic support. Rather, each has developed skills (or added to their role repertoires) that formerly had been exercised primarily or exclusively by the other. One father explained how he has developed into a cook.

I can't fix them [the kids] a gourmet meal . . . anything like that. I go look at a book, I'll make something. And they eat it. They don't throw it away. We had spaghetti last night and it's fine. I was buying Stouffer's type lasagna at one point. We got tired of that. I made my own lasagna from scratch.

The mother described the way in which she too has become self-reliant in domestic matters.

He asked me to sign some paperwork on the car. I took it to him, gave it to him because it wasn't in my name. I had been doing the paperwork and put a lot of money into it. . . . I decided to go and get a new car. . . . This man thinks that I cannot function without him. In the meantime, I had a new car sitting in a parking lot. Mine. And I had done all of it, without him.

Although they manage their households independently of one another, they view themselves as a parenting team and cooperate in support of their children's well-being. The father explained:

Even though we're divorced . . . our interests and our decisions for the kids . . . [are] the same. There wouldn't be any kind of conflict there. We're able to work it out as parents together as opposed to they're with me, I'll make the decision type of situation. As a matter of fact today we were talking about Bobby's stud- ies. And we both sat and discussed it and mutually agreed what we should, if he doesn't do well in the school, that he will not be allowed to pursue athletics in eighth grade. And that kind of a thing we do work out.

They also keep each other informed about their children, as is evident in the father's comment regarding school meetings:

[W]e attend most things together where the kids are concerned. And if there's a meeting at the school for some particular reason . . . because of a problem, some- thing like that, we will . . . we will go together. And we understand what our roles are. And both . . . and everybody knows that we're separated . . . but we still are parenting this child. Not as one individual parent carrying the whole load.

Resources

Sharing parental responsibility between households produced problems in re- source allocations. Most of the mothers and fathers we interviewed attempted to minimize their contributions to the households of the other parent, which might lead to arguments over which parent was responsible for the costs of children's expenses such as clothing or camp fees. In other couples, fathers provided a set amount to the mothers' households. In these couples, too, there could be arguments over how to deal with such unanticipated costs as med- ical bills. The father in one of these couples said:

There was an issue, back when we were looking at the divorce agreement, where she wanted me to be responsible for all unpaid medical bills and all glasses and all unpaid dental bills. And I said, "No way, they'll be down at the doctor every day. I'll be flat broke." We finally came to what the lawyers said would be the only thing that would really pass, is that we split the bills.

Expenditures in the other household became, in one instance, a matter of dispute. The mother objected to the father giving the children money as a re- ward for the chores they performed in his household. The father was aware of the mother's objections and her feeling that his practice made more difficult her own relationship with the children:

She absolutely hates it when I give the kids money on a weekend. It's not every weekend, but occasionally I'll take them out and buy them something, just give them ten bucks or something at the end of the weekend, for doing a whole bunch of things for me. And she says, "That's no good for them and I find that they won't do anything for me and I don't know how to deal with that." But I'm not going to be cheap with them because she thinks it's a bad idea.

It is not the father's practice in itself that is problematic for the mother so much as its being a practice to which she had explicitly objected.

In general, what seemed to work best were arrangements understood and accepted by both mothers and fathers. Although the availability of resources is certainly problematic when parenting from separate households (as it is in other types of households), the parents' assumptions about those resources are critical: what they are or should be, how they should be managed, and who should decide about their distribution.

Most couples defined the household, rather than the family, as the proper reference point in making economic decisions. They believed that resources should be available to all within households, but that households should be economically independent of each other. The unit of resource management is the newly established parental household (mother's and father's), not the parenting couple nor the (former) family of parents and children.

Parental Partners

A peculiarity of the two-household parenting arrangement is the advent of new partners, some of whom live part of the time within the mother's or father's household. The new figures may become quasi-parents to the children, although only one of the parents we interviewed has given them this role. The parent in the other household can accept the new figure, complain about or otherwise oppose the new figure's presence, or attempt to avoid confronting the reality of the new figure. Yet, inevitably, the new figure affects everyone.

When one parent objects strongly to the other parent's new partner, communication and coordination between the parents can suffer, and the children can be put into difficult situations. One father permitted his preoccupation with his ex-wife's new partner to lead to interrogations of their children. The children felt forced to lie in order to protect the mother and, also, to prevent the father from becoming irrational. The older child, a girl of about fourteen, described dealing with the father when he brought her and her younger brother back from a visit and the mother wasn't at home to receive them.

> We'd just kind of tell him, she must have just run to the store. Or that she said that she was going out but she'll be back in a few minutes. Or she ran over to a friend's house. Something like that. And most of the time lately she's been home. It went through . . . this period of time when she'd be home like a half hour after the visit ended. Which was fine with us, but then we'd have to listen to him. She was usually out with her boyfriend. And we didn't want to tell my father that.

These are situations in which children feel caught in the middle between parents in conflict (Buchanan, Maccoby, and Dornbusch 1996). The children, because they wanted to retain honest and caring relationships with both parents, hated the experience. Most parents recognized that the children wanted to protect their relationships with each parent. In consequence, most parents avoided intruding into their children's relationships with the other parent. Parents told us repeatedly, "I never ask." Asked what she knew about the children's experience in the father's home, a mother said: "Well they don't want to talk about it and I don't ask too much."

There were problems with the policy of not discussing events in the other household. It meant not talking about a vital part of the children's lives. Questioning of the children about their lives between visits constantly impinged on a sort of blocked out area, the area of things the parent and children implicitly have agreed not to discuss. Parents become less accessible to children in the area of the children's relationships with the other parent.

The appearance of a new partner was often disturbing to children. Some children eventually learned to accept the new household arrangement, but many maintained reservations, and a few seemed bitterly resentful of a new figure, despite the passage of time. From the children's perspective, the mother's boyfriend and the father's girlfriend are strangers in their households with whom they must compete for their parent's attention and, occasionally, for other resources as well. A few of the children with whom we spoke had learned to accept a parent's boyfriend or girlfriend, but most had reservations and some were quite resentful. However, parents might give unjustified weight to indicators that their potential new partners were accepted by the children. Their own need for someone who might share their lives easily gave rise to a misreading of how their children actually felt about the new figure. For example, one father said about his adolescent daughter and his girlfriend: "Actually my daughter and my girlfriend probably get along. My daughter and my girlfriend both went to the ballet and they had a great time." The daughter, however, was quietly resentful of the new girlfriend. She felt that her father was unnecessarily considerate of the girlfriend, sometimes to his children's disadvantage. She gave as an example, the way the father had people sit in his car:

> When we're around his girlfriend, he treats her like the queen. She always gets to sit up front in his car. Me and my brother are squashed in the back, because it's a little sports car.

Logistics

Parents may differ in their views about household boundaries, parental relationships, and resources, but they can, through a process of negotiation, minimize those differences or at least manage them. However, even when people can agree on the tasks and responsibilities of co-parenting, logistical problems appear to be unavoidable. These were most evident in establishing, maintaining, and implementing the movement of children between households, especially when the households were geographically distant and the children were small.

Here, too, parental flexibility seemed valuable. However, most couples, whatever their willingness to be flexible, had to deal with schedules that were not only complicated but were also constantly changing. A shift in the work schedule of either parent, the event of a vacation, a change in the children's school schedule, an after-school program, or a child's invitation to a friend's weekend birthday party could require parents to modify their times with the children, and thus change what may have been long-established plans. As a result, parents were required almost constantly to give attention to the scheduling of the children's movement between households.

Even without these inescapable changes, moving the children between residences could be complicated. One father said:

> I know it's tough on the kids because they spend at least two days a week with me, and then three days, four days with my ex-wife, and every Saturday and Saturday night or Saturday night and Sunday during the day with my parents, depending on what my schedule is. And the kids are basically living out of a suitcase. It's tough on them that way.

Parental insistence on a particular visiting schedule can sometimes be hard on the children, especially on older children who may have scheduled activities of their own. If the parents live in the same neighborhood this can be less of a problem. But if they live far enough from each other so that going with one parent removes a child from the milieu of the other, there can be cost to the child. An early adolescent girl said:

> My cousin and her friend had a party at my friend's dancing school place. And I was with my Dad that weekend and I said, "Dad, can I please stay with Mom just this weekend, so I can go to the party?" And he said, "Well, I'm not sacrificing a weekend with you. If you go with your Mom two weekends then you're coming with me two weekends." So I tried to make it that I would go with him two weekends and with my Mom two weekends, but I couldn't fit it that way, because I had too much homework. So I had to miss the party because of my weekend with him. I heard it was really a lot of fun. My best friend goes, "Why didn't you go to the party?" And I had to tell her. And I asked her if it was fun, and she said it was a blast. They had music, I guess they had kind of like a pizza party. They had a lot of fun. And I wish I could have been there.

It seemed that those couples who could maintain flexibility in scheduling, so that they could respond to their own needs and the needs of their children, did best in managing the logistical complexities of co-parenting from separate households.

The Emotional Experience of Parents and Children in Two-Household Arrangements

In two-household parenting, parents may alternate between being a single parent with sole custodial responsibility for the children and being the noncustodial parent separated from the children. The mothers and fathers we interviewed were with the children very different amounts of time. Most of the children lived most of the time with their mothers. In several of the cases, the children were resident in the father's household only for two days every other weekend, with additional occasional visits to the father for an evening. In several other cases, this pattern was understood as basic, but the father and mother shifted from it as the father found time to see the children or the mother desired time away from them.

Given couples' typical child care arrangements, mothers were more likely than fathers to feel overwhelmed by child care responsibilities and relieved to have time without the children, although they might be worried about the children when they were in the care of their fathers. Fathers, on the other hand, were more apt to experience visits as too brief and harried, and times spent without the children as desolate.

One father spoke poignantly about his alternating feelings of joy when his children appeared and loss when his children left:

> One of the things I've learned from all this is that I think I need my kids more than they need me. Because kids, believe it or not, they want you when they need you. Other than that they have their own separate lives, even at two and three, four years old. But when they need you, that's when they need you. And that's why I want to be available to them at every opportunity that I possibly can. It is tough on the weekends that I don't have them. There's a lot of times when I say, Oh, I wish they were here to see this or that. And I do miss a lot of seeing them every day and being able to help with their homework or get excited about my daughter trying to learn to play the piano, and things like that. Its like when I pick them up I feel euphoric, when I drop them off it's a letdown, because they're gone. And if they need me, I won't be there. I feel a little empty, a little incomplete, a little lost, because I feel like no one depends on me for anything. And I am the kind of person, I need for someone to depend on me. I need to feel responsible. So I feel less complete at this point.

Part-time parenthood is different from having the children as a normal part of one's life. Each parent continually has the cyclic experience of losing the children and regaining them. Each parent has to adapt to the children being with them sometimes, and away sometimes. When the children are resident in the household, it is a single-parent family, and if the parent works full time, there is the single-parent problem of vulnerability to overload. In addition to the usual work responsibilities, the parent then has to manage the household chores of shopping, cooking, cleaning, and keeping clothes in order, as well as attend to her or his own needs and the children's need for reestablishing a sense of closeness.

Fathers who have their children only on weekends complain that there is not nearly enough time to give the children the kind of attention they want to give them. One father described his experience as an intermittent parent to his three children:

I pick them up and rush to get dinner prepared. Which is always a challenge, because no one ever likes to eat what you are going to fix, everybody wants something different. And get the food prepared, at the same time trying to answer questions from every kid, because everybody has a question to ask me. And to divide your attention among the three of them becomes a real challenge. At the same time, trying to make sure homework is done. And get them prepared for a bath and ready for the next day. And before you know it, you're looking at 9:30, and you know the kids should be in bed already. And you try to be somewhat flexible, because you have not seen them. You certainly don't want to just pick them up and put them right in bed, because that doesn't serve any kind of purpose for you. And none of us ever gets a chance to sort of . . . sit back and relax and enjoy ourselves.

The demands of single parenting come to a sudden end when the children leave for the other parent's household. Now the parent is entirely free to pursue his or her own concerns. The parent may see a boyfriend or girlfriend, or read, or watch television, or catch up on sleep. Often, though, the parent worries about how the children are doing in the other household.

Parent couples differ in the extent to which the children become inaccessible to one parent when in the other parent's household. If parents live near each other and the children are older and the parental relationship is cordial, children can move easily between households, although even in the best case the children are likely to treat one household as more nearly home than the other. Most of the parents we interviewed lived too far from each other, or had children too young for the children to visit a parent's household as they wished, and a few of the couples tried to discourage the other parent's telephone calls to the children.

Although for some children traveling between the parents' households is a minor price to pay for feeling that both parents remain accessible, most children dislike it. One early adolescent girl who saw her father quite often in the week said that a twenty-minute walk to her father's house was very different from having her father right there.

When I was doing my homework I had like six pages in every subject and I just started crying. I was like, "Why can't my parents just be back together again so that they can both help me? So I can get both their opinions on math homework and stuff? So I won't have to get a tutor?" Before, they used to always be with me, but now I have to go to the next town in order to see Dad. I mean it's only a twenty-minute walk from my house, but still I like him being here instead of me having to go over to his house. I don't like switching back and forth every day.

The repeated loss and rejoining that goes on between parents and children contributes to problems in maintaining the continuity of parental relationships. It is difficult for parents to keep up with what has happened in their children's lives and it is difficult for children to have ready access to both parents whenever they need them.

Parents find themselves asking their children to report something that happened on the days in which the children were with the other parent. The children in the two-household family do not have the option of saying that they have already told the other parent, so why not ask the other parent. Instead, the children have to repeat their stories. And by the time the children see the second parent, the stories the parent wants to hear no longer hold the same meaning for the children; new events now occupy their minds. A father said:

> My oldest child says, "I get tired of coming home and I got to tell you stuff and then I got to tell Mommy stuff, got to show you papers, got to show Mommy papers. I just want to tell it one time."

For the children, the biggest problem in two-household parenting is that one parent is always absent. Furthermore, the parent, who for the time being is the noncustodial parent, can be hard for the children to reach. Usually, it is the father who isn't there, and often a telephone call will not reach him. The children cannot count on being able to contact their fathers when they want to. A boy said about his father, "Seems like I hardly ever get to talk to him, because when he calls us I'm outside, and when I call him, he's not home."

Some children worry that the parent who for the moment is the noncustodial parent will be unable to reach them. They worry that the noncustodial parent may fall ill or encounter some other emergency. Or that the noncustodial parent will be worried about them, or have something to tell them, or want them back. An early adolescent girl said:

> When I go away on the weekends, I always worry about my mom. I always wonder what happens if something happens? They're not going to know the phone number so I can get contacted. What if I come home and there's something wrong, like she's in the hospital, or something happened? And now I worry about my friends too, and even my brother's friends, because early in the year, my brother's friend died in a boat accident. One night there was a problem with my mother and she had no way of getting in touch with us because we were over there. We were outside my father's apartment and my father wouldn't let me go back up to watch TV because he and my brother were playing catch. And I was extremely bored. And if I had gone upstairs I would have gotten this call from my mother. And she had been trying and trying to call us. She had no idea what was going on.

A few children mentioned as one advantage of two-household parenting that their fathers were more available. No children thought two-household parenting was an improvement over having the parents together in a home they also shared. All children found reason for complaint. In addition to disliking a situation in which they could only be with their parents one at a time, they disliked traveling between the households. There is, to begin with, the small irritations of having to plan for the move, then there is having to pack and having to leave their neighborhoods and friends, and at the end of a visit, fearing that possessions would be left behind when they changed households.

Some children said they didn't adapt well to the alternating bedrooms. A father said:

> One of our biggest concerns about this whole situation is that we recognize that it's tiring packing a kid up and moving him two days a week. You know, just picking them up and spending some time with them, and taking them back.

Going from one parent to the other often meant leaving friends and it sometimes meant being unavailable for parties or sports events. Adolescents, especially, were likely to complain about this. An early adolescent girl said:

> I remember I had a report to do for school and I was assigned to do it with another friend. And we couldn't get together any day in the week. And that weekend I was with my dad. And he said, "Well, you better find a way that you can do it during the week, because I'm not sacrificing my weekend for you for a stupid project." So she had to cancel a music lesson or something so that we could get together on a Thursday, and then I could be with my dad that weekend.

Conclusion

Parenting from separate households entails negotiating agreement on boundaries and their permeability. Parents who are no longer partners have to negotiate the nature of the boundaries of their households, their relationships, and their resources. They have to negotiate accessibility. On the other hand, parents and children assume they have access to one another even when they are not coresidents. An assumption of continuing accessibility between parents and children, regardless of their ages or stages of life, seems to explain why the boundaries of the households of grandparents and grandchildren are relatively permeable and unproblematic. On the other hand, an assumption of a lack of accessibility between ex-spouses appears to account for the relative impermeability of the boundaries between their households and/or the problematic nature of those boundaries.

Among the people we describe in this paper, different perspectives on the permeability of such boundaries correlate with the degree of difficulty in co-parenting from separate households. People who viewed household boundaries as permeable had less difficulty in co-parenting, and people who conceptualized the rights and duties of parental roles as divisible and distributable among different persons had less difficulty in co-parenting. Conversely, people who saw the boundaries of households, roles, and relationships as closed had more difficulty in co-parenting.

The problems associated with parenting from separate households derive from the persistence of cultural ideas about relationships and resources that are more appropriate to the household form in which parents are coresidential. The two-household form of co-parenting requires that those involved in it establish new understandings or "tiny cultures" (Goldner 1982) consistent with their situation. Among the understandings that have to be developed are those concerning the permeability of household boundaries, the movement of children from household to household, and the particulars of the allocation of resources between the households. Parents will have to establish a shared understanding of the extent to which they will make decisions jointly, the conditions under which one parent can ask help of the other, and the children's events for which the parents will appear together. Differences in the ways in which our informants have accomplished these goals help to explain the variability of their experiences in parenting from separate households. Moreover, the process of forming new understandings suggests that the two-household family form is not inevitably problematic. Rather, what is inevitable are the difficulties entailed in the process of developing new understandings.

Notes

We gratefully acknowledge the help of Susan Clark, Stephanie Howard, and Amy Koel in the recruitment of families for this study, and Stephanie Howard for interviewing the children. All three have contributed significantly to the preparation of this manuscript. We also thank Linda Stone for her editorial suggestions.

References

Abu, Katharine. 1983. The Separateness of Spouses: Conjugal Resources in an Ashanti Town. In *Female and Male in West Africa*, ed. Christine Oppong. Boston: Allen and Unwin.

Bohannan, Paul. 1971. Dyad Dominance and Household Maintenance. In *Kinship and Culture*, ed. Francis Hsu. Chicago: Aldine.

Bray, James H., and Charlene E. Depner. 1993. Perspectives on Nonresidential Parenting. In *Nonresidental Parenting: New Vistas in Family Living*, ed. Charlene E. Depner and James H. Bray. Newbury Park, Calif.: Sage.

Buchanan, Christy M., Eleanor E. Maccoby, and Sanford Dornbusch. 1996. *Adolescents After Divorce*. Cambridge, Mass: Harvard University Press.

Clark, Gracia. 1989. Money, Sex, and Cooking: Manipulation of the Paid/Unpaid Boundary by Ashanti Market Women. In *The Social Economy of Consumption*, ed. Henry Rutz and Benjamin S. Orlove. Lanham, Md.: University Press of America.

Del Carmen, Rebecca, and Gabrielle N. Virgo. 1993. Marital Disruption and Nonresidential Parenting. In *Nonresidental Parenting: New Vistas in Family Living*, ed. Charlene E. Depner and James H. Bray. Newbury Park, Calif.: Sage.

———. 1993. Nonresidential Parenting: Multidimensional Approaches in Research, Policy, and Practice. In *Nonresidental Parenting: New Vistas in Family Living*, ed. Charlene E. Depner and James H. Bray. Newbury Park, Calif.: Sage.

Fortes, Meyer. 1949. Time and Social Structure: An Ashanti Case Study. In *Social Structure*, ed. Meyer Fortes. New York: Russell and Russell.

———. 1950. Kinship and Marriage Among the Ashanti. In *African Systems of Kinship and Marriage*, ed. A. R. Radcliffe-Brown and Daryl Forde. New York: Oxford University Press.

———. 1969. *Kinship and the Social Order*. Chicago: Aldine.

Goldner, Virginia. 1982. Remarriage Family: Structure, System, Future. In *Therapy with Remarriage Families*, ed. Lillian Messinger. Rockville, Md.: Aspen Systems Corp.

Howard, Stephanie E. 1996. Post-Divorce Influences on Fathering and Their Implications for Children's Well-Being. Ph.D. diss., University of Massachusetts at Boston.

Maccoby, Eleanor E., and Robert H. Mnookin. 1992. *Dividing the Child: Social and Legal Dilemmas of Custody.* Cambridge, Mass.: Harvard University Press.

Skolnick, Arlene. 1991. *Embattled Paradise: The American Family in an Age of Uncertainty.* New York: Basic.

Weiss, Robert S. 1994. *Learning From Strangers.* New York: Free Press.

Chapter Fourteen

Open Adoption: Extending Families, Exchanging Facts

Judith S. Modell

On October 25, 1998, the *New York Times* printed a photograph on its front page of two mothers "sharing" a child. The accompanying article, "In Search of a Child: The New Openness," went on to discuss, among other aspects of American adoption, the spread of *open adoptions*. The photograph was full of implications, not all plumbed in the accompanying article: a scene of two mothers cuddling an infant evokes assumptions about parenthood and family, nurture and love that uphold adoption in the United States. Those evoked assumptions simultaneously cover over the real significance of "openness" in American adoption.

The photo in the *Times* suggested that open adoption brings a birth parent and an adoptive parent together, their mutual concern for and involvement with the child marking the establishment of an "extended family." That may be the popular view of open adoption, a view that inspires a tingle of dread in individuals contemplating adoption from within—the participants in—or from without—the spectators of—created kinship. In truth, open adoption has about as many meanings as there are individuals embarking on adoptive family relationships. Even agencies, the arbiters of adoption in the United States, do not agree on definitions, and one must expect that the social workers within those agencies accommodate practices to their personal viewpoints.

Practices that now come under the rubric of openness include an exchange of nonidentifying information between birth parent and adoptive parent; a face-to-face meeting without an exchange of names; exchanges of photographs, letters, and names at the time of contact; ongoing contact between birth parent, adoptive parent, and, at parental discretion, the child (Rappaport 1992; Silber and Dorner 1990; Demick and Wapner 1988). In the 1990s, most American adoption agencies offered the possibility of openness among their services. One scholar of adoption estimates that 80 to 90 percent of adoption agencies encourage information sharing and that about 20 percent have families participating in fully disclosed adoptions in which anonymity is dropped (McRoy 1991). The breadth of these practices and the lack of precision in defining openness reveal several things about American adoption. First, use of the term to cover the exchange of information reveals exactly how *closed* adoption became over the course of the twentieth century.[1] Sealed in state records, locked in agency files, and protected by court orders, "information" is a precious commodity. Second, the breadth of definition exposes a particularistic approach long characteristic of American adoption: each case is treated as special and distinct in practice. Particularism makes sense in the child-centered climate of American placement policy; the perceived tragedy (or expediency) of transferring a child away from her or his biological parent is modified by emphasizing the child's special needs, personality, and vulnerabilities. The effect of particularism is to throw everything up for grabs—including the lines of kinship adoption follows.

I think there is a third explanation for the expansiveness and, one might say, chaos of meanings of open adoption. The bustle and bounty of referents for the phrase haze over and obscure the real threat opening adoption poses. Unmistakably and overall, open adoption challenges the confidentiality and sealed-record policies of American adoption. The challenge is severe for two reasons: (1) confidentiality is crucial to the ideal of family that adoption practice implements, and (2) confidentiality accords control over constructed families to social workers and other professionals who manage the transfer of children in the United States. Opening adoption weakens the boundaries of family, defies conceptualizations of kinship, and undermines customary regulations of placement in ways that have no precedent in American history. Opening adoption disrupts the function adoption has served in the United States of enforcing the normative nuclear family: father, mother, and children attached to one another forever. Interpreted as sharing a child, open adoption implies that divorce, stepfamilies, and sequential parenting are *fine*. In short, open adoption throws a gauntlet at the consanguineal core of kinship that until now adoptive arrangements scrupulously, vividly, and persuasively represented (see Modell 1994 and Modell 2001).

Open adoption requires a whole new model of parent–child ties. The energy of resistance to such a change is evident in the fierce opposition openness arouses. More importantly, resistance is evident in the hazy way openness is defined—its meaning accommodated to the predilections, the principles, and the unarticulated assumptions of those who practice, oversee, and write about adoption. As other chapters in this book argue, redrawing the lines of kinship is rarely easy or harmonious; in the case of adoption, as in other cases, redrawing kinship happens person by person, day by day. The subject of open adoption extends the analytic perspectives of kinship studies inasmuch as adoption prompts—and always has prompted—an *articulation* of the principles and signs of relatedness. Controversies over open adoption are indicative of the process of change the institution has consistently manifested. In turn, the controversies show how American adoption offsets substantial revisions of notions of parenthood, family, and kinship.

My argument is more than that. A close look at open adoption reveals an emphasis on "information" that enlarges its impact farther than researchers suspect, participants acknowledge, and historians document.[2] Several features of the arrangements deemed "open" stand out; these frame my discussion in the following pages. First, opening adoption is premised on the value of information, not on the extension of kinship ties. Second, opening adoption reflects a postmodern isolation of the parent–child tie from family and from continuity over generations.Third, opening adoption has more to do with individual choice than with family. Sounding paradoxical and odd, each of these statements merits discussion—though in the end, they are not separable from one another.

What Does "Open" Mean in Open Adoption?

The term "open adoption" applies to what are called stranger or nonrelative adoptions. These are the adoptions that form popular stereotypes: a child, previously unknown and unrelated, is adopted by an adult or a couple. Relative adoptions occur between individuals who know one another, and increasingly adoptions are undertaken within a family and by new partners of a biological parent. Different assumptions about information attach to each form of adoption. In stranger adoptions, the assumption is that necessary information will be passed from birth parent to adoptive parent, traditionally through a social worker or other intermediary. In relative adoptions, the assumption is that the participating adults know the child and have relevant information about her or him. Recently, too, the rise in foster child and older child adoptions means the child herself or himself carries a wealth of information into the adopting family. These developments have the dual effect of bringing information to the forefront, since it differs from one type to another, and of confounding the meaning of the word. In this chapter, I focus on openness in the conventional stranger adoption.

Many reasons are given for the shift away from closed and confidential adoptions. (The story, of course, is complicated by the plethora of interpretations of "closed" and of "open.") Probably the least disputed reason is one that focuses on adoptees. In the 1960s, in a movement well described elsewhere, adoptee demands for more information about themselves intensified and, in an increasing number of cases, led to a search for members of a birth family (see e.g., Carp 1998; Modell 1994). Birth parents followed soon after, with claims for "information" that at once resembled and extended the claims adoptees were making. In response to demands, and alert to the number of achieved reunions, agencies began offering more information at the onset of an adoption; such information was thought to forestall later dissatisfaction and possible disruption of the adoptive family. The perceptible groundswell out there energized agencies into attending to client demands, among which "information" took the lead.

Another explanation for openness exists, intertwined with the presumed significance of information. This second explanation might be called the market factor in American adoption. In the United States, adoption depends on the willingness of a parent to relinquish her child—to offer a child for distribution, as it were—and on the willingness of an adult to take in (permanently) the child produced by another person. The ratio of supply and demand, furthermore, is not just a matter of balancing product availability and consumer need, but also of negotiating the principles of exchange held by those who enter an adoption market. Supply as well as interpretations of the transaction changed in the 1960s and 1970s. Fewer parents relinquished and those that did joined the chorus calling for information. More potential adopters entered the market and they, too, chafed against the secrecy and confidentiality agencies imposed.[3]

Clients came to agencies no longer assuming they had to be docile about the terms of adopting. Agencies had to comply with the mobilization of client interests or lose their business. Information became both the centerpiece and the cover for a profound sea change in cultural understandings of kinship, parenthood, and identity.

The emphasis on information itself needs to be explained. All members of the adoption triad were influenced by the preoccupation with background, ancestry, and, eventually, genetics spreading through American culture. Publicized in various ways, including the poignant personal memoirs displayed in print and on television, the urge to *know* won converts right and left—and still does. Controversial and heated, the subject of releasing or protecting information touches deep roots in American culture. The debate around confidentiality exceeds that occurring in European nations, which, by and large, approach adoption with similar goals and understandings. A scholar of adoption from Finland, herself an adoptee, Wegar (1997: xi) remarked on her surprise at the persistence of closed records in the United States. Exploring "the structures of belief, perception and appreciation that shape the controversy" over sealed records, her book hints at the distinctive importance information—its content, storage, and distribution—plays in the United States. My discussion concentrates on the role of information in open adoption, and shows the emphasis on "facts" to be a major break in the links between adoptive kinship, kinship, and cultural values.

Practicing Openness in Adoption

The move toward openness, in any of its guises, has been slow and cautious. "Meetings between birthparents and adoptive parents started in 1974 at the

Children's Home Society of California (CHSC)," reported McRoy, a prominent researcher on American adoption. "As of 1984, 10 percent of their adoptions could be classified as *open*, in some respects. Less than 1 percent included the exchange of last names, addresses, and phone numbers" (McRoy,
Grotevant, and White 1998: 16). Ten percent is not abundant, especially when
qualified by "in some respects." Other agencies followed the California example, also offering openness *in some respects*. Most often, the practice involves
providing the birth parents and the adoptive parents with much more information about each other than had been the case in twentieth-century American adoptions. A few agencies encourage, even advise, face-to-face meetings,
but these meetings do not necessarily include an exchange of names, addresses, or other identifying information.

I have been working with an agency in my community that introduced a
policy of openness ten years ago. Like other agencies in the country, this one
defined the move as innovative and has moved cautiously in implementing
new practices. The data for my discussion below come from my research with
this agency (supplemented by contact with other agencies in the community),
as well as from the studies of open adoption now available. These studies,
while expanding, are still preliminary: new practices have not produced
enough cases to warrant a large-scale research project (Gross 1993). When research with families is done, the population is small, self-selective, and, generally, consists of the articulate and the forthright members of an adoption
community. In addition, the subjects of a majority of these research projects,
including my own, are primarily white, middle-class—mainstream—Americans. The agency is old, elite, and well respected in the community. While customarily accepting clients—birth and adoptive parents—who have resources
and options, along with introducing open adoption, the agency has also expanded its community to include nonwhite and less well-off clients. My initial findings suggest that the clients willing to try some form of openness are
individuals with higher education and income.

Like other agencies in the country, the placement agency I work with practiced caution by attending to the expressed wishes and needs of clients. Like
other agencies in the country, this one also attributed its change in policy primarily to the swelling of demand for information on the part of adoptees. Social workers also reported that parents contemplating relinquishment, as well
as individuals applying for adoption, request more detailed information
about the "other" parents of their child. The thumbnail sketch, with its summary of health, habits, and hobbies, no longer suffices.[4] In addition, the
agency had been losing business, with the shortage of infants remarked all
over the country and the consequent turn to international or independent
adoptions by potential parents.[5] A wider swath had to be cut in order to at-
tract clients.

In the 1980s, the agency began offering three different types of adoption:
traditional (closed), semiopen, and fully disclosed adoption. Traditional

adoption preserves the confidentiality and sealed-records policy of American adoption. In semiopen arrangements, letters and photos are exchanged along with information, but identifying information is not provided.[6] In fully disclosed adoptions, the parties meet one another face to face, have phone conversations, and exchange names—though, I discovered, often not addresses.

Potential adoptive parents come to the agency expecting a conventional, closed adoption. This may be because they know the "normal" rules of American adoption or it may be that, like many adoptive parents before them, they value the protection and insurance that secrecy (presumably) provides. A certain number of birth parents, too, request anonymity, for the reasons that have always existed: the stigma attached to an unplanned pregnancy, perhaps personal shame at a "mistake," and often simply the desire to be private about a decision still regarded as odd or unnatural in American culture. These clients indicate the hold secrecy has, preserving as it does the closure and permanency of transfer that adoption is supposed to effect in the United States. Operating in a context in which "openness" (in some form) receives the approval of the Child Welfare League of America as well as of a number of individuals already engaged in adoptive relationships, the agency intervenes with a presentation of the advantages of "disclosure."

These presentations occur in group meetings and at carefully structured panels. The presentations do not concentrate on the best interests of the child, recognizably not the total issue, but on the expectations, comfort level, and understandings of family that clients bring to the table. To the credit of the agency, presentations do not force a point of view; they do address common fears and concerns that haunt participants in adoptive kinship in American society. Based on my interviews, attendance at a number of meetings and panels, and anthropological-style immersion in this adoption community, the concerns voiced by birth parents and adoptive parents resemble those discussed in studies of adoption in general. Confronted with the idea of limited or no confidentiality—of knowing about and even knowing in person—the other parents of one's child, birth and adoptive parents worry about similar things. How will the presence of a birth parent (or family) affect adoptive parent attachment to and bonding with the child? How important are biological factors (or genetics) to a child's development and identity? What role is a birth parent to play in the child's life? How does a child handle the presence of several different mothers and fathers in her or his life? Elaborated and generalized, these are also the issues that come up in debates over openness in adoption literature, in the media, and in casual conversations about a nonsecret, nonconfidential "transaction in parenthood."[7]

Like the debates, concerns voiced by potential birth and adoptive parents often "forget" the child. This sounds paradoxical, especially since the language manifestly focuses on the child. In fact, one of the most frequently cited reasons for opening adoption is that "more information" facilitates the process of telling the child about adoption. There are no gaps or mysteries, no secrets or confusions on the part of the parents; consequently, in conversations with the child about adoption, parents do not need to hesitate, fabricate, or romanticize. Entering the large body of literature on telling, the pros and cons of open adoption still leave the content of information, the significance of "knowing," a matter of individual, and diversified, understanding and application.[8]

Close examination of most texts on open adoption, including those I gathered in my fieldwork, reveals that the child is regarded as a recipient, a beneficiary of his or her parents' satisfaction with the arrangement they have made. The assumption within my adoption community, as in much adoption literature, is that when birth parent and adoptive parent are content, the child will be well served, her or his interests carefully nurtured and protected. The child's changing perceptions, experiences, cognitive and emotional growth are less prominent in group discussions and on panels than the level of comfort the adults achieve.[9] And while the child may slide away from direct focus because there are not enough children experiencing new types of openness to constitute a study population, the primary reason is that open adoption in the end has to do first with the adults and secondarily with the child. Moreover, open adoption has less to do with kinship among individuals than with control over information and, with that, identity.

One Case

One sunny spring morning, I spent three hours with a wife and husband who were participating in an open or *fully disclosed* adoption, in the language the agency used. I arrived at their urban townhouse around 10:00 A.M., and was greeted with coffee, fresh fruit, and cookies that "Danny helped bake." Danny, age four, was around, playing with his cars and trucks. Unlike other adoptive parents I interviewed, Marilyn and Daniel did not "hide things" from young Danny.[10] They were very happy to talk about open adoption and told me they wanted to "help others make the decision we made." Admitting to fear at first, they were comforted by attending a panel of birth parents who had met and knew the adoptive parents of their children. "There was nothing frightening about them. They were just young girls who had made a mistake, or couldn't tell their parents, or wanted to go to college." Marilyn and Daniel both expressed appreciation at the amount of exposure to various types of adoptive arrangements they had received at the agency.

After considering the pros and cons, Marilyn and Daniel agreed to try a fully disclosed adoption. They met the young mother and exchanged information about themselves with her. "We felt comfortable with her," they told me, and were overjoyed when, five months later, she handed the baby to them in person. Certainly there seemed to be no secrets here; or, rather, the secrets were not imposed by the agency but by the participants themselves. Social workers are present during initial meetings to facilitate and to make sure that each person is satisfied with the exchange of information. Personal reports, and my observations, suggest that the exchange of information expands but never breaks the envelope sanctified in adoption practice over the years. With or without intervention by a social worker, the "facts" people offer one another resemble the conventional sketches American adoption agencies have always provided: health, background, interests, hobbies, attitudes toward children, and feelings about family. Added to this information are whatever details can be learned from reading the gestures and facial expressions of another person. And because theirs was "fully disclosed," Marilyn, Daniel, and the birth mother, Sally, also exchanged identifying information, primarily names and phone numbers.

As important as the initial meeting for all three was the opportunity to keep lines of communication open after the baby had been placed and legally adopted. To meet this goal, Marilyn and Daniel regularly sent letters and photographs to Sally documenting Danny's growth and development. Sally called at first regularly, and then sporadically; every Christmas, Marilyn and Daniel brought Danny to visit Sally and her mother. When Danny was two, Sally left the state, stopped phoning, and ended contact. Marilyn and Daniel still visit with Sally's mother on Christmas, but Sally is not a major topic of conversation. Marilyn and Daniel are pleased that Danny has contact with the birth grandmother. They frankly admitted that they were "relieved" that Sally was not more interested in the child. At age twenty-one, she probably would "move on with her life."

Redrawing Kinship or Disclosing Information?

This is one story. What does it mean in the larger discussion of changed adoption practices? Nearly a decade ago, Caplan (1990) published a step-by-step narrative of an open adoption in the *New Yorker*. The piece follows the fortunes of Peggy, who would not relinquish her child unless she could know the parents; Tom, the child's father and Peggy's boyfriend whom she did not want to marry; and Lee and Dan, the adoptive parents who accepted the requests Peggy made. Both analytic and sensitive in its descriptive thickness, Caplan's story reveals the cultural complexities embedded in changed adoptive arrangements. Similarly, the story of Sally, Marilyn, Daniel, and Danny exposes the difficulties and dilemmas in a shift to openness.

The complexities are different, without being contradictory. Caplan tells a story of unsuccessfully redrawn kinship. The story I told (much more briefly) demonstrates the significance and the multiple meanings of *disclosure*. Together, the two cases illuminate what opening adoption meant and did not mean in late 1990s American society. As Caplan tells the story, Peggy and Tom developed a close, familial relationship with Lee and Dan before the birth of the child. The four spent time together, drawing and redrawing the lines of relationship that connected them to one another. Peggy, like other birth mothers in studies, seemed to consider Lee a mother figure; Lee, in turn, nurtured and worried over Peggy. The fathers had a different approach to family, one equally gendered: the two men took responsibility for the ties between all four adults. After the baby was born, problems arose, unresolvable even with an *as-if* kinship map. Caplan's narrative, with the strikingly unambiguous title "An Open Adoption," ends with Peggy gone from the lives of Lee, Dan, and the baby, and with Tom only a voice on the answering machine. In the last scene, the adoptive family is alone in the kitchen, preparing breakfast—just like any other "real" family.

In one way a failure, in another way the adoption suggests what "open" may really mean to those who practice and those who support the practice within agencies. (For the moment, I leave out the most militant supporters of open adoption, those who insist on "new" families. I come back to the point in my conclusion.) The completion of the story comes from my fieldwork, from Sally, Marilyn, Daniel, and Danny. They participated in what the agency carefully calls "fully disclosed" adoption. By rejecting the word "open," the agency avoids the vagueness of that term, the titillating publicity surrounding the idea (for instance, "two mothers sharing a child"), and the suggestion of completely fluid family boundaries. Instead, taking the phrase "fully disclosed" maintains the positive aura the word "open" has in an American context and emphasizes *the transfer of information rather than the creation of kinship ties.*

"Fully disclosed" speaks to the end of sealed records and closed files, hidden facts and doctored data. "Fully disclosed" underlines the documentary aspect of any form of adoption in 1990s American society; it refers to the composed and coherent representation of crucial actors, not to the emotional and familial minefield through which Peggy, Tom, Dan, and Lee walked. Sally chose a disclosed adoption (according to Marilyn and Daniel) because she wanted to *know* the parents of her child; she wanted to learn their outstanding traits and personal perspectives, as well as the lineaments of their social and domestic worlds. Marilyn and Daniel, in turn, emphasized the importance of *knowing* Sally. For them, too, the word had a particular meaning, which had nothing to do with intimacy and everything to do with a perception of important information. One might even say (without losing sight of the feelings Marilyn and Daniel had about adoption and their adoptive family) that "knowing" distanced them from an intimacy with Sally, putting the contact into a clear and manageable arena.

"Fully disclosed" uncovers the significant feature of opening adoption as it occurred in late twentieth-century American society: each party to the transaction received an elaborated description of the other, a more complete life history, a thicker file folder. Birth parents and adoptive parents entered the arrangement with the desire to provide and to acquire a thorough dossier on the key actors in the event. The content ultimately depends on personal definitions, decisions, and responses to the inevitable changes a lifetime brings.

Knowing is not the beginning of a relationship. Marilyn and Daniel were relieved when Sally moved away. And Sally did, after all, move away and stop phoning. With some exceptions, participants in open adoptions tend to reduce contact quickly. "For all studies, the actual amount of contact . . . is in the range of two to four contacts a year" (Gross 1993: 273). Adoptive parents in other studies admit being "tired out" by the visit of a birth parent. "Sometimes I think I'm tired of sharing. It's getting ready for the visits. The kids will fight and punch each other and you say, 'Oh Lord, please don't do this in front of them [birth parents].' When they leave, I say, 'Whew, that's another visit over with' " (quoted in McRoy, Grotevant, and White 1988: 89). While this might be the comment of any harried mother, the word "sharing" suggests the deeper problems adoptive parents perceive in continued contact. As the mother's remark reveals, the arrival of a birth parent is not just that of another relative but of someone who actually shares the child. No matter what term the "visitor" is given, aunty or first name, she (or he) evokes an uncomfortable, because not delineated, participation in the child's life and identity. Contact is not a first draft of kinship but a smudged picture of interactions.

Birth parents end contact, but for somewhat different reasons. Apparently, a number do accept the "move on with life" prescription so deeply embedded in relinquishment rhetoric in the United States (Modell 1994). From this vantage point, staying in contact with the adoptive family signifies remaining in a niche without a future. Plus the relationship birth parents find themselves in is not *sharing* but *being* a child. Statements like "the adoptive mother is like a mother to me," or "I can always depend on her," run through reports on contact between birth and adoptive parents. Continued contact seems to work only for a small segment of the American population. In her book *Open Adoption* (1987), Lindsay described satisfactory relationships between birth parents and adoptive parents. Participants tended to be members of religiously based adoption communities. Homogeneity was the rule, and reference to "God's gift" of a child smoothed over the problems of defining behaviors and relationships among the individuals participating in the adoption. Like other studies, Lindsay's is horizontal: there is no time scale through which to track changes in the relationships established at the onset of an adoption. As she recognizes, longitudinal studies are vital; this does not, however, vitiate her findings that something else is needed if contact is to last: religious beliefs, a tight community, a charismatic social worker.

Another group reportedly able to manage ongoing contact is loosely deemed "intellectuals." As used, the term not only covers a mélange of so-called daring, somewhat marginal members of American society, but also underlines the intellectual dimension of engaging in openness. "Some liberal people think that they can handle all this [openness] but I personally wouldn't want to" (quoted in McRoy, Grotevant, and White 1988: 77). A recent book on the experience of being adopted reiterates the idea: "As happens in any innovation, the pioneers of open adoptions are a very select group of parents: highly educated, liberal, open-minded, nondefensive, experimental individuals who are not tied to traditional mores and lifestyles" (Brodzinsky, Schechter, and Henig 1992: 190). The implication is that opening is a politically correct thing to do, which, as well, introduces a dependence on information that has nothing to do with "real" parenthood. From one point of view, then, "facts" intrude in the creation of loving, unconditional parental ties; from another point of view—for those who choose disclosed adoption—facts cement the tie between parent and child. Both viewpoints stress the informational aspects of opening adoption, not the establishment or the continuity of contact between birth and adoptive parents.

It's very 1990s American culture to stress information. The intrusion of "freedom of information" into adoption has been striking in the past three decades, as it has been in other areas of American life. To get information is culturally considered better than being denied information. In the case of adoption, one must ask "what information?" and "why better?" Under the auspices of their agency's fully disclosed practice, Sally, Marilyn, and Daniel gleaned more information about each other than they would have in a conventional confidential arrangement: they saw each other, they asked questions of one another, they presented themselves in person, not just on paper. Marilyn and Daniel told me they felt they could be better parents of Danny knowing his background, knowing "where he came from." Sally felt better placing her child in an environment she knew.

The remarks seem to focus on parental satisfaction and on the factors that make adults happy with an adoption. Yet Marilyn, Daniel, and Sally were not being self-interested. Rather, their views on the adoptive arrangement reflect a principle in American culture that the well-being of a child depends on the nature of his attachment to parents. The three also seem to accept the (connected) assumption that parental bonds are strengthened, even ensured, by feelings of comfort on the part of parents.[11] In the case of the birth parent, the assumption refers back to—and explains—the oft-repeated conviction that a contented birth parent does not try to "snatch back" her child. In the case of the adoptive parents, the assumption refers back to—and explains—the conviction that adoptive parents bond better when there are no "mysteries" about the child or the child's past. Open adoption expands and penetrates these assumptions by inserting "knowing" or, interchangeably, "information" into the equation.

Overall, then, open adoption accentuates the importance of documents and data in late twentieth-century American adoption. While couched in the framework of parental ties, attachment, and bonding, the desire for information on the part of birth parents and adoptive parents alters the institution of adoption more thoroughly than may first appear. *The quest for facts removes adoption from its basis in family and in kinship.* And that needs an explanation.

Opening onto Chosen, Contingent Ties

Open adoption fits into a longer history of adoption in the United States. Like earlier changes in that institution, the move toward openness stems less from policy decisions or ideological shifts than from particular actions and demands. Like the passage of state laws in the mid-nineteenth century, the challenge to law in the late twentieth century emerges from lots of individual behaviors, under the pressure of changed demographic, economic, and political circumstances. Open adoption fits the history of American adoption in another way. The practice of opening records, in its several variations, perpetuates the oscillation in the functions adoption serves in an American context: caring for runaway and/or needy children; providing an heir to carry on name and property; making a couple into a family.[12] Is adoption for the child or for the adults, the individual or a kinship group? Is adoption a personal or a social phenomenon? The questions persist, as appropriate to alternative as to conventional adoptions.

Open adoption also extracts a theme often subdued in the history of American adoption: a focus on the individual, on personal needs and satisfactions, and on a quest for "identity" that has a long pedigree in American culture. Justification for disclosure, an end to sealed records and secrecy, comes in terms of "helping" individuals through the process of transacting a child and living with the implications of bringing parenthood into the public, legal domain. Not only is this justification on an individual level and not a social one, but it also has little to do with family, with the conceptualization of affectionate affinity that Fortes (1969) inserted into kinship studies. Furthermore, the emphasis on lasting bonds suggests how thoroughly American adoption has come to replace other seemingly frail and impermanent bonds, including marriage and genealogical links between parent and child. In my reading, American adoption has come to represent a permanency missing in a postmodern society in which virtually all relationships seem fluid, flowing, and temporary. An open adoption position claims that facts substantiate the tie between parent and child; in the perspective of those who support disclosure, facts thicken the fictive (or as-if) bond.[13] Simultaneously, the tie between parent and child becomes the centerpiece, the function and the goal of an adoption. Not continuing a bloodline or completing a family but ensuring (at least) one permanent relationship is the raison d'être of American adoption.

With its emphasis on facts and information, fully disclosed adoption pushes American adoption farther from the "core of kinship" than it has ever been before.

In the media, and probably for most people who pay attention, "open adoption" represents expanded kinship. Popularly, "open" evokes ongoing contact between birth and adoptive parents and new forms of an extended family. More than that, in some versions, open adoption suggests deeper and more intimate bonds than those developing out of "ordinary" kinship. As the *New York Times* photo caption put it: two mothers *share* a child. Given the "genealogical core of kinship" in American culture, that's a pretty profound closeness.

My research, and that of others, indicates that complete and continued contact is a rare scenario; the initial plan often gives way to thin and sporadic contact. Letters, phone calls, and e-mail step in, constituting an exchange and replacing the visits and interactions touted by the press. "Fully disclosed," the term in the agency I work with, most aptly describes the phenomenon in its current state. Openness in American adoption is, at the moment, best defined as keeping channels of communication open, not as ongoing contact, sharing a child, or extending a family.

Why should an emphasis on exchanging information and disclosing facts distance adoption from the core of kinship? And what might the consequences be of such a development? The cultural core of American kinship is genealogical, as Schneider (1968, 1984) argued in his crucial contributions to kinship studies. Historically and ideally, adoption in the United States replicates this genealogical principle. Replication is accomplished in three ways: in the insistence that the adopted child is just like a child born to its adoptive parents, the "as if begotten" premise of American adoption law; in the prescription (until recently) that the created family look just like a family established by marriage and the birth of children; and in the disappearance of a birth parent so the adoptive family can be a normative nuclear unit. Modified in practice over the course of the twentieth century, all three necessitate the sealed records, anonymity, and secrecy of conventional American adoption.

State laws of adoption were followed speedily by laws assuring confidentiality to all parties to the transaction. Laws of confidentiality created the "closed" adoption to which "open" adoption is now juxtaposed. The juxtaposition further illuminates the nature of openness and underlines the extent to which openness *in any respect* refers to "freedom of information" and not to realization of relationship.

"Freedom" is not simply a cliché in this context. Tapping into notions of choice and contract, as well as into cultural notions of the person and of personal autonomy, openness represents a bid for control. "Full disclosure" also represents a move away from the metaphors of fate and destiny that once diffused from biological to legal relationships (Modell 1994). The word openness points to, among other things, a principle that no person should deny information that he or she has to an interested party. The principle implies the "rightness" of control over information on the part of actors in an adoptive arrangement: to be deprived of facts is thought to signal lack of leverage. Similarly, a relationship phrased in terms of fate or destiny comes to seem to be one over which a person has no control. Partially a reaction to the strictures and constraints social workers imposed on transactions in parenthood, openness stretches beyond that to draw on values of honesty and "coming out" that resonate throughout an American cultural context. Walking in the sunshine, proverbs (and laws) announce, is better than hiding in darkness.

Connotations of honesty and straightforwardness render the word "open" appealing while allowing the denotations to be arbitrary and idiosyncratic. Positively valenced, openness diversifies the meaning of information; content varies with each person's perspective and circumstances. Ideally, in open adoptions information is not supposed to be constricted and systematized, but loose and individualized. Like adoptees and birth parents who reject their sealed-record adoptions and search for one another, participants in open adoptions decide on the content of information step by step, moment by moment. When Marilyn, Daniel, and Sally sat together, discussing the transfer of the as-yet unborn Danny, each brought to the demand for disclosure a wealth of opinions, experiences, and interpretations of kinship, family, and identity. Despite the presence of a social worker, each acquired a degree of control over the transaction in parenthood that would not have been available in an agency adoption even a decade ago.

Debate over opening adoption and disclosing information takes different forms. The critique may be draped in the principle of "best interests," but this is merely the inherited discourse for a quite different issue. Behind the banner of best interests, I argue, lies apprehension at what opening adoption bodes for the cultural ideologies that conventional adoption has upheld in the United States. Ideologies include expectations about good families, fit parents, and proper kinship. These expectations, in turn, have been supervised and regulated by social workers since the Progressive era in the United States. Awareness of the loss of a supervisory role enters the debate over open adoption in two ways: (1) framing a negative response in terms of the chaos and confusion that will result if "everyone" can arrange her or his own adoption, and (2) pushing experts who advocate disclosure into adding the requirement that clients who embark on open adoption visit the agency from time to time for counseling. And as always in the history of adoption, clients absorb and activate the messages, taking them on as their own. "Because Amy [birth mother] doesn't want to hurt Tricia and Mike [adoptive parents], and because Tricia and Mike care and are concerned about Amy, it's working. And especially because there's an understanding counselor acting as an intermediary when needed, it's working" (Lindsay 1987: 104).

Both advocacy of counseling and acceptance of the advice show how qualified the approval of opening adoption is. Genuine reference to a child's best interests could lead to support for complete openness, ongoing contact, and new relationships as logically as the principle presently leads to either condemnation of the change or close supervision of its implementation. Qualification of approval cannot be attributed solely to ambition and greed for power (or status) on the part of child welfare experts. Nor can it be simply attributed to adoptive parent fear that a birth parent will share, intervene in, and ultimately repossess the child. And arguments that open adoption prevents a birth parent from "moving on" also carry small weight. Yet, qualification of "disclosure" is apparent in many adoption communities, within the practice of opening itself, as well as in some literature on adoption in the United States.

My first impulse was to conclude that qualified approval resulted from the problems of shared parenthood, for the child and for the adults. Along with this, I considered the difficulty of opening family boundaries in new and unscripted ways. Second thoughts revealed that by framing my conclusion in that way, I, too, had accepted the available discourse: best interests and the connection between a child's interests and *a particular kinship*. Further examination of my data and of existing studies led to another conclusion: the threat a demand for information poses to the conceptualization of "real" kinship in the United States.

Especially in adoption, an arena of deliberately constructed parenthood, emphasis on "facts" is viewed as (potentially) antithetical to enduring solidarity. The view implicates birth parents and adoptive parents who insist on *knowing* before giving and receiving a child. From this, it is one small step to predicting a (consequently) less-than-secure bond between adoptive parents and child. Beyond the voiced concern that bowing to demands for information will release a chaos of motivations, desires, and actions exists an unvoiced cultural assumption that "facts" are not the foundation for affective ties, intimacy, and parental love.

Conclusion

Arguments for and against open adoption are passionate, often inflammatory, and, at the moment, lacking in substantial data.[14] The heat these arguments generate signals their impact beyond the parameters of adoptive kinship. Extending families and stretching kinship boundaries is not what fuels the passion of the debate. Even "two mothers sharing a child" can be incorporated into a culture of kinship these days, given high rates of divorce and remarriage in the United States. Rather, the insistence by participants in adoption that "facts" can permanently seal the bonds, perpetuate the contracts, and protect the child involved in an adoption troubles some observers and some participants. Discomfort at what seems to be a relentless societal move toward "knowing all" before any relationship can be formed energizes the controversy over open adoption. *Full disclosure*, then, captures the heart of the matter more accurately than "open."

Three reasons can be cited for discomfort at the insistence that information is crucial to a transaction in parenthood. First, a demand for full disclosure violates the romantic mysticism about kinship in American culture summed up in the dictum blood is thicker than water; second, full disclosure introduces rational, "cold" calculation into an arrangement supposedly based on love, need, charity, and selflessness; and third, full disclosure alters the historically hierarchical relationship between giver and receiver of a child.

These three reasons enter the debate on both the pro and the con sides. For supporters of openness, information fills in for the perceived thinness of a constructed parent–child tie, gives a solid foundation for the love that evolves between parent and child, and regulates the relationship between giver and receiver of a child. Advocates argue that the "more ties" a child has, the more secure her or his identity: connections with biological kin, from this position, intensify the connection with adoptive parents. As Marilyn and Daniel explained to me, knowing more about Danny's background would help them be "better parents," more confident in expressions of love, and wiser in child rearing. Knowing Sally herself removed for them the mystery and secrecy that make a birth parent a shadowy and therefore threatening figure. "The children have the love and attention of another adult and come to know the birth parent as a real (as opposed to a fantasized) person" (McRoy, Grotevant, and White 1988: 128). Marilyn, Daniel, and Sally accepted the idea that "in the sunshine," neither birth nor adoptive parents will break the contracts they have made with one another. The straightforwardness and honesty "open" connotes keep everyone from acting in a deceptive fashion.

The latent function of open adoption is linked to the positive valence of "sunshine." Forthright and in the open, birth parent and adoptive parent face down the stigmas that attach to both their roles in the United States. They are "out of the closet."

Like every development in American adoption history, the turn to open adoption has multiple causes. Like every other development, too, this one proceeds by fits and starts—fits and starts that result from the particular actions and interpretations of particular individuals. Despite the persistent use of one term, the landscape of open adoption contains a wealth of different niches. In religiously based adoption communities, open adoption establishes ongoing bonds between birth and adoptive families, solidified by similar beliefs and backgrounds (see e.g., Lindsay 1987; Silber and Dorner 1990). In so-called innovative adoption communities, individuals establish chosen and contingent ties that leave behind a model for kinship that rests on a "genealogical core."[15]

With its rejection of the definition of kinship that "blood" and "birth" create, open adoption enters a postmodern world. Relationships are based on knowledge, on choice, and on individual determination of satisfaction and fulfillment. In an American cultural context, findings on open adoption reveal that these relationships are not designated *kinship*, but friendship or "closeness." Individuals I interviewed, like those quoted in other studies, did not use kinship terms for one another. Furthermore, they emphasized the communication and not the contact, the letters and not the visits. An inclination to redraw the contact into a process of communication, planned and (frequently) ceremonial visits, and casual "chat" between interested individuals indicates how far from kinship the arrangement strays. In real kinship, Americans tend to claim, contact is affective and expressive of profound feelings, not just a matter of casual conversation and sporadic news. Although this is certainly an idealized (and media-influenced) view, the contrast with the general outcome of an open adoption is clear. At the end of the *New York Times* article that began with "shared" motherhood, a birth mother admitted that she had no idea what will happen next.

Historically, adoption in the United States has replicated and enforced the cultural core of kinship, the genealogical link between parent (mother) and child. Especially after state laws were passed, more than elsewhere adoption in American society insisted on the sanctity of the blood relationship. Insistence led to the tangles evident in the arrangement and recently exposed (and condemned) by participants in adoption: erasure of the birth parent's "natural" blood tie in order to legitimize the adoptive parent's "cultural" blood tie. Open adoption and opened forms of contact cut through the tangles, deceptions, and symbolic subterfuges characteristic of twentieth-century adoptive arrangements in the United States. The distinction between real, with its connotations of good and true, and fictive, with its connotations of second-best and frail, disappear. Parents and children in adoptive relationships do not need to measure their bonds against a mystical blood tie. They negotiate their bonds within a context of evolving communication—not a bad thing, and certainly appropriate to the world the millennium seems to be bringing.

Notes

1. For a fine history of sealed records in American adoption, see Carp (1998).

2. I put the word in quotation marks to indicate that it has no clear meaning.

3. The story I have briefly told here can be developed at much greater length, in terms of other developments in American society of the period—for instance, the Freedom of Information Act. But that would constitute another paper.

4. This is one descriptive phrase for the presumably objective and stringently nonidentifying information a birth parent and an adoptive parent were likely to receive about one another until recently.

5. Independent adoptions occur outside of an agency, though in some states an agency must do a home study before the adoption goes to court. That was true in my state, and the placement agency did such studies. Still, this is not the same as arranging adoptions from first to last.

6. Some parents I met—birth and adoptive—went to lengths to disguise their identities while providing informative photographs to the other members of the triad.

7. I borrow the phrase from Goodenough (1970).

8. David Brodzinsky has done thorough research on telling children about adoption, in the sense of paying close attention to children's changing understandings, and cognitive capacities, over time. These appear in a number of different articles.

9. There are exceptions: Silber and Dorner (1990) interviewed the children of open adoption; McRoy (1991) and McRoy and her associates (1988), and Harriet Gross (1993) all recognize the importance of drawing children more fully into adoption studies. Several projects, including my own, are currently under way.

10. I have changed names and certain details, to protect the identity of this family.

11. Kirk (1964, 1981) has done important work on parental comfort with adoptive parenthood; he does not apply his findings to birth parents.

12. I discuss these issues more fully in Modell, *A Sealed and Secret Kinship: Policies and Practices in American Adoption* (New York: Berghahn Press, 2001).

13. I refer to the cultural proverb, blood is thicker than water.

14. Many individuals who enter the debate admit to the lack of data, awaiting further study of the phenomenon.

15. This is implied by the findings in McRoy, Grotevant, and White (1988), and Gross (1993).

References

Brodzinsky, D. M., M. D. Schechter, and R. M. Henig. 1992. *Being Adopted: The Lifelong Search for Self.* New York: Doubleday Anchor.

Caplan, Lincoln. 1990. An Open Adoption. Parts 1 and 2. *The New Yorker* (May 21 and May 28): 40–65; 73–95.

Carp, Wayne. 1998. *Family Matters: Secrecy and Disclosure in the History of Adoption.* Cambridge, Mass.: Harvard University Press.

Demick, Jack, and Seymour Wapner. 1988. Open and Closed Adoption: A Developmental Conceptualization. *Family Process* 27:229–49.

Fortes, Meyer. 1969. *Kinship and the Social Order.* Chicago: Aldine.

Goodenough, Ward. 1970. Transactions in Parenthood. In *Adoption in Eastern Oceania,* ed. Vern Carroll. Honolulu: University of Hawaii Press.

Gross, Harriet. 1993. Open Adoption: A Research-Based Literature Review and New Data. *Child Welfare* 72, no. 3:269–84.

Kirk, H. David. 1964. *Shared Fate: A Theory of Adoption and Mental Health.* Glencoe, Ill.: Free Press.

———. 1981. *Adoptive Kinship: A Modern Institution in Need of Reform.* Toronto: Butterworth.

Lindsay, Jeanne W. 1987. *Open Adoption: A Caring Option.* Buena Park, Calif.: Morning Glory Press.

Mason, Mary Ann. 1994. *From Father's Property to Children's Rights.* New York: Columbia University Press.

McRoy, Ruth G. 1991. American Experience and Research on Openness. *Adoption and Fostering* 15, no. 4:99–111.

McRoy, Ruth G., Harold D. Grotevant, and Kerry L. White. 1988. *Openness in Adoption.* New York: Praeger.

Modell, Judith. 1994. *Kinship with Strangers: Interpretations of Adoption in American Culture.* Berkeley: University of California Press.

———. 1999. Freely Given: Open Adoption and the Rhetoric of the Gift. In *Transformative Motherhood,* ed. Linda Layne. Albany, N.Y.: SUNY Press.

———. 2001. *A Sealed and Secret Kinship: Policies and Practices in American Adoption.* New York: Berghahn Press.

Rappaport, Bruce M. 1992. *The Open Adoption Book: A Guide to Adoption without Tears.* New York: Macmillan.

Schneider, David M. 1968. *American Kinship: A Cultural Account.* Chicago: University of Chicago Press.

———. 1984. *A Critique of the Study of Kinship.* Ann Arbor: University of Michigan Press.

Silber, Kathleen, and Patricia Martinez Dorner. 1990. *Children of Open Adoption and Their Families.* San Antonio, Tex.: Corona.

Wegar, Katarina. 1997. *Adoption, Identity, and Kinship: The Debate over Sealed Birth Records.* New Haven, Conn.: Yale University Press.

Chapter Fifteen

In the Name of the Father: Theology, Kinship, and Charisma in an American Polygynous Community

William Jankowiak

Religious meanings, like all cultural meanings, invariably reflect the interplay between official creed and other structural and psycho-cultural factors. Because every culture must adjust to individual and collective interests (Bourdieu 1977; Giddens 1991, 1992), religious tenets are seldom upheld as consistently or as uniformly as religious leaders prefer, or the practitioners profess. I contend that this interplay between theological axioms and social realities accounts, in large measure, for the institutionalization of what I call father glorification or adoration in the fundamentalist Mormon cosmology. As we will see, father adoration is pivotal to fundamentalist constructions of kinship and family in a way that links individuals to their church and its cosmology.[1]

In this chapter, I explore the origins, persistence, and meaning of the phenomenon of father glorification. Father adoration is a complex psycho-cultural configuration that arises from three separate yet intertwined factors: (1) a theology that endows men with a supernatural essence that commands the regeneration of a religious organization primarily, but not exclusively, through copious reproduction; (2) a closed-corporate, theological community that confers its greatest esteem on men in leadership positions as members of the church's priesthood council and/or on men who are independently wealthy; (3) a polygynous family system organized around a father/husband, who is the primary focal point, at least at the symbolic level, and who unites the often competing female-centered natal family units.

I explore how these factors not only foster the formation of father adoration but also account, in large part, for the variation found within that formation. Specifically, I examine father adoration as it manifests itself most powerfully: a fondly remembered, or deeply troubling, but socially salient experience that is remembered most acutely in adulthood. Because father adoration is volatile, it can serve as a litmus test for the issues that unite and divide the polygynous family.[2] The data presented in this chapter were collected between 1993 and 1999, in a fundamentalist Mormon polygynous community in Angel Park (pseudonym), a small township located in the intermountain region of the western United States.[3]

Angel Park: The Social Community

Given the uniqueness of the Mormon polygynous family system, it is easy to overlook the commonalities that fundamentalist Mormons share with mainstream American culture. Forged out of the nineteenth-century American frontier experience, fundamentalist Mormonism embraces many American middle-class values: a basic frugality of means, emphasis on controlling one's destiny, a striving of upward mobility, and a belief in individual responsibility.

Although the residents of Angel Park feel that certain aspects of the larger culture are immoral (e.g., X-rated movies), most members of the community participate as interested spectators and, at times, disgruntled critics of national and international events. Several polygynous families have even appeared on various talk shows to defend their religiously based lifestyle. Contemporary fundamentalists are not like the Hutterites, who disapprove of, and strive to withdraw from, mainstream American culture. For most of Angel Park's residents, life is to be enjoyed and they do not hesitate to partake of some of life's delights (e.g., drink coffee and alcohol, visit the national parks, shop at a nearby mall, and feast at all-you-can-eat $6.99 buffets). Common dinner topics range from religious issues, current events, the entertainment value of *The Mask of Zorro* and *Saving Private Ryan*, Clinton's impeachment trial and its reflection of changes in American culture, to the benefits of flaxseed oil for preventing illness.

Fundamentalist Mormons never rejected mainstream culture as much as they feared provoking its wrath. For most of its seventy-year existence, the community has repeatedly encountered social harassment and political persecution. From 1882 on, federal and state governments sought to disenfranchise the Mormons in Utah. As a result, many who were practicing polygyny went into hiding, fleeing into remote areas of Utah, Idaho, Arizona, and Mexico. By 1897, almost two hundred Mormons had been sent to prison for practicing polygyny (Bohannan 1985: 81). However, despite the arrests and the opposition from Americans outside the community, several church leaders, including some of the founders of the Angel Park community, believed that by giving up polygyny the church would be compromising fundamental religious principles and they therefore refused to do so. Their refusal has resulted in more than two generations of strife between Angel Park and the mainstream Mormon church, which after 1890, officially prohibited polygyny. Polygyny is the primary issue that theologically separates the fundamentalist from the mainstream Mormons.

Thus began an ongoing antagonistic and sometimes bitter conflict between Mormon fundamentalists, the mainstream Mormon church, and state and federal governments. From the 1930s until the 1950s, Angel Park was the site of numerous governmental raids. The last and largest took place in 1953, which resulted in the arrest of 39 men and 86 women, and in their 263 children being placed in foster homes for up to two years (Bradley 1993: 110; Van Wagoner 1986). An unintended consequence of the raids was to "strengthen everyone's conviction and dedication to maintain their life-style. Outside pressure had in effect turned everyone into a community of believers" (Bradley 1993: 110). In this way, Angel Park remains an "enclave culture."

Since the late 1960s there has emerged a greater tolerance, albeit a reluctant one, of the State of Arizona for the polygynous community. Although the western states remain adamant in their insistence that the polygynous lifestyle is illegal, they have tacitly adopted a "live and let live" posture toward the more than 30,000 polygynous people living in western North America (Quinn 1991). Given American mainstream culture's tolerance toward cohabitation, alternative child rearing practices, and other related social experiments in family living, the polygynous community has become a "public secret" and is culturally tolerated.

Angel Park is a sectarian religious community that forms one of five polygynous communities found in western North America and northern Mexico. Each community is separately governed and maintains only nominal, if any, contact with the others. The population of Angel Park is approximately 6,500, with over half of the population under the age of twelve.

Angel Park is an intentional community where members live, or expect to live, in a plural family. Unlike nineteenth-century Mormonism, where an estimated 10 to 20 percent of the families were polygynous (Foster 1992), more than 45 percent (158 out of 350 Angel Park families) form a polygynous household.

On the whole, the town on first sight appears quaint and rather ordinary. Like other small American rural communities, its main roads (seven in all) are paved, whereas its side streets are not. Its houses, however, are anything but ordinary. Because people practice "Big House" polygyny where everyone lives together, the houses range in size from three-bedroom mobile trailers to huge 35,000-square-foot mansions that are in various stages of completion or renovation.

Because of its location, Angel Park's economy cannot support all of its residents. The lack of a well-developed local infrastructure necessitates that most residents find employment outside the community. Most men work in the booming regional construction and interstate trucking industries, while women and other men work in a variety of jobs that include accountants, architects, janitors, masseuses, caretakers, principals, teachers, nurses, and mechanics. Despite the inconvenience of working outside the community, most people find employment, and the town boasts a remarkable zero unemployment rate. Angel Park nonetheless is not a wealthy town. Although its $14,500 average income is nearly double Appalachia's $8,595, it is still one of the lowest median incomes in the western United States, according to a front-page article titled "Polygamy on the Dole" by Tom Zoellner in the *Salt Lake Tribune*, June 28, 1998.

Mormon Theology, Christianity, and Honoring Thy Father

Several elements of the fundamentalist Mormon religious creed provide salient components of the culture's cosmology, which, in turn, accounts for the institutionalization of father glorification in that cosmology.[4] There are two main nonnegotiable tenets at the core of this theology: (1) God is a polygamist who loves all his children but confers on men, in particular, an elevated spiritual essence that ensures that men who live "righteously" will obtain a higher spiritual standing in the next life, and (2) men occupy leadership positions in their families and on the church council and have the potential in the next life to become godheads with dominion over all their descendants. Priesthood council members in the second ward (a church division) become gods to their constituents. Their kingdom, much like the Salt Lake valley Allredites, "is ranked higher than other men's kingdom[s]" (Bennion 1998: 44). Within this cosmological creed, the father is charged with the duty to constantly expand his kingdom by entering into the institution of plural marriage (Musser 1944).

Women's standing, on the other hand, is determined by their performance in the highly valued complementary roles of mother and wife. Like Southern Baptists, Mormon fundamentalists interpret the scripture literally; "A woman should submit herself graciously" to her husband's leadership and a husband should "provide for, protect, and lead his family" (*New York Times*, June 15, 1998, p. A1).

In fundamentalism, women achieve salvation through obedience, first to their fathers and then to their husbands by becoming sister-wives (i.e., co-wives) in a "celestial," or plural, family. The marital contract "seals" a man and woman together "for time and eternity" in the Heavenly Kingdom (Musser 1944). Because this bond extends beyond the grave into an eternal world, it is in a woman's "best interest to advance her husband's interests" (i.e., she should bear a large number of children [Bohannan 1985: 81]), while at the same time strive to uphold her husband's authority, especially in front of his children.

Another religious tenet holds that the father–son relationship is the core axis for the transmission of cultural and spiritual essence. First articulated by Joseph Smith in 1832, this tenet is a "theme that predominates throughout the Book of Mormon" (Clark and Clark 1991: 286). It is based on the belief of a Melchizedek priesthood whose line began when the great priest Melchizedek ordained Abraham, who handed down the keys of the kingdom to his son

Isaac, who passed them to his sons, and so forth.[5] All literal descendants of Abraham are eligible to receive the priesthood that will unlock the "keys of the mysteries of [God's] kingdom, even the key of the knowledge of God" (Palmer 1964: 19). This belief constitutes the primary legitimization of Angel Park's insistence that the only acceptable basis or form of religious expression is that based in the Melchizedek priesthood.

The polygynous family's behavioral expectations are derived from these theological axioms that uphold men as the religious center and authority in the family. From an organizational perspective, serious and consistent familial attention should be on the father/husband as both the ultimate adjudicator of family affairs and the representative of spiritual authority. In effect, this becomes a patriarchal family system.

A patriarch is the head of a family who holds the right to rule its members with unquestioned authority. Technically, a patriarch is a member of the upper or Melchizedek priesthood who has been appointed within the church ward (or stake) to pronounce blessings upon those members who call upon him. His centrality is routinely reinforced as he leads the family in Sunday school service (usually conducted in his home), conducts daily family prayers, arranges the marriages of his children, disburses the family income, and reveals his religious dreams to his wives and children.

The fundamentalists' conviction is that they are God's chosen people born to live "the fullness of the Gospel" and, thus, to create what the prophet Smith declared was God's ideal: the Celestial Kingdom on earth (Baur 1988). Angel Park, like other Mormon fundamentalist communities, believes that the mainstream Mormon church erred when, under threat of invasion from the federal government, it renounced polygyny as an earthly ideal. The fundamentalists believe that God expects them to try to create his family ideal while living on earth. Some fundamentalists point out that after death they will be granted special abilities to live in harmony within a plural family in the afterlife. The best they can do in this life is learn character-building experiences that prepare them to live in the plural family in the next life. Unlike Islamic societies that tolerate polygynous marriage but do not make it the bedrock for salvation, fundamentalists have made polygynous marriages the key to salvation. The religious leaders continuously lecture their congregations about the importance of living up to the plural marriage. They regularly note that "If you have two wives, and you are a monogamist at heart, I am afraid the One Mighty and Strong will not be able to use you."

In time, the community made plural marriage a kind of cultural fetish, whereby men who had three or more wives were regarded as spiritually more pure than those who had only two or one. It is the plural family that lies at the heart of the fundamentalist communities' communitarian impulses to create a spiritually unified and harmonious society. The maintenance of harmony, unity, and regularity depends on the strength and vitality of not only father–son relationships and mother–children relationships, but also the relationships between co-wives. The plural family is held together as much by a collective will, or communal effort, to maintain a strong image of a harmonious family as it is by individuals' actions and decisions.

Recent disagreements within the community have resulted in the split of Angel Park into two rival religious communities or wards (i.e., first and second wards). With the exception of theological differences concerning political succession within the church organization, both wards are similar in their cultural orientation. In this and every other way, Angel Park has remained, throughout its history, both demographically and culturally, a male-centered, family-oriented, theologically governed, religious community.

Honoring of Fathers/Idealizing the Father

Social standing in every American town is organized around wealth, religious membership, and ethical conduct. This is certainly true in Angel Park, a small town governed by a religious elite who are "called by God," in a rank order of succession, to the office of the Brethren or the priesthood council. The community constitutes, as such, a sacred charter dedicated to establishing a social environment conducive to supporting the polygynous family system.

To achieve this ideal, Angel Park was formally incorporated into a religious trust in order to provide economic and social assistance to its members.[6] The idea was to create a supportive environment that would enable individuals to transcend their preoccupation with basic human needs and become, in the process, a more cooperative and spiritually focused people and, thus, worthy to enter into the kingdom of God. Within this religiously inspired framework, men, as fathers, occupy the dominant role. Not only are they the religious specialists in their families, the final arbiters of all spiritual and ethical conflicts, but they are also eligible, by virtue of their gender, to become high priests of the entire community.

The history of any group is often shaped through the stories it tells itself. None are as powerful as the historical testimonials that people tell one another in public gatherings. In Angel Park, these testimonials invariably focus on the laudable deeds and accomplishments of fathers that ultimately advanced or improved the community. These testimonials, devotional in tone and presentation, honor the deceased father's memory through the selection of hagiographic accounts that ritualistically praise the father's actions, while, at the same time, overlook his shortcomings.

The hagiographies are remarkably alike in their content. They typically tell a story of a just and honorable man whose steadfastness to his religious convictions, often in the face of personal hardship and financial loss, demonstrate his commitment to cherished community ideals or participation in important community activities. These activities can include the building of some structure, such as a drainage ditch, the operation of a much-needed saw mill, the creation of a mortgage company capable of employing residents, making large contributions to the congregation's legal defense, or generally striving to uphold the idea that human cooperation promotes a spiritually refined life and harmonious social order (sometimes referred to as the United Order).

The public testimonials, which are usually delivered during church services, family gatherings, and, on occasion, in discussions with friends, are customarily received as wonderful tales of loving devotion.[7] By providing an opportunity for the community to idealize an individual's life, the core values to which everyone professes to aspire are remembered and reaffirmed. The devotional tone of the testimonials can be heard in the remembrance of a woman in her mid-twenties of the role her deceased father played in her life. Delivered during a church service, she stressed how "my father always explained the importance and meaning of the gospel to his family. Although he was strict and diligent in his work, he was also a concerned and loving parent who always worked with his children so they never got in trouble." She concluded by saying how she loved to "see him in the morning, pouring milk into his coffee and that even today, every time I make coffee, the smell reminds me of his wonderful presence." This palpable visionary presence of the father is not uncommon in the memories of adult children everywhere, but at Angel Park, it becomes a part of religious ritual.

The love of the father is found, too, in the public remarks of a woman in her mid-thirties who fondly recalled that, as a young girl, she used to go on walks with her father who never failed to explain the importance of living God's law (i.e., polygyny). She declared, with an emotional timbre in her voice, that through "his kindness and love, I am a better person." An unmarried teenage girl, whose father had passed away when she was eight years old, remembered her father as a sensitive man whom "I appreciated for his kindness and commitment to the family." She added that "he will always be an inspiration to me."

Father glorification is often expressed outside of church as well. At a family's Sunday dinner, the special time when the entire family tries to eat together, a man in his forties said to his wives and children that his father had always stressed the importance of eating at least one meal a week together as a family. "Dad always said," he added (with tears in his eyes), "the family that eats together stays together." He dwelt on his father's enlightenment and how he, too, as a father, wanted to continue what was, for him, a memorable family tradition.

The honoring of the father as either an important founder of the community or the founder of a family line is reinforced by Angel Park's private school's requirement that every graduating senior write a report about his or her family's history or about the history of a significant community founder. Such a man is regarded as a kind of father to the whole community and, in a way, is everyone's father. Significantly, women, as mothers or wives, while revered in conversation, are seldom the subject of these student essays. Nor are they ever commemorated during church service.[8] Hagiographies, in Angel Park, are reserved only for fathers.

These examples do not mean that mothers are less loved or regarded as unimportant in Angel Park. Privately, adults are quick to acknowledge their mother's contribution to their development as a person (discussed below). In the public arena, however, fundamentalists speak almost entirely in the idiom of father adoration and seldom in terms of mother love. Typically, after the father has "passed to the other side," he is commemorated by the placement of his photo in a prominent place in the family living room. A deceased mother's photo, however, is usually smaller or is placed under his, or inconspicuously on an adjacent wall. In this sense, there is a form of ancestor reverence in Angel Park, with prominent focus on one's father.

Familism: Competing with a Father's Reputation

Although fundamentalist Mormon theology and church leadership actively discourage familial ranking (i.e., the ranking of families into a hierarchy of relative social worth) the practice unofficially flourishes in Angel Park. Its social repercussions encourage a kind of clannishness whereby individuals seek to advance their family status and, indirectly, their own reputations through economic achievement and superior moral performance. Status competition often involves the advancing, or smearing, of a father's reputation. It is not surprising that Angel Park children often believe their relative social standing depends upon advancing or criticizing one another's accomplishments. What is significant is the fact that gentle and not so gentle "digs" are couched in a father-centered discourse, which is often nothing more than an exercise in status-leveling or status assertion. Such interfamily competition takes place in a variety of settings: "song duels" between children of rival families, general peer group teasing, and public criticism and ridicule of another's behavior.

One popular form of competition, the song duel, takes place only between children and never, as in the case of the Eskimo song duel, between adults. As an example, an eight-year-old girl encounters two seven-year-old half sisters from the rival religious faction and immediately sings: "Your family is too simple, just too simple." The seven-year-olds, just as quickly, repeat the song fragment but substitute the eight-year-old's family name in place of their own. Claims and counterclaims are flung back and forth by the peer group.

Teasing among children always involves mockery in the name of one's father. Another child's supposed family-centered personality traits (wherein the family and its figurehead, the father, are implicated in the defect) can be seen in the interaction of children playing a game of basketball. When one boy repeatedly kicked the ball, some children ridiculed his physical clumsiness as "typical of all the Jacksons." In a reversal of father adoration, the Jacksons' father is belittled as the source of the clumsiness. Positive attributes are also seen as a trait typical of a certain family. For example, when a particularly gifted musician performed at her school reception, she was warmly applauded with many in attendance noting in appreciation that "all the Boyds are gifted musicians, just like their father." Whether one wants to raise up in awe or to mock, the image of the father is inevitably invoked.

Unlike children's status competitions that take place in a semipublic arena and are directed at a specific person, adults voice their negative evaluations in private settings among family members and close friends. These evaluations invariably take the form of teasing put-downs such as the so-and-so family "puts on airs" or "they think they are so special," in order to uphold, on one hand, a community ethos of equality and fellowship while also defending, if not advancing, one's own family reputation. There is, thus, in Angel Park a kind of balance of power involving mockery of fathers and adoration of them as a way of preserving or challenging the historical continuity of status. Mockery is one way of keeping certain fathers and their descendants in their place within the local social hierarchy.

The Charismatic Father: Imagining the Polygynous Family

The polygynous family's social organization is derived, in part, from theological axioms that uphold a man as the religious specialist and authority in the family and, in part, from the social dynamics of polygynous family life that make men, as fathers and husbands, the pivotal axes by which wives and children organize attention and internalize family identity. From an organizational perspective, intense and persistent familial attention is on the father, as the ultimate adjudicator of family affairs as well as the representative of spiritual authority.

For children of a plural marriage, the notion of familism, and thus belongingness, stems from an image of the all-powerful father who is the biological source and the social and religious authority for his children. In a very practical way, the plural family is held together as much by the effort to maintain an image of a strong family as it is by the actual memories of interacting with one's father. It is an image that needs the active involvement, participation, and affirmation of fathers and co-wives.

Psychologists have long noted that for American children of both sexes, the mother is the most important parental figure (Sered 1994: 57). Because families tend to be organized around the mother, there is a general tendency, especially among white American middle-class families, toward developing greater emotional ties between mothers and children than between fathers and children. Sered (1994) points out that matrifocal units often arise within patrilineal social organizations. In Angel Park a tendency toward matrifocality is undermined by the cultural emphasis on the spiritual and administrative authority of the father.

Women's Places: Courtship and Placement Marriage

The Mormon conception of true love closely resembles that of nineteenth-century Victorian England, which Seidman told us, was "essentially spiritual, not physical or carnal in origin and essence" (1991: 45). In reality, however, sexual love in fundamentalist Mormon society, as it was in Victorian society, is often highly eroticized. Mormon polygnists throughout history have insisted that sexual pleasure is an appropriate desire provided it is the by-product of spousal affection and, hence, marital love. However, Angel Park fundamentalists, while disapproving of premarital sex, are mixed over whether or not sexual pleasure should be an aspect of every marriage.

Mormon cosmology holds that, before birth, everyone lives with God as a spirit. In this preexistence state, men and women are promised to one another for time (or this life) and eternity. Individuals must therefore strive to find their "true love" and, in a sense, remarry. Failure to do so can potentially lead to an awkward situation whereby one's earthly spouse will differ from one's heavenly designated spouse. To ensure that death will not result in the separation of the earthly spouses, it is imperative that the couple follow God's will. To this end, individuals are asked to pray alone and together for guidance before deciding to marry.

There are a number of different ways an individual can obtain a spouse. The most common is for a man to ask a woman's father. If the father approves and the daughter agrees, then the couple will go to the priesthood council and ask for its approval and blessing. If there are no complications, such as someone else also desiring the young woman's hand, the request is readily granted.

In the early 1950s and 1960s, when the community operated as if it were a closed corporate community, fathers often exchanged their daughters with each other. These daughters then entered the man's home as a plural wife. Since these exchanges were seldom immediate—often some had to wait until the girl passed puberty and became a teenager—there was always anxiety that the promised daughter might be given to someone else, or worse, that the girl might refuse and run away with someone else. Consequently, these agreements were fragile and seldom became institutionalized agreements between family lines. Rather, they remained privately negotiated "deals" that usually ended once the exchange was completed. A system of delayed or immediate wife exchanges popular among tribal groups in southeast Asia (Lévi-Strauss 1969) was never institutionalized in Angel Park. One factor that undermined the development of a marital exchange system was the absence of lineages.

A bedrock principle of Angel Park family life is that each man's home is his kingdom. No one has the right to tell another man how to organize and govern his family. This ideal contributes to a reluctance to intervene in families that are abusive toward a spouse or the children. Upon marriage, a daughter is regarded as having entered into someone else's kingdom, and a son is perceived as having started his own kingdom that is independent of his father's.

In a way, he becomes an individual who is in competition with his father for future mates. This competition combined with the lack of a financial base for descent groups ensured that Angel Park's social organization would be family-centered and not lineage-centered.

A separate, albeit related, factor is the community's preference to give daughters to the prophet (a senior religious leader who communicates directly with God), who because of a seniority rank system, is often in his seventies when he assumes leadership over community affairs. At this age, he seldom consummates his union with his young wives, preferring to wait until the next life when his body will be replenished and he can again begin to produce spiritual children. The primary reason for fathers (often with a wife's encouragement) to give the prophet their daughter(s) is to obtain material benefits (e.g., not paying rent, taxes, water and power bills, and other types of assistance). On a symbolic level, the father gains prestige for having married a daughter to the prophet. Unless the man is regarded as an elite member of the community, the prophet will never reciprocate.

It should not be assumed that placement marriages result in unhappiness and misery. Some do and others do not. In these marriages, individuals, particularly teenage women, follow the matrimonial recommendations of their parents and the priesthood council. These marriages seldom bring about intergenerational conflict or personal turmoil. The individual, who is usually not deeply emotionally involved with a spouse, enters marriage expecting, as in many cultures, that in time, "love will come." As a twenty-seven-year-old woman on the eve of her tenth wedding anniversary said, "During the first three years of my marriage, I did not even like my husband, but now I can say I truly love him." Hers is not an atypical case.

Nevertheless, dilemmas do arise, usually when youths develop romantic interests that can lead them to not follow their parents' wishes. There are times when parents disapprove of a daughter's (though to a lesser extent a son's) choice or, more importantly, the priesthood council considers the relationship inappropriate. When this occurs, individuals must reconcile their romantic feelings with their deep-seated religious beliefs, which include the priesthood council's role in guiding the community and its members to salvation and eternal happiness. This is never an easy task. In the face of such resistance, many couples break up and marry whomever the priesthood council recommends.

Yet, some couples do resist their parents or the priesthood council's recommendation. There are numerous precedents for individuals asserting that their romantic experience is authentic and, thus, sanctioned by God. Because Mormon theology is derived, in part, from nineteenth-century transcendentalism, it holds that God's will can be known through acts of private introspection and personal revelation. Accordingly, it honors individual conviction, and this religious tenet gives romantically entangled couples solid ground on which to argue that the council might be mistaken in its judgment. Although an individual's testimony of being divinely inspired is never directly challenged, the common response of the council is to wonder whether God or the Devil is the real source of the inspiration. Still, the notion of "agency," or personal choice, serves as an effective counterpoint to the community's formal organization, its male-centered priesthood council. It is accepted that the individual has the right to agree or disagree with any recommended marriage proposal.

Marriage negotiations are just that, negotiations that take place between the priesthood council and the couple, with the woman serving as both the object and the arbitrator of the negotiations. If the bride-to-be cannot be persuaded to change her mind, the council will often, albeit reluctantly, support her marital choice. For, as one informant said, "who can deny God and God's love" (i.e., choice). However, in those instances where either the parents or the council refuse to sanction the marriage, the individual will either recognize and submit to the council's authority or the couple will elope and marry outside the community; then, once a suitable time has elapsed, return as a legitimate couple.

A twenty-seven-year-old man who eloped with his wife told me that "my wife's parents liked me until they found out that I wanted to marry their daughter. Her father wanted her to marry someone else. But we loved each other and knew we were meant to be together. My wife was only 16 and I was 26 when we left the community and married. A few months later, we returned and were accepted back into the family." In this instance, the disagreement was between the girl's parents and the boy and not the council, which had taken no strong position in the matter.

Another example of intergenerational antagonism is found in the tale of a young woman, who at the age of fifteen, refused her parents' and the priesthood council's insistence that she marry a sixty-two-year-old man. She recalled:

> he was so sure that I would agree that he immediately began to build a new house for me, while keeping his first wife in an old trailer. After six years of waiting and pleading, he finally got the hint and accepted the fact that I never would marry him. I wanted to marry someone who I love, and I did.

In this way, marriages in Angel Park are often quasi-arranged but only with the tacit support of some members of the younger generation who were not able to find someone on their own, and so had less difficulty acceding to the wishes of their parents or the priesthood council's marital recommendations.

It is the desire for romantic intimacy, however, that intensifies a woman's identification with the role of wife/lover in addition to that of mother. This orientation stands in sharp contrast to the religious ideal that marriage is primarily a procreative institution organized around an ethos of harmonious love.

Family Politics, Co-Wives, and Father Glorification

The Mormon polygynous family is centered on the notion of harmonious familial love. Harmonious love is somewhat akin to communitas (Turner 1969) in being unbounded in its potential for forging, strengthening, and sustaining affectionate bonds. Because it encourages respect, empathy, helpfulness, and lasting affection, harmonious love often serves as the principal means to bind and unite the polygynous family. Its non-dyadic focus stands in sharp contrast to romantic love, a tolerated but seldom glorified emotional experience. Although harmonious love is fervently stressed as the preferred ideal, it is vulnerable, as we have seen, to personal desires.

Social relations in the Mormon polygynous family, unlike other polygynous societies, revolve around personal sentiment as much as duty. This is a twin pull of almost equal force. Whenever a conflict arises, an individual response is unpredictable and thus threatening to the family order: will he or she uphold family harmony or seek to satisfy personal gratification? This question is especially relevant in terms of romantic love that, more than any other emotional experience, not only overwhelms a person's judgment but also can reorder his or her priorities for an uncertain period of time.

There is a continuum in both men's and women's involvement in plural marriage that ranges from shared equality to outright favoritism. Men, as the symbolic center of the family, must balance each wife's emotional and economic interests. Conscious of the impact of favoritism on family harmony, men strive to modify some of its harmful impact. To this end, most husbands are diligent in spending quality time (e.g., dinners and trips), if not equal time, with each co-wife. In this regard, women intently study and assess their husband's actions and are quick to note acts that suggest favoritism. If a husband can avoid pursuing his own interests or, in their words, if he can "sacrifice" in order to uphold the religious principles, the household ambience will be relatively harmonious and content.

The most delicate and potentially dangerous situations arise whenever a new wife enters the family. This is the most unstable time in a fundamentalist household and often tests a woman's religious convictions and, in turn, her willingness to participate in a plural marriage. During this liminal state, the new wife usually receives the husband's undivided attention, and co-wives do not complain about their husband spending a lot of time with the new wife. It is understood that the intimacy will continue once the couple returns from their honeymoon trip. However, if the intimacy continues beyond a few weeks, it will engender a round of questions and doubts and, ultimately, trigger intense jealousy among the co-wives.

It is romantic passion's volatility that makes it a feared, resented, and yet compelling emotional experience. For the fundamentalists of Angel Park, it tests the faith and commitment of long-term co-wives as well as newlyweds' religious faith. For example, in the case of a new wife, her emotions and expectations are often challenged by the reality of sharing a spouse. The adjustment is never easy. A young woman, who had recently taken a new "sister-wife," told us that "sometimes I want to always be with my husband, but I know that it is selfish so I encourage him to see his other wife." Not every wife is as generous or as noble. Some are confused, experiencing doubt and distress. A young woman told us that "I did not think my husband's second marriage would bother me—I was ready to live the principle. But I stayed awake at nights, unable to sleep. I felt so alone and abandoned." Other co-wives cease believing in the spiritual nobility of harmonious love and focus entirely on getting their fair share of emotional attention. This attitude is exemplified in the following account of a new wife's surprise and eventual resignation that her co-wife did not believe in, nor did she want to work to create, a "united polygamous" family. She reported that

> right before I married my husband, he, his first wife, and myself went for a walk. My husband had his arms around both of us as we walked down the street. As we walked, I put my arm around my husband's waist, just below the first wife's arm who was already holding on to him. Later that evening, the first wife told me, "When I felt your arm around our husband's waist it made my blood boil." I was shocked at her comment because I thought she wanted to live the principle and create a harmonious large family. . . . This marriage has been a challenge from that day forward, because the first wife refuses to accept God's law [i.e., polygyny].

Unlike other polygynous societies, Mormon polygynous women expect to develop strong, intensely emotional relationships with their husband. However, such strong husband–wife relationships are counter to church teachings about the nature of a man's role, which emphasizes an emotionally neutral posture toward his wives. This accounts for the continuous evaluation of every potential marital prospect and the ongoing reevaluation of the place of marital unions in the larger family system.

Often in competition for their husband's attention, co-wives contribute to the father glorification process by vying with each other. In this struggle, the children are often used as a means to an end: to become the desired object of their husband's attention. Mothers instruct their children to love and cherish their father. By thus cultivating father adoration, mothers hope to demonstrate their superior worth among co-wives and to draw their husband's attention to themselves. This tactic can be deliberate as well as unconscious. Also, as wives focus their attention on their husband, the children, wanting to please their mother and father, follow suit. All this enhances the father's status and esteem.

In Angel Park, as I have noted, the husband is the hub around which women articulate; over and above their attachment to the man himself is their commitment to the fundamentalist theology. At the same time, the wives assert and maintain affective bonds with their own children. Women tacitly seek to balance their duties to uphold their husband's reputation and thus the family's public image, while, at the same time, look for ways to demarcate their status and that of their children as distinct and valuable entities within the often contentious polygynous family. One way that women seek this is by resisting the doctrinal mandate to surrender their children into the melting pot of their husband's progeny.[9]

This division in familial loyalty also results in the children identifying with two different kinship nodes—the mother's line and the father's line—within the overarching patriarchal social order. For example, when asked about their position in the family's birth order, everyone, regardless of age or gender, responded first by noting their birth position in relation to their birth mother, only secondarily identifying their position within the larger family. Significantly, only sons added their relative positions; daughters never noted their relative positions compared to other half siblings. For example, one man noted that he was the first child in his mother's family and the sixth child within the larger family, and his father's thirteenth son.

Spiritual Affirmation: Visions and Dreams

The experience of visions and dreams are the most vivid evidence of a person's ability to interact with the spirit world. By imparting such religious visions and their meaning to his children and wives, a father's authority is unmistakably affirmed. It is understood that personal visions are of profound religious significance and must be taken very seriously.

Mormon fundamentalists seek to understand God's will through the aid of visions and dreams. Prayer, visionary dreams, and one's own inner prompting are evaluated in an attempt to understand one's spiritual mission. The process is not unlike the approach taken by American Puritans to spiritual conflicts. Belief in the validity of dreams as a vehicle of truth is so strong in the fundamentalist religion that dreams are often the critical guide in making important decisions. A middle-aged man, for example, told his family about an angel who instructed him that his oldest son would live the fullness of the gospel (i.e., would stay in the community and form a plural family). In another dream, a father told of his son's ability to support the family and sustain the family unity. Still another father reminded his wives of a vision he had when he was a young man, which signaled that he would live a short but very fulfilling life. This dream affirmed his religious righteousness and the need to follow his instructions, cherishing his time with them. Stories of such dreams circulate within the family and, at times, into the community, serving to uphold the father's authority (directly supported by God) and to make him not only a moral force but a charismatic presence within the family.

In every moral community there is identification of the self with the leader. If "identification is the process of developing bonds to an object and altering one's actions because of these attachments" (Ross 1994: 58), then the peculiar interdynamics of the American Mormon polygynous family likewise contribute to transforming the father from an important, albeit respected parent, into an all-powerful charismatic figure whose memory is privately cherished and socially adored. Since the father is given God's will, he is the voice of spiritual idealism and thus imposes the conditions for transcendence derived, in part, from social organization and, in part, from emotional identification with the father, the man. As this voice, he must be heeded.

Love, Ambivalence, and Hostility: Resolving the Father

The internal dynamics of polygynous family life contribute to the production of charismatic awe felt toward the father. It is an adoration that will continue throughout most people's lives. It is, however, an adoration tempered by the actual quality of the childhood and teenage relationship with the father. For those whose father passed away when they were children, there is only an unqualified adoration of the father. However, long-term interaction with a father produces memories that are less clouded with idealization based on fantasy and more grounded in reality. The reality forces or compels many sons and daughters to assimilate the cultural ideal to their own more personal encounter, which may be less than perfect. Before exploring the darker side of father–child interaction, I will look at the children's perspective, especially those whose father died when they were too young to have many meaningful or memorable interactions.

A common theme and a consistent lament in Angel Park is the yearning of children for the experience of having had a closer relationship with their deceased father. This is common because of the practice of older men fathering children with younger wives, then dying before the child is grown. When asked about the importance of a father, a fourteen-year-old boy whose father had passed away six years earlier said that "a father is so important for a boy. He will give you guidance, leadership, and direction. I regret I didn't have a closer relationship with my dad, before he passed to the other side." The intensity of such idealization is revealed in the following event. An eleven-year-old girl was walking up a mountain path when she spontaneously exclaimed, "I remember going up here with Dad. It was so wonderful." She turned to her mother and asked, "Mom, did I go up here with Dad? The mom nodded, and the girl said: "Yes! I remember it was so wonderful."

Another example of how yearnings for closer intimacy contribute to generating an idealized image of one's father can be seen in a twenty-five-year-old married woman's efforts to come to terms with her biological father who abandoned her mother and left the community when she was a toddler, only to return to the community when she was a teenager. She had refused to accept her stepfather but rather maintained a detached, but respectful, posture toward him. Toward her biological father, however, she maintained a positive, albeit fantasy-grounded, relationship. Although now in her late twenties and with seven children, she calls her biological father twice a week "just to talk about things with the man I adore." One's ego identification is based, in part, on recognizing one's biological roots and, in part, on rendering homage, regardless of biology, to whomever is the patriarchal family head. In this instance, however, the daughter refused to accept her stepfather and preferred to dwell on an idealized image of her biological father who, recalling her child-hood years, she had hoped would someday return and be worthy of her love.

Although this example seems typical by mainstream standards, it goes against the community's theological tenet that holds that only those who re-main in good standing in the church are worthy candidates for honor. For this woman, her preference for an emotional bond with her biological father over-rides the religious mandate to honor the current male head of the family.

Although fundamentalist Mormons want nothing more than to honor and admire their fathers, often as not, despite their best efforts, it is a qualified honor. It is, nonetheless, the depth and the persistence of the desire to do so that indicates the power of father adoration as an institution. Because the fa-ther's actual involvement with his family ranges from intimacy to outright in-difference, it is not surprising that there is a deep underlying ambivalence to-ward one's father who, as a valued social symbol, is the focal point of family organization and identity. In effect, the father is the key symbol that links the church and self together into a unified cultural system.

There are two often competing images of the father in Angel Park. The cherished and revered public image (discussed above) is often modified, in private conversation, by a more guarded and obviously ambivalent attitude. Given the community's social dynamics and the core tenets of its religious creed, most are uncomfortable in acknowledging their ambivalence and pre-fer instead to praise their deceased father's memory. However, the actual real-ity of their father–child interaction often gets in the way.

I found that if the father had a warm relationship with his children, there was no contradiction between the father's public image and the child's actual remembrance (as an adult) of their interaction. However, if the father–child relationship was grounded in what a child believed was an abusive relation-ship, then that adult daughter's or son's attitude could veer from absolute ado-ration and denial to smoldering resentment. For those who felt anger toward their father and remained in Angel Park, that anger would have to be recon-ciled with the cultural ideal of the father as a figure vital to their own com-munity identity and managed accordingly.

This reconciliation often takes place in one of three ways: absolute devo-tion, guarded adoration, or rejection. Guarded adoration, by far the most common attitude toward the father, is characterized by maintaining a clear distinction between the symbolic accomplishments of the father and the qual-ities of the father as a man. For example, sons of a prominent family repeat-edly praised their father's accomplishments and what he meant to them. In private, they acknowledged their lack of real closeness and the emotional gap it left in their lives. Significantly, brothers, more than sisters, admitted a fear of their father and even, at times, a deep resentment. One brother recalled that he admired his father deeply but often wondered if he loved him. He noted that he had no difficulty in distinguishing his father as a cultural symbol from his actions as a man. Such an ability to compartmentalize is not shared by most of his nineteen other brothers who feared the consequences of a failure to completely honor their father's memory. This man further observed that "My brothers are afraid that if they acknowledge the chinks in our father's character, they might completely hate him. They do not want to look at or acknowledge that he was also a man. They can only handle him as our honored father. They think they have to adore him in every way or not at all." For them, there could never be guarded adoration, only an absolute one.

An example of guarded adoration can be heard in one middle-aged woman's reminiscence that she "wasn't that close to my dad. The only reason I want to write my father's life history is to do it before someone else does. Then I can read it at our church service." For her, it is celebrating the father's public image and her role in the public performance that holds the greater appeal.

Another attitude is total rejection. When a son or daughter rejects, especially in conversation, his or her father, it usually means that he or she no longer participates in the community's social life. By rejecting the father as an admirable symbol, the individual effectively severs his ties to the wider cultural and religious order. Rejection of the father entails a kind of self exile from Angel Park. So deep is the cultural ideal of father adoration that when rejection occurs, the child will often bitterly curse his or her father. Invariably, these individuals leave the church, if not the community.

The various attitudes toward the father hide a deep-seated ambivalence and emotional volatility that can fuel the idealization of him as bearer of the family pride and identity. I believe that ambivalent anger toward the father actually contributes to the institutionalization of father adoration in Angel Park, primarily by rechanneling the guilt that accompanies the rejection. The characteristic ambivalence does not satisfactorily reconcile the father–child relationship and, as such, constitutes an emotional reservoir for the unresolved emotions that shape the style in which father adoration is manifested in ceremonial and ordinary life in Angel Park. The bifurcation of the father into two parts, the symbol and the man, is one means that men and women in Angel Park use to manage what is, for many, a ghost they can never shake.

Conclusion

I have explored the interplay between the psycho-cultural dynamics of the polygynous family and its male-centered theology and how this interplay transforms the father into a revered cultural, if not personal, symbol. I have suggested that the emergence of father adoration arises from the peculiar social dynamics of the polygynous family household as much as it does from the theological centrality of the father in the fundamentalist Mormon religious system. From this perspective, the fundamentalist Mormons' institution of fatherhood is a product of numerous factors, each in itself suggestive, but when they cohere as they do in Angel Park, father glorification is unavoidable.

I have explained the effects of charismatic awe that, in death, becomes transformed into a psycho-cultural phenomenon I call father adoration. Together, these forces introduced new factors into the fundamentalist cosmology that, over time, became incorporated as a new, albeit sacred, aspect of the community's worldview. Within this worldview, fathers are the most valued social category.

It is the transformation of the father into a venerable, powerful, and nearly deified figure that distinguishes the contemporary fundamentalist Mormon community from the mainstream Mormon church. In periodically gathering together in the name of the father, the family and the community celebrate their cultural heritage as well as renew their dedication to the creation and maintenance of what it believes to be their Heavenly Father's ideal family unit—the polygynous family.

Notes

1. The data that form much of this research are part of a larger ongoing research project that began in 1992. The work is partially supported by a minigrant from the Nevada National Endowment for the Humanities and a University of Nevada, Las Vegas, Research Grant and Fellowship Award. I would like to thank Emilie Allen, Janet Bennion, Jim Bell, Monique Dietrich, Tish Diskin, Mindy Gebaide, Barry Hewlett, Philip Kilbride, Katherine Peek, Thomas Paladino, Gary Palmer, and Elizabeth Witt.

2. Polygyny has been studied primarily from a structural perspective that seeks to understand its evolution as a form of adaptation to certain ecological restraints. With the notable exceptions of Young (1954) and Bohannan (1985), analysis of an individual's experiences in a polygynous household is, for the most part, overlooked.

3. The fundamentalist Mormons themselves use the term "polygamy" (plural spouses) to describe their marriage system. Technically, their practice is "polygyny," or the marriage of a man to two or more wives at the same time.

4. Fundamentalist Mormon theology is grounded in the teachings of three books: the Bible, *The Book of Mormon*, and *The Doctrine and Covenants*. The latter two books are prescribed as holy scripture, the words of God revealed directly to Joseph Smith (Musser 1944).

5. Adam is not believed to have been the first man on earth but rather a god who married several wives, including Eve and Mary, the mother of Jesus. Jesus, his first son, later became the supreme god over earth.

6. Until the 1985 religious split, Angel Park was unified in its commitment to create a more benevolent collective order. The principal was incorporated into a religious trust that facilitated the distribution of food supplies, practical assistance in homes, and, most importantly, access to land. An unintended consequence was conferral on the leaders of the trust an enormous fund of power. Historically, the trust provided the church leadership with the means to reward its followers while evicting those who failed to conform. Because families merely lease their land and do not own it, the church leadership is able to evict "undesirable" members from their homes by terminating their lease. However, the recent religious split has generated additional problems for the members who want to leave the church but retain control of their homes that they built with their own money. In the past, expulsion was reserved only for the marginally deviant; today, it is being used to evict the entire membership of the rival religious faction. The disagreement has become a legal matter, and after being tied up in the state courts for more than five years, was final resolved by the court upholding the original religious trust while extending exemption sta-

tus to those family founders who still lived in the community. The court declared that they would be able to live in their homes without threat of eviction. However, upon their death, their house would revert to the trust.

7. If private criticism is motivated by a zero-sum prestigious economy, then public adoration of the father is perceived to be based on an ever-expanding sphere of possibilities. In a way, parental or noble love is an unlimited substance that is potentially available to everyone. It is never seen as a zero-sum commodity: the more I have, the less you can get. Its potential is vast and it is open to everyone.

8. Among children, the primary identification is with the father's role. However, among adults, especially women, the mother's contribution is also acknowledged. Thus, Mother's Day, as in mainstream culture, is more important than Father's Day.

9. Women are the custodians of family memory. They preserve and nurture important cultural values in their children. Nothing reflects the dual role—of family memory and cultural values—that women play as much as remarriage when they must manage their bond with their children and reaffirm their loyalties to their new husband while not abandoning their former husband's memory. The division is a classic American experience. They continue to honor their deceased husband's memory in the name of their children or his children while simultaneously placing a photograph of the new husband into the intimate space of their bedroom. In this way, women strive to balance twin demands. Again, we see that women must mediate competing or coexisting duties.

References

Baur, Hans. 1988. *Utopia in the Desert.* New York: SUNY Press.

Bennion, Janet. 1998. *Women of Principle: Female Networking in Contemporary Mormon Polygyny.* New York: Oxford University Press.

Bohannan, Paul. 1985. *All the Happy Families.* New York: McGraw-Hill.

Bourdieu, Pierre. 1977. *Outline of a Theory of Practice,* trans. Richard Nice. Cambridge, U.K.: Cambridge University Press.

Bradley, Martha. 1993. *Kidnapped from That Land.* Provo: University of Utah Press.

Cannon, Janet. 1992. My Sister, My Wife: An Examination of Sororal Polygyny in a Contemporary Mormon Fundamentalist Sect. *Syzygy* 1, no. 4:315–20.

Clark, Aaron, and Ivin Clark. 1991. *Fathers and Sons in the Book of Mormon.* Salt Lake City: Deseret.

Foster, Lawerence. 1992. *Women, Family, and Utopia.* Syracuse, N.Y.: Syracuse University Press.

Giddens, Anthony. 1991. *Modernity and Self-Identity: Self and Society in the Late Modern Age.* Cambridge: Polity.

———. 1992. *The Transformation of Intimacy: Sexuality, Love, and Eroticism in Modern Societies.* Cambridge: Polity.

Jankowiak, William. 1993. *Sex, Death, and Hierarchy in a Chinese City.* New York: Columbia University Press.

Musser, Joseph. 1944. *Celestial or Plural Marriage.* Salt Lake City: Truth Publishing.

Palmer, Lee. 1964. *Aaronic Priesthood: Through the Centuries.* Salt Lake City: Deseret.

Parker, Steve, Janet Smith, and Joseph Ginat. 1973. Father Absence and Cross-Sex Identity: The Puberty Rites Controversy Revisited. *American Ethnology* 2, no. 4:687–706.

Quinn, D. Michael. 1991. Plural Marriage and Mormon Fundamentalism. In *Fundamentalism and Society,* ed. Martin E. Marty and R. Scott Appleby. Chicago: University of Chicago Press.

Ross, Marc. 1994. *The Culture of Conflict.* New Haven, Conn.: Yale University Press.

Lévi-Strauss, Claude. 1969. *The Elementary Structures of Kinship.* Boston: Beacon.

Sered, Helen. 1994. *The Mother Goddess.* New York: Oxford University Press.

Seidman, Steve. 1991. *Romantic Longings.* Malden, Mass.: Blackwell.

Shipps, Jan. 1985. *Mormonism: The Story of a New Religious Tradition.* Urbana: University of Illinois Press.

Turner, Victor. 1969. *The Ritual Process: Structure and Anti-Structure.* Chicago: Aldine.

Van Wagoner, Robert. 1986. *Mormon Polygamy: A History.* Salt Lake City: Signature.

Young, Kimball. 1954. *Isn't One Wife Enough?* New York: Crown.

Zablocki, Bob. 1980. *Alienation and Charisma.* New York: Free Press.

Chapter Sixteen

Fictive Kinship in American Biomedicine

Richard E. Maddy

In the interview prior to one's acceptance into medical school, one is asked the obligatory question: Why do you want to become a doctor? I don't know what you said, but my answer had to do with Virgil. In the Aeneid, there is an old doctor who arrives at the siege of Troy to tend the wound of Aeneas, who has been struck by an arrow. The doctor's name is Iapyx. Now it happened that when Iapyx was a boy, Apollo fell in love with him, and offered him, as a gift, music, wisdom, prophecy or swift arrows. Iapyx chose none of these, and asked for Medicine instead. For he wished only to prolong the life of the father he loved. But as the battle of Troy raged all around him, Iapyx realized that he could not save Aeneas. All his skill was to no avail. He cried out to the gods to help him. Suddenly, the arrow, of its own accord, fell from the wound of Aeneas. Iapyx surmised that more than man had wrought this cure. Iapyx was right. Venus, the mother of Aeneas, had placed a healing herb in the water that Iapyx was using to bathe the wound of her son, and the arrow was miraculously extruded.

I became a doctor to prolong my father's life, and many times since, I have summoned the gods to my side for consultation.

—Richard Selzer, M.D., *Letters To A Young Doctor*

Systems of social organization characterize and, to an extent, define the group with which they are identified. Such systems may be referenced under a number of differing designations, all carrying with them the concept of relatedness, either through shared beliefs, ideologies, or blood. Blood relationships and those emanating from such consanguineal ties are referred to as systems of kinship. Consanguinity and affinity typify most classic systems of kinship. The orientation of kinship systems may vary widely with reference to focality, lineality, marriage patterns, incest taboos, and a host of other cultural measurements. Consanguinity and affinity are not, however, essential for the validity of the term "kinship system" as a social descriptor. It is within the realm of non-consanguineal relationships that systems of "fictive" kinship are described.

Fictive kinship systems are those relationships that are not characterized by consanguinity. Among the most familiar of these relationships are the systems of ritual co-parenthood that are practiced among Hispanic cultural groups, known collectively as *compadrazgo*. The co-parents, known as the *padrino* (co-father) or *madrina* (co-mother) are individuals chosen by a parent or parents as a type of spiritual guardian, godfather, or godmother for their children. The responsibility assumed by the *padrino* or *madrina* within the scope of co-par-enthood is one of social vigilance on behalf of the godchild by means of the extension of the dyadic *compadre/comadre* relationship beyond the family of the child into their own kin groups. This serves to increase the social network, thereby providing the participants freer access to systems of reciprocity, social and economic power, as well as the moral obligations inherent within the system. It is also, in many instances, the responsibility of the *padrino* or the *madrina* to ensure that the child is given the necessary resources in the event of the parents' deaths or inability to fulfill normal parental roles. The spiritual aspect of the relationship is oftentimes as important, if not more so, as the economic considerations of *compadrazgo* (Keesing 1975: 129, 130). Other, less formalized systems of fictive kinship exist within many cultures, whereby an individual assumes a role that would ordinarily be reserved for a blood relative. These relationships, while informal, can, nevertheless, exhibit characteristics as strong as consanguineal and affinal ties. This chapter examines a distinctive sector of American life—professional biomedicine—and analyzes relationships within the system itself in terms of fictive kinship. Taking narrative data gathered during interviews with biomedical practitioners, I present three cases of fictive kinship, demonstrating the value of this anthropological construct in the elucidation of these particular social relationships within the cultural system of biomedicine.

American Biomedicine as a Fictive Kinship System

Professions, while replete with shared values and objectives, have not routinely been identified with fictive kinship systems. Legal, medical, and various academic professionals tend not to be looked upon as having any unique relationship within their respective disciplines that would qualify as fictive systems of kinship. Within the field of medicine, however, a paradigm exists that has, for over two millennia, exerted an influence upon its members that warrants consideration as the catalyst for a type of fictive kinship. The paradigm lies partially hidden in the text of the Hippocratic Oath. The first portion of the oath, written in approximately 430 B.C., reads as follows:

> I swear by Apollo the physician, by Aesculapius, Hygeia, and Panacea, and I take to witness all the gods, all the goddesses, to keep according to my ability and my judgment the following oath:

"To consider dear to me as my parents him who taught me this art; to live in common with him and if necessary to share my goods with him; to look upon his children as my own brothers, to teach them this art if they so desire without fee or written promise." (Hippocrates 1994)

The Hippocratic Oath represents the cognitive orientation of the practitioner of medicine as it has been transmitted from medicine's ancient forbears to the present. While, for the most part, the oath is viewed as a historical artifact that sets forth the moral ideal of the day in which it was written, it is, nevertheless, the document to which many medical practitioners look as their ideological touchstone. It could be argued that the Hippocratic admonition to "consider dear to me as my parents him who taught me this art" forms the basis for a system of fictive kinship that is demonstrable even in today's biomedical environment. Selzer, a physician and author of numerous medically-related literary works, described such relationships in his book *Letters To A Young Doctor,* in which he recorded the following discourse written to a young friend upon the young man's entry into a surgical residency program.

> I send as your graduation present my father's old textbook of physical diagnosis. It was published in 1918. Lifted yesterday from a trunk in the attic it is still faintly redolent of formaldehyde, and stained with Heaven only knows what ancient liquid. I love my old books—Longfellow, Virgil, Romeo and Juliet and Moby Dick—but I love this Textbook of Physical Diagnosis more. I can think of no better thing to give you as a reminder that all of Medicine is a continuum of which you are now a part. Within you is the gesture of the prehistoric surgeon who trephined his neighbor's skull on the floor of a cave. Within you, the poultice of cool mud applied to a burn by an old African woman. The work of all doctors before you is in your blood. Yours will enter the veins of whosoever comes after you. (Selzer 1982: 13)

Selzer's letter to his young friend identifies a relationship that exceeds the bond of professional commonality and extends itself into a realm that resembles a familial tie. His metaphoric use of the term "blood" as a purveyor of the healing art further exemplifies the professional bonding that, as will be witnessed through subsequent interview data, serves to create relationships that correspond to consanguineal bonds. The image also engenders a sense of the spiritual or metaphysical aspect of healing; an almost sacred transmission of the ability and desire to restore the injured or the infirm. The fact that the author is passing on a book that belonged to *his* father, a physician, is suggestive of a relationship that carries a depth of emotion that would be atypical of a strictly professional relationship. Selzer appears, in effect, to be assuming the role of *fictive father.* Cassell, in her book *Expected Miracles: Surgeons at Work,* identified within the medical subspecialty of surgery an organizational complex that she refers to as a "fellowship of surgeons." She then proceeded to characterize the "fellowship" by a series of qualities that typify the relationships within the social organization that she observed. These characteristics closely resemble those typical of many kinship groups (Cassell 1991: 60–66). Cassell has also noted the power of influence that fictive kin relationships might wield on the individual. In her research, she interviewed one surgeon who had given up smoking after having been asked to do so by his mentor when previous requests by his actual father had been ignored (Cassell 1996).

In his valedictory address entitled "Aequanimitas," delivered to the graduates of the medical school of the University of Pennsylvania in the spring of 1889, Sir William Osler, whose imprimatur on the form and structure of systematic medical education is evident to this day, wrote of a relationship that transcended the professional. In recalling his mentor, Osler wrote,

> Personally I mourn the loss of a preceptor, dear to me as a father,
> the man from whom more than any other I received inspiration,
> and to whose example and precept I owe the position which
> enables me to address you to-day. There are those present who
> will feel it no exaggeration when I say that to have known
> Palmer Howard was, in the deepest and truest sense of the
> phrase, a liberal education.

> "Whatever way my days decline,
> I felt and feel, tho' left alone,
> His being working in mine own,
> The footsteps of his life in mine."
> (Osler 1906: 10)

From an anthropological perspective, Osler is describing a relationship to his mentor that could quite accurately be characterized as a type of fictive kinship. His mentor, the late Robert Palmer Howard, was depicted by Osler as being "dear" to him "as a father," a description nearly identical to that employed by Hippocrates in the oath. Cushing, former chief of surgery at Harvard and student of Osler, in his two-volume work *The Life of Sir William Osler*, wrote of the relationship between Osler and his mentor as "truly filial." In depicting Howard's affection toward his famous student, Cushing noted, "Howard, in turn, had loved Osler as a son, and the three younger children (Howard's children), who from now on came to be regarded after a fashion as Osler's wards, had always looked upon him from their earliest years as a combination of elder brother, playmate and father confessor" (Cushing 1925, 1: 304–5).

Based upon the Hippocratic writings and the above observations from the record of medical history, it is clear that close professional and mentor–student relationships exist within the field of biomedicine that create a cultural solidarity within the discipline. When viewed in the context of fictive kinship, the nature and meaning of these bonds will be demonstrated.

Systems of kinship, apart from conferring identity both symbolically and literally, offer advantages to the individual through an extension of the familial or fictive bonds. In the example of *compadrazgo*, not the least among these advantages is the network that is established between the child and the *co-madre* and/or *compadre*. These networks serve to provide economic, spiritual, emotional, and physical benefits to the individual in time of need. In like manner, ties of fictive kinship within American biomedicine create networks that link individuals together through which benefits are bestowed, identity conferred, and social position established.

Thus, systems of fictive kinship within American biomedicine, serve *at least* a twofold purpose. In the initial sense, these systems identify their members as participants in a close-knit social organization with its own primary level culture (Hall 1983), thereby creating a sense of identity among members of the association. Second, such systems serve as networks through which members and initiates may communicate and interact with each other for the benefit of individuals within the group. These networks may form the bases for informal psychosocial support systems as well as vehicles through which members protect and perpetuate their economic viability.

This study of fictive kinship within the culture of American biomedicine was, of necessity, small, and confined to several biomedical fictive kinship clusters that I had previously identified as typifying a kinlike organization. I conducted a series of interviews with biomedical practitioners to elicit information from them that might be suggestive of fictive kinship systems within American biomedical culture.[1] While the exploration of the possibility of such systems remained the focus of the interviews, it was not my intention to invent systems of fictive kinship where they did not exist. It should be noted that physicians, for the most part, do not characterize their participation in these systems as a form of kinship nor do they describe such relationships with kinship terminology. Close relationships are acknowledged (as in the case of Osler) as being "as close" or "similar" to familial bonds, yet the anthropological construct of fictive kinship is a foreign concept to most biomedical practitioners. These relationships are typically referenced by their participants with nomenclature that is suggestive of a bond that is more meaningful than mere networking, yet, most practitioners do not use terms associated with kinship as descriptors.

Since the premise of fictive kinship in biomedicine was initially based upon the admonition in the Hippocratic Oath to the adherent to "consider dear to me as my parents him who taught me this art," it was necessary to operationalize this concept. I determined that the Oath itself would be employed in order to define the relationship Hippocrates spoke of as one of fictive kinship. I worded the questions (see appendix) to enable the informant to identify an initial fictive relationship. Thus, the informant was able to emically identify and define individuals within his social organization (Geertz 1983: 58). This format was employed for case one and for case three. Case two, a social discourse evaluation, represented an examination of group structure within an established medical practice. The purpose of this observation was to determine the nature and scope of relationships within the group itself, as well as the effects of the group dynamic on its individual members.

During the course of the research, it became apparent to me that fictive relationships did not exist or were not identified as frequently within the specialties of family medicine, general medicine, and internal medicine as they appeared to occur within biomedical subspecialties such as cardiology, nephrology, gastroenterology, and so on. For this reason, the data that appear below reflect relationships within subspecialties of internal medicine (i.e., epidemiology, cardiology, and gastroenterology).[2]

Case One: The Making of a Medical Kin Group; Matters of the Heart

The formation of a kin group within the American model is, by many non-Western standards, relatively simplistic since kinship, within this model, is defined biogenetically (Schneider 1980: 23). Fictive relationships, on the other hand, are defined in a volitional manner; that is, they tend to trace their beginning to someone's choice. The choice may be made by the individual or, as in the instance of *compadrazgo*, on the individual's behalf. Nevertheless, such choices represent voluntary associations. Voluntary associations may be based upon varying degrees of commonality between members, ideological similarity, perceptual necessity (e.g., national defense, public safety), or in the instance of adoption, a desire on the part of individuals to create a kinship association in an environment in which direct biogenetic reproduction is either impractical or impossible.

Fictive relationships within biomedicine represent voluntary associations based upon common intellectual and ideological orientations that are shared by its members and initiates. The introductory phase of medical education is still Oslerian in outlook, owing its form and substance to the systematic theories of medical education set forth by Osler (Nuland 1988: 401; Cushing 1925, 1: 440). Osler's system of clinical clerkships, itself heavily influenced by the German educational model (Nuland 1988: 423–28) that has evolved into today's residency and fellowship programs, created a predisposition on the part of those who have been thus trained toward a hierarchical network through which scientific thought is disseminated. Such networks provide fertile ground for the formation of alliances among biomedical practitioners that assume characteristics of kin groups.

One such group came to my attention during a series of interactions with an individual who later became a principal informant. The individual noted that his relationship with medical school colleagues was similar to that of an "extended family" and that he maintained close personal ties to members of his "group" nearly thirty years later. During subsequent meetings and conversations, it became apparent that this "group" had definable form, structure, and organization, very similar to that of any traditional kin group.

The informant (hereafter referred to as M) is a board-certified cardiologist with a clinical cardiology and internal medicine practice in Texas. He has been in clinical practice since the early 1970s. He received his undergraduate degree from Harvard University (A.B.), proceeding from there to a well-known university school of medicine in the southeastern United States where he received his M.D. degree and completed a fellowship in cardiology.

I began the interview by asking M his motivation for pursuing a career in medicine. He indicated that a member of the faculty at Harvard Medical School, a Dr. T, had been extremely influential in directing him toward a medical career pathway. M had worked for T as a research assistant at Massachusetts General Hospital. Although the informant was attending Harvard on an academic scholarship, outside employment was necessary in order to supplement his income during his course of undergraduate study. M had originally intended to attend law school after receiving his degree from Harvard. During the course of his research assistantship, M participated in research projects that were subsequently published in scientific journals. The intellectual reward of having his name included among the investigators in the publication, coupled with the positive reinforcement from T, who encouraged him to attend medical school, provided the impetus necessary to convince M to consider applying to a leading medical institution. The medical school that M was to attend was chosen based upon T's recommendation, which itself was based upon T's personal friendship with several of the school's faculty members. M applied to the institution and was accepted. (It should be noted that although T played an important mentoring role in M's undergraduate development, the relationship was not characterized by the informant as one that would typify a fictive kinship relationship.)

The department of internal medicine at the institution and particularly the research efforts associated with that department were, at the time of M's attendance, under the direction of Dr. E, an epidemiologist who had come to the school from a prestigious medical center in the southern United States. E (while not considered by M to be a direct fictive kin relation) occupied a position similar to that of a spiritual patriarch. This relationship was reminiscent of Douglas's description of the Nuer's concept of the "founding ancestor" (Douglas 1986: 73). E represented an ideological leader to the members of the research group within the Department of Medicine. When M spoke of E, his references carried an almost reverential tone, denoting the great respect that he continues to hold for the individual.

During the beginning of M's medical training, he made the decision to pursue cardiology as a medical specialty. This decision was based upon his interest in preventive cardiology and the cardiovascular research that was being conducted at the institution. It was at this time that M was befriended by a faculty member in the cardiology department, Dr. D. It was D who, in M's own view, became his fictive father. This relationship was based upon D's personal interest in M's pursuit of a cardiology fellowship, a personal affinity based upon their congruent personalities, and their commonly held religious beliefs. Although M points to D as a type of fictive father figure, he was quick to point out that this relationship had greater social implications than it did professional ties. His relationship to D was characterized by social activities at D's home, interaction with D's family, and joint attendance of nonprofessionally related events or activities.[3]

M also acknowledged a relationship with his fictive "siblings," however, these connections were not the result of his relationship with D. The sibling relationships were formed within the department of medicine with individuals with whom M shared common interests. These interests were usually characterized as being partly professional and partly personal. A principal factor in the fictive siblings' relationship was their mutual participation in the developmental phase of an organization within the department of cardiology dedicated to cardiovascular research. This organization was developed primarily as an epidemiologic data center for cardiovascular disease. The aforementioned fictive founding ancestor was instrumental in the establishment of the research center. The sibling relationships that developed as a result of the common research interests within the research organization were between M himself; R, M's chief resident in medical school; F, a contemporary of M who now practices cardiology in the midwestern United States; G, currently a cardiologist on staff at the research facility; and C, a cardiologist also practicing in the midwestern sector of the United States. All five physicians continue to work with and contribute data to the cardiology research database. Another who was mentioned by M, a Dr. K, was a junior physician at the time of the informant's residency and fellowship. M was K's resident physician during K's early medical training. K now holds a position of prominence within a large medical institution and maintains a connection to the research center yet does not enjoy the fictive sibling relationship that is shared by the other five physicians. M attributed this to what he perceived as K's inability to view the research program in the same perspective as that of the five fictive siblings; an epidemiologic database, capable of providing insight into the etiology and potential treatment strategies for a host of cardiovascular diseases. K's interest in the research organization is, according to M, motivated by less altruistic concerns.

Thus, the fictive lineage that began with D the father, M the son, and M's siblings R, F, G, and C, and that remains nearly thirty years later is based, according to M, on a commonality of purpose within biomedicine. It is this intellectual/professional commonality that maintains these relationships over time and distance. It can be argued that M's "group," which I characterize as a "biomedical fictive kinship cluster," was, by the very nature of its members' proscribed training, culturally predisposed to a common connection with its foundations in interventional cardiology. This predisposition, coupled with common professional objectives and shared paradigms of the members of the group, is one explanation of the group's continuing connection.

Case Two: Rituals, Rites of Passage, and a Trip to New York City

Citing examples from the writings of Max Gluckman, Mary Douglas and Victor Turner, anthropologist Peacock notes that communities are "embodied in ritual." Peacock goes on to say that "ritual sustains belief, and belief is part of culture" (1986: 40). The truth of this statement extends well beyond traditional concepts of culture into the "cultural system" (Rhodes 1996) of American biomedicine. The rituals of biomedicine serve several functions, among them being the psychological assurance the practitioner receives during difficult procedures (Koenig 1988: 465–96) as well as the creation of solidarity among members of a medical practice. From a psychological perspective, it is necessary that the biomedical practitioner view the practice of medicine as a set of constants with as few variations as possible. It is, after all, the *rules* and the *paradigms* of biomedicine that the practitioner must follow in order to alleviate suffering, heal the sick, and eradicate disease. When imprecision can be transformed into certainty, particularly when the outcome involves the prolongation of human life, the psychological comfort for the practitioner is immeasurable. Thus, the rituals of medicine, whether based on the results of hard scientific research or biomedical tradition, represent an important source of emotional, psychological, and professional power for biomedical practitioners. When the social aspect of ritual is invoked, as in the instance of rites of passage, its function becomes one of either committing the individual more intimately to the group or separating the individual from the group entirely.

The second case illustrates the traditions and rituals that are evident among many groups of physicians. It is based on interviews that I conducted with a group of physicians who are members of a specialty practice that is affiliated with a major medical teaching institution. The group is actively involved in patient care as well as in the training of physician fellows who have chosen the particular specialty as their area of professional concentration. For the purpose of the interview, members of the group were allowed to invite spouses or significant others.[4] It was my intention to gain additional insight into the interactions and group dynamics of the physician group from spouses or others who have had the opportunity to observe these individuals over time. A second interview with two senior members of the practice was conducted at the academic institution in order to elucidate some comments made during the first session, elicit additional information, and verify my interpretation of the previous encounter.

My initial meeting with the director of the division, the two senior associates (hereafter referred to as Dr. Davis and Dr. Eggerton), and two junior members of the practice and their spouses took place at an arranged social event.[5] The participants had been informed that they would be asked to participate in ethnographic research focusing on the group dynamics within their medical practice. All agreed to participate. They also understood that I was there to observe group interaction as well. Once introductions were made, I asked Dr. Davis, who had been acting as the group's spokesperson, to explain each individual physician's function and position within the practice. This enabled me to understand each individual from the group's perspective and to determine how each member of the practice was emically defined.

The spatial organization of the meeting place, while not seminal to the social evaluation of the group per se, was of interest as a cultural artifact. At the center of the room was a large elliptical table where all members of the practice and their spouses would be seated. I was seated at one end of the table. I had assumed that the director of the practice would be seated at the opposite end. This did not occur. Dr. Davis systematically seated each member of the group. Spouses were not seated next to each other. The arrangement did not inhibit interaction but rather appeared to stimulate conversation among the members of the group. The interactions appeared, in fact, to be more suggestive of the interchange that one would expect from a consanguineal kinship group, with the preponderance of the conversations focusing on personal vis-à-vis professional issues. While the director of the practice did not assume the headship of the table, his positional station of leadership was clearly recognized from the deference shown him by the other members of the group. The majority of the evening's discourse consisted of narrative accounts of interactions with the director by each member of the practice, usually delivered in a humorous manner. These anecdotes are typified by the following narrative delivered by Dr. Eggerton regarding his brother, a former member of the practice, now practicing in a large metropolitan area in the eastern United States.

> My brother was scheduled to come in to the hospital early one morning for patient rounds and he was late. He lived in the extreme northern section of the city and had to take the tollway in to the medical school. Since he was late, he was driving about eighty miles an hour down the tollway, hoping to get to the hospital quickly enough so that maybe he wouldn't be missed during rounds. Well, a cop was shooting radar and pulled him over when he was just about to get to his exit. The cop saw that he was in his hospital scrubs and asked him if he was on his way to a medical emergency. My brother said, "I can't lie to you. I'm late for work. But if you knew the guy that I worked for, you'd understand why I'm driving this fast." The cop asked him, "Who do you work for?" My brother said, "Doctor X." The cop said, "You can go ahead and go," and didn't even write him a warning ticket.

Upon the completion of the narrative, all of the individuals present were laughing while leveling mock criticism at the director for inciting such fear in his subordinates. The director, who was also laughing, was genuinely amazed that he had been viewed as such a source of intimidation by anyone in the group.

The conversation then turned to a recent trip that Dr. Davis and the director had just taken to New York City. Dr. Davis said that he and the director had gone to see a football game between the director's alma mater Columbia, and its rival, Princeton. During the recounting of the trip, Dr. Davis noted that they shopped for neckties, as they "always do," got haircuts at the "same place that [they] always do," ate at the same restaurant that they "always go to," and saw a Broadway production, just like they "always do." During the second interview, conducted with Dr. Davis and Dr. Eggerton, the trip to New York became the primary focus of discussion. The original trip, which had taken place a number of years ago, began as an excursion by the director and Dr. Davis shortly after Dr. Davis completed his fellowship and joined the practice as a permanent member. The initial itinerary was to see the Columbia and Princeton game and to take a sightseeing tour of New York City. It was during this first trip that the traditions of the haircut, the purchase of neckties, the restaurant, and the Broadway production were established. The trip has been repeated every year since. Dr. Davis said that as the practice grows, thereby providing more coverage for members who are away or on vacation, it will be possible for more members of the group to participate in the trip. The trip, at this point, has taken on the characteristics of a social ritual.

The sense of community among the members of this particular medical practice has been fostered and perpetuated over the years by the director and by his senior members. This solidarity encompasses both professional and personal aspects of the members' lives, influencing their biomedical methodology, their scientific paradigms, their professional identity, and their commitment to the practice itself. The spouses' participation within the context of the interactions of the members of the practice indicated that they were very familiar with the day-to-day exchange that takes place between the members of the group. The sense of connection, therefore, extended well beyond the individual to include members of the individual's consanguineal/affinal family, expanding the scope and influence of the fictive kinship cluster.

Case Three: Paradigmatic Development: I Will Teach You How to Think

In his classic book *The Structure of Scientific Revolutions*, Kuhn detailed the essential nature of paradigms and paradigmatic development as a means of informing "normal" scientific thought (1996). So powerful is the paradigm, argued Kuhn, that scientists need no discoverable set of rules to legitimize the paradigm's validity. Kuhn noted, "Scientists work from models acquired through education and though subsequent exposure to the literature often without quite knowing or needing to know what characteristics have given these models the status of community paradigms. And because they do so, they need no full set of rules." He further stated that "Paradigms may be prior to, more binding, and more complete than any set of rules for research that could be unequivocally abstracted from them" (1996: 42). Paradigmatic development occurs during periods of discovery. While it may be argued that biomedicine has passed through delineable periods of discovery, it is equally valid to assert that scientific discovery, when applied to biomedicine, is best represented by a continuum of discovery that either builds upon or replaces previous theory. Such minor revolutions are attributable, according to Kuhn, to the applications of scientific theory or "law" in specific areas of research within the general scientific tradition. Paradigmatic development within particular subspecialties of science takes place, therefore, with little or no noticeable disruption to the accepted tenets of science. These *minor* revolutions of science have occurred and

continue to occur within biomedical thought with great regularity. The paradigmatic development that underlies these revolutions falls to those who have
assumed the responsibility, either implicitly or explicitly, for the direction of
scientific thought within a particular medical subspecialty. One need look no
further than the accepted medical texts to determine who the so-called *experts*
in any given field are. It is within the context of paradigmatic development that
the third course of interviews took place.

I conducted a third series of interviews with two former members of a specialty fellowship program in a large academic medical institution. Several of
the original members of the program are still affiliated with the department,
although the founding physician of the group has since assumed a role in private medical practice. The principal informant, Dr. S, who trained under the
founder more than twenty years ago, is the current chief of medicine of a
major academic institution. A second informant, Dr. A, occupies a prominent
position within the same institution. Both doctors trained under the founding physician, who became a mentor and type of fictive father to each.

During one interview, Dr. S was asked to recount his initial meeting with
the individual who became his mentor/fictive father. In the course of the narrative, the informant revealed the basis for his decision to enter into an affiliation with his mentor. He noted, "I don't remember a lot about the interview
other than a few things; one is he had his sleeves rolled up, he had no sport
jacket on, he was very informal, he was very easy to talk to, he was very relaxed
and . . . I think he had a can of Dr. Pepper in his hand, and he told me if I came
here *he would teach me how to think.* And that intrigued me" (italics added).[6]

The defining moment of the interview was the mentor's statement, "I will
teach you how to think." The statement hearkens back to Kuhn's assertion regarding the priority of the paradigm to normal science (1996: 43–51). It is the
paradigm that contextualizes scientific thought. It is the paradigm that gives
meaning to research. It is the paradigm that constitutes the *lens* through which
the scientist views the world in which he or she lives and works. The mentor
was, in effect, saying, "I will enable you to see the world in the correct manner."
This "intrigued" the informant to the degree that he chose to affiliate himself
with the mentor and to enter into a relationship that would significantly influence his way of comprehending medicine. When asked if he considered the remark, "I will teach you how to think" to be a sort of challenge to his abilities, the
informant replied, "I considered it, not so much a challenge in the sense that I
would prove to him that I already knew how to think; I considered it more of a
mystery; what exactly did he mean? I knew that . . . I had done some research, I
had done very little; I knew that he had been very successful as a researcher and
so I wasn't exactly sure what he meant, but I thought what he probably meant
was that he would teach me how to think analytically and critically about research and that it would make me a better researcher. So I viewed it as he was
going to open some magical door and expose me to a world that I had not been
exposed to before, and I found it a little bit titillating."

When asked whether or not his mentor had influenced his mentoring of students, Dr. S responded affirmatively. He indicated that even the style in which he related to his students bore similarities to the mannerisms exhibited by his mentor more than twenty years previously.

Dr. A, a colleague and contemporary of Dr. S, is actively engaged in research as well as in the instruction and mentoring of residents and fellows within his subspecialty. His exposure to the mentor/fictive father bore similarities to that of Dr. S, yet his emphasis focused primarily on the deontological nature of the mentor's instruction. For Dr. A, the manner in which scientific inquiry *ought* to be conducted was unmistakable. The mentor provided a clear-cut, systematic methodology for the execution of the tasks that were assigned to those under his tutelage. These were set forth both tacitly and explicitly in a series of dictums that were issued with repetitive frequency, acquiring, at times, the air of ritual. Dr. A recalled several instances during which members of the program were called upon to present research data to the attendees of scientific symposia. The mentor would routinely call meetings of those who were responsible for the presentations that amounted to formal rehearsals, ensuring that the presentation would adequately reflect the proficiency of the program. These rehearsals themselves proved to be defining activities, serving to identify the individual with the standards set forth by the mentor.

Discussion

The fictive kin relationships that Dr. M in Case One described, based upon the reverence and fondness that were evident in his discourse, clearly went beyond a purely academic or professional identification. Each relationship remains active after more than twenty-five years. Although the members of this group do not meet or necessarily correspond on a routine basis, the relationships still exist and are maintained, irrespective of time or distance. The relationships described possess several key components that are extant in many consanguineal or affinal kinship systems. First, a commonality of professional and personal interests existed that were responsible for forming the initial relationship. In some instances, the academic interest took precedence (F and G), while in others, the relationship came into being via a social or personal interest (D and R). This could be looked upon conceptually as a form of *affiliation*, linking those of like interest through, in this instance, fictive kinship (see Fox 1967: 134). Second, all members exhibited a close identification with the social or public personae represented by the individuals in the group. This identification was implicit within the informant's references to his colleagues. Third, a dedication to a concept outside of themselves (in this case, the cardiovascular research organization) served as the "social mortar" that continues to hold the group together. The *institution* (i.e., the research center), in effect, conferred upon each member his identity (Douglas 1986: 55–67).

The relationships that emerge in Case One appear to align with aspects of kinship. This group is not a fictive kinship system within itself, but rather what I have designated as a fictive kinship "cluster," somewhat analogous to "agnatic clusters" as noted within tribal societies.[7] Biomedical fictive clusters in many instances form ideological connections with other clusters in other institutions. For example, the ideological ties between the schools of medicine from which the fictive patriarchs, fathers and mentors, originated all represent institutions that are connected via fictive kin within each secondary or tertiary institution. Many members of the faculty at the institution in Case One received their training at the same institution in the eastern United States. E continued to maintain a strong affiliation with the southern medical school where he had previously served. Interviews that I have conducted in other institutions have uncovered similar connections.

Case Two, involving a group of medical professionals, revealed not only the relational aspect of the interactions between participants, but also the social dynamics that occur within the group. The concept of the "social father" (Keesing 1975: 13) accurately describes the role that the director of the medical practice assumed in the professional and, to a degree, the personal lives of his subordinates. Within the social milieu of the group dynamic, the positions of father, elder brother, and younger brother could clearly be identified. These positions carried with them both privileges and expectations implicit within the culture of the group.

Case Three represented an assessment of the extant relationships within a group that had been maintained over time, primarily by the psychodynamic authority of the primary mentor/fictive father. This authority, although tacit in nature, nonetheless represented the ideological basis upon which the relationships were founded and maintained. The authority further served to perpetuate a subsequent fictive generation, unrelated directly to the fictive father, yet dependent upon him for its existence. The foundation for this authority rests in the paradigm. The mentor's defining remark, "I will teach you how to think" speaks volumes. Ideological connection is strong. It requires a volitional surrender on the part of the individual to a particular way of thinking; a way of thinking with which she or he closely identifies. Ideology may change over time. The initial connection, however, appears to remain. It represents the intellectual touchstone to which the individual returns during times of uncertainty. Nuland, professor of surgery at Yale and author of *Doctors: The Biography of Medicine*, wrote of his own experience:

> Even after almost thirty years of being a surgeon, my own occasional flutterings of self-doubt in the operating room can always be stilled by reminding myself that my professor was Gustav Lindskog, whose professor was Samuel Harvey, whose professor was Harvey Cushing, whose professor was William Halsted. The process of remembering is instantaneous, and the quiverings are gone in the wink of an eye. (1988: 406)

Bosk (1979) pointed out the protective nature in the resident/attending relationship. The relationship is a hybridization of peer-to-peer and subordinate-to-superordinate alliances, based primarily on their clinical association. To a certain extent, however, the attending (superordinate) is professionally defined by the proficiency of his resident (subordinate). This creates a functional bond that, in my view, tends to evolve into a fictive kinship relationship (1979: 134–35).

Mentoring relationships are often sought out by many physicians and medical students during the course of their training experiences. These relationships as well tend to evolve into relationships of fictive kinship (Kaufman 1993: 112–13; Cassell 1996).

The relationships and social organizations that exist within the biomedical community all contribute to the character and viability of the profession itself. Just as kinship systems tend to define certain cultural groups, so too, the fictive kinship of biomedicine characterizes the biomedical complex.

Although viewing biomedicine as a cultural system has given it some theoretical importance, few have sought to analyze the system itself. Much of what is written constitutes a cultural critique of how the system either acts, reacts, or fails to do either within the framework of other systems (Rhodes 1996: 165–80). A notable few have attempted to describe and define the system of biomedicine as it is (Cassell 1991; Bosk 1979; Starr 1982). When biomedicine is seen for what it is, a distinct cultural system, only then will it be properly contextualized within its appropriate setting. Seldom is biomedicine viewed in this light. Biomedical practitioners themselves rarely, if ever, characterize their organizational structure as a social system. As members of the system, they are seldom able to view the system itself with any degree of detachment that would lend itself to objective ethnographic analysis. I was made acutely aware of this fact when I presented much of the descriptive data that is discussed above to the faculty and staff of a medical department in a biomedical educational facility, located in the midwestern United States. During the question and answer session, which extended well beyond the allotted time for the discussion, numerous questions pertaining to the view of biomedicine as a cultural system were posed. The manner in which the questions were phrased and the types of questions that were presented indicated that the concept of viewing biomedicine as a cultural system was a foreign proposition, albeit one that evoked a great deal of positive inquiry. Possibly the most poignant question came from a cardiologist who had practiced medicine for more than thirty years and who had taught in various capacities over two decades. His question was extremely relevant for two reasons. First, it represented a legitimate inquiry into the utility of research directed at the culture of biomedicine. Second, and for me the more important reason, was that his query forced me, the researcher, to think more critically of the work that I had done with reference to its application. During the question and answer session, this gentleman offered the following statement and question: "When I attend these lectures, I go through a process that I refer to as 'afterlearning,' during which I ruminate over the information that I've heard, and try to apply it practically. My question to you is, what can we as practitioners take back with us into our day-to-day activities and use?"

My answer, while spontaneous, was, I hope, adequate. My suggestion to the physician, based on the above research, was simple, yet, I believe, important to the application of such ethnographic work. Cultural systems are profoundly powerful in their ability to convey meaning and shape lives. Biomedicine as a cultural system is no different in this sense than any other clearly identifiable cultural group. The "afterlearning" that the physician sought can be stated very simply: As a biomedical practitioner who is engaged in the education of future practitioners, make certain that all that you convey, both explicitly and implicitly, is directed toward the benefit of the ultimate recipient of your teaching, the patient. Make certain that your instruction is founded upon that which has been adequately tested and found to be, inasmuch as is possible, consistently true. What you tell your students and those who look to you as a mentor, or, in the case of the above, a fictive parent, they believe you. They believe that everything that you tell them is unquestionably valid. Thus, they put into practice what you have told them, thereby affecting the lives of the patients who are placed in their care. The biomedical practitioner who is involved to any degree in teaching or mentoring should, therefore, approach his or her duties with no small sense of responsibility, both to the student and, ultimately, the patient.

The relationships that undergird biomedicine, when properly understood, enable the outsider to more accurately define the system. It is from such contextualization that the clinically applied medical anthropologist, in the role of cultural "broker," will be able to negotiate the differing cognitive orientations present in the practitioner/patient/institutional continuum. It is then incumbent upon the anthropologist to champion the interests of the patient (the ultimate beneficiary of medical care) as these differing orientations are evaluated, merged, modified, and adapted in pursuit of the ultimate goal, which is the healing of humankind.

Appendix

Please read the following excerpt from the Hippocratic Oath:
"I swear by Apollo the physician, by Aesculapius, Hygeia, and Panacea, and I take to witness all the gods, all the goddesses, to keep according to my ability and my judgment the following oath:

To consider dear to me as my parents him who taught me this art; to live in common with him and if necessary to share my goods with him; to look upon his children as my own brothers, to teach them this art if they so desire without fee or written promise. (Hippocrates 1994)

When you read the above quote, who, if anyone, comes to mind? Please write three or more sentences that would describe your current relationship with this individual.

Notes

1. The interviews took place during periods between the fall of 1995 and the spring of 1999. The settings for the interviews varied from locations away from the informants' offices and hospital practices, to on-site interviews in the office, hospital, or teaching situation. Informed consent was obtained from each of the informants and every effort has been taken in the course of this writing to protect the anonymity of the informants.

2. Initial contact with the informants was made by phone, during which time an explanation of the purpose and scope of the interview was discussed. The informants in cases one and three, as previously noted, agreed to a meeting at a time that was convenient to their academic and clinical commitments. A copy of the questionnaire (see Appendix) employed in the first and third series of interviews was made available to the informants prior to the time of the initial meeting and the interview. The informants were assured that the information gathered during the interview was for anthropological research only and that no names would be used in subsequent publications.

3. For a nonfictive explanation, see Keesing's (1975: 13) remarks on "social fathers."

4. The interview itself took place at a facility that was removed from the academic site of the practice.

5. The names Dr. Davis and Dr. Eggerton are pseudonyms.

6. It is of interest that the informant indicates that he did not remember a great deal about the interview, yet proceeds with a recounting of the interview in minute detail (e.g., "he had his sleeves rolled up, he had no sport jacket on, he was very informal").

7. Although structurally similar to an agnatic cluster (i.e., a group within a group), they are functionally unrelated. See Hammond-Tooke (1984).

References

Bosk, Charles L. 1979. *Forgive and Remember: Managing Medical Failure.* Chicago: University of Chicago Press.

Cassell, Joan. 1991. *Expected Miracles: Surgeons At Work.* Philadelphia: Temple University Press.

———. 1996. Personal communication, November 26, 1996.

Cushing, Harvey. 1925. *The Life of Sir William Osler,* 2 vols. Oxford, U.K.: Clarendon Press.

Douglas, Mary. 1986. *How Institutions Think.* Syracuse, N.Y.: Syracuse University Press.

Fox, Robin. 1967. *Kinship and Marriage.* Cambridge, U.K.: Cambridge University Press.

Geertz, Clifford. 1983. *Local Knowledge: Further Essays in Interpretive Anthropology.* New York: Basic.

Hall, Edward T. 1983. *The Dance of Life: The Other Dimension of Time.* New York: Doubleday.

Hammond-Tooke, William D. 1984. In Search of the Lineage: The Cape Nguni Case. *Man* 19:76–83.

Hippocrates. 1994. *Hippocrates,* vol. 1, ed. and trans. Wesley D. Smith. Cambridge, Mass.: Loeb Classical Library, Harvard University Press.

Kaufman, Sharon. 1993. *The Healer's Tale: Transforming Medicine and Culture.* Madison: University of Wisconsin Press.

Keesing, Roger M. 1975. *Kin Groups and Social Structure.* Orlando, Fla.: Harcourt Brace Jovanovich.

Koenig, Barbara A. 1988. The Technological Imperative in Medical Practice: The Social Creation of a "Routine" Treatment. In *Biomedicine Examined*, ed. Margaret Lock and Deborah R. Gordon. Boston: Kluwer Academic Publishers.

Kuhn, Thomas S. 1996. *The Structure of Scientific Revolutions*, 3d ed. Chicago: University of Chicago Press (original date of publication, 1962).

Nuland, Sherwin. 1988. *Doctors: The Biography of Medicine*. New York: Random House.

Osler, William. 1906. *Aequanimitas: With other Addresses to Medical Students, Nurses, and Practitioners of Medicine*, 3d ed. New York: McGraw-Hill.

———. 1913. *A Way Of Life*. Philadelphia: Lippincott.

Peacock, James L. 1986. *The Anthropological Lens: Harsh Light, Soft Focus*. Cambridge, U.K.: Cambridge University Press.

Rhodes, Lorna Amarasingham. 1996. Studying Biomedicine as a Cultural System. In *Medical Anthropology: Contemporary Theory and Method*, ed. Thomas M. Johnson and Carolyn F. Sargent. Rev. ed. New York: Praeger.

Schneider, David M. 1980. *American Kinship: A Cultural Account*. 2d ed. Chicago: Chicago University Press.

Selzer, Richard. 1982. *Letters To A Young Doctor*. New York: Simon & Schuster.

Starr, Paul. 1982. *The Social Transformation of American Medicine: The Rise of a Sovereign Profession and the Making of a Vast Industry*. New York: Basic.

Chapter Seventeen

Going Nuclear: New Zealand Bureaucratic Fantasies of Samoan Extended Families

Ilana Gershon

Now that diversity is in vogue in multicultural nations, government welfare bureaucracies face a thorny dilemma. Their workers must encourage families in two tasks that are often contradictory. Government agencies expect families to raise productive citizens. At the same time, government workers try to support culturally different families in families' efforts to maintain their uniqueness. To what extent are these two tasks necessarily at odds? I heard one optimistic view while I was discussing a new government project, "Strengthening Families," with a New Zealand public relations officer at a regional social welfare office. When I asked her how her agency defined families, she explained that families, broadly defined, were similar to her family—a team, with every member contributing a fair share. She viewed all families as social mechanisms leading to good citizens. I had this interview toward the end of a sixteen-month period of fieldwork (August 1996 to December 1997) among Samoan migrants, New Zealand's largest Pacific island migrant group (approximately 90,000). Since I spent considerable time listening to Samoans' discomfort with the Eurocentric prejudices they found in government policy, my first reaction upon hearing the officer's assertions was to think "pure unadulterated ideology." Here, I want to take a step back, and take a serious look at both Samoan discomfort and government officials' optimism. I explore the question: "When and how does keeping families Samoan come into conflict with raising children to be productive New Zealanders?"

In *Democracy and Ethnography*, Greenhouse (1998: 1) suggested that this conflict arises because liberal democratic governments' conception of difference creates difficulties in accommodating cultural diversity. She argued that the conflicts are generated because governments protect collective identities using the same principles that promote individual welfare and equality. By beginning the debate at the intersection between the person and the nation, the demands of other collectivities become awkward when they violate the nation's conceptualizations of the individual's best interests. Povinelli offered an example of this dilemma in her account of how female circumcision brings to the fore the paradoxes of the modern liberal and strategically guilt-ridden nation-state:

> Liberal democratic societies are now haunted by the specter of mistaken intolerance. . . . Liberal members of democratic societies stumbling, lose their breath, panic, even if ever so slightly, when asked to say why, on what grounds, according to whom, a practice is a moral, national limit of tolerance. (1998: 578–79)

Nonnational collectives offer alternative ways in which people can belong to groups, potentially making a specific nationalism that much more arbitrary. These other collectives risk becoming the treacherous third term, the categorical interlocutor encouraging citizens to behave destructively toward the nation. In this tense mix, families play a problematical role. Essential as social mechanisms for producing future citizens, they are also collectives that can promote actions contrary to national interest. At the core of this potential conflict is a concern familiar to kinship theorists from the discipline's initial explorations: namely, what forms do the webs of obligations take that link people to their families, as opposed to other collectivities?

As kinship theorists addressed this question, they discovered that certain kin relations were better at articulating the paradoxes of a specific kinship system. For example, Fortes discusses how the Tallensi's version of patrilineality made father–son relationships the locus for tensions surrounding jural or economic group membership. The structural contradictions surrounding what it means to belong to a Tallensi group tended to unfold in father–son relationships (Fortes 1949). In this chapter, I build on the insight that certain kinship ties are particularly good to think with when people reflect upon group membership.

One of a multicultural nation's problems is that the structures of group membership vary from community to community and from family to family. This becomes apparent when groups use the same relationship to articulate substantively different assumptions about what it means to belong to a family. The contradictions between becoming a Samoan and becoming a New Zealand citizen emerge when the parent–child relationship is at issue. For the Samoan families I spoke with, as well as for the New Zealand social services representatives I interviewed, the parent–child relationship is the vehicle for thinking about how resources and information should flow within the family. Yet the assumptions underlying these distributions are substantively different, leading to miscommunications at the sites where Samoan families meet New Zealand government bureaucracy.

The Hierarchies in Samoan Kinship

Readers familiar with Samoan ethnography may be surprised that I have sin-
gled out the parent–child relationship since ethnographers of Samoa (Shore
1981; Schoeffel 1978, 1995; Tcherkezoff 1993) have focused upon the
sister–brother tie as the key relationship through which Samoans understand
their social obligations. However, migration has sparked a transition from
Samoan families' focus on the sister–brother tie to the parent–child bond.
Here, I discuss this shift as well as changes in how resources and knowledge
circulate within Samoan migrant families, practices that New Zealand government agencies have difficulty addressing.

When ethnographers analyze the Samoan sister–brother bond as a powerfully metaphorical relationship, they are describing an ideological relationship
that can serve as an ordering principle for the daily negotiations of contradictory hierarchies. In Samoa, people experience social organization as a cluster
of hierarchies that interweave, sometimes discordantly, and that define appropriate displays of respect and competition as contexts shift.[1] Walking through
a Samoan village, a Samoan man might have to show proper deference to a
church minister, another family's *matai* (chief), his older sister, and his paternal grandfather's brother. Age, gender, degree of relatedness, and chiefly status
all contribute to determining a given social relationship. Within families, the
hierarchical relationships are made visible at mealtimes, in which ideally the
matai and elders of the family are served first, then the adult family members,
the children, and finally the daughters-in-law of the household. Yet if the
daughter-in-law is a foreigner, or is married to the only son in the family who
is a minister, she might be asked to eat with the other siblings. The status of
foreigner or minister's wife is honored along different hierarchical axes than
husband–wife relations, and these different axes can collide at meals. While
every social relationship in Samoa is hierarchical, not every hierarchical relationship is constituted along the same principles.

Anthropologists explored this tension between hierarchies by examining
Samoan concepts of gender (Shore 1981; Schoeffel 1978, 1995; Tcherkezoff
1993). They focus on the fact that in Samoa, a person's sex does not determine
his or her status. Rather, the dominant social relationship in a given setting
will decide the hierarchical structure of the event. Samoan constructions of
gender present an apt example of how hierarchical relationships in Samoa are
all inherently contextual.

All three anthropologists cited above agree that in Samoa, husband–wife
relationships are substantively different from sister–brother relationships.
Samoan wives invariably owe respect to their husbands and are obligated to
serve their husband's family by performing the household chores, preparing
meals, cleaning, and eating last (Schoeffel 1978). Wives are subservient to their
affines. In contrast, Samoan sisters, in relation to brothers, are far more passive,

embodying a role owed respect, obedience and, in general, representing the family's honor (Schoeffel 1978: 308; Shore 1981: 200). Thus, a woman is either a wife or a sister—not only a woman. She is always defined in terms of a dyadic relationship. Gender is not based on a contrast between men versus women, but rather as a contrast between husband–wife and sister–brother (Schoeffel 1978; Tcherkezoff 1993).

While each scholar disagrees about the precise nature of the dyadic relationships, all agree on the basic Samoan structural interaction between power and social relationships. In Samoa, power is never embodied wholly in one person. Power is inherently dyadic, with each person in the relationship embodying one pole. In the most abstract form, power is expressed in a passive and active form, with, for example, the sister as an instantiation of the passive form of power, and the brother as the active form. The husband–wife tie is not a social relationship on the same order as the sister–brother link. When a woman moves from a sister–brother link to one of husband–wife, she is moving between ways in which social relationships can channel expressions of power. All three scholars argue that the *feagaiga*, the dyadic power relationship modeled often upon the sister–brother tie, is a metaphorical vehicle for understanding Samoan society as a whole.

While ideologically some hierarchical relationships may be privileged over others, this does not serve as a practical guideline for Samoans on the ground. In daily life, Samoans are constantly juggling their different hierarchical roles. A child could easily be in a quagmire, trying to figure out which of the two mutually exclusive requests to fulfill—the minister's or her father's sister's. In his thesis, St. Christian captured this tension elegantly in the following passage:

> A command from one authority can be superseded by a command from another, and obligations to one powerful figure can be overruled by obligations to some other. As such, obedience in any context is premised on a calculation of how accepting the authority of person X relates to, and effects, conditions of obligation and obedience to persons Y and Z. (St. Christian 1997: 156)

In lived experience, the differing hierarchies are contradictory demands to be negotiated. So while the *feagaiga* may be Samoan society's self-reflexive relationship, through which Samoans can know society as a whole, in practice, this knowledge is continually juxtaposed with daily fragmented mediations of hierarchies.

Migrating Hierarchies

Because Samoans are continually negotiating a constellation of hierarchies, different hierarchies can be privileged upon migration. Among Samoan New Zealand families, at the family level, the *feagaiga* as a formalized brother–sister relationship is no longer practiced systematically. Brothers and sisters

discuss each other's love lives openly, share clothes readily, and no longer al-
locate chores as in Samoa. Once I observed to a middle-aged Samoan-raised
woman that it did not seem as though the younger generation practices the
feagaiga anymore. She agreed, and with what felt like typical Samoan humor
and succinctness, said: "The boys are just like their fathers now. They lie
around the house with their legs up and their things up." In one sentence, she
managed to convey two significant lapses in the *feagaiga*. The young men no
longer perform the regular gendered chores that encapsulate a brother–sister
division. In addition, in her pithy summary, for the young men an expression
of sexuality becomes more dominant than an expression of respect.[2] The
sister–brother bond has shifted valences in migration. It no longer acts as the
self-description for Samoan society, the familial metaphor guiding Samoans
into understanding how power and sociality are channeled and articulated.
Instead, it has become just another hierarchical relationship that Samoan migrants must manage.

What has changed in migration that Samoan families would no longer find
the sister–brother bond good to think with? Luhmann (1990) offers some insights into understanding the dynamics of this transformation. He claimed
that a characteristic feature of societies such as New Zealand is that they exist
in a state of "functional differentiation." The various functional systems (such
as families and governments) each have their own form of self-representation,
which is fundamentally incompatible with that of other systems. Luhmann argued that this incompatibility is a symptom of modernity. In societies that are
not functionally differentiated, one relationship can provide a vehicle for reflecting upon the relationships between people and social collectivities. In
Samoa, the representations of society function metaphorically—the
sister–brother bond is like the bond between God and the minister, which is
like the bond between the *ali'i* (high chief) and the *tulafale* (the talking chief).
This is a society in which one hierarchy is particularly useful as a self-
description for all other forms.[3] In New Zealand, society can no longer be realized as a whole, and no functional system can provide an unassailable representation of society to itself. As a result, Samoan communities in New
Zealand are not finding relationships that can stand for all of sociality. Instead, they explore relationships that can stand for how they experience
Samoanness within the broader New Zealand society. Their self-description as
Samoans has shifted from a totality of already existing power relationships to
a specific differentiated subsystem based on a constantly reasserted identity.

In many ways, the relationship that has taken the place of the sister–brother
bond for Samoan migrants is the parent–child relationship. While the
parent–child bond doesn't play the same role as the sister–brother link in
Samoa, it is becoming the relationship through which Samoan migrants articulate their links to Samoa and "Samoanness." The relationship with parents
has become the foci for thinking about Samoanness in two ways—in terms of
transmitting knowledge and managing resources. How people know what to

do in Samoan contexts, how they learn what behaviors are typically Samoan, or how they decide how to spend their money and time, are all issues that become linked to the parent–child relationship after migration.

The parent–child relationship articulates Samoanness in different ways, depending on whether or not a person was raised in Samoa. If Samoans are New Zealand–raised, then parents become the conduit through which the children learn how to be Samoan. In Samoa, children would learn expected behavior from a wide variety of people, partially as a by-product of the multiple hierarchical relationships Samoans are constantly navigating (Ochs 1988). Once they move to New Zealand, parents become a much more important source for teaching appropriate behavior.

Several of my New Zealand–raised Samoan friends described how they learned about Samoan practices from their parents or grandparents. However, just as often, I was told about how strained the learning process was. New Zealand–raised Samoans told me that their parents seemed to expect them to know what to do automatically. When they made a mistake, the parents would criticize them publicly. As a result, many of them experienced Samoan practices as implicit and rigid expectations that their parents' generation seemed to grasp intuitively.

While Samoan-raised migrants do not share the New Zealand–raised Samoans' anxieties about their parents, the structure of Samoan ritual exchanges (*fa'alavelave*) ensures that their relationships with their parents become the relationship through which they think about their connection to Samoa. *Fa'alavelave* are ritual exchanges of food, fine mats, and money for occasions such as weddings, funerals, major birthdays, and so on. They have become an important vehicle for Samoan migrants to express their connection to their family and to Samoa.

When they first began to arrive in the 1950s, Samoan migrants were more concerned with sending resources back to Samoa than in building demanding exchange networks within New Zealand. When Samoans initially began establishing communities in New Zealand, they were not actively participating in local *fa'alavelave*. The first large-scale exchanges began within the newly formed Pacific Island churches. While Samoan migrants began building exchange networks from within the churches and with family members who had also migrated, the depth of historical relationships represented by the exchanges was far more shallow than in Samoa. Samoans were often commemorating relationships forged only over the past decade or so, rather than over generations.

This initial shift created changes in the ways in which Samoan migrants use *fa'alavelave* to express their connections with their family even to this day. Just as with knowledge transmission for New Zealand–raised Samoans, parents often become the primary vehicle through which those living in New Zealand stay connected to the Samoan exchange system. For example, a village back in Samoa might decide that it needs to build a new church and ask each family in the village to contribute money. The parents will start calling their children in New Zealand, asking them to send some money for the church. The children will not necessarily feel very connected to the village itself—they might not have lived there for twenty years.[4] But because their parents are asking, they will send money back to Samoa.

How Samoan migrants decide the amount to donate for a *fa'alavelave* also reinforces this new emphasis on the parent–child link. In my interviews, Samoans described two basic patterns for determining how much to give, and to whom. In some instances, the *matai* (which in migration was a parent or a parent's oldest local sibling) of the New Zealand branch of the family learns that one of their relatives soon will be having a funeral or a wedding. The *matai* decides how much he or she would like the family as a whole to donate and then calls up each family member and tells them how much to give. Occasionally, the *matai* simply tells the family members that a *fa'alavelave* is looming, and asks them to "give as much as you can afford." If the *matai* can't collect a sufficient amount of money, he or she will (as most informed me) supplement the amount with an even larger personal donation, so that the family is not shamed in the exchange. Alternatively, a parent (who is often the *matai* of the family as well) calls a family meeting where members will determine how much the parents and sibling set as a unit will contribute.

I have noticed two themes emerging from people's accounts of family meetings. First, not everyone speaks freely. Certain people (such as affines) do not have the right to speak, and often are not even present. Second, parents will make the final decision, determining how much money is given, and how much each of their children will contribute. In short, the private techniques with which money and fine mats are gathered for a *fa'alavelave* are part and parcel of the hierarchical relationships that shape family dynamics. Among Samoan migrants, these hierarchical relationships now reflect the shift from a focus on brother–sister ties to parent–child links.

This shift has also been accompanied by a change in the ways in which extended families make themselves visible as collectivities to their members and others in Samoan communities. In Samoa, *fa'alavelave* are but one, albeit the most public one, of the avenues through which extended families articulate forms of relatedness. But after migration to New Zealand, *fa'alavelave* are often the only means through which Samoan families explore their interconnectedness.[5] Siblings who haven't seen each other for twenty years might be compelled to interact because of wedding expenses.

To sum up, in Samoa, *fa'alavelave* serve as a public arena for exploring the boundaries between families, defining family membership, and revealing the collective strength of a family through its exchanges. In New Zealand, the emphasis of *fa'alavelave* has gradually rested on the strength of the family in terms of the money and fine mats the family gather for the event. Being part of a Samoan collectivity has become largely defined in terms of these exchanges. This shift has also affected the parent–child relationship as Samoans increasingly rely on this relationship as a model for imagining being part of a Samoan collective.

Between Governments and Families

The ways in which Samoans have restructured their networks for exchanging information and resources do not reflect the techniques or priorities that the New Zealand government agencies imagine for families. Both government agencies and Samoan migrant families stress the parent–child relationship, yet for quite different reasons. For government agencies, children are supposed to grow independent of their families. For Samoan migrant families, this independence is fraught with the potential for a negligent assimilation that they struggle to prevent. This gap becomes an issue when New Zealand government social workers intervene in bureaucratically determined cases of child abuse or juvenile delinquency among Samoan families. Having explored how information and resources can flow between parents and children in Samoan migrant families, I will now discuss the assumptions about the parent–child relationship underlying the New Zealand Department of Social Welfare policies.

In moving to the sites where governments and Samoan families intersect, I turn to Donzelot (1979) and Luhmann (1982, 1987, 1990), both of whom emphasized the interrelations between government agencies and families. Donzelot offered a historical perspective and suggested that over two centuries Euro-American families gradually emerged as essential counterpoints to modern governments. He suggested that a great deal of bureaucratic energy has gone into answering the question that underlies the junctures in which government and family have come to circle each other—how should the government and the family divide the labor of producing citizens? Government and family are entities that regulate the complicated paths through which an individual enters into a relationship with society (cf. Strathern 1992) and between which battles are fought over the allocation of responsibility, roles, and obligations.

Luhmann (1990) provided a framework for examining this tension between government agencies and families in his discussion of functionally differentiated societies, referred to above. His approach serves as a theoretical context for exploring the ways in which Samoan migrants and New Zealand social workers, as conduits of divergent systems, misunderstand each other. Luhmann argued that the historical processes Donzelot traced have resulted in societies that are functionally differentiated systems. They are composed of a variety of autopoetic systems, that is, systems that produce internally all the elements, including self-referential operations, necessary to continue functioning. These societies are uneasy alliances between subsystems, all performing necessary tasks for society as a whole to continue, but each operating according to its own insular logic. So the political system and the family system are interdependent at the same time as their functioning depends upon fundamental misrecognitions of each other's processes. In order to interact, each system must translate the input of the other systems into forms that it can process. Thus, for example, political systems interpret legal decisions not in terms of legality, but rather in terms of whether these decisions support the government or its political opposition.

In practical terms, this translation ensures that there will be a particular type of tension underpinning the relationships between government welfare agencies and the families they serve. Because the political subsystem is driven by the binary tension of having or not having political authority, the problems generated by other subsystems often become arenas for contestations of power. Policy decisions about health and unemployment benefits, job training programs, or child abuse interventions become sites for legitimating power. As a result, government agencies are continually compelled to justify their existence. Bureaucracies urgently need to have subsystems, such as families, which generate problems for their citizens that state apparatuses can appear to resolve. From the political subsystem's perspective, when families fail to perform their function, this legitimates government agencies. The agencies then can step in and justify their existence by solving specific problems with a backdrop of normative families in mind. Thus citizens exist in family systems whose initial structures exclude government involvement, but whose failures (often generated by the mismatch between the political and the familial subsystems) require it. The struggle to determine what is the state's responsibility versus what is the family's responsibility is in fact the product of the political subsystem's requirements for its own existence.

To be a potential site for failure that can be remedied, families need to be imagined in a very specific way—as systems that circulate information and resources. Families are seen as providing the education that the schools should not—offering ethical and etiquette guidelines that will help transform children into socially adept citizens (cf. Smith 1998). In addition, families act as resource bases in relationship to each of its members, providing its members with basic needs such as food, shelter, and clothing. What happens, however, is that at the moment of imagining families as systems for circulating knowledge and resources, the government overlooks the precise dynamics through which knowledge and resources do circulate. In other words, government welfare regulations treat families as unified, with all members working toward a common goal, in which hierarchy only emerges in the parent–child relationship.

Placed within the context of a welfare bureaucracy, this approach to families encourages certain presuppositions that elide kinship rather than engage with different forms of relatedness as structuring principles. As Fleming (1997) pointed out, policy makers believe that resources circulate among members of the household, and the central priority is to ensure that the resources are used first for household members' basic needs. Surplus, if there is surplus, should ideally go to the younger members of the household. This creates the context for social workers to read certain family dynamics as problems. This approach predicts that when individuals spend resources at their disposal for their own self-interest, and on items considered luxuries and not necessities, there will be conflict within the family.[6]

The relationship between parents and children is a marked exception to this ethos of familial equality, partially because, for New Zealand government agencies, families' central function is to socialize the children into being productive citizens. From this standpoint, the central tension within a family is between the parent and the child, in which the child is continually attempting to reach a level of independence in the context of parental attempts to instruct the child properly. The parent–child relationship is a momentary hierarchical stage in the child's progress towards becoming an equal member of its own family (Strathern 1992: 15).

European New Zealander parents do not struggle for independence from their children—the quest for independence only flows in one direction. As a result, children are often seen as withholding information. They don't tell their parents who their friends are, what they do in school, or how involved they are in drugs. The parents labor to uncover this information and understand what is happening in their child's life by forging communicative ties that will encourage the necessary flow of information. The opposite is not true. The child is not expected to know about the travails of the parent's life, and, in fact, this type of knowledge is often seen as inappropriate.

However, other family relationships are not seen as highly charged in terms of the circulation of knowledge. Information ideally circulates within the family easily. The principal tension surrounding information flow, from this perspective, emerges from the family's central project—to form productive citizens. This perspective is at odds with Samoan families in general, where most relationships are highly charged in terms of knowledge transmission, although the specific tensions vary from relationship to relationship.

New Zealand government bureaucracies assume that, with the exception of the parent–child relationship, families act as cohesive units for information transmission and resource management. There is a belief that any adult member of a household will serve as a liaison in terms of information transmission. When the social worker informs one parent about the court procedures by which a juvenile delinquent is to be tried, he or she is telling all the responsible adults in the family. Anyone can represent that family and carry the necessary knowledge back to all the other members.[7] Because adult siblings, cousins, spouses, parents, and even grandparents are all equal, knowledge is supposed to be distributed equally between all of them. Secrecy is seen as destructive and is normally associated with disruptive activities that are meant to prioritize individual pleasures over family needs or boundaries, practices such as adultery or drug use.

For European New Zealanders, a main goal of all families is to raise children properly. Toward this end, the family is imagined to circulate knowledge and resources as a coordinated and unified group. As a result, European New Zealanders often view extended families through a nuclear family lens. Samoan migrant families have completely different goals, such as making the family visible as a collective that can gather ample resources for ritual exchanges. When New Zealand's social welfare departments have Samoan families as clients, the Samoan ways of practicing family unity expose the nuclear family biases within the European New Zealand system. In short, when social workers assume that Samoan extended families function as specific unified systems, they are making the intricacies of Samoan kinship invisible.

Legislating Families

The reactions of Samoan migrant social workers to New Zealand family legislation provides insights into how these tensions unfold. In this section, I want to focus on the impact of legislation designed to overhaul New Zealand's child protection services and the juvenile justice system. When I interviewed Samoan migrant social workers about implementing this piece of family legislation called the Children, Young Persons and Their Families Act (CYPFS) (1989), several responded in a way that puzzled me. They told me that the act "in its [the family's] raw form" couldn't be brought straight to the Samoan family "in its raw form." The social worker, in their view, has the difficult task of raising the level of the family to the level of the act. At the same time, social workers have to shift the way that they present the act to their clients so that it can be more easily introduced into the Samoan family. Their descriptions confused me, since they indicated that the act was not unfolding as the stories about its origins would have predicted.

Before the New Zealand Parliament passed this piece of legislation, government representatives consulted extensively with both Maori and Pacific Islanders (migrants from various Pacific Islands, largely Samoans, Cook Islanders, Tongans, Niueans, Tokelauans, and Fijians). These consultations had a profound effect on how the Department of Social Welfare would subsequently approach cases of child abuse and juvenile crime; in particular the act helped to establish a new process called Family Group Conferences. These conferences were supposed to be based on Maori and Pacific Island techniques for resolving family conflict. They provided an arena where the family members and all interested parties could deliberate over the best course of action for the abused or delinquent child in question.

This act was designed to herald in a new era of family policy, one which was intended to accommodate a multicultural citizenry by modeling itself upon Maori and Pacific Island extended-family practices. So why, when I spoke with Samoan social workers in 1997, eight years after implementation, did they tell me about their difficulties mediating between their Samoan clients and the act itself? The social workers were voicing the tensions caused by a mismatch of cultural expectations, yet the act was written to circumvent precisely these problems. As mentioned, when discussing this mismatch, social workers referred to the need to raise the level upon which Samoan families operated, and change the level upon which the act functioned so that they could coexist on the same level.[8] Initially, I thought that they were talking about the divide between an abstract piece of legislation and the nitty-gritty realities of daily family life. When I asked one man if this is what he meant, he agreed uneasily, and then explained how the act in its raw form could not be effectively introduced to Samoan families in their raw form. He taught me that Samoan social workers must take unarticulated aspects of Samoan family life and transfigure these into explicit topics for conflict resolution within the parameters established by the act. At the same time, they must contend with the ways in which the act invokes family systems that re-inscribe nuclear family dynamics. The legislation often presumes an egalitarian circulation of knowledge and resources, thus seeing extended families through a nuclear lens.

The hallmark innovation introduced by the CYPFS is the Family Group Conferences referred to earlier. The family conferences are geared toward creating a forum in which family members and other interested people can, under the guidance of a CYPFS social worker, develop a plan to protect and support the minor. In the case of juvenile crime, the emphasis is on ensuring that the youth makes restitution, both to the victim and to the government. By introducing family group conferences, the government took an explicit stance on the essential goodwill of all families. The bill itself makes clear that "given the resources, the information, and the power, a family group will generally make safe and appropriate decisions for children." The ostensible purpose of the bill is to reconfigure the dynamics between government and family, with government no longer in the role of savior. While government officials still intervene when families fail to uphold their side of the division of labor, social workers are merely supposed to create a forum for families to develop their own solutions to the institutionally defined problems. The premise is that families are basically functional systems that circulate information and resources in such a way that the needs of the individual members are met. Failure, from this perspective, occurs because of a breakdown in these flows, which social workers can mend by creating an arena for the family to heal itself.

The bill in its final form was significantly different than when it was first introduced to the parliament in December 1986, partially because of Maori input. This legislation was introduced at a politically charged moment, when Maori had successfully wrested a strong commitment from the New Zealand government to forge bicultural policies. Various Maori responses to the initial version of the CYPFS Bill were not favorable. They felt that the bill recreated European New Zealander assumptions about the nature of the family and did not take into account Maori cultural practices. In its submission, the Department of Maori Affairs wrote:

> However, the current bill fragments Maori structures of care and control and weakens the *whanau, hapu,* and *iwi* structure. In so doing, it disregards the Treaty of Waitangi and weakens Maoridom in general. It is not consistent with the goals of a bicultural society. (Department of Maori Affairs, Submission Re: The Children and Young Person Bill 1986)

These concerns pointed to the underlying paradox in how government agencies had been structuring their relationship to families. In effect, the Department of Social Welfare had been only offering lip service to the idea that families exist as separate systems. In the efforts to create a division of labor between government organizations and the family, invariably government officials stepped in when they decided that families had failed. While Maori and Pacific Islander interests do not always overlap, in this instance the groups shared mutual concerns over the Eurocentric prejudices in the government's family policies.[9] And while not all of the Maoris' and Pacific Islanders' wide-ranging critiques were answered in the act's final version, they did promote two significant changes: no more mandatory reporting of child abuse, and social workers now deemed the child's interests paramount only in the final instance. These two changes had the potential to encourage family systems and government agencies to function as two distinct systems, and it was this distinction that the New Zealand government had officially supported but did not practice.

Ending mandatory reporting of child abuse was a crucial step in allowing families to function as independent systems.[10] Under mandatory reporting, families were unable to control the information that flowed across the divide between family knowledge systems and bureaucratic paperwork. In addition, families had little input in the Department of Social Welfare's definitions of their success or failure as a system. Mandatory reporting ensured that outsiders could participate as the eyes and ears of the government's regulatory function. As the Department of Maori Affairs submission on the Children and Young Persons Bill of 1986 explicitly stated, this ran the risk of encouraging racism, since people were more likely to project systemic failure on families that functioned differently from their own. In effect, mandatory reporting ensured that the government agencies had far greater control over how information produced by families circulated and entered into the bureaucratic system, undercutting any attempt at allowing families to be independent.

When the act declared that families (not children) are paramount, it asserted that families are typically functioning systems that will solve problems holistically. By refusing to make the child's interests paramount throughout the entire process, the act is enabling families to evolve their own solutions to the perceived crisis. And this is, in fact, precisely the way in which Family Group Conferences are ideally structured. The role of the social worker is to insist on defining the abuse and/or juvenile misdemeanor as a crisis that the family as a unit must address. The social worker still carries out some of the agency's former task of defining certain activities as crises, but the families are not compelled to agree. Even the CYPFS pamphlet for families, "Family Group Conferences—Care and Protection," said:

> The family has the right to decide whether or not it agrees that the child/young person is in need of care and protection. (If the family doesn't agree, the matter is referred back to the social worker or agency who presented the case and who will then consider what action to take. The case may go to the Family Court.)

If the family agrees, it is expected to develop its own solutions in the conferences. The social worker is simply facilitating this by creating a space in which families can act as systems.

When the act posits families as systems, it deliberately attempts to avoid defining what constitutes a family. The legislative intent was to allow for a plurality of social relationships to count as family—ranging from stereotypically European New Zealand nuclear families to numerous forms of extended families. The act makes two fundamental assumptions in an attempt to legislate for such diversity. First, it presumes that all families function as systems with common aims. While there may be different kinds of families and multiple paths toward the same goal, each family has, as its foundational purpose, the function of caring for the needs and well-being of each of its members. Secondly, as a corollary, families are unified systems in which every member contributes to ensuring that the system stays functional. From this perspective, families are dysfunctional when members do not cooperate toward a common goal—which is ensuring that the family as a unified system satisfies the needs of each of its members. This form of unity emerges from nuclear family ideology, in which family conflict is negative, and is the exception rather than the norm. In fact, Samoan extended families emerge out of a sociality in which unity is only an occasional goal, and who gets to define the unity is a hotly contested issue. Social workers are then caught between the realities of Samoan migrant families and a government policy that forces them to render "families" into unified and harmonious systems.

Through the generosity of counselors at a Samoan nonprofit organization, I had the opportunity to attend a few counseling sessions with Samoan mothers who had been involved with family group conferences. The organization treated these clients because the local CYPFS workers had sought culturally appropriate treatment for them. I watched the aftermath of these conferences—for reasons of confidentiality and bureaucracy—I never witnessed an actual conference. But the telltale traces of mismatch lingered for months afterwards. I will summarize the details of one typical case, which captures the ways in which the intricacies of kinship do not translate through CYPFS policy.

Before I actually met the client, I knew that her counselor, Lupe, saw this case as one of the tragedies of migration. The mother had three children, each of whom had been removed by CYPFS, one by one. Lupe did not think that she was a bad mother, she was simply inexperienced. Lupe said that she took care of her children's basic needs, ensuring that they were clothed and fed. But she had no understanding of their emotional needs, and was not careful about who she let into the house and who she turned away. She had her children quite young, which Lupe felt would not have been a problem if she had stayed in Samoa. There, her mother or another older female relative would have been able to supplement the skills that she lacked. But in New Zealand, she was expected to display the full range of parenting skills. Lupe explained with a gentle sigh that this mother acted as though she was her children's older sister, not their actual mother. Lupe wished that her client had just one older relative in New Zealand, but that had not been the pattern of her family's migration. Instead, she was the oldest in her sibling set in New Zealand. Her younger siblings had no authority to take over some of her parenting responsibilities, or control the flow of guests into their house.

The mother was in her late twenties, hesitant and soft-spoken, never initiating a conversation or line of thought. She responded to Lupe's gentle questioning, and as the questions slowly built one upon the other, a story of communication gaps began to emerge. Her children were staying with her younger sister as the result of a CYPFS-initiated Family Conference. She wanted her children to visit her over Christmas, but these were not the arrangements that had been made by others. Her younger sister, in violation of Samoan family hierarchical principles, had made arrangements with the CYPFS social worker for the children to visit their mother two weeks before Christmas. The mother wasn't allowed to be with her children unsupervised. The younger sister or other relatives had to be present. As Lupe continued asking about the arrangements, it became apparent that Lupe had been negotiating with both the social worker and the sister for permission for the children to have Christmas dinner with their mother. Lupe had been making all sorts of tentative schedules, with everyone's knowledge but the client's. The client had been kept in the dark about this likely change in plans. It was only in the way that Lupe kept asking questions that this alternative was gradually revealed to the mother.

This case reveals many of the consequences of a clash between forms of systemic explicitness created when Samoan families must respond to CYPFS policy. First, Lupe was constantly forced to teach her client to regard mothering as a problematic arena to which she must consciously tend. The client did not think that mothering required any form of self-reflexivity, and hence found the reasons for her children's removal hard to fathom. Second, the client was suffering from a hierarchy spread across too much geographical distance. She had no larger structures of authority in the guise of older relatives to turn to in New Zealand. As a result, she was expected to be a parent who managed all parental responsibilities instead of having them distributed among an extended family. Finally, the information that formed the basis for most decisions circulated in an unpredictable fashion, from a CYPFS perspective. The mother did not know about plans for herself or her children and had little say in the matter. Rather than assuming, as CYPFS does, that it was transparent who knew what and when, this was precisely what the Samoan counselor had to establish. She was using the counseling sessions to ensure flows of information that her contractor, CYPFS, took for granted.

Knowledge plays a particularly revelatory role in the implicit narrative of how families function. For New Zealand social workers, one of the major causes of dysfunctionality is sheer ignorance—if people knew better, they would manage their families properly. Thus social workers are cast in the roles of bringing transformative knowledge—once everyone in the family knows the same things, the family can start functioning properly again. At times, this is expressed in slightly different terms—that families are unaware of the services the government can offer to assist them in their efforts to resolve crises. Families would access government resources if only they knew about them. In these cases, social workers are information brokers, the nodes through which families can enter into the government agencies' flow of resources and information.

Alongside this assumption is the belief that in Family Group Conferences, people are interacting on an equal playing field. Family Group Conferences are meant to recreate ritually each person's commitment to the family as a functioning system. Everyone has an opportunity to speak and be heard at a Family Group Conference. At the same time, each has the opportunity to articulate his or her own needs, which the family is expected to satisfy. This takes place in a context where everyone is presumed equal and seen as actively choosing to participate in the family. This presumption of equality is, as I discussed, antithetical to the way Samoans structure their relationships. For Samoans, family meetings, which CYPFS Family Group Conferences are supposedly modeled upon, are not sites for asserting a baseline equality. On the contrary, family meetings are contexts in which the hierarchies of who gets to speak and for whom are challenged and reasserted. Family meetings are attended by local extended family members and occasionally a sibling set's affines. The meetings can be moments for airing and delaying well-established tensions. Samoans presume neither family unity nor individual equality in these settings. For Samoans, the work of kinship is to express different forms of hierarchy—of reaching a hotly contested public unity that is an achievement precisely because of the private conflicts.

Conclusion

Migration encourages Samoans to reconceptualize their relationship to their extended families by affecting the ways Samoans can share knowledge and resources. The change in emphasis within the Samoan family from brother–sister relations to parent–child bonds indexes a transformation in migrants' experiences of Samoan sociality itself. In Samoa, people used to experience Samoan sociality in terms of dyadic relationships, in which each role in an intertwined relationship expresses a form of sociality. As a result, while exchange of knowledge and objects shaped the ways in which Samoans made hierarchy visible, the emphasis was far more on the paradoxes of conflicting hierarchies that were cohesive ideologically. This changes when Samoans migrate to a functionally differentiated society. In New Zealand, government and families are posited against each other as systems, and thus both appear to each other as unified networks of circulating resources and information. The internal hierarchical distinctions are often invisible in these moments of interplay between two systems. As a result, the government agencies hold a distorted view of how knowledge circulates within these systems—family members are expected to share a uniform base of information. This is antithetical to the ways in which Samoan extended families operate. For Samoan extended families, knowledge is always contingent and used to create hierarchy, not establish equality.

I have argued that equality and diversity are not inherently at odds in multicultural nations. They become antithetical through the ways government bureaucracies imagine difference. In New Zealand, social welfare agencies view all families as sharing a common project—raising children to be productive citizens. From this perspective, cultures are different styles—the many avenues for reaching a common goal. As long as the families can appear to agree with this principle, legislative acts such as CYPFS (1989) will endeavor to accommodate diversity. When, as is the case with many Samoans, child rearing is an activity that the families do not find particularly good to think with, a conflict between diversity and equality emerges. The families no longer share the same project as the nation–state, and becoming Samoan is not the road to being a productive citizen.

Notes

I would like to thank the following for their generous and helpful insights: Toeutu Fale'ava, Henry Goldschmidt, Phil Parnell, Michael W. Scott, Teri Silvio, Linda Stone, James Rizzo, and Susan Williams.

1. Western Samoa changed its name to Samoa in 1997. In this article, Samoa refers to Western Samoa.

2. Practicing the *feagaiga* has not gone completely out of fashion. One instance in which the *feagaiga* still holds occurs when Samoans are watching television. Several younger Samoans told me that they still can't watch romantic scenes on television if their cross-sex siblings, or parents for that matter, are in the room. They immediately change the channel the moment it looks as though the actors might kiss. While channel switching is a sign of respect for one's cross-sex sibling, it is not a sign of respect reserved only for that particular relationship. In contrast, other instances of the *feagaiga* practiced in Samoa such as not sharing clothes had been explicitly banned only between sisters and brothers.

3. As might be expected, given this argument, the other distinctions that the sister–brother bond metaphorically stand for also become less relevant in migration. When I first began interviewing New Zealand–raised Samoans, I would ask them who the chiefs were in their family. When they told me, I would ask if the chief was an *ali'i* or a *tulafale*. Many times, people told me that they didn't actually know the difference between the two. This distinction has lost its significance, and it can now be enough for a generation of Samoans to know that someone is a chief.

4. According to people I interviewed in Wellington, Samoans in New Zealand have begun fund-raising for their villages in Samoa as a whole group only in the past five or ten years. Until then, Samoans were either raising money as a family or as a church.

5. I want to thank Toeutu Fale'ava for this insight.

6. While spending money to form one's individual consumer identity can also be a source of tension among Samoan families, this was not how the tension about spending money was expressed to me. For the most part, the Samoans I interviewed talked about balancing their household's economic needs against the demands of their extended families.

7. From what I have seen of Samoan families, this is not the case. Information does not flow smoothly between siblings, spouses, or across any generation gap.

8. Because of the exigencies of fieldwork, I never used a tape recorder during these discussions. As a result, I am relying upon my field notes, rather than a verbatim transcript.

9. In fact, various government policies are structured to create unequal competition among minority groups.

10. Mandatory reporting can be an obligation for all employees who work with children, such as teachers or doctors.

References

Donzelot, Jacques. 1979. *The Policing of the Family*. Baltimore: Johns Hopkins University Press.

Fleming, Robin. 1997. *The Common Purse: Income Sharing in New Zealand Families*. Auckland: University of Auckland Press.

Fortes, Meyer. 1949. *The Web of Kinship among the Tallensi*. New York: Oxford University Press.

Greenhouse, Carol, ed. 1998. *Democracy and Ethnography: Constructing Identities in Multicultural Liberal States*. New York: SUNY Press.

Luhmann, Niklas. 1982. *The Differentiation of Society*. New York: Columbia University Press.

———. 1987. *Political Theory in the Welfare State*. Berlin: Walter de Gruyter.

———. 1990. *Essays on Self-Reference*. New York: Columbia University Press.

Miller, Max. 1994. Intersystemic Discourse and Coordinated Dissent: A Critique of Luhmann's Concept of Ecological Communication Theory. *Culture and Society* 11:101–21.

Ochs, Elinor. 1988. *Culture and Language Development: Language Acquisition and Language Socialization in a Samoan Village*. Cambridge, U.K.: Cambridge University Press.

Pitt, David C., and Cluny Macpherson. 1974. *Emerging Pluralism: Samoan Migrants in New Zealand*. Auckland: Longman Paul.

Povinelli, Elizabeth A. 1998. The State of Shame: Australian Multiculturalism and the Crisis of Indigenous Citizenship. *Critical Inquiry* 24:575–610.

Schoeffel, Penelope. 1978. Gender Status and Power in Samoa. *Canberra Anthropology* 1, no. 2:69–81.

———. 1995. *Tonga and Samoa: Images of Gender and Polity*, ed. Judith Huntsman. Christchurch: Macmillan Brown Center for Pacific Studies.

Shore, Bradd. 1981. Sexuality and Gender in Samoa: Conceptions and Missed Conceptions. In *Sexual Meanings: The Cultural Construction of Gender and Sexuality*, ed. Sherry B. Ortner and Harriet Whitehead. Cambridge, U.K.: Cambridge University Press.

———. 1982. *Sala'ilua: A Samoan Mystery*. New York: Columbia University Press.

Smith, Dorothy. 1998. The Underside of Schooling: Restructuring, Privatization, and Women's Unpaid Work. *Journal for a Just and Caring Education* 4, no. 1:11–30.

St. Christian, Douglas. 1997. Body/Work: Aspects of Embodiment in Western Samoa. Ph.D. diss., McMaster University, Ontario, Canada.

Strathern, Marilyn. 1992. *After Nature: English Kinship in the Late Twentieth Century.* Cambridge, U.K.: Cambridge University Press.

Tcherkezoff, Serge. 1993. The Illusion of Dualism in Samoa: "Brothers-and-Sisters" Are Not "Men-and-Women." In *Gendered Anthropology*, ed. Theresa del Valle. London: Routledge.

Chapter Eighteen

Women's Organizations, the Ideology of Kinship, and the State in Postindependence Mali

Rosa De Jorio

Until very recently, women were absent from scholarly accounts of Malian politics. Only in the past few years and with the work of Ba Konaré (1991, 1993) and Turrittin (1993), have women's contributions to local and national politics begun to be taken into account. In general, however, these authors present a limited vision of women's national associations as essentially subordinated to the single-party state—the political system that dominated Mali from its independence in 1960 to the coup d'état of 1991, which finally led to the progressive democratization of state institutions.[1] Missing from these studies are analyses of both the symbolic order underlying women's associations and the power relationships between women. The complexity of women's associations is reduced to the level of gender analyses, without much consideration for other relevant social distinctions, such as class, or the distinctions between the semiendogamous professional groups (Meillassoux 1970; McNaughton 1988; Conrad and Frank 1995). In contrast, the inclusion of issues such as class and local social distinctions ultimately leads me to suggest a more complex relation between women and the state, a relation not only of subordination, but also of gender specialization in partially independent political domains (cf. Okonjo 1976). Central to my analysis is a discussion of how both Malian women themselves as well as state officials are employing ideas and metaphors of kinship to reformulate women's relationship to the state.

In this chapter, I contribute to current debates on women's political activism by highlighting the pervasiveness of patron–client relations across Malian society (Amselle 1978, 1985, 1992) and, in particular, its structuring force within Malian women's official organizations (De Jorio 1997). In fact, during my fieldwork, it soon became quite clear how some women, far from being voiceless witnesses of male-dominated historical processes, had progressively succeeded in carving out distinctive spaces in the political arena.[2] A consideration of women elites brings me to problematize the unifying and victimizing portrait of local women we find in most of the available literature for this area. This does not mean that gender becomes an irrelevant category for the analysis of the leadership of women's associations. Indeed, in Mali, women leaders built upon women's specific competencies and women's distinctive political contributions to push forward and legitimize their ascent to power.

My perspective leads me to problematize a vision according to which the study of women elites is not pertinent to gender studies. Scholars such as Moore justified this exclusion by arguing that elites' privileges would not have any impact on the status of women in general: "In any event it [elite privilege] only effectively empowers elite individuals and groups within the community rather than working to improve women's overall political representation and decision-making power" (Moore 1988: 154).

In an approach similar to that of authors such as Anthias and Yuval-Davis (1989) and Ortner (1996), I intend to bring some complexity to the study of gender relations. I show how the organization of women's groups as well as women's political practices cannot be understood without taking into account power relations between women in addition to gender dynamics.

In this chapter, I first question the image of women's past subordination to the state prior to 1991 and present a more diversified account of women's relations to the state. Second, I focus on the ways in which the relationship between women's national associations and the state was imagined in the general public discourse. In this respect, I show how kinship categories played a crucial mediating role in the formation of new forms of citizenship and national identity. More to the point, kinship categories mediated the specific contribution of women's organizations to the national enterprise. This leads me to suggest that Malian nationalism, far from constituting an egalitarian message, found in kinship a seemingly egalitarian idiom through which to enforce gender and status differences. Third, I examine the organization of women's groups and the structuring role of patron–client relations within women's associations. This system of patronage reflects and contributes to the development of a dynastic model within the Malian national rhetoric—again linking the domains of politics and kinship at the level of practices.

From One to Many: Changes in Women's Organizations, from Single-Party State to Democracy

Malian historian Ba Konaré (who is also the wife of the president of Mali, Alpha Oumar Konaré) has analyzed the relationship between the state and women's national organizations prior to the coup d'état of 1991. Her work stresses women's subordination to the one-party system and women's reduction to the role of puppets in the hands of male politicians (1991, 1993).

Ba Konaré's work represents a sort of founding charter of contemporary women's organizations and has indeed inspired recent institutional changes. According to her account, women's national associations were subordinated to the one-party structure prior to 1991, but the progressive democratization of Malian state institutions, which began with the coup d'état of 1991, has basically freed women from such relations of subordination.

In contrast to Ba Konaré, I suggest that while women's relations of subordination to the state did not end with the coming of Malian democracy, subordination is not the only way to describe the relationship between women and the state. Indeed, women have been progressively able to carve out independent political spaces in the postcolonial nation after independence in 1960.[3] To appreciate the complexity of women's participation in the national enterprise, we have to go beyond institutional political changes and look at women's political and symbolic practices in the long term. Let me start with some background information on the history of women's groups in postcolonial times.

From 1960 to 1991, the Republic of Mali was governed by a one-party system—the Union Soudanaise-Rassemblement Démocratique Africain (US-RDA) from 1960 to 1968, and the Union Démocratique du Peuple Malien (UDPM) from 1979 to 1991 (Imperato 1989).[4] Two women's national organizations corresponded to these parties, the Commission Sociale des Femmes (CSF, 1962–1967) and the Union Nationale des Femmes du Mali (UNFM, 1974–1991). These organizations represented the only accepted medium for women's political expression for three decades. The CSF was the women's branch of the US-RDA. Its general secretary was automatically a member of the national political bureau of the US-RDA. She was understood to be the go-between between women and the party; in other words, she was to inform party leaders of women's activities and transmit the party's orders to female militants. This situation did not substantially change during the years of the UNFM. Though this association was initially created in 1974 as an independent force, it was integrated into the UDPM party structure following that party's creation in 1979. From then on, the UNFM president was automatically appointed to the board of the UDPM—the Bureau Exécutif Central (BEN)—where she played a function similar to that of the general secretary of the CSF (Ba Konaré 1993: 73).

According to Ba Konaré, during the first thirty years of the single-party state, women's participation was limited to specific political events such as elections, visits of political delegations, and participation in national holidays. In her view, women, mobilized by their leaders, worked mostly as supporters and facilitators of political events, certainly not as their main actors. As Ba Konaré detailed, there is little doubt that women participated as cooks, hosts, and entertainers for official political events. However, Ba Konaré did not fully examine the meanings and implications of women's discursive practices in the political arena. In the course of their supposedly "subordinating" activities, women developed competencies and strategies of political action that they could claim as their own, thus symbolically mobilizing a "traditional" competence and authority (that is, based on culturally specific gender distinctions) to exert active and novel political influence in the emerging Malian nation-state. To this day, Malian women do not question traditional gender roles within the family, yet they do claim, based on these traditional values, a greater level of women's participation in state institutions.

A connection between women and the domestic sphere was indeed clearly articulated by women leaders. Since the establishment of the CSF, the household was perceived by male and female political leaders alike as women's specific field of political intervention (Anonymous 1965a, 1965b, 1965c; A. Touré 1965; UNFM 1974). This perception was reflected at the public level where women in practice came to play a "maternal" role. In other words, women's initial political contribution consisted of the extension of their role within the household to the national level. For instance, in one 1982 interview, the then UNFM president described women's contributions to the Biennale Artistique, a landmark of the cultural policy of the first two Malian Republics (Y. Touré 1996), mostly in terms of the service that women offered to the Malian youth who had come as delegates to Bamako from all parts of Mali. Women's participation consisted of "the reception of [youth] delegates, their accommodation, and their nourishment" (Anonymous 1982: 5).

Nonetheless, while women were playing this conservative role, they extended their national organizations throughout the whole of Malian territory and came to play a progressively greater role in local decision-making. Indeed, oftentimes scholars forget that although women were scarcely represented in the institutions of the state, they were indeed well represented in the party structure. Since the time of the CSF, and even more so during the earlier UNFM time, women's branches were formed in every neighborhood and village in Mali. Women leaders sat on all local party boards, and their weight in decision-making grew significantly with time.

While we thus have to recognize that gender-based discourses opened up real opportunities for women's political intervention, I do not agree with the vision of Ba Konaré that women's subordination to the rule of the party is a past affair. The process of democratization of Mali, which began with the coup d'état of 1991 that overthrew Moussa Traoré's dictatorship, did not change the dominant one-party logic of Malian politics. The Malian case shows the difficulties of overcoming thirty years of one-party rule and of developing a culture of opposition.

On the one hand, there has been a progressive segmentation of the women's movement—which reflects segmentary trends running across the whole of Malian society. Since 1991, Malian women have formed more than a thousand groups, including nongovernmental organizations (NGOs) specializing in women's development and women's associations. The aspirations and strategies of these organizations are so different as to make any coordinating attempt a rather fruitless endeavor. There is a profound gap between the aspirations and political goals of Western-style women's associations and the more traditional, often religiously inspired women's associations. For instance, these organizations differ radically on the issue of female circumcision—the elimination of which is energetically pursued by one of the largest women's organizations, L'Association pour le Progrès et la Défense des Droits des Femmes Maliennes (APDF, with 25,000 members), while being resisted by the Moslem national association.[5]

On the other hand (and partly in reaction to the segmentation of women's forces), the current democratic government is becoming increasingly more involved in the coordination of women's associations, claiming a need for a more cohesive development program for women. This has resulted in a number of institutional changes such as the formation of a ministry for women (Ministère de la Promotion de la Femme, de l'Enfant et de la Famille, MPFEF)[6] and the institutionalization of the links between this ministry and a presumably grassroots umbrella organization, the Coordination des Associations et Organisations Non-gouvernementales Féminines (CAFO), which is composed of eighty-five different women's groups.[7] However, such institutional changes are clearly favoring certain women's groups—those closer to the majority party—over others. The CAFO was initially created by women themselves to coordinate their activities and thus make their voices more widely heard at the national level. In 1994, some women leaders decided to transform the CAFO into a structure of coordination between the women's associations and the state.[8] Yet it was clear that the CAFO was not representing all women's groups across the Malian territory, but only a fraction. Thus, early on, the CAFO and its representatives developed a privileged link with state institutions, whose ideology and strategies the CAFO came to embody.

Criticisms of the current government's program and strategies quickly developed. During my last visit to Mali in the summer of 1999, several women inside and outside the CAFO lamented how this umbrella organization has increasingly become the voice of the majority party rule and a means to control women's activities. Women do feel that some important political goals have been partially achieved, such as a greater freedom of association and a greater representation of women in national politics; however, they feel that these goals are yet not satisfactorily realized and that certain democratic gains are in jeopardy. Women's associations as well as other sectors of Malian civil society are currently struggling to maintain a voice independent of the dominant party logic.

Imagining Women's Contribution to Nation Building

It is important to analyze the ways in which the relationship between the women and the Malian state was imagined in the public sphere and, in particular, how it was viewed by the women themselves.[9] This analysis will also lead us to problematize certain discussions of nationalism (Anderson 1991). Indeed, the Malian case suggests that nationalism may not be a homogeneous and coherent public discourse, but a complex and often contradictory one. The Malian national community, even at the level of discourse, is far from being represented and articulated in terms of a close community tied together by linkages of comradeship and solidarity (Anderson 1991). Malian nationalism is full of conceptual references that highlight the differential contributions that women and men make to the national enterprise, but is also full of references to the complex Malian system of social stratification.[10] Let us now turn to the analysis of such gendered national discourse by reconstructing the role of kinship tropes in politics.

During the struggle for independence from French colonialism and then during Mali's first postcolonial government, US-RDA political leaders dedicated only limited attention to the "woman question." The subject of political concern were the masses, the Malian people, without apparent recognition of social distinctions. Paradoxically, given this focus on homogeneous masses, women were attributed a limited role in the enterprise of nation building in the rare instances in which gender issues were directly addressed. At the approach of independence, Modibo Keita, who was to be Mali's first president from 1960 to 1968, commented:

> Women must be concerned with the defense of women's specific interests, with the protection of women and children, with the modernization of family life through the exploitation of local resources. Women must be convinced of the relevance of their role in the achievement of an African personality, of the creation and development of a national consciousness. (Anonymous 1959)

For Keita, women's contribution to the emerging independent nation was conceived primarily in terms of their role as mothers and wives.[11] They were to "modernize" consumer practices (to make better use of local resources) and family care as well as to ensure the transmission of African values and nationalistic sentiments to the new generations. Women's contribution to nation building was confined to the domestic sphere, to prepare the new (male) generations for a responsible and engaged participation in politics. Keita's opinion was certainly not unique, and we can find examples of this very same attitude in the speeches of several female and male politicians of this period (see Gologo 1960; Doumbia 1966; Camara, pers. comm. 1994).

And yet, almost ironically, women played an important role as cementing forces in nation building.[12] To develop an awareness of national unity, Malian politicians engaged in what I call the feminization of public politics. Even more paradoxically, this process was paralleled by the initial exclusion of women from public politics. Women's images—in particular, kinship terms indicating links through the mother's side—became the language through which new political (nationalistic) concepts were conveyed. It is in this frame that we have to understand one of the most advertised national values since independence: the reference to national solidarity. Local politicians translated the word *solidarity* (used mostly in French, the national language) into Bamana (the most widely used local language) as *sinjya* or *badenya*,[13] terms that express the relationship between siblings of the same mother, a relationship characterized by feelings of affection and mutual care.[14]

The concept of *sinjya* (see Bagayogo 1987) stresses the "physical" bond created between children who "have been fed by the same breast" (Béréhima Wulalé, pers. comm. 1994). This concept allows me to bring to the fore the specificity of the Malian notion of motherhood in a predominantly patrilocal and patrilineal society (to be juxtaposed to popular notions of motherhood in the West; see, for instance, Stone 1997). The mother in the Mande language (the largest family of languages in Mali) and cultural universe is not necessarily the biological mother; she is the woman who has actually raised the child. There are a number of occasions in which a mother may give one of her children in fosterage to a co-wife or sister. For instance, this may be done in the event of the other woman's sterility or in an attempt to overcome the jealousy between different co-wives and the competition between children of different mothers. Thus, in my host family in Ségou (Mali's second largest city), two of the co-wives had raised each other's sons in the hope of developing a better mutual understanding. Likewise, on certain social occasions, women other than the biological mother may take on certain attributes of motherhood in relation to a child. Today, when a girl is to be married, it is often the mother's co-wife or a mother's sister who acts as the "main mother" (*denba*) in front of the community. In this context, being a mother is not necessarily an individualizing experience, but rather a transferable property, as is indicated by the term *sinjya*. Motherhood is seen not so much as founded on an individual biological relationship, but as based on a reproductive capacity that unites all women and that finds its full realization in the praxis of motherhood. Indeed, children's education is one of the major attributes of motherhood in national public discourse. Thus motherhood is a process more than a status; it is based on the development of common experiences between the mother and the child. From this comes the idea that women's contribution to their children is not automatic at birth, but rather is a gradually transmitted influence. More precisely, women's contribution is seen as directly dependent on their behavior within the household; the household, in turn, is viewed as the locus for the transmission of traditional knowledge and traditional values from a mother to her children.

In Bamana, the trade language of Mali, there are two proverbs that capture the differential contributions that fathers and mothers make to the development of their children. According to the proverb *Ba ye barika ye* (lit. the mother is the success), it is the woman who, through her behavior, and in particular, her capacity to passively withstand her often bitter fate as a spouse, secures her children's success in life (*barika* or *fanga*). According to the other proverb, *Fa ye togo ye* (the father is the name), it is the father who automatically transfers at birth a name to his child. Through his father, a child receives a position within a chain of birth events and comes to partake of the reputation of his patrilineage (Karim Traoré, pers. comm. 1999).[15] The father's contribution to molding his child's identity seems to be less subject to verifications and trials than is the mother's.

This idea of the maternal contribution is directly linked to another crucial aspect of the Mande conception of human nature (in Bamana, *maaya*). I refer to the idea of honor (*danbe*) whose retention is based on the ability of individuals to adapt their behavior to expected social norms. *Danbe* is something that one inherits from the past and must be preserved if not further accrued in the present. As the female Malian sociologist Maiga observed, *danbe* is a very conservative force that encourages women to comply with society's expectations and continue to fulfill a traditional role within the family (pers. comm. 1999). This *danbe* is not the same for everybody, as different categories of people in the complex hierarchy of the Mande social universe follow different rules of conduct.[16]

There are three important points to emphasize about this conception of womanhood. First, *danbe*, far from being a leveling concept, ratifies differences among women. For instance, women from different social strata are expected to follow different norms of conduct. The idea of *danbe* is attached to a specific worldview, one that emphasizes the reproduction of precise distinctions between women and men, and between nobles and those of perceived lower social status such as the *nyamankalaw* (a semiendogamous group of professional workers such as smiths, leatherworkers, and praise singers). As Bird and Kendall (1980) have remarked, *nyamankalaw* women and, in particular, women bards or praise singers (*griottes* in French; *jelimusow* in Bamana) can afford to subvert the strict code of honor followed by women of noble status or noble aspirations (*horonw* in Bamana). Both *jelimusow* and women whose ancestry can be traced to former-slave origins can be much more expressive, direct, and ironic than noblewomen can afford to be. Noblewomen are expected to exhibit a much more discreet and austere conduct. For instance, "To speak loudly in public was a sacrilege for a woman from a good family" (Keita 1975: 298).

The idea of honor, or *danbe*, rests on a historical and, I would say, stratigraphic conception of personhood. Indeed, according to a leading *jeli*, Bakary Soumano, *danbe* can be best translated as "prestige of genealogy [origin]" (*le prestige de la souche*, pers. comm. 1999). Family members are seen as drawing their success from their ancestors' exceptional conduct. Indeed, according to Bakary Soumano, a person's *danbe* is measured with respect to the *danbe* of his ancestors. Moreover, the *danbe* can generate a symbolic struggle between descendants and their ancestors in that the descendant must aim to equal the ancestor's prestige. For instance, members of my host family in Ségou still capitalize on the sacrifice of one of their ancestors, Fassighi, who gave his life for the victory of the army of the Islamic warrior El Hadj Omar Tall (1794–1864). Thanks to Fassighi's selfless act, his descendants are men who have distinguished themselves in the arts of trade (for example, the transport company La Bonne Etoile) and politics. Likewise, the rupture of deep-rooted social norms is seen as being capable of bringing misfortune onto the following generations and must be eliminated whenever possible. Thus, one of the daughters of Modibo Keita supposedly committed suicide because of her liaison with a *jeli* (bard), which had resulted in an undesired pregnancy. Her behavior subverted expected social norms—that nobles should neither have intercourse with nor marry people of lower social status—and was to some extent redeemed by her suicide (it is significant that the mother of the woman who committed suicide was blamed for her dead daughter's unconventional behavior).

This leads me to my second point: this conception of motherhood has important implications at the level of popular explanations for social problems. In Mali, as elsewhere, women are often the scapegoats for larger social problems, as seen, for instance, in the media's representation of Mariam Traoré as the main culprit for her husband's political flaws. In the rhetorical struggle against corruption that periodically resurfaced during the dictatorship of Moussa Traoré, there were a number of newspaper articles inflating women's responsibility in the process. Women were scolded for their "lack of civic maturity" and their "useless sumptuary expenses" on the occasions of family events, acts that, according to the articles, led their men willy-nilly on the path to corruption. It may not be a surprise that the writer of those articles was a female journalist who traditionally dealt with women's issues for *L'Essor*, the oldest, and for a long time the only, Malian national newspaper.

My third point is that Malian women and their leaders did not question their association with the domestic sphere. On the contrary, they made it their main reason for participating in national politics—who else could take care of their specific interests and concerns if not women themselves? In an article published several years ago, Okonjo (1976) rightly defined this pattern of political action as an example of the dual political systems that have characterized many African societies since precolonial times. This indeed had been a recurring characteristic of the Malian women's movement since the struggle for independence. Since the US-RDA days, women militants have emphasized the transformative role of women at the household level—even though this political strategy that did not allow for radical changes in terms of the gender division of labor within the household. As I mentioned earlier, women's contribution to household changes was seen as their major contribution to nation building. Women were asked to improve their family members' health; to substantially change consumer practices, thus privileging nationally produced goods over imported goods; and to inculcate an appreciation for Malian cultural traditions and a love for their country in their children. Similarly to the

CSF, UNFM leaders adopted like goals. Most of the UNFM initiatives consisted of small and narrowly conceived development projects mostly aimed at reducing women's daily work. UNFM leaders never questioned the gender distribution of work within the household.

Instead of challenging their association with the domestic sphere, women challenged the distinction between the public and the private by making political use of the private and, thus, internally subverting the excluding power of the dichotomy between public and private.[17] In other words, women responded to their initial exclusion from postcolonial politics by politicizing the domestic sphere. UNFM women campaigned even more aggressively than CSF leaders for their rights to be represented in greater numbers in state institutions and they based their requests on the specificity of their contribution to the national enterprise. Women were directly involved in questions that were considered relevant to their specific competence, such as issues pertaining to the family, women's activities, and children's health.[18] In recent times they have been able to move somewhat outside these boundaries and enter—if still as minorities—more traditionally male-dominated political fields.

Patronage, Gender, and Power

I suggest that patron–client relations constituted an important structuring force within women's associations.[19] In other words, I argue that some women built on their dynastic capital (real or fictitious) to establish relations of patronage with other women. On the basis of their women followers' political support, leaders claimed a right to enter the political arena. My discussion starts with an analysis of the strategies by which the newly emerging female elites—who belong to what Amselle (1987) has called the bureaucratic classes—legitimized their power position in the public sphere (Amselle and Grégoire 1987).

It is well known that the Malian bureaucratic classes engaged in "the reproduction of the aristocratic model of state domination" (Bagayogo 1987: 106). However, this process has not yet been accounted for from the perspective of the actors involved in it—the authors quoted above have indeed privileged a third-person perspective—nor from within a frame of systematic discussion of the relationships between politics and kinship in Mali. Moreover, very few scholars have analyzed the patronage system from the women's perspective, with the exception of the work of Lambert de Frondeville (1987) on women traders. In addition, the women I talk about are not simply negotiating with male authority but are in a position to form relations of patronage with other women.

The appeal to the dynastic model was the most effective strategy of power legitimization for the new Malian elites after independence. On the one hand, the new female elites allied with representatives from local noble families by involving the noble women in the organization of their groups, thus benefiting from their prestige and social support. This was a tactic systematically pursued by US-RDA leaders since the emergence of the first women's groups in the mid-1950s during the struggle for independence. For instance, Aoua Keita (1975: 300–301), presumably from a noble family but most importantly a representative of the new literate elites, made sure that the presidency of the women's association of Nara in the Koulikoro region was given to Yâ Diallo—a woman from a well-respected local family.[20] Keita took for herself the position of general secretary, which involved literacy skills and competence in the handling of bureaucratic procedures. The process of leadership construction did not just reproduce traditional power positions, but also entailed a more creative dimension. While seeking the support and involvement of traditional leaders, party representatives such as Keita were contributing to the remaking of traditional leadership roles, as Yâ Diallo's recruitment within women's political groups shows.[21] The authority, though, was often in the hands of the general secretaries who had the necessary knowledge of the bureaucratic system to actually run the group and represent it in appropriate institutional contexts.

On the other hand, the new elites[22] often claimed prestigious ancestry and adopted aristocratic practices on the basis of which they justified their claims to political leadership. Indeed, they relied on the generous use of their resources and the dedicated services of *griottes* and women of humble origin (such as women who could trace their ancestry back to former slave families).[23] In particular, the *griottes*, as the master of words and authoritative reinterpreters of local histories, were quintessential in helping leaders refashion their family backgrounds. In other words, the formation of women's associations— which essentially consisted of local female branches of the ruling party—was a quintessential step for those literate women in search of upward social mobility. It provided women's leaders with the possibility of extending their patronage relationships well beyond the habitual sphere of the nobility.

Women's associations came to constitute microcosms reflecting the complexity of the local social structure, but they also allowed for new syncretic fusion between old and new elites through the strategies described above. This was possible because there was no strictly unified system of social distinctions in Mali: "It is difficult to make clear distinctions among the social classes. Indeed, people still belong to various milieus, old and new, which interpenetrate" (Meillassoux 1968: 40). It has rightly been suggested that in Mali, classes per se (as conceived in sociologies of Western societies) are in an embryonic phase, since the Malian elites did not reinvest their capital in product-generating activities (Bagayogo 1987, 1989). Modern leaders, following traditional noble practices, made systematic use of *griottes* in their organizations, and not only as praise singers for ritual events (which is not to diminish the importance of their praises in the process of leadership construction). Certain positions in the exclusive directive boards (*bureaux*) of women's associations were typically occupied by *griottes*, such as the positions of *commissaire aux conflits* and *commissaire à l'information*. In other words, *griottes* (but also apparently *wolomusow*, women of slave origins) took up the tasks such as disseminating information and appeasing conflicts among group members, which represented an extension of the roles that these categories of people played in Mande societies (Wulalé, pers. comm. 1994). Leaders' success was based on their ability to rethink and negotiate between partly competing social distinctions (e.g., nobility vs. class). Through social practices and processes such as these, women's associations de facto became very effective pressure groups in the hands of their leaders.

From the previous discussion of the pervasiveness of patron–client relationships throughout Malian society, it follows that membership in women's associations is based primarily on personal connections rather than explicit ideological similarities (see also Bagayogo 1987). For instance, many women's political groups are known not so much under their official name, but as "the women of such-and-such leader." This practice also reflects people's awareness of the differential role women play within their organizations. Another consequence of this focus on an individualized approach to politics is the continuity of the country's political leadership despite coups and governmental changes. An extreme case in this direction was represented by a Ségouvian female leader who has been the president of the women's association of her neighborhood since 1962. Likewise, very few UNFM leaders withdrew from the political arena after the coup d'état of 1991—many have by now entered the ADEMA, the majority party, or the parties of the governmental coalition.[24] Several among them have become deputies or local political representatives. In my last visit to Ségou in July 1999, I was informed that of the two former UNFM presidents of women's political associations who had initially withdrawn from politics in 1991, one had recently become a political deputy to the ADEMA.[25]

Personal considerations also constitute the main reason women join a women's group. Rather than following ideological convictions, women members have a myriad of social and economic motives. Given the low literacy rate among Malian women (approximately 20 percent), women leaders are able to secure access to the benefits of the development bureaucracy (NGO projects, bank accounts, employment opportunities, new technologies, and so on). Indeed, women leaders put their professional knowledge and their entrepreneurial capacity at the service of their female constituents. For instance, one neighborhood leader, Ina, who was also a retired nurse, had transformed her house into a clinic for pregnant women. Moreover, female leaders often organize small-scale development projects for the production and commercialization of items such as soap, spices, and so on. Finally, they often serve as mediators and resources in times of family crisis. As one prominent Ségouvian woman leader said to me, speaking of the recipients of leaders' help: "This really makes a moral debt that the women have incurred vis-à-vis you. . . . So that when you take a side, all the other women follow you. . . . They know that if they do not follow, you can break that link."

The relationship between leaders and group members has an economic component, particularly in times of draconian state budget cuts and devaluation of the local currency by international monetary institutions and donors. During a family's food or money shortages and/or during a period of tension within the household, female political leaders are frequently asked to intervene, which they often do. This obviously creates some obligations on the part of those who benefit from the leaders' help.

Another characteristic of such a personalistic conception of power in Mali is its extreme centralization. Decision-making is firmly in the hands of the leader–patron, who shares her programs and their rationales with a handful of selected board members. Group members typically follow their leaders' objectives (political, development-oriented) and often compete with each other in the attempt to gain their leader's attention and recognition.

A similar hierarchy is also present among local leaders. For instance, several former UNFM neighborhood leaders in Ségou claimed limited knowledge of the internal affairs of the organization. They were not involved in the decision-making process, but rather at the level at which such decisions are executed. For instance, the aforementioned leader Ina described her participation in local politics simply in terms of readiness to mobilize her own and her followers' efforts in response to the requests of more powerful women. Even today, meetings among former UNFM leaders are kept very secret, and attendance by current ordinary members and other observers is discouraged—as I experienced on more than one occasion.

The fuzziness of the boundaries between the personal and public and between kinship and politics also finds expression at the level of activities in which women engage within their associations.[26] Indeed, as I mentioned early on, the activities of women's groups never consisted solely in participating in meetings or national festivities and welcoming official delegations. Besides small-scale development activities, women invest time and energy in the celebration and partial sponsorship of each other's family events such as marriages, naming ceremonies, and the like. These constitute important moments for the renewal of social bonds among the members of existing groups but also are occasions for the formation of totally new political enterprises. The president of a Ségouvian branch of the APDF stated that she recruited most of her group members on occasions of such ritual events. Participation in other women's family lives, during ritual events and life crises, represents one of the most effective strategies for political persuasion and one of the reasons for leaders' public success. This political strategy has been actively pursued since the time of Modibo, Keita and according to some women leaders, this was the very reason for the US-RDA's political success over the competing party, the PSP, in the 1950s. In fact, during my fieldwork in Ségou, this was the political strategy systematically used by one of the most appreciated local leaders—a woman who rose to success during the heyday of the UNFM and is today one of the ADEMA deputies at the National Assembly.

To sum up, modern political leaders rely upon a dynastic model—based upon a claim to aristocratic prerogatives—to legitimize their political power and recruit political followers (via the establishment of patron–client relations). This model finds expression at the level of practices in the establishment of patron–client relations between the woman leader and her female constituency. Leaders contribute part of their intellectual and financial capital to help their constituency, while in return, their followers both directly and indirectly help the leaders to achieve noteworthy political and economic power—indeed, most leaders have a standard of living well beyond what their salaries would allow. Thus, rather than simply being sites of mutual help, women's groups are aggregates of people who concentrate around the figure of the leader in contexts where women of different social status exchange different goods and services.

Conclusion

This chapter has analyzed Malian women's discursive practices from at least three different angles. First, I have challenged the image of women's subordination to state institutions before the coup of 1991. I have suggested that Malian women did not reject what they perceived as the prerogatives of womanhood. On the contrary, they built on their gender identity to claim their own space within Malian politics (such as women's organizations, women's branches of political parties, and a governmental ministry for women). In recent times they have built bridges to justify their presence outside their perceived fields of competence and have begun to assume typically male-dominated political positions, though without radically challenging what are locally perceived as typical gender roles (including women's domestic tasks).[27]

Second, I have looked at cultural images of Malian women and in particular at the ways in which women were imagined in the process of national construction. I examined the ways in which kinship relations have been reinterpreted and used to mediate new political situations. Overall, I have argued that kinship is erroneously read as a unifying and leveling idiom, since it reproduces a symbolic order of gender and social distinctions as inscribed in the Malian worldview. Within this framework, I have discussed the feminization of Malian politics and the trope of motherhood as a cementing force in nation building. However, I have also remarked that although women share certain experiences, their *danbe* reminds them of their substantive differences.[28] The *danbe* is a mechanism, or, better, a motivating force, that divides rather than unites women along status lines. The rules underlining the notion of *danbe* are not the same for all women, since women are expected to follow the norms of conduct proper to their position in the social hierarchy (that is, according to people's genealogy), a position that is based on a seemingly ancient, yet profoundly modified, logic of status differences.

Third, I have analyzed patron–client relations as an important structuring force within women's associations. Patron–client relations are the outcome of the adoption by the modern elites of a dynastic model, a model that legitimizes their current claims to power. I have also observed that, in spite of the existing power structures among members of women's associations, there are certain forms of solidarity between women—although they follow an aristocratic code of behavior and are governed by the principle of noblesse oblige. This chapter ultimately shows the relevance of considering both gender and power practices, and how they intertwine, in an analysis of women's organizations in Mali. Women elites are the core of women's associations that can be viewed as an extension and formalization of their client groups. Women's access to the state depends on these elites, and in turn, the state asks these leader–patrons to interpret and represent women's needs in institutional contexts.

Notes

I would like to thank Alma Gottlieb, Hans Herbert Kögler, and Linda Stone for their comments and suggestions on earlier versions of this chapter.

1. Ba Konaré and Turrittin give some attention to the political contributions of some exceptional woman—in the style of classic historiography whose limits were already recognized by British structural functionalists (e.g., Nadel 1951).

2. This essay is based on my doctoral fieldwork on women's official organizations in Mali in 1993–94, and recent follow-up research in the summer of 1999.

3. During the struggle for independence, Malian women had hoped for a higher degree of involvement in postcolonial politics. Over time they in fact succeeded in reversing male party representatives' attempts to delimit women's contribution to the household level.

4. From 1968 to 1979, Mali was ruled by a military committee, Comité Militaire de Libération Nationale (CMLN), which was presided over by Moussa Traoré, the future leader of the UDPM party and president of the country from 1968 to 1991.

5. Indeed, one of the leaders of the APDF declared that she had received numerous death threats from the Association Malienne pour l'Unité et le Progrès de l'Islam (AMUPI) to induce her to abandon the organization's objective of immediate elimination of the practice of excision from Malian society.

6. The Ministère de la Promotion de la Femme, de l'Enfant et de la Famille is the heir of the Commissariat à la Promotion des Femmes. CAFO's first president, Mme Diarra Afoussatou Thieró, is now the new minister for women.

7. The CAFO is composed of eighty-five women's associations and nongovernmental organizations, according to a document issued by the Commissariat à la Promotion des Femmes.

8. In 1994, the state institution in charge of women's issues was the Commissariat à la Promotion des Femmes. This organism was recently replaced by the MPFEF.

9. During my recent stay, many Malians severely criticized the current effort by international financial institutions and donors to impose a Western-conceived model of democracy upon Mali. For reasons of space I cannot take up this important question, but I feel obliged at least to mention it.

10. For a similar analysis in another geographical context, see McClintock 1993, Hassim 1993, and Joseph 1997.

11. The same idea was expressed by Mali's second president in a 1970s speech published in *L'Essor*: "It is a commonplace to emphasize the three attributes of a woman, who, more than a citizen, is also a mother and a spouse" (Anonymous 1970, my translation).

12. This representation of women as a unifying force at the national level is certainly not unique to Mali. However, its articulation takes culturally specific forms that I want to elucidate here. For the development of this theme in other cultural contexts, see Hassim 1993, McClintock 1993, and Joseph 1997.

13. *Badenya* connotes cooperation, mutual support, and solidarity among the children of the same mother.

14. This choice finds some justification in the gender polarity typical of this cultural area before colonization. According to Camara (1992), the Mande woman was encouraged to develop a more emotional and more compassionate side than was the Mande man. On the other hand, the Mande male noble was encouraged to be more competitive, fierce, and proud. If Camara's analysis is valid, it should not be a surprise that to foster a sense of unity, solidarity, and harmony, Malian politicians appealed to the extension of feminine values to the general population.

15. However, not all births have this power, for the precondition for the passing of a family name (*togo*) from a father to his children is that the union be legitimate. On strategies for the acceptance of premarital motherhood, see Brand 1996.

16. Traditionally, Malian societies were divided into *horonw*, people of free or noble origin; *nyamankalaw*, a group of semiendogamous professionals sometimes termed "castes," such as bards, smiths, leatherworkers, and other occupational groups; and *jonw*, slaves (e.g., Meillassoux 1968 and McNaughton 1988). For a critique of traditional approaches to the study of social distinctions in Mali, and in particular, those overemphasizing the rigidity of social boundaries between different social groups, see Conrad and Frank 1995.

17. One character of Malian politics in general seems to me to be the rejection of the Western distinction between the private and the public (or, better, the fusion of those two elements). Malians are proud of their politicians' social sensitivity (their willingness to engage personally with their electorate), which they often juxtapose to the inhumanity of Western politics.

18. Women's political participation is also the outcome of narrowly conceived international development projects whose impact on the construction of gender identities still needs to be systematically appraised in this specific historical context. Development projects for women have at best consisted of income-generating activities, and initiatives geared toward the reduction of labor tasks, and so on. In other words, such development projects have not entailed a deeper reflection upon traditional gender roles. According to Ba Konaré, the developmental approach to women's problems "has increased women's subordination to men" (Ba Konaré 1993: 76).

19. On other aspects of the patronage system, see Amselle 1987, 1992; Lambert de Frondeville 1987; Bagayogo 1987, 1989; and Fay 1995.

20. In a similar vein: "The election of the other board members took place as planned, for a preliminary selection had already been conducted to single out influential and respected people in the different neighborhoods" (Keita 1975: 301, my translation).

21. One reason for this strategy of involvement of the local elites was also the greater mobility of the new literate elite (a strategy consciously pursued by the state to foster national unity among the elites). The new elites were, so to speak, in need of the connection and reputation that only longtime residents could offer (Hopkins 1972).

22. Most of the leaders are literate and professional women in a country where only 7.1 percent of women have a secondary education or higher.

23. This new elite became the new opinion makers and forged new cultural trends. It is interesting to note that the term that is most commonly used to refer to Mali's political leadership is *nyemògò* (people who are before the masses). Thus, in the 1950s, the electoral victory of the US-RDA depended on the party's capacity to recruit and involve the new elites such as the local doctor, the merchant, and the notable in party activities (Keita 1975).

24. ADEMA stands for Association pour la Démocracie au Mali (1991 to present).

25. Women's forms of patronage have been effective in helping women conquer a greater space in the political sphere—although such methods have not radically changed or questioned certain traditional gender dynamics (e.g., women's domestic tasks). Indeed, Malian women have become unavoidable centers of power. For instance, during the 1997 elections, many of today's male political leaders formed alliances with some of the most powerful women leaders to achieve power positions. The difference with regard to the past is that women today are more determined to secure positions for their own leaders within the state administration.

26. I agree with Bagayogo that "the economic, the political, the cultural, art and history do not constitute yet autonomous categories" (Bagayogo 1987: 104). Thus, rather than being sites of mutual help, women's groups are aggregates of people who concentrate around the figure of the leader in contexts where women of different social status exchange different goods and services.

27. It should also be clear that women's political participation does not go unchallenged but must be constantly reasserted and defended. Despite current enthusiasms for the democratization of Malian state institutions, some women's groups are experiencing marginalization in the public sphere.

28. The concepts of personhood (*maaya*) and family honor (*danbè*) are rooted in a stratigraphic conception of personhood that strongly depends on one's family origin and the behavior of one's parents (in particular, one's social mother).

References

Amselle, Jean-Loup. 1978. Le Mali socialiste (1960–1968). *Cahiers d'Etudes africaines* 72, XVIII–4:631–34.

———. 1985. Socialisme, capitalisme, et précapitalisme au Mali (1960–1982). In *Contradictions of Accumulation in Africa*, ed. Henry Bernstein and Bonnie K. Campbell. Newbury Park, Calif.: Sage.

———. 1987. Fonctionnaires et hommes d'affaires au Mali. *Politique africaine* 26:63–72.

———. 1992. La corruption et le clientélisme au Mali et en Europe de l'Est: quelques points de comparison. *Cahiers d'Etudes africaines* 128, XXXII–IV:629–42.

Amselle, Jean-Loup, and Emmanuel Grégoire. 1987. Complicités et conflits entre bourgeoisies d'Etat et bourgeoisies d'affaires: au Mali et au Niger. In *L'Etat contemporain en Afrique*, ed. Emmanuel Terray. Paris: L'Harmattan.

Anderson, Benedict. 1991. *Imagined Communities*. London: Verso.

Anonymous. 1959. Mali. *Le Magazine Illustré d'Information du Gouvernement Fédéral* 2:6.

———. 1965a. Chronique féminine: la femme et son foyer, elle devra accorder une attention particulière à la salubrité des aliments. *L'Essor Quotidien* (jeudi, le 14 janvier): 4.

———. 1965b. Le militant vu de près: "Nous femmes de l'U.S.–R.D.A. Notre participation sera toujours effective dans la construction socialiste de notre pays." *L'Essor Quotidien* (vendredi, le 15 janvier): 4.

———. 1965c. Après le vote de la loi portant statut général de la profession de commerçant, le ministre des finances et du commerce nous accorde une interview. L'Essor Quotidien (samedi, le 3 avril): 1–3.

———. 1970. Discours par Moussa Traoré en réponse aux Voeux au chef de l'Etat. *L'Essor Quotidien* (samedi, le 3 janvier): 4.

———. 1982. Interview de Madame la présidente de l'UNFM. *Quotidien de la 7ème Biennale Artistique et Culturelle* 2:5–6.

Anthias, Floya, and Nira Yuval-Davis. 1989. Introduction to *Woman, Nation, State*. New York: St. Martin's.

Ba Konaré, Adam. 1991. Role et image de la femme dans l'histoire politique du Mali (1960–1991): perspectives pour une meilleure participation de la femme au processus démocratique. CODESRIA Workshop on Gender Analysis and African Social Science, 16 to 20 September, in Dakar, Senegal.

————. 1993. *Dictionnaire des Femmes Célèbres du Mali*. Bamako, Mali: Editions Jamana.

Bagayogo, Shaka. 1987. L'Etat au Mali: représentation, autonomie et mode de fonctionnement. In *L'Etat Contemporain en Afrique*, ed. Emmanuel Terray. Paris: L'Harmattan.

————. 1989. Lieux et théorie du pouvoir dans le monde mandé: passé et présent. *Cahiers des sciences humaines* (ORSTOM) 25, no. 4:445–60.

Bird, Charles S., and Martha B. Kendall. 1980. The Mandé Hero. In *Explorations in African Systems of Thought*, ed. Ivan Karp and Charles S. Bird. Bloomington: Indiana University Press.

Brand, Saskia. 1996. Premarital Motherhood in Bamako (Mali): Negotiating Acceptance. Paper presented at the thirty-ninth annual meeting of the African Studies Association, 23 to 26 November, in San Francisco.

Camara, Sory. 1992. *Gens de la parole*. Paris: Karthala.

Commissariat à la Promotion des Femmes. n.d. Plan d'Action Pour la Promotion des Femmes 1996–2000. Bamako, Mali.

Conrad, David C., and Barbara E. Frank. 1995. *Status and Identity in West Africa*. Bloomington: Indiana University Press.

De Jorio, Rosa. 1997. Female Elites, Women's Formal Associations, and Political Practices in Urban Mali (West Africa). Ph.D. diss., Department of Anthropology, University of Illinois.

Doumbia, Dramane. 1966. Visite d'une délégation parlementaire à Ségou. *L'Essor Quotidien* (mercredi, le 2 mars): 3.

Fay, Claude. 1995. La démocratie au Mali, ou le pouvoir en pâture. *Cahiers d'Etudes africaines* 137, XXXV–I:19–53.

Gologo, Mamadou. 1960. Le rôle des femmes dans la construction nationale. *Rencontres Africaines* 25:3–9. First published in *L'Essor Quotidien* (le 20 mai).

Hassim, Shireen. 1993. Family, Motherhood, and Zulu Nationalism: The Politics of the Inkatha Women's Brigade. *Feminist Review* 43:1–25.

Hopkins, Nicholas S. 1972. *Popular Government in an African Town: Kita, Mali*. Chicago: University of Chicago Press.

Imperato, James. 1989. *Mali: A Search for Direction*. Boulder, Colo.: Westview.

Joseph, Suad. 1997. The Public/Private—The Imagined Boundary in the Imagined Nation/State/Community. *Feminist Review* 57:73–92.

Keita, Aoua. 1975. *Femme d'Afrique. La vie d'Aoua Keita racontée par elle-même*. Paris: Editions Présence Africaine.

Lambert de Frondeville, Agnès. 1987. Une alliance tumultueuse: les commerçantes maliennes du Dakar-Niger et les agents de l'Etat. *Cahiers des sciences humaines* (ORSTOM) 23, no. 1:89–103.

McClintock, Anne. 1993. Family Feuds: Gender, Nationalism, and the Family. *Feminist Review* 44:61–81.

McNaughton, Patrick R. 1988. *The Mandé Blacksmiths. Knowledge, Power, and Art in West Africa*. Bloomington: Indiana University Press.

Meillassoux, Claude. 1968. *Urbanization of an African Community*. Seattle: University of Washington Press.

————. 1970. A Class Analysis of the Bureaucratic Process in Mali. *Journal of Development Studies* 6, no. 2:97–110.

Ministère de la Promotion de la Femme, de l'Enfant et de la Famille. 1998. *La Malienne en chiffres edition 1998*. Bamako, Mali.

Moore, Henrietta. 1988. *Feminism and Anthropology*. Minneapolis: University of Minnesota Press.

Nadel, Siegfried Frederick. 1951. *The Foundations of Social Anthropology*. London: Cohen & West.

Okonjo, Kamene. 1976. The Dual-Sex Political System in Operation: Igbo Women and Community Politics in Midwestern Nigeria. In *Women in Africa*, ed. Nancy I. Hafkin and Edna G. Bay. Stanford: Stanford University Press.

Ortner, Sherry B. 1996. *Making Gender: The Politics and Erotics of Culture*. Boston: Beacon.

Stone, Linda. 1997. *Kinship and Gender: An Introduction*. Boulder, Colo.: Westview.

Touré, Adrienne. 1965. La malienne et ses tâches: "Elle doive rationaliser les dépenses familiales," déclare la camarade Aoua Kéita à la réunion des femmes de l'U.S.-R.D.A. *L'Essor Quotidien* (vendredi, le 8 janvier): 3.

Touré, Younoussa. 1996. La Biennale artistique et culturelle du Mali (1962–1988): socio-anthropologie d'une action de politique culturelle africaine. Doctorat nouveau régime. Sous la direction de M. Jean-Pierre Olivier de Sardan, directeur d'études à l'Ecole des Hautes Etudes en Sciences Sociales (EHESS), directeur de recherche à l'ORSTOM, Marseille, France.

Turrittin, Jane. 1993. Aoua Keita and the Nascent Women's Movement in the French Soudan. *African Studies Review* 36, no. 1:59–89.

Union Nationale des Femmes du Mali (UNFM). 1974. Chart and Programme d'Action pour l'Année Internationale de la Femme. Bamako, Mali.

Index

Aberle, David, 25, 38
Aborigines, 100, 102
abortions, 198
Abu-Lughod, Lila, 30, 58, 60
acculturation models, 34–35
adaptive mechanisms, 97–99
ADEMA. *See* Association pour la
    Démocracie au Mali (ADEMA)
adoptees, 248, 249
adoption, 28, 54–56, 147–48, 150,
    152n14, 153n16; best interest of child
    principle, 259; changes in
    information exchanged, 250–51,
    262n4; clientele, 250, 262n4; closed,
    15, 247, 251; confidentiality of
    records, 247, 248–49, 251, 258;
    disclosures, 253–56, 258, 260;
    information transfer, 15, 248–49,
    262n4; kinship and, 247–48; sealed
    records, 258–59; types, 250–51;
    Weismantel's analysis of, 115, 121;
    see also open adoption
adoption agencies, 246–47
advice columns, 175–77
affiliative relationships, 79, 82–83, 85n5
aging, 57
agnatic kinship, 50–51, 58, 61, 63n9, 298,
    301n7

Åkesson, Lynn, 125–38
the alien, 135, 136n13
ali'I, 307, 320n3
alliance theory, 60, 77, 80
Altorki, Soraya, 56
altruistic behavior, 71–73, 75, 77, 84n1,
    95, 99–100
American Anthropological Association,
    ix, 27
American Kinship: A Cultural Account,
    109–14
Amerindianization, 50
Anderson-Levy, Lisa M., 14, 185–203
Angel Park, 265–67, 268–71, 273–77,
    280–81, 283n7
Angela's Ashes, 132
"Ann Landers," 175–76, 182n2
Anthias, Floya, 323
antikinship school, 8
Apache, 44n15
Appadurai, Arjun, 52
archaeology, 14
arranged marriages, 30, 35–38,
    43nn10–11
artificial fertilization, 139–40, 144–45,
    152n2, 152n4, 152nn10–11
ascription, 157
Ashanti households, 231

About the Contributors

Lynn Åkesson is a Research Fellow and Associate Professor at the Department of European Ethnology, Lund University, Sweden. Her research has focused on culturally defined normality and deviance, most recently in relation to modern technology. Together with Susanne Lundin, she is leading the interdisciplinary research project *Genetics, Genetic Engineering, and Everyday Ethics* at Lund University and participating in the EU-founded project *Educating the European People for Biotechnology*. Recent books include *Amalgamations: Fusing Technology and Culture* (1999, eds. Lundin and Åkesson) and *Arvets Kultur—essäer om genetic och samhälle* (2000, The Culture of Heritage—Essays on Genetics and Society, eds. Lundin and Åkesson).

Lisa M. Anderson-Levy is a Ph.D. student in anthropology and a member of the Center for Advanced Feminist Studies at the University of Minnesota. Her research interests include the production of racial identity, and her dissertation focuses on construction of whiteness(es) among whites in Jamaica.

Caroline B. Brettell is Professor and Chair of the Department of Anthropology at Southern Methodist University. In addition to numerous book chapters and journal articles, she is the author of *We Have Already Cried Many Tears: The Stories of Three Portuguese Migrant Women* (1982, 1995) and *Writing Against the Wind: A Mother's Life History* (1999); editor of *When They Read What We Write: The Politics of Ethnography* (1993); and co-editor of *Gender in Cross-Cultural Perspective* (1993, 1997, 2001), *Gender and Health: An International Perspective* (1996), and *Migration Theory: Talking Across Disciplines* (2001).

Rosa De Jorio received her Ph.D. from the University of Illinois at Urbana–Champaign. She is Assistant Professor of Cultural Anthropology at the University of North Florida in Jacksonville. Her geographic area of specialization is urban Mali, West Africa, where she has carried out fieldwork since 1991. Her research interests and publications center on gender politics, the globalization of local economies (in particular its impact at the level of local conceptions and practices of work), as well as nationalism and cultural heritage in Mali. She is working on a book about transnationalism and gender politics in Mali.

Allen S. Ehrlich received his Ph.D. from the University of Michigan. He is Professor of Anthropology at Eastern Michigan University. His earlier research focused on Caribbean studies involving East Indian cane workers. He has published articles on cultural ecological adaptation, ethnic identification, and political integration of East Indians in rural Jamaica.

Kathey-Lee Galvin is a Ph.D. student in anthropology at Washington State University. Her research focuses on South Asia, kinship, and gender. She is in Nepal conducting fieldwork for her dissertation on Nepalese widowhood under a Fulbright Fellowship.

Ilana Gerson is a graduate student in cultural anthropology at the University of Chicago. She writes on Samoan migrant experiences of modern nation-states, asking how Samoans make differences cultural within their families and in government contexts. She is also staff associate editor at *American Ethnologist.*

Barry S. Hewlett is Professor of Anthropology at Washington State University in Vancouver. He is the author of *Intimate Fathers* (1991) and several articles on infant and child development in forager and farmer cultures. He has published articles utilizing the human behavioral ecological and dual transmission approaches discussed in his chapter: "Demography and Childcare in Preindustrial Societies, *Journal of Anthropological Research* 47:1–37, and "Cultural Transmission among Aka Pygmies," *American Anthropologist* 88:922–34.

David Jacobson is Associate Professor of Anthropology at Brandeis University. One of his research interests is the social organization of families and households, and he has done fieldwork on stepfamilies and the cultural context of household resource management. In addition to his recent articles on stepfamily households, he is the author of *Itinerant Townsmen: Friendship and Social Order in Urban Uganda* (1986) and *Reading Ethnography* (1991). He is also co-author with Charles Ziegler of *Spine without Spies* (1994).

William Jankowiak is Associate Professor of Anthropology at the University of Nevada in Las Vegas. Among his numerous publications are *Sex, Death and Hierarchy in a Chinese City* (1993) and *Romantic Passion* (1995). He is completing an ethnography of the largest and oldest polygynous community in North America. In addition, he has begun an in-depth restudy of Hohhot, the capital of Inner Mongolia, PRC.

Louise Lamphere is University Regents Professor of Anthropology at the University of New Mexico in Albuquerque and President of the American Anthropological Association (1999–2001). She has carried out extensive fieldwork in the northeastern and southwestern United States with a specific focus on women, immigration, work, family, and kinship. She co-edited *Woman, Culture and Society* with Michelle Zimbalist Rosaldo (1974), an important early collection on feminist anthropology. She has also written *From Working Daughters to Working Mothers: Immigrant Women in a New England Community* (1987), co-authored *Sunbelt Working Mothers: Reconciling Family and Factory* (1993), edited *Structuring Diversity: Ethnographic Perspectives on the New Immigration* (1992), and co-edited *Situated Lives: Gender and Culture in Everyday Life* (1997). Her early field research on Navajo family and kinship is found in *To Run After Them: The Social and Cultural Bases of Cooperation in a Navajo Community* (1977), and she is completing a biography of three Navajo women entitled *Weaving Together Women's Lives: Three Generations in a Navajo Family.*

Joan H. Liem is Associate Professor of Psychology and Director of Clinical Training at the University of Massachusetts in Boston. Her research focuses on individual and family responses to a variety of stressful experiences including unemployment, divorce, childhood sexual abuse, and dropping out of high school. She has published a number of articles on these topics in journals such as *Child Abuse and Neglect, The American Journal of Orthopsychiatry*, and *Journal of Traumatic Stress.*

Susanne Lundin is a Research Fellow and Associate Professor at the Department of European Ethnology, Lund University, Sweden. She has worked on several projects focusing on biology and culture, which has resulted in *Bodytime* (1996, eds. Lundin and Åkesson), *Gene Technology and the Public* (1997, eds. Lundin and Ideland), *Guldägget: Föräldraskap i biomedicinens tid* (1997, The Golden Egg: Parenthood in the Age of Biomedicine), and *Amalgamations: Fusing Technology and Culture* (1999, eds. Lundin and Åkesson). Since 1997 she has, together with Lynn Åkesson, been leading the project *Genetics, Genetic Engineering, and Everyday Ethics.* Since 1998 she has been the head of the project *Cultural Perspectives on Xenotransplantation.*

Richard E. Maddy is a Ph.D. student in anthropology at Southern Methodist University. His research focus is in medical anthropology, specifically biomedicine as a cultural system. His dissertation explores how biomedical practitioners have responded to the proliferation of managed care organizations. In addition to his research on the culture of biomedicine, he has co-authored an article in the journal *Postgraduate Medicine* in which he examines barriers to the effective control of hypertension in patients with diabetes.

Judith S. Modell received her Ph.D. from the University of Minnesota. She is Professor of Anthropology, History, and Art at Carnegie Mellon University. Publications include *Kinship with Strangers* (1994), *A Town without Steel: Envisioning*

Homestead (1998), and *A Sealed and Secret Kinship: Adoption and Policy* (2001). Her most recent studies of adoption and foster care involve closer scrutiny of federal and state laws and practices. A new project involves gathering photographs, stories, and drawings from children who are "in the system" (i.e., foster care) in Pittsburgh, Pennsylvania. She is also working on a life-study of a man who identifies himself as "one hundred percent Hawaiian" and represents important developments in Hawaiian history.

Cynthia Robin is Assistant Professor of Anthropology at Northwestern University. The theoretical and methodological focus of her research is on everyday life. Other research interests include gender theory, social organization, household, and settlements. An archaeologist, she bases her fieldwork primarily in Mesoamerica. She has just completed a multiyear research project focusing on the everyday lives of ancient Maya farmers living in the vicinity of the civic-ceremonial center of Xunantunich, Belize (1994–97). This project culminated in the 1999 Ph.D. dissertation from the University of Pennsylvania entitled *Towards an Archaeology of Everyday Life: Maya Farmers of Chan Nòohol and Dos Chombitos Cik'in, Belize.*

Joan B. Silk is Professor and Chair of the Department of Anthropology at the University of California in Los Angeles. Her work focuses on the evolution of social behavior among nonhuman primates, and she has conducted empirical research on chimpanzees, baboons, and bonnet macaques. She is co-author with Robert Boyd of *How Humans Evolved* (2nd ed., 2000) and the author of a number of articles in refereed journals, including *Animal Behavior, The American Naturalist,* and *Behaviour.*

Karen Sinclair received her Ph.D. from Brown University. She is Professor of Anthropology at Eastern Michigan University. Her fieldwork with the Maori of New Zealand began in 1972 and has continued into the present. She has received grants from the Fulbright Foundation, National Endowment for the Humanities, National Science Foundation, and National Institute of Mental Health. Eastern Michigan University has also provided research fellowships, summer awards, sabbaticals, and research support. In addition to numerous articles on Maori culture, she has just completed a book on the contemporary Maori to be published by Rowman & Littlefield.

Linda Stone received her Ph.D. from Brown University. She is Professor of Anthropology at Washington State University. Her specializations cover kinship, gender, medical anthropology, and religion. She has conducted research in Nepal, Thailand, Indonesia, Italy, and the United States. Her previous books include *Illness Beliefs and Feeding the Dead in Hindu Nepal* (1989) and *Kinship and Gender: An Introduction* (2nd ed., 2000). She is also co-author of *Gender and Culture in America* (1999).

Robert S. Weiss is Emeritus Professor of Sociology and Senior Fellow at the Gerontology Institute at the University of Massachusetts in Boston. He has extensively researched families, focusing on divorce and single parents. He is the author of *Marital Separation: Managing After a Marriage Ends* (1975) and *Going It Alone: The Family Life and Social Situation of the Single Parent* (1979), as well as several other books and articles.